MAN, LAW AND MODERN FORMS OF LIFE

LAW AND PHILOSOPHY LIBRARY

MAN, LAW AND MODERN FORMS OF LIFE

Edited by

EUGENIO BULYGIN

Faculty of Law, University of Buenos Aires

JEAN-LOUIS GARDIES

Department of Philosophy, University of Nantes

and

ILKKA NIINILUOTO

Department of Philosophy, University of Helsinki

Introduction by

MICHAEL D. BAYLES

Department of Philosophy, University of Florida

D. REIDEL PUBLISHING COMPANY

A MEMBER OF THE KLUWER ACADEMIC PUBLISHERS GROUP

DORDRECHT / BOSTON / LANCASTER

Library of Congress Cataloging in Publication Data
Main entry under title:

CIP

Man, law, and modern forms of life.
(Law and philosophy library)
"Proceedings of the 11th IVR World Congress on Philosophy of Law and Social Philosophy ... held on August 14-20, 1983 in Helsinki"–Introd.
Includes bibliographies and index.
1. Law–Congresses. 2. Law and anthropology–Congresses. 3. Law Methodology–Congresses. I. Bulygin, Eugenio. II. Gardies, Jean-Louis. III. Niiniluoto, Ilkka. IV. International Association for Philosophy of Law and Social Philosophy. V. World Congress on Philosophy of Law and Social Philosophy (11th. : 1983 : Helsinki, Finland) VI. Series.
K225.M36 1985 340'.1 85-11749

Published by D. Reidel Publishing Company,
P.O. Box 17, 3300 AA Dordrecht, Holland.

Sold and distributed in the U.S.A. and Canada
by Kluwer Academic Publishers
190 Old Derby Street, Hingham, MA 02043, U.S.A.

In all other countries, sold and distributed
by Kluwer Academic Publishers Group,
P.O. Box 322, 3300 AH Dordrecht, Holland.

ISBN 978-90-481-8409-5

PROCEEDINGS OF THE 11th WORLD CONGRESS ON PHILOSOPHY OF LAW AND SOCIAL PHILOSOPHY

TABLE OF CONTENTS

III. IS AND OUGHT: PRESENT ISSUES IN ARGUMENTATION AND LEGAL THINKING

EDITORIAL PREFACE

During the last half of the twentieth century, legal philosophy (or legal theory or jurisprudence) has grown significantly. It is no longer the domain of a few isolated scholars in law and philosophy. Hundreds of scholars from diverse fields attend international meetings on the subject. In some universities, large lecture courses of five hundred students or more study it.

The primary aim of the Law and Philosophy Library is to present some of the best original work on legal philosophy from both the Anglo-American and European traditions. Not only does it help make some of the best work available to an international audience, but it also encourages increased awareness of, and interaction between, the two major traditions. The primary focus is on full-length scholarly monographs, although some edited volumes of original papers are also included. The Library editors are assisted by an Editorial Advisory Board of internationally renowned scholars.

Legal philosophy should not be considered a narrowly circumscribed field. Insights into law and legal institutions can come from diverse disciplines on a wide range of topics. Among the relevant disciplines or perspectives contributing to legal philosophy, besides law and philosophy, are anthropology, economics, political science, and sociology. Among the topics included in legal philosophy are theories of law; the concepts of law and legal institutions; legal reasoning and adjudication; epistemological issues of evidence and procedure; law and justice, economics, politics, or morality; legal ethics; and theories of legal fields such as criminal law, contracts, and property.

ALAN MABE
MICHAEL BAYLES

MICHAEL D. BAYLES

INTRODUCTION

This volume belongs to two important book series in legal philosophy – the Law and Philosophy Library and the Proceedings of the 11th IVR World Congress on Philosophy of Law and Social Philosophy. As a member of the first, it illustrates the broad range of international interest in legal philosophy to which the Law and Philosophy Library is directed. The contributors to this book represent many countries and traditions in legal philosophy and science. Readers can learn much from a thorough study of their different approaches to similar problems and themes. Although the Law and Philosophy Library will primarily publish works by single authors, from time to time it will publish collections of important and previously unpublished essays. As a volume of the Proceedings, this book provides a thematic selection of papers given at the 1983 World Congress in Helsinki. (Detailed information on the rest of the Proceedings volumes is provided at the end of this one.) Readers owe a debt of gratitude to the Finnish Cultural Foundation and the Finnish Foundation for Economic Education for financially supporting the editing of this book and to Mr. Jyrki Uusitalo for serving efficiently as Editorial Assistant.

The 11th World Congress, held on August 14–20, 1983, in Helsinki, brought together about four hundred legal scholars to examine the Philosophical Foundations of the Legal and Social Sciences. The working sessions of the Congress were organized around eight general topics with several subtopics each. The working groups were as follows:

I. Law and Society
II. Law and Morality
III. Models of Legal Reasoning
IV. System and Systematization in Law
V. Knowledge and Values in Law
VI. Theory of Law and the Social Sciences
VII. Law and Anthropology
VIII. Philosophical Problems of the Social Sciences

In reviewing the papers for publication, the Proceedings committee and the editors regrouped them to exhibit better the themes of contemporary scholarly discussion.

As a result, several points about the presentation of the papers at the

E. Bulygin et al. (eds.), Man, Law and Modern Forms of Life, xi–xvi.

Congress should be noted. First, although it is third to last in this volume, Professor von Wright's paper was the opening lecture of the Congress. Second, several of the papers were co-reports. Those by Professor Klami and Dr. Karlsson were co-reports at the plenary session on Legal Philosophy in the Nordic Countries. Professor Stening's is a co-report to the main paper by Professor Hintikka for the working group session on Evidence and Plausibility in Legal Reasoning. Third, some papers are commentaries to main papers. Thus, Professor Airaksinen's paper is a commentary to Professor Stroup's paper, and Professor Stroup has a brief reply to the commentary. Professor de Cervera's is a commentary to Professor Wróblewski's.

From the titles of the sections of this book – Anthropological and Epistemological Dimensions of Law, Schools and Perspectives in Legal Theory, and Is and Ought: Present Issues in Argumentation and Legal Thinking – one might surmise that there is little connection between them. However, several important themes and issues run through the various sections. It is not possible here to develop them in detail, let alone to summarize the various papers. Consequently, I shall merely note a number of themes and issues that run through the papers.

Many of the papers are concerned with the implications of anthropological information for law, legal institutions, or legal theory. Anthropology is here to be understood broadly as including biological, psychological, geographical, and cultural knowledge. There are at least three general ways in which anthropological information can relate to law, legal institutions, and legal theory. First, anthropology can indicate how culture causally influences law, legal institutions, and legal theory, and how they in turn causally influence culture. For example, in his paper Klami indicates how Finnish legal theory emphasized legal conceptualism as a defense of Finnish culture and autonomy against Czarist Russian oppressive tendencies at the beginning of the 20th century. In an earlier era, civil law spread across much of Europe with the Napoleonic armies. Much has also been written about whether legal positivism contributed to the development or success of Naziism in Germany. At a more specific level, schools of legal thought often develop from the influence of a few prominent scholars which frequently crosses national borders.

Second, as several papers in the first section discuss, anthropological information can indicate empirical constraints on and possibilities for law. Sociobiological theory, which tries to explain certain cultural features as the expression of biological factors, is currently of much interest. Some sociobiologists contend that aspects of kinship systems are natural expressions of biological characteristics of human beings. If they are correct, one could expect most legal systems to support these kinship relations and legal systems contrary to these relations to fail. At a more specific level, there might be biological bases for human desires, such as to know one's biological parents. Although it is possible to deny the satisfaction of these desires (as in adoption), there might be an inevitable cost of frustration that should be considered in establishing adoption laws.

Anthropological information can also indicate possibilities for law, legal institutions, and legal theory. If one of the kinship theories of sociobiology is correct, then these kinship ties might be used to support lawful behavior. Similarly, anthropological information can indicate how other societies have responded, for better or worse, to problems similar to those confronted in a society. Put simply, one can learn much from other cultures. It is very easy for human beings, even highly intelligent and sophisticated persons, to believe that the development and institutions of their society represent the only way societies can develop and be structured. Such beliefs can find expression in legal theory. Some legal theories seem to presuppose that all legal systems evolve similarly. Anthropological information may dispel this belief, opening new possibilities in legal theory. In particular, Broekman's essay in this volume emphasizes the benefits from an anthropological-epistemological approach which examines the law as a particular form of "discourse."

Third, anthropological information might be relevant to the justification of legal or ethical theories. For instance, natural law theory has always claimed to rest on general features of human nature. Anthropology can show whether or not such features are universal human traits. Similarly, many arguments for ethical egoism rest on psychological egoism. And many thinkers, especially during this century, have taken anthropological information to support ethical relativism or some form of ethical subjectivism. In this volume, Stroup's and Airaksinen's discussion of Edward Westermarck's theory show that a careful and plausible relativistic analysis is useful for a causal inquiry into morality and the law. Yet, because anthropological material is alleged to support a wide variety of incompatible ethical theories, doubt is cast on the soundness of all such arguments from anthropology to normative theory.

The use of anthropological information to support legal theories is closely related to one of several epistemological issues that are discussed in this volume, namely, the relation between is and ought. During this century, the problem of relations between is and ought sentences, or descriptions and prescriptions, has been widely debated, as shown in von Wright's comprehensive essay where the author also develops his own standpoint on the problem. The central dispute has been whether prescriptions can be derived from descriptions, with many theorists contending that they cannot. This issue is centrally important for both legal theory and the analysis of legal reasoning. If prescriptions cannot be derived from descriptions, then anthropological information cannot be a basis for adopting one normative legal theory rather than another. Some prescriptive assumptions must be made before prescriptive conclusions can be drawn from anthropological information, and these assumptions cannot themselves be justified solely by anthropological information.

The is-ought problem has not often been thought to pose a problem in legal reasoning. The standard view has been that the law provides normative rules or principles (prescriptions), the facts indicate that a case should be subsumed under one or another rule, and the particular legal judgment then follows from the application of the normative legal rule. However, this account is now widely recognized to be inadequate. It assumes that facts are given in a neatly labeled form for the application of normative rules, thus ignoring the difficulties in establishing the facts of a case. It says nothing about how a legal norm is determined to be appropriate for a case. Moreover, it provides no assistance in analyzing how legal rules and principles are justified.

Thus, several epistemological and logical issues arise in addition to the relation of descriptions to prescriptions. One issue concerns the possibility of logical relations between norms (prescriptions). If, as many theorists contend, prescriptions are neither true nor false, then how can logical relations hold between them? The traditional account of logical reasoning is based on truth relations, but if prescriptions cannot be true or false, then it seems that logical relations cannot hold between them. Three possible ways out of this difficulty are (1) to hold that prescriptions can be true or false; (2) to hold that although themselves not capable of being true or false, prescriptions imply sentences that can be true or false; or (3) to develop a revised concept of logical relations.

Even if logical relations can be shown to hold between prescriptions, other problems arise. Legal systems seem to violate the fundamental law of noncontradiction, since conflicting norms can both be justified and even used within a legal system. Some account of this possibility is needed; Hilpinen's paper in this volume is a contribution to this discussion. Moreover, the logical relations between norms are not always deductive. Some legal norms (principles, doctrines) are weighed and balanced against one another. An account of the logic of this reasoning is also needed. In short, reasoning with legal norms does not fit the traditional models of deductive and inductive reasoning. The new field of deontic logic began developing in the early 1950's to try to account for this reasoning. Further interesting perspectives seem to be opened by the application of new models of reasoning in this domain, such as the "logic of questions" advocated by Hintikka in his paper here.

Not all the problems of legal reasoning and epistemology relate to normative sentences. In recent years, there has been a growing interest in the way courts reason about facts. The problem is not merely that courts often exclude as irrelevant information that science and ordinary reasoning treat as relevant. It is more fundamental. Courts use probabilistic information to support factual claims. The traditional model of legal reasoning simply ignores this feature. Once it is recognized, difficulties arise. One difficulty concerns the relation of statistical information to individual cases. Stening, in his paper, presents a good example. If the police have statistical evidence that nine out of ten drivers were speeding, would a court be justified in convicting all ten, because in each case there is a ninety percent chance the person was speeding?

Another difficulty stems from the facts being only probably true. The traditional model of reasoning assumes that, however arrived at, the facts of a case are facts, that is, the factual sentences are simply true if the evidentiary requirement (balance of probabilities, beyond a reasonable doubt) is met. However, descriptions that are only probably true leave some uncertainty. Shoud this uncertainty be taken into account? And if so, how? For example, suppose in case 1 it is sixty percent probable that factual elements *A, B, C*, and not *D* obtain, but in case 2 it is sixty percent probable that factual elements *A, B, C*, and *D* obtain. The difference between the cases is only twenty percent as to whether or not *D* obtains. Is that a sufficient basis for distinguishing them so that the plaintiff wins in case 2 but not in case 1? Recognition of factual uncertainty may call for differences in substantive legal norms.

The foregoing provides only a brief glimpse of some of the many issues discussed in this volume. One other general theme of legal theory is evidenced in all the sections – the relevance of other disciplines to legal theory and philosophy. The papers in this volume draw on a wide spectrum of other disciplines – anthropology, sociobiology, linguistics, history, logic, and probability theory, among others. Legal philosophy is not an isolated, self-contained discipline. The law both reflects and shapes society, and the understanding of law requires the use of all the tools available for understanding society. The papers in this volume exhibit a healthy awareness of this fact. They, and the papers in the other Proceedings volumes, also indicate that legal philosophy is alive and thriving around the world.

University of Florida

I

ANTHROPOLOGICAL AND EPISTEMOLOGICAL DIMENSIONS OF LAW AND ETHICS

EDGAR BODENHEIMER

ANTHROPOLOGICAL FOUNDATIONS OF LAW

In his valuable work on Legal Anthropology, Professor Ernst-Joachim Lampe points out that the institution of law serves human needs and human interests, and that it appraises actions and events with regard to human needs and human interests. He concludes that any general analysis of law must take as its starting point the nature of man. For this reason, he believes firmly in the value and necessity of an anthropology which directs its focus at the institution of law.[1] I find myself in agreement with him on this issue.

In the framework of the present paper, the term "anthropology" is being used in a broad sense. It is meant to encompass scholarly efforts on a wide range that endeavor to probe into human nature as a whole. This holistic approach will include the biological and psychological traits of the human person as well as the noetic component of human nature, that is, man's mind or spirit. This form of anthropology is usually referred to as "philosophical anthropology," but I do not wish to use this term in contradistinction to scientific anthropology. It seems to me that a philosophical theory which disregards firmly established propositions of science is not of great value. On the other hand, where scientists are in seemingly hopeless disagreement on a question – which, as you know, happens frequently – the philosopher should be free, to the extent that he is able to form an intelligent judgment on the controversy, to adopt the view which he considers most convincing.

I shall divide my paper into a descriptive and a critical part. I shall first discuss some views on human nature which appear to have some bearing on the normative design of a legal system. I shall then criticize these views and explain my own position on the question. Finally, I shall attempt to trace the impact which my position would be likely to have on the most basic social policies underlying a legal system. The key problem to which I shall address my attention, the Wagnerian "leitmotif," so-to-speak, will be the following: Are there any genetically inborn propensities of human beings that will place significant constraints on the ability of the human mind to fashion and effectuate social and legal systems according to some ideal-inspired masterplan? Differently expressed, is there a biological human nature, characterized by some more or less constant qualities, that will put limitations on the realization of political, economic, and cultural aims

E. Bulygin et al. (eds.), Man, Law and Modern Forms of Life, 3–13.

which the architects of society, partly through the device of the law, may wish to accomplish?

There are two groups of thinkers, far apart in their general attitude toward social problems, who would give a resounding negative answer to this question. Some existentialist philosophers have vigorously denied that there exists some essence that may be called "the nature of man." A prominent advocate of this viewpoint was Jean-Paul Sartre, who declared in a point-blank fashion that "there is no human nature."[2] He was convinced that "man is nothing else but what he makes of himself," and that his freedom to choose a certain form of self-actualization was not limited by pressures resulting from innate traits controlling behavior.[3] The inference may be drawn from this position that, according to Sartre, a collectivity of radically free individuals could build a legal system based on some agreed-upon social ideal. Karl Jaspers has taken a view similar to that of Sartre; he has declared his opposition to any philosophical anthropology designed to expatiate on a common nature of man.[4]

While existentialists believe strongly in the creative powers of unique human personalities, a more passive conception of man has prevailed in the writings of American behaviorists. John Watson attempted to explain human conduct almost exclusively in terms of responses to sensorial stimuli, without reference to concepts such as "mind," "purpose," or "consciousness." Personality, in his opinion, was nothing but the outgrowth of habits. The habits of the "assembled organic machine" called man were, in turn, decisively formed by environmental influences, such as education and training.[5] More recently, B. F. Skinner has played down the importance of aims, ideals, and philosophies of life as motivating forces in human behavior.[6] Although he acknowledges a hereditary component in human conduct, he believes that such conduct is primarily shaped by "operant conditioning" administered by forces outside the individual. "It is the environment which acts upon the perceiving person," he asserts, "not the perceiving person who acts upon the environment."[7] It seems obvious that behaviorism comes close to the view that effective environmental conditioning can mold human beings into almost any type of specimen favored by the controlling authorities in society.

The strong influence which behaviorism had upon thinking in the United States for many decades has suffered some decline in recent years. The theories of the influential linguist Noam Chomsky, for example, mark a partial return to the rationalist philosophy of the seventeenth and eighteenth centuries. Chomsky ventures the hypothesis that the human mind is endowed with innate ability to use language creatively far beyond the scope of learning experiences and direct instruction supplied by the environment.[8] More directly relevant to the theme of this paper is the recent development of sociobiology, a discipline which has engendered an unusual amount of interest and controversy in the United States. According to its chief exponent, Professor Edward O. Wilson of Harvard University, sociobiology is "the systematic study of the biological basis of all social behavior."[9] This approach to biology is decisively shaped by Neo-Darwinian doctrine. According to this view, individual survival and perpetuation of a person's genotype in future generations constitute the chief factors in man's biologically-induced striving.[10]

This fundamental belief strongly colors Wilson's position toward the ethical (and also partly legal) problems of altruism and cooperation. Wilson maintains that altruism "enhances the personal genetic fitness of others at the cost of the genetic fitness on the part of the altruist; the altruist either reduces his own survival capacity, or curtails his own reproduction, or both."[11] (I have great difficulty in understanding why this should be so as a generalized proposition.) This conviction leads Wilson to the assumption that natural selection favors altruistic behavior toward close relatives (called by him "kin selection"), because close relatives share a large proportion of genes with the altruistic actor which will be passed on to subsequent generations. Natural selection, on the other hand, discourages unselfish conduct on behalf of unrelated persons or the social group as a whole.[12] Wilson admits that people sometimes commit themselves to a common task that transcends the bounds of purely personal pursuits. He suggests, however, that such social cooperation, unless repaid by tangible rewards, is bound to be "grudging."[13]

Other genetically implanted tendencies of human conduct, according to Wilson, are aggressivity, at least toward strangers,[14] defense of territory and warfare,[15] the desire to dominate, visible particularly in the attitude of the male toward the female sex,[16] spiteful behavior and deceptive practices,[17] and the incest taboo.[18] Wilson also suggests that, according to the findings of sociobiological research, ideals of justice may not, in fact, be justified. "While few will disagree," he says, "that justice as fairness is an ideal state for disembodied spirits, the conception is in no way explanatory or predictive with reference to human beings."[19] He recommends that we should retain a sense of reserve about proposals for radical social change based on utopian intuition. "It is a misconception," he maintains, "among many of the traditional Marxists, some learning theorists, and a still surprising proportion of anthropologists and sociologists that social behavior can be shaped into virtually any form."[20]

In a recent book entitled *Promethean Fire*, which Wilson coauthored with the physicist Charles Lumsden, a stronger emphasis is placed on the interaction between biology and culture than in Wilson's earlier publications. The authors admit the justification of some criticisms of sociobiology which have pointed out that culture has achieved a life of its own beyond the ordinary limits of biology.[21] The authors develop a theory of what they call "gene-culture coevolution." Culture is generated and shaped by biological imperatives, while biological traits are altered by genetic evolution in response to cultural innovation.[22] Notwithstanding the reciprocal influence of culture, the authors are convinced that the genes hold culture on an elastic but unbreakable leash.[23]

When we look at the authors' definition of culture, we find that it is quite narrow. Culture is defined as "the sum of all the artifacts, behavior, institutions, and mental concepts transmitted by learning among the members of a society."[24] This definition deemphasizes the great products of the human mind, such as philosophy, literature and other creative writing, and outstanding works of architecture, art, and music. The narrowness of the definition becomes understandable when we comb the book for an explanation of the purposes of culture. The authors make it clear in several places that culture is primarily designed to promote individual survival and maximization of a person's genotype.[25] Any other position would not have been consistent with the decisive role attributed by sociobiology to natural selection in the evolution of the human race.

Wilson's view of innate human nature has its antecedents in the pessimistic psychology of Thomas Hobbes and Sigmund Freud.[26] All three authors emphasize the self-regarding impulses of human beings and play down the social components of human nature. According to Wilson, selfishness is of great help to man in attaining his goals, and deception and hypocrisy are "very human devices for conducting the complex daily business of human life," as he puts it.[27] We have also seen that he limits the biological value of altruism to kin selection, which he regards as an extension of individual selection.[28]

While the center of gravity in Wilson's sociobiology lies in man's self-assertive and egotistical traits, other writers have accentuated the social side of human nature. In the work *De Jure Belli ac Pacis* by Hugo Grotius, the following statement appears:[29]

Among the traits characteristic of man is an impelling desire for society, that is, for the social life – not of any and every sort, but peaceful, and organized according to the measure of his intelligence, with those who are his own kind; this social trend the Stoics called 'sociableness.' Stated as a universal truth, therefore, the assertion that every animal is impelled by nature to seek only its own good cannot be conceded.

From this optimistic view of human nature Grotius deduced the possibility of a universal world order guaranteeing peace and social cooperation.[30] While Hobbes saw the natural condition of mankind, before the institution of a strong-arm government, as one of ceaseless conflict, Grotius believed that human beings were by nature essentially good and altruistic.

In the nineteenth century, Prince Peter Kropotkin charged in his book *Mutual Aid* that many writers had overrated the antisocial manifestations of human self-assertiveness.[31] In his opinion, sociability was as much a law of nature as mutual struggle. Although a great deal of warfare was going on between different species of animals, and different societies of human beings, there existed at the same time "as much, and perhaps even more" evidence of mutual support, mutual aid, and mutual defense.[32]

According to Karl Marx, the rallying point of the new materialism was going to be "human society, or social humanity."[33] He stressed the "species existence of man," without denying that self-assertion was necessary in certain definite circumstances.[34] "Only when real, individual man," he said, "has become a *species-being* in his empirical life, his individual work and his individual relationships, only when man has recognized and organized his *forces propres* as *social* forces so that social force is no longer separated from him in the form of *political* force, only then will human emancipation be completed."[35] In a communist society, he maintained, social development would be determined by the "connection of individuals," a connection which ensures the development of all through solidarity and the "universal" character of the activity of individuals.[36]

The sociologist Emile Durkheim voiced the opinion that man can be happy only as a member of an integrated cohesive society.[37] The contemporary biologist Ashley Montagu took the position that "man is born with the strongest cooperative impulses, and all that they require is the proper support and cultivation."[38] Quite recently, the American biologist George E. Pugh has developed a theory of innate values which include the other-regarding, altruistic values. The genetic selection process, he points out, is not concerned with just individual survival but rather with the survival of the species. If this is true, a certain amount of individual self-abnegation is necessitated to keep the development of the group viable and intact. Pugh believes that genetic evolution will have a positive tendency to favor socially cooperative behavioral traits.[39] He stated that the general ideas underlying his work showed a remarkable correspondence with the findings of sociobiology, but the specific conclusions he reached with respect to the nature of genetically inborn values are almost diametrically opposed to those of Wilson.

I now come to the critical part of my presentation. In my opinion, both the existentialist view as to man's complete freedom of self-realization and the behaviorist theory of the almost total malleability of the personality through operant conditioning must be rejected. I find myself in agreement with John Wild's statement to the effect that "man possesses a common nature which determines the general direction of essential tendencies."[40] This common nature is evidenced by typical reactions of human beings to benevolent or hostile behavior on the part of others. These typical reactions account for the manifold congruences in the world's ethical and legal systems. Without such universal or at least preponderant traits, a science of psychology would be entirely impossible.

I believe that this common nature of man normally has an individual and self-centered, as well as a social and other-regarding component. While there is variation in the strength of these two elements in particular persons, we rarely encounter a total egomaniac or a radically self-abnegating individual.

As I pointed out earlier, the sociobiology of Edward Wilson lays its chief stress on the self-regarding ingredient of the human personality. From a genetic perspective, he says, man is mainly interested in his own survival and the survival of his genes in his descendants; he will often exhibit aggressivity and ruthless egotism to promote these goals. "True selfishness," he has said, "if obedient to the other constraints of mammalian biology, is the key to a more nearly perfect social contract."[41] It is obvious that this statement has implications for law and justice.

Wilson's whole position, apart from other defects, is reductionist in character because it ignores man's spirit and reason, which are part of his biological equipment in a broader sense.[42] The human spirit has some ability to fashion blueprints for the overcoming of the most deleterious forms of aggression, deception, and power abuse (i.e., of qualities which according to Wilson inhere in the biological makeup of man). A reasonable person is aware that cooperative attitudes and concern for his fellowmen will not only be of personal advantage to him but will also be indispensable in building a worthwhile society. In such a society, the variegated capabilities of individuals will be pooled, and benefits and sacrifices will be borne equitably.[43] The psychiatrist Viktor Frankl has argued that it is part of man's nature to commit himself to a common task or cause that transcends the bounds of his purely personal ego gratification.[44]

I do wish to make a concession to Wilson, however. I do believe that the self-serving impulses of most human beings are sufficiently strong so as to place constraints on a fully harmonious pursuit of economic or cultural community objectives. It is not very likely that we shall ever see the emergence of a society in which men have been completely socialized and will pursue common aims in a collective spirit without substantial socio-economic incentives appealing to individual self-interest. "The view of 'nature, red in tooth and claw,' " said Dobzhansky, "in which every living being has only the alternative of 'eat or be eaten' is just as unfounded as the sentimentalist view that all is sweetness and light in unspoiled nature."[45]

We thus arrive at the conclusion that the duality of individual self-seeking and social concern for others is anchored in man's nature, understood as an amalgam of physiological, psychological, and spiritual components. It is, of course, possible through social persuasion, education, and even some use of force to strengthen one of the two sides of human nature at the expense of the other. But it would seem that a viable society should give support to the affirmative and constructive attributes of both of these components. It is desirable that an individual should attend to his personal needs and interests and do everything in his power to develop his personality. This objective may not be realizable without the presence of a certain amount of ego-centered assertiveness. It is also desirable that an individual should exhibit social interest and take part in the collective endeavors of his civilization. The pursuit of this aim requires some degree of self-abnegation and dedication to group objectives.

A society that blends in its political, social, and legal system individualistic and trans-subjective elements may be called a "symbiotic society." Such a society will endeavor to achieve a delicate integration of individual rights and public responsibilities. It will, in principle, endorse the civil, political, economic and social rights recognized in the Universal Declaration of Human Rights adopted by the United Nations General Assembly in 1948. It will, on the other hand, favor limitations on some of these rights which are required in the interests of public safety, public health, and public morals, and for the protection of the reputations and rights of others.[46]

The right to life will, of course, figure prominently among the rights to be protected by law; Edward Wilson's strong emphasis on survival as an innate biological urge will serve as an anthropological foundation for this right, though not necessarily the only one. As long as wars and civil wars exist, society will restrict the right of self-preservation for purposes of collective self-defense; and it is possible that the law of the future will continue to deny an individual the right to life in some (and hopefully rare) instances as a punishment for outrageous crimes.

The symbiotic society will be aware, however, that individuals desire not merely bare survival but survival as intact persons under tolerable conditions of life. The right to life will therefore be complemented by the right to bodily and psychic integrity, which will require protection not only against physical assaults but also against the destruction of reputations. The overall promotion of public health and the furthering of decent conditions of life would also rank high among the legal aims of such a society.

Sociobiology's repeated insistence on man's desire to perpetuate his genotype in future generations might find some support in unsuccessful attempts by some countries to limit reproduction by measures designed to achieve voluntary cooperation in population control. It is possible that – in the absence of a large-scale war – this problem may some day attain proportions requiring the taking of efficacious measures in the interest of collective survival. As a general proposition, I feel that sociobiology has greatly exaggerated the motivational force of gene perpetuation, especially in our own time.

Some versions of psychology have recognized innate needs of men which Darwinian biology has – consciously or unconsciously – neglected. Abraham Maslow, for example, has accentuated man's need for self-esteem, self-actualization, and creativity.[47] The desire of most people to engage in productive work useful to society would be a normal concomitant of these psychological needs. The symbiotic society would therefore recognize a right to work and at the same time set up incentives and reinforcements designed to instill a sense of duty in individuals to take part in the building and maintenance of civilization. The establishment of a right to education would be an indispensable precondition to the fulfillment of such societal tasks.[48]

The attitude of the symbiotic society toward the acquisition of personal property would be favorable; such property may be regarded as an extension of the individual person who wishes to be surrounded by objects congenial to his tastes. A use of such property, however, which would endanger the enjoyment of life by others or injure the public weal ought to be proscribed. As far as property in the means of production is concerned, the symbiotic society would have no all-embracive ideology preferring either public or private ownership. The choice between these two forms of ownership would depend, among others, on the question of accretion of unduly strong political power resulting from substantial controls over a branch of industry or commerce.

The right to liberty of expression would enjoy a high status of recognition in such a society. Constructive and responsible criticism of existing institutions may prevent societal stagnation or regression. But there appears no good reason for extending the right of free speech to unscrupulous or destructive attempts to undermine social cohesion, especially attempts to denounce racial, national, or religious minorities with the aim to reduce them to an inferior social status.

The concept of justice prevailing in the symbiotic society would be one which ensures the enjoyment of individual rights, such as freedom, a reasonable degree of equality, and security against violence and serious want, to the greatest extent consistent with the public good. The public good would be measured chiefly in terms of the highest economic and cultural development.[49] Such a conception of justice demands a resourceful balancing of private and public interests. Care would have to be taken that some institutional control be exercised over the decisions of legislators, upon whom the primary authority to undertake the difficult task of reconciling freedom and authority would devolve.[50]

University of California, Davis

NOTES

1 E.-J. Lampe, *Rechtsanthropologie* 1, Berlin 1970, 17.
2 J.-P. Sartre, *Existentialism*, New York 1947, 18.
3 *Ibid.*, 18-20.
4 K. Jaspers, *Die Geistige Situation der Zeit*, Berlin 1931, 146.
5 J. B. Watson, *Behaviorism*, New York 1924, Lectures I, X and XII.
6 B. F. Skinner, *About Behaviorism*, New York 1974, Chapters 4 and 14.
7 B. F. Skinner, *Beyond Freedom and Dignity*, New York 1971, 188.
8 N. Chomsky, *Language and Mind*, rev. ed., New York 1972, 6. See also *ibid.*, 9: "Normal human intelligence is capable of acquiring knowledge through its own internal resources." Cf. Chomsky, *Reflections on Language*, New York 1975, Chapter 1.
9 E. O. Wilson, *Sociobiology: The New Synthesis*, Cambridge, Mass. 1975, 4.
10 E. O. Wilson, *On Human Nature*, Cambridge, Mass. 1978a, 2–3, 199; D. P. Barash, *Sociobiology and Behavior*, 2d ed., New York 1980, 45; 'Reports of Three Group Discussions', in G. S. Stent (ed.), *Morality as a Biological Phenomenon*, rev. ed., Berkeley 1980, 256, 263.
11 E. O. Wilson, 'The Genetic Evolution of Altruism', in L. Wispé (ed.), *Altruism, Sympathy, and Helping*, New York 1978b, 11.
12 Wilson (1975), 117–118, 120; Wilson (1978b), 11–13, 29–35.
13 Wilson (1978a), 199.

[14] Wilson (1975), 575. See also the more general statement in Wilson (1978a), 99, to the effect that human beings are innately aggressive.
[15] Wilson (1975), 564-565; Wilson, 'Academic Vigilantism and the Political Significance of Sociobiology', *BioScience* 26 (1976), 187; Wilson (1978a), 99. In the last-mentioned work Wilson points out, however, that the more violent forms of aggression are not necessarily based on genetic factors but are in part the result of environmental influences. Wilson (1978a), 105–106.
[16] Wilson (1975), 575; Wilson (1978a), 126–128.
[17] Wilson (1975), 119, 553; Wilson (1978a), 159.
[18] Wilson (1978a), 36.
[19] Wilson (1975), 562. See also Stent, *op. cit.*, 254.
[20] Wilson (1978a), 18. See also Wilson (1976), 189.
[21] C. J. Lumsden and E. O. Wilson, *Promethean Fire: Reflections on the Origin of Mind*, Cambridge, Mass. 1983, 45.
[22] *Ibid.*, 19.
[23] *Ibid.*, 60.
[24] *Ibid.*, 187.
[25] *Ibid.*, 20, 119, 173. See also Wilson (1978a), 2. Wilson has also described culture as a "system of environmental tracking devices". Wilson (1975), 560.
[26] T. Hobbes, *De Cive*, S. P. Lamprecht ed., New York 1949, Chapter I; S. Freud, *Civilization and Its Discontents*, J. Strachey ed., New York 1961, 58–63, Chapter V.
[27] Wilson (1978b), 31; Wilson (1975), 553.
[28] Wilson (1978b), 27.
[29] H. Grotius, *De Jure Belli ac Pacis* 2, F. Kelsey transl., Oxford and London 1925, Prolegomena Sec. 6.
[30] See C. F. Murphy, 'The Grotian Vision of World Order', *American Journal of International Law* 76 (1982), 477.
[31] P. Kropotkin, *Mutual Aid: A Factor of Evolution*, Boston 1955.
[32] *Ibid.*, 5, 76–77, 292–300.
[33] K. Marx, 'Concerning Feuerbach', Thesis X, in: *Early Writings*, Vintage Books ed., New York 1975, 423.
[34] K. Marx, 'On the Jewish Question', *ibid.*, 241; K. Marx and F. Engels, *The German Ideology*, J. C. Arthur ed., New York 1970, 104–105.
[35] Marx (1975), 234.
[36] Marx and Engels (1970), 118.
[37] E. Durkheim, *Suicide*, New York 1951, 209–210, 376; Durkheim, *Sociology and Philosophy*, London 1953, 54–55, 91; J. Piaget, *Biology and Knowledge*, Chicago 1971, 98.
[38] M. Ashley Montagu, *The Direction of Human Development*, New York 1955, 30.
[39] G. E. Pugh, *The Biological Origin of Human Values*, New York 1977, 115–116, 227–229.
[40] J. D. Wild, *The Challenge of Existentialism*, Bloomington 1955, 267.
[41] Wilson (1978a), 157.
[42] For the view that the mind is a distinctive form of energy which gives directions to the brain, whereas the brain (as a sort of computer) either executes these directions or transmits them to other organs of the body see W. Penfield, *The Mystery of the Mind*, Princeton 1975, 11, 46–48, 75–76, 81; K. Popper and J. C. Eccles, *The Self and Its*

Brain, Berlin and New York 1977, 335–336, 362. Penfield is an outstanding neurosurgeon and Eccles a well-known neurophysiologist, and their conclusions are based on neurological experiments rather than on metaphysical speculations. See also W. H. Thorpe, *Biology and the Nature of Man*, London and New York 1962, 21, 27; P. Teilhard de Chardin, 'The Formation of the Noosphere', in *The Future of Man*, New York 1964, 161–191. Wilson, on the other hand, characterizes the mind as a mere "epiphenomenon of the neuronal machinery of the brain." Wilson (1978a), 195.

[43] According to Theodosius Dobzhansky, natural selection has been achieved not only by competition and struggle, but – to an even greater extent – by cooperation. See T. Dobzhansky, *The Biological Basis of Human Freedom*, New York 1956, 65.

[44] V. Frankl, *The Will to Meaning*, New York 1969, 38, 50; Frankl, *The Unheard Cry for Meaning*, New York 1978, 35–36.

[45] Dobzhansky, *op. cit.*, 64.

[46] See in this connection Art. 29 (2) of the Universal Declaration of Human Rights and Art. 10 (2) of the European Convention on Human Rights. For the text of these provisions see I. Brownlie (ed.), *Basic Documents in International Law*, Oxford 1967, 137, 199.

[47] A. H. Maslow, *Motivation and Personality*, 2d ed., New York 1970, 45–46, 170–171.

[48] The United States Supreme Court has denied a right to education under the U.S. Constitution in *San Antonio Independent School District v. Rodriguez*, 411 U. S. 1 (1973), but appears to have cautiously moved away from this position in *Plyler v. Doe*, 457 U. S. 202 (1982).

[49] See E. Bodenheimer, *Jurisprudence: The Philosophy and Method of the Law*, rev. ed., Cambridge, Mass. 1974, 240–245.

[50] A special constitutional court consisting of fifteen members, endowed with power to invalidate legislation on specified grounds by a two-thirds majority, appears to me to be the most desirable form of supervision.

JAN M. BROEKMAN

LAW, ANTHROPOLOGY AND EPISTEMOLOGY

INTRODUCTION

Quite often studies concerning the relationship between law and anthropology are considered in the light of *cultural anthropology*. The comparison between legal system and cultural system provides impressive possibilities for reaching an understanding of human structures. At the same time it provides the opportunity to study the whole of law as a unique cultural form. Against the background of increasing internationalisation of relations between states, people, legal systems and cultures, the comparative approach just mentioned would seem to be the way forward. This is even more pertinent because international, economic, industrial, constitutional and other branches of law will assume proportionately greater perspectives with considerable practical import. In this connection one also has in mind the strong Anglo-Saxon tradition which is progressively gaining ground in continental legal thinking.

Closely related to the above is the starting-point of a more legal philosophic orientation. In this latter the same theme is considered from the standpoint of *philosophical anthropology*. In this context, the basic attitude is that law is an expression of the being or existence of man. Such notions are apparent in scholasticism, the period of natural law and thinking based on the social contract theory, and are also present in the works of Kant and Hegel. The same can be said with regard to Herder whose work may indeed on a number of points be said to be the precursor of the philosophical anthropology of the twenties in our century. The discussion around Gehlen's theory of institutionalisation illustrates how quickly a fixated image of human existence leads to untenable political and juridical conservatism. The reason for the untenability is that ultimately such conservatism comes into conflict with whatever conceivable political value including every contemporary anthropological insight. This danger is evident despite all the modern anthropological insights which are attributable not only to phenomenology, existentialist philosophy and structuralism but also to the integration of insights derived from biology, physiology, systems theory and other studies.

The problem, as indicated above, could be resolved by taking every expression about the human being no longer as a *point of departure* but as a *speech*

E. Bulygin et al. (eds.), Man, Law and Modern Forms of Life, 15–42.

act. On this basis the human being (person) is to be viewed as a being in and of the law. Human being and law are together moments of a more encompassing speech structure. The relationship between law and anthropology is embedded in one unit of actions, thoughts and speeches – a veritable unit of speech acts called "discourse". This leads to a criticism of the traditional way of thinking about the foundations of law. According to such thinking law is founded in anthropology. But even critical rationalism, in a large measure a critique of the traditional way of thinking, also failed to discover the discoursive dimension of law. Yet it is this latter dimension which brings to light a legal theory appearing as a unit of dogmatic and ideological criticism. Such legal theory may deservingly be called non-Cartesian. In contraposition there is legalism which, as the ideal contemporary theory, is part and parcel of Cartesian legal theory.

Anthropology understood as the study of man as a speaking being provides with respect to law a particular insight which is specifically instantiated in three discoursive practices. One of these is the process of *individualisation*. In practice this involves the establishment of one's own causality in the sense of being one's own authority or sovereign and the creation of equilibrium. The positivist legal necessity for individualisation thus becomes apparent in every concrete juridical setting. In particular Marxist legal theory has pointed out this necessity and subjected it to criticism. The second, *juridical causality*, does in the same light appear to be a moment in the construction of a whole legal discourse. Ultimately, law reaches its self-realisation in the search for and the actualisation of *equilibrium*. In this tripartite vision lie the fundamental concepts of law and anthropology. Such concepts are the usable material in the quest for equilibrium. Since the self-realisation and the actualisation of law culminate in the achievement of the condition of equilibrium, it is clear that the fundamental concepts of law and anthropology will be utilised to bring about the law and the man conducive to the desired condition. Precisely here is the locus of the deep-seated foundations of the relationship between law and anthropology on the one hand and their specific epistemology on the other.

1. THE LEGAL IMAGE OF MAN

There is widespread disaffection concerning the function of law in contemporary society. At bottom the discontent relates to the manner in which theory formulation occurs in legal science and how the particularity of this science is to be understood in relation to other sciences. It is evident that the former aspect cannot simply be regarded as a sociological and exclusively theoretical question of science. In fact both aspects have assumed such great importance that they may no longer be viewed merely as introductions to specific problem areas. These aspects converge at one important point, namely, the question concerning *man as an image of law*. This basic question immediately spurts out of a series of related questions: what are we in the eyes of the law and according to its principles; which qualities does the law attribute to us; what conditions should we fulfil in order to acquire legal rights? What kind of man does the jurist have in mind whenever he addresses a question to me? How does the response to his question reach his mode of thought and what does it say about law in general? As a whole these questions illustrate that it is cognitively important to know the kind of images of man upon which law is based and upon which specific images of man the law actually orientates its decisions.

The preceding questions can therefore not be confined to a more or less sociological perspective. Notwithstanding the important and interesting problem concerning the character of legal provision, the access to legal procedure and the desideratum to establish order in the structures of social relations, it is clear that the answers as well as the variables provided by way of response to all the questions already raised remain somewhat fragmentary. Dogmatic delineations and legal techniques are actually oriented towards fixed and specific images of man. For example, it happens quite frequently that the question concerning the image of man is raised in criminal law. The same holds true with regard to the Christian-humanistic orientation which finds expression in the decisions handed down as law by the appeal court. A close look at these latter aspects will also reveal the fragmentary character of the answers and the variables provided.

The way out of the limitations indicated above is to proceed along a general structural and epistemological level.[1] An important consideration in this connection is that it is hardly possible to determine precisely whether or not such an approach as well as the effort to clarify certain aspects of the foundations of law, is ultimately the result of an over-optimistic and simplistic belief in progress. One frequently encounters this kind of scientific optimism in discussions on legal theory.[2] In conjunction with such scientific theoretical optimism there is the generally accepted presupposition that far from being a nebulous, abstract, anonymous and overwhelming structure, law appears as a clear and concrete sphere susceptible to change. In support of this latter view, it is often argued that a critical attitude, the will to change and a certain human rationality are not only present but they are also effective in law. This is discernible in the various experiences of delinquents and sometimes even of jurists! Apparently this happens because the issue here concerns qualities which we would like to attribute to ourselves. It therefore requires courage to go against matters which are held to be self-evident. This observation applies not only with regard to one's own position but it is also generally applicable.

The image of man in contemporary Western positive law consists in:

(a) the *subject* (an individual, the elementary unit in discourse, juridical identity, source, capability),

(b) *with causalities* (rationality, conceptuality; reconstructibility of acts and liabilities; biography as a unity of complex articulations),

(c) *engaged in a situation of intercourse with conflict or disturbed equilibrium* (otherwise there is hardly any need to establish order or to resolve problems; legal factuality comes into being as a specific perception out of the total situation of balance or equilibrium; without this aspect there can be no sensible talk about 'the other'),

(d) *which tends towards conflict resolution and the restoration of equilibrium* (the restoration of the overwhelming silence; legal speech is but an articulation of a transitory character; equilibrium is the return to the sphere of the existing legal equality and its identity with civil reality.[3])

The above position provides a robot-photo of legal man and indicates the great extent to which this man is the embodiment of legal dogmatics. Legal dogmatics is understood here not only as a legal theory on the finding of the law, or the formation and construction of the law, but also as a system of rules which the legal practitioner must come to terms with in order to remain within the confines of valid positive law. This means that legal dogmatics rule the construction of the legal discourse as such. These rules are different but equally important in the common law system as in the codified legal systems of Western Europe. Our analysis implies therefore a generality, and touches upon both legal systems of the Western hemisphere. This includes yet another important aspect, namely, that the determinable as well as the well-defined man of the law is at the same time the embodiment of the conditions for the necessity of law as law. Whoever knows legal man is also cognisant of the epistemological conditions which must be fulfilled before there can be any talk about law. This insight forms the basic statement of our problem concerning the relationship between law, anthropology and epistemology. In this connection we lay particular emphasis upon the distinction between legal dogmatics (*Rechtslehre*), legal theory (*Rechtstheorie*) and legal philosophy (*Rechtsphilosophie*). The interconnection with anthropology is also underlined by Jenkins in his *Social Order and the Limits of Law*:

Every legal system rests, consciously or unconsciously, upon a theory of man. In both cases (and especially the latter), the underlying theory is apt to be present only implicitly. But this does not lessen its influence . . . .[4]

The same is also affirmed by Miaille in his *Une Introduction Critique au Droit*. In this latter text Miaille stresses particularly the epistemological dimension thus:

Pour développer une étude scientifique du droit, nous devons forcer trois obstacles d'autant plus solides qu'ils paraissent plus 'naturels': L'apparente transparance de l'objet d'étude, l'idéalisme traditionnel de l'analyse juridique, la croyance enfin qu'une science n'acquiert son statut qu'en isolant de toutes les autres recherches.[5]

In this same context it must be stated quite explicitly that the characteristics of legal man in our law including the conditions for the necessity of law as law are simultaneously expressive of the basic values of our culture. On this level it is important to keep in mind that law is a cultural element. Accordingly, law is an expression of that which is deemed to be valuable in a given culture.

This position with its three components: (1) the characteristics of legal man in our law, (2) the necessaritarian conditionality of these characteristics for law as law, and (3) the fact that at the same time these qualities and conditions are expressive of values, forms the basic organising concept or principle.

(1) *Individuality* is a social datum. This assertion brings to light one of the deeply-rooted conflicts relative to juridical assumption and reality. There are those like Althusser and Edelman who speak in this connection about *the* legal ideology. The ideology springs from the denial of the fact that individuality is the result of a long and important process of cultural assimilation. The ideology proceeds simply to speak about individuality in terms of autonomy as the foundation of a fundamental legal principle according to which each one is by nature a bearer of rights and duties. This principle, unchanged up to the present, is regarded as 'the principle of material entitlement'. Every human being has, on this view, the right to do or not to do whatever he or she wishes. However, none has the right to handle another's personality or proprietary rights without the period consent of the former. Each one owns his possessions and is master of himself only. This, it is argued, is the principle of law.

In this way the already stated fact is suppressed and cast into oblivion. The individual thus identifies himself with the first-person singular only through a rather risky phase of development which is of the utmost importance biologically, spiritually, socially and for the individual as well. But in this perspective the juridical mode of thought is once more expressive of the basic values of Western culture. From the Renaissance onward individuality has been taken as the basis for all the actuality of life including the coming into being of scientific truth. *Cogito ergo sum*. The real character of individuality thus became not only suppressed and forgotten but it was also reified. These transformations subsequently became hypostasized data upon which juridical structures and forms of social life rest.

(2) *Contractuality* is closely related to the already mentioned individuality. This notion is partly associated with the fact that up to the present day law and social life are explained and legitimated, excogitated and lived through in terms of the social contract. The terms and the concepts employed in this context reveal striking affinities with the ideas of either Hobbes or Locke. This fact is complemented and preserved by more subtle and deeply anchored forms of thinking in terms of contract. The latter are discernible in our linguistic patterns, in scientific and philosophic conceptualisation as well as in the everyday life of social reality. However, it still requires a great deal of effort to detect and discern this dimension of contractuality.[6] The forms are viewed as the radicalisation and the absolutisation of the variable forms of reflexive thinking. The latter were already operative in antiquity. *Do ut des*. Thus the question is whether or not we are still capable of thinking about law and justice, state and society, ourselves and others without reference to the implicit form-giving reflexivity that inheres to the idea of contract. It appears that this latter idea is entertained simply as a matter of natural course. Thus it is pertinent to ask if we are still capable of going through life without the prior implicit assimilation of contractuality and the subsequent living out thereof in our everyday life.

(3) This two-pronged material rationale is supported by two more formal trends. In the first place both individuality and contractuality are indeed demonstrable as the depth-structures of legal dogmatics. This leads to a more general point of departure, notably, the *demonstrability* of analyses in the sphere of concrete legal practice. This insight is supported by the fact that such thought-forms, fixations and legal conceptualisations on legal dogmatics (here understood as being representative of the forms of legal thinking as such) as well as the actual social bond are taken to be together or in community. This in turn gives rise to the question if between the two – namely, legal discourse and the general every-day discourse – there is no immediate direct relationship or some kind of possibility whereby one kind of discourse may be transformed into another. It would seem that there is such a possibility. It must therefore be constantly borne in mind that the

claim to demonstrability in legal praxis and legal thought leads necessarily away from ontologistic and essentialistic questioning with regard to law. Whoever observes legal dogmatics, analyses cases and arrests and investigates theories of law and the state according to the above mentioned conceptualisations, can hardly be said to be interested in the existence of the law, debates concerning the being of law or the definitions thereof. He recognises a pragmatic-analytic position which might grow into a critical attitude towards ideology. It is equally important to keep in mind that demonstrability is not the same thing as applicability. But this inclination is nevertheless rather strong in legal thinking. Two reasons may be adduced for this tendency. One is that legal practice is directed towards the application of principles to reality and another is that legal dogmatics exerts considerable influence upon all theory formulation concerning legal science. In this connection the question is not, in the first instance, a philosophical clarification of 'demonstrability' as such (Wittgenstein). Rather the issue is a pragmatic position which on the one hand never loses sight of legal practice while on the other it does not become theory for theory's sake nor a ready instrument useful for the circumscription of legal practice.[7]

These basic lines are supported by the utilisation of the concept of discourse (*discours*). The concept originates from French philosophy of the second half of our century. It means to express the truth and simultaneously to recognise that the speech of the subject is *not* 'his' or does *not* 'belong' to him! It is crucially important to grasp together the instrumentalist connotation and its subversive counterpart (that is, the Freudian oedipal experience that my actual speech is never properly 'mine' but that of the other taken *grosso modo* as culture). This occurs also when legal discourse refers to 'the law' as the particularity of a general culture and everyday-life actuality which in turn is characterised as 'bourgeois discourse'.[8] It may be important to point out here that the concept of discourse is at the root for the interpretation of that which we call *speech* performances.[9] It is therefore fitting to define the concept of discourse through the aid of the concept of *speech act* (in no way an exclusive concept of Anglosaxon analysis[10]). 'Discourse' indicates a *specific* unity of speech acts. Ultimately the unity and subsistence of the legal discourse are brought about by the speech acts performed by Highest Courts: Supreme Court, Cour de Cassation, Hof van Cassatie, Hoge Raad, etc. The specificity of the Supreme Court is created and maintained by legal dogmatics. It must be noted that in the case of the legal discourse the issues are much clearer than in the case of a description of medical, economic or another integral discourse. However, the specificity of bourgeois discourse and a description thereof is even more complex and involves more profound sociological and narrative analytical investigations.[11] In any case it must be stressed that even with regard to the concept of 'legal discourse' the ambiguity already described, that is, the recoilability of language from perfect instrumentality and from being the product of the speaking subject, must never be lost sight of.

2. FOUNDATIONS OF LAW

The three closely related perspectives mentioned below are particularly important for a vision of the foundations of law and anthropology:

The fact that every legal thought and every legal action are the work of man may be viewed as a generally accepted principle. In spite of this it is difficult to avoid the impression that a one-sided interpretation of this principle seems to be overwhelming. Indeed law is neither a Moloch nor is the state a Leviathan. There are various efforts to present law as the work of man and to try to make it of service to their direct interests.

Yet such efforts do not overcome the one-sidedness already outlined. *Law is not only the work of man but the man of today is also the work of law*! Whoever fails to comprehend this will similarly fail to make a good jurist. Every speech made by the jurist affirms a specific image of man, sustains it and even delineates it more closely. Surely, it behooves every jurist to know this and to comprehend how it comes about. The central issue here is not some abstract philosophical expression which might be excogitated alongside legal reality. On the contrary, the issue is the concrete fact through and through. The hallmark of this fact is that it is accepted as self-evident and therefore requires no discussion.

Every legal speech act forms and reaffirms a specific image of man and the legal subject is expected to be at home with such imaging. This is concretely demonstrable and it is operative in all the branches of law. As a matter of fact there is no choice. According to the concealed juridical thought which in fact gives form to social life, the point is that you either experience yourself as legal man or the law is simply not for you. Consequently, if the latter is your experience then you can neither acquire nor enjoy your rights. This fact often lies hidden from the jurist because it is embedded in a certain non-cognitivity of speech, writing, text and conversation in a general sense. Legal science proceeds from the assumption that everyone knows what this kind of language is. In this way a very specific and well-defined traditional position continues to be frequently repeated and quite uncritically. According to this position speech and writing, text and conversation are regarded merely as *means* of communication. The jurist literally takes this means to hand. Thus equipped the jurist acquires a position of power which he perpetuates by coming to terms with the whole differentiated system of what he calls legal techniques. The first word that the jurist utters to me by way of his typical manner of speech already transforms me into a legal subject. I am not a legal subject by nature but nevertheless I must be such because it is the tacit price that I have to pay for being in society and enjoying my rights therein. This condition must be satisfied so that I can exercise my freedom in society. Such an insight about myself belongs at the same time to the insight concerning the foundations of law.

A complication immediately arises. The speech acts of the jurist as already described will generally be perceived as non-deviations from the manner in which we speak to one another. Is it not the case that our manner of speech is such that we persistently try to make one another the subject of speech? Surely, everyone is so thrown-down (subjected) by speech that it is well-nigh impossible to talk about free or liberated speech acts. Indeed this complication means that the forms of juridical cognition and their corresponding speech acts constitute such an exceptional variation from the reality of general discourse that one may aptly call it *legal discourse*. The relationship between the two, their points of difference and convergence shall have to be closely studied. But caution! The method here is that it is our collective responsibility to debunk from our speech performances all the specific responsibility that the jurist takes with regard to his own speech acts relative to us. In fact it is precisely at this point that the courage and the critical attitude already referred to, emerge. These can be drawn not only from objective scientific perception but also from anxiety, restlessness and an uneasy feeling of fatalism.

Related to all this is the fact that today many people do not perceive themselves as the law sees them. This is manifested in diverse forms: often a feeling of helplessness expressing itself as disaffection or sometimes desperate violence appearing in the form of terrorism. Violence and disaffection with existing legal rules, legal assumptions, laws, legal systems and juridical interpretations are by no means the last word on the matter. But quite often this is hardly realised and the result is that immediately the symptom is mistaken for the cause. No doubt this is a simplistic solution which can be nothing more than a defence mechanism. Disaffection and violence are the *manifestation* of a profound conflict in the law itself. If the man created by law is the only condition for the possibility of that law then it would appear that many no longer regard themselves as that kind of man and consequently the legal image of man can no longer be accepted as a self-evident life-form. Thus law is hit directly at its very foundations. Nowadays this happens repeatedly. One wonders if the man created by law is really human. What is the true relationship between law and humanity, law and love? Could one realistically draw a sharp line between law and love? Do law and anthropology relate to each other on a tense footing?

In addition, the two perspectives already sketched must appear to be somewhat ominous for the legal practitioner. *De facto* he has to deal with whatever has to do with the legal process. This appears to have obscured anthropology long ago and as a whole it is no longer relevant. At some point it is concerned with equality or the power of self-expression of the parties involved. At yet another point it is concerned with arguments or the range of interpretation. One wonders whether or not it is still important nowadays to use all the techniques and considerations in order to create the image of legal man which could be used to determine if legal man would consider himself to be even worse off either because of such an image or on account of the fact that he had lost a case. This course would obviously be difficult to chart and to verify. Talk about legal man can conceivably come to an end either during the proceedings or in the construction of a legal argument. Similarly, one hardly talks to the operating surgeon about the political attitude of the multinational concerns which have developed his apparatus.

In the light of the foregoing it is clear that it is only through a thorough knowledge of speech and writing, text and conversation that another type of legal dogmatics can be developed. On this basis a more effective argumentation could be constructed, provided the knowledge of man created by the law could be used for the establishment of a relatively just legal order. Such an achievement would almost certainly compel the legal practitioner to pay attention to the theme "law and anthropology" and to debate the whole matter openly. In all other cases there is a looming threat that law cannot be ameliorated and if the threat materialises then the entire theme would be through and through superfluous. Thus juridical activity relies upon complete taciturnity over the anthropological dimension. Juridical self-evidence maintains a rather loud silence: anthropology is the *concealed discourse* in law.

3. NATURAL AND LEGAL PERSON

The life of every individual is spanned out in a network of social relationships. An important aspect of the latter is the complex of juridical relationships.

It is in the context of such relationships that legal rights and obligations are formulated. Of particular importance here is the fact that there is a tendency to forget that in such circumstances the issue centers on the one hand around legal construction and the dogmatic consequences flowing from it whereas on the other it is a question of the creation of a legal reality which is nonetheless not exclusively juridical. Legal constructions create the reality of rights and duties. Without such constructions the reality in question can simply not exist. The speech act character of the law becomes apparent in this situation. 'Behind' legal reality there is no other concealed actuality. Therefore, legal reality cannot through the application of legal formulae function as an instrument for the expression of the supposedly concealed reality. This must really be emphasised because that which is expressed is thus reality itself. The performative character of the legal speech act is usually not consciously identified. The reason for this is that the illusion that there is yet another reality subsisting independently 'behind' the actuality of juridical construction is eagerly sustained. Thus the question that comes to the fore is whether or not the particular juridical articulation may be regarded as being more or less adequate. The question is instrumentalistic in its nature and setting. An answer to this question provides the opportunity over which one has got power. Every underlying thought over an encompassing responsibility for the existence of the legal speech act as such becomes suppressed. Thus one is confined only to effective construction and argumentation on the basis of the already given reality! According to current dominant opinion the jurist may appositely be described as the magician of language. For this reason the jurist considers his activity *grosso modo* as a naming activity.

The organisation of the legal person must be seen in the same light. In this connection it is important to realise that law excogitates the natural person exclusively from the viewpoint of the legal person. For the jurist the natural person operates as the reality 'behind' the legal person. In this way the natural person becomes the necessary point of reference for every speech concerning the legal person. This is borne out by the suggestion that the naturalness of the natural person is entirely outside the legal person so that the former would appear as an anthropological datum from which juridical thought and knowledge could take their point of departure. But this is simply not the case. The concept of a natural person is alien to anthropology. The same holds true with regard to theological, philosophical and biological anthropology. But in legal thinking the remarkability of the concept of 'natural person' is not brought into question. It is hardly clarified that in fact legal dogmatics conceptualises both the natural and the legal person. The former is necessary as the point of reference for the latter. On this showing it is then suggested that the legal person is nothing more than the natural person endowed with exceptional quality! This mechanism of conceptualisation is discernible as soon as one discovers that even the natural person is a legal construction.

But whenever this point of departure remains concealed then rights and duties, whether as privileges or possibilities and capabilities, become the attributes of the natural person, 'every human existent'. In this way pronouncements such as the following have become familiar, particularly in civil law. 'Every individual, every human existent, is generally speaking a legal subject.' For this reason it is not every individual who is in fact the owner of goods, a debtor, a creditor and so on. However, the individual may acquire certain privileges under specific conditions and he may in specific circumstances be obliged to fulfil certain obligations. Thus the attribute of legal subject is in reality the possibility to acquire specific rights or be related to other individuals in such a manner that one may be held liable for the fulfilment of specific obligations.

The natural person is a juridical construction. He is in turn the condition for the juridical construction of legal subjectivity. The fact that such a figure can come into existence is an indication that the naturalness of the person is deemed to be a value. The same value reappears as a fixed juridical dogmatic reasoning manifesting itself in legal speech.

A possible counterargument to this type of reasoning including its philosophical background with regard to the performative character of the legal speech act, is that the idea of a 'person' is much older than law. Surely, the social reality of an argument, a delict, guilt, marriage and so on is anterior to the form which has been inscribed into it by law. In general, most social relations which are currently the object of legal regulation cannot be viewed as either the discovery or the creation of law. It is therefore difficult to see how one can successfully maintain that one is the result of juridical construction. Clearly, a thorough investigation of this aspect must involve a high degree of differentiation leading up to the spheres of linguistic philosophy, epistemology and critique of ideology. But before moving into the latter area it is pertinent to observe that those elements of social reality which are under the grip of legal thinking are *structurally altered*. Transformations have occurred. This simply means that the one reality is not the other. Legal provisions form a unique whole of its own kind which is a special category of human experience.[12] One cannot understand a contract or a delict unless one recognises one's being as *de iure*.

4. THE CONSTRUCTION OF THE LEGAL PERSON

In much the same way as the natural person is not considered to be a concept in terms of legal dogmatics, also the conditions which law attaches to legal subjectivity are disregarded. Put differently, specific laws apply unreservedly once an individual belongs to a particular state, is a member of specific sex, has reached a legally determined age, and has acquired a fixed domicile. Only then can one rent a house, exercise the right of freedom of expression and commit a delict. The conditionality is such deeper than the technical-juridical and political dimensions relative to the capacity to act and being the subject of a specific state. The cardinal point here centres around the relationship between law and anthropology. One *ought to* take a specific name and a fixed domicile and even *exercise* rights over some patrimony in other to become a legal person. In this way the individual, the rational being, is bound towards the purposefulness of the orientation to restore equilibrium.[13] However, the legal subject is seldom aware of this because being human in the eyes of the law involves simultaneously enclosure in a concealed discourse. The fact that the individual has a name[14] and a fixed domicile reflects two separate moments of legal individualism. The appearance of such moments strikes us blind. Indeed the lightning-flash of these moments obscures our vision because we seldom, if ever, recognise the logic of such moments. This means that we fail to recognise these moments as *conditions which come about* because of the impact of legal construction upon reality. The same holds true with regard to the values pertaining to such moments. Here we refer specifically to the legal consequences that could flow from the construction already mentioned. The former remain in abeyance but they become operational as soon as a fresh need to create order arises. Whoever takes up a name is accordingly in some way or another embedded in the rigorous system of the civil status. Thus the fact that one's civil status is intimately related to one's name means that the name provides the possibility for identifying the individual within the system whereas it also means that the individual is identifiable via the system. Against this background the significance of juridical localisation through residence and domicile is shatteringly obvious. The bearer of the name is deemed to be present (even though he may be absent) in his domicile because he *ought* to have a domicile. It is hardly surprising therefore that all the legal texts should mention the domicile and even have dealings with it. Provided that these conditions are satisfied then the legal subject can speak of his rights and duties in the sense that they are his 'property'. Here appropriation and expropriation go hand in hand –

incurring the duty to perform in return for a reciprocal right to performance. It is the close interconnection between these two aspects which fulfils so perfectly the basic value of contractuality.[15]

To all this must be added the consideration that all these conditions, insofar as they signify the freedom of the individual, do respectively relate to the individual as a legal subject. The *freedom* is conceived of in terms of *autonomy*. It is the kind of autonomy that must remain bound to the legal system without which it cannot stand on its own.

Thus the construction of the legal person is closely related to the problem of freedom in law and politics. The construction finds its mirror image and necessary complement in the constitution of the state and the Treaty of Europe. On this showing, freedom and legal subjectivity become the most important theoretical components of legal dogmatics. They were specific themes of thought about law and the state in the bourgeois period of West European civilisation. Finico and Pico della Mirandola, Hobbes, Locke and Descartes all develop this theme having a more or less similar understanding of it. Ultimately this boils down to a process of creating the new man in terms of political freedom. Evidently, the process is far from complete. More and more people would like to be grafted into the process. They claim that they could rediscover their true selves within the process. English thought in particular wields considerable influence in this sphere. Witness, for example, the impact of Anglosaxon analytical philosophy relative to the development of political theory. Thus the inquiry into freedom has become transformed into a question about law. In this latter connection freedom in contemporary life is perceived as being inextricably connected to rights and duties, legal subjectivity, constitutional and human rights. A necessary corollary to this is that freedom cannot be excogitated otherwise than in terms of *autonomy*. On the one hand this autonomy is coupled with the capacity to act and contractuality on the other. Juridically everything is geared towards promoting, deepening and defending progress or development. For this reason it is much more apparent that the crucial issue here is the basic value of Western culture and its articulation through the law. The constitution as well as the activities leading to the Treaty of Europe reflect freedom as autonomy (Title 1, art. 5, 13, 14). They reflect a well-defined juridical interpretation. It is an interpretation which is presented as one single big thing. Thus it emerges that contemporary law is intent upon a radical *auto-representation*. Legal man is simply fitted into the latter.

The most important point with regard to all this is that the self-evidence with which this trend of thought has captured our perception now determines our relationship to ourselves, to others and to the world around us. It surely requires no special argument to make the point that this mode of thought is to a very large extent determined by legal practice. Legal practice is indeed the means through which considerable pressure is brought to bear upon legal theory. No doubt legal practice together with its peculiar legal dogmatics dominate the interpretation and construction of the juridical conceptual world including its rationality.

The mechanisms that sustain the legal construction of reality can be outlined and clarified by way of a critique of ideology. One could also focus one's criticism upon the function of human images in law. It would appear, however, that no answer can be provided to the question how a less dogmatic tie between human images, positive law and legal theory can actually grow. Baruzzi attempted to answer this question in his analysis of criticisms of human images in law as they function in the judgements handed down by the Supreme Court.[16] The first criticism is that of W. Weischedel[17] who considers that the problem lies in the ethical foundation of law. According to these authors the ethical foundation is partly attributable to the autonomy-ethic of Kant and the material value-ethic of Max Scheler. However, both moments converge in their reference to a Christian-humanistic image of man. The three components already indicated are, according to Weischedel's criticism, historically determined data. In the foundations of legal dogmatics the said data are dealt with as though they are extra-temporal entities. In addition there is the instrumentalist and free use of arguments in legal argumentation. Correlatively, there is the more philosophical problem which pertains to the question whether or not law can indeed be founded on ethics. In this connection it is proper to ask if the preceding line of inquiry does not immediately provide a built-in *fixated anthropologicum.*[18] The second criticism is juridico-technical, and politically it is something completely different. The criticism is advanced by E. Denninger who attempted to criticise the constitution of the Federal Republic of Germany relative to its image of man.[19] By means of his critique Denninger demonstrates that law necessarily requires institutional decision-making mechanisms and that these latter are already endowed with an image of man. But such an image of man is frequently concealed in the normative realm. It becomes operationalised at a very abstract level. Above all it is also already functional within the decision-making logic of the law itself.

Both criticisms, the first more philosophical and the second juridical and functionalist, agree on one point, namely, that the relationship between positive law and its image of man must simultaneously be that of *relativisation* and *fixation*. This may be illustrated by reference to the interpretation of clauses which appear in many constitutions and have a bearing upon the inviolability of the dignity of the human person and his value. In order to guarantee this inviolability effectively, it is necessary that legal dogmatics should transform it into that which it is not, notably, a reified and very important quality. The latter immediately receive an occupant and the occupant is none other than a legal party. Baruzzi makes the following observation:

> Hinsichtlich der glänzenden Gründungsversuche, die uns in den Wissenschaften und der Technik gelingen spiegelt die Verfassung den Versuch, uns zunächst in einem Abgrund anzusiedeln. Wissenschaft und Technik müssen vor dem Menschen haltmachen. Er ist letzlich nicht der Gegenstand, sondern der Widerstand zu allen Verhältnissen. Wenn er sich dies getraut zu sagen, wenn die Verfassung als der Gesamtrahmen der *res publica* sich auf den Menschen stellt, nicht auf ein Wesen oder bestimmtes Bild, vielmehr auf die Menschlichkeit schlechthin, dann lösen wir uns von allen konkreten Bildern. Das Bild wird diffus und ist damit das uns wirklich zeigende Urbild des Menschen. Dem entspricht die Formulierung: Die Würde des Menschen ist unantastbar.[20]

The overall critique of the image of man in law as outlined above is rather inadequate. The critique boils down to a call to the goodwill to mount a struggle against the reification of the image of man. Yet such a call does not in itself alter the structure of concrete legal dogmatics. It may well be that ultimately the critique is no more than the philosophical position of *re-presentation* which as such could leave legal dogmatics intact. In order to be in a position to judge this line of criticism it is necessary to attain some insight into the complex relationship between legal dogmatics, legal theory and legal philosophy. It is only in the latter context that one can meaningfully study the character and the operation of legal dogmatics.

5. LEGAL DOGMATICS, LEGAL THEORY AND LEGAL PHILOSOPHY

The question concerning the precise delimitation of the sphere of legal science as well as the question of justice, is in essence a legalistic question which recurs in every discussion on legal theory. Here the positivity of law is at some point touched upon directly. Knowledge of the limits of law is necessary because without it it is impossible to ascribe legitimate enforceability to the law. This attitude means that theoretical and philosophical questions concerning law should preferably be brought within the sphere of legal science, particularly, legal dogmatics. In this way legal science would assume the character of a *closed* system of knowledge. But the latter is always under threat of *dogmatism*. Theoretical investigation in this connection is coupled with the fact that law appears as an *ideological* datum in our society. The ideological aspect of law is seldom subjected to a critique of ideology. For example, law as an ideological datum is unmasked by Machiavelli's understanding of it as an instrument in the hands of a few or by Marx's characterisation of it as a weapon of the dominant class. Such views are also applicable to legal dogmatics. The claim to knowledge of its own boundaries and internal control mechanism renders legal dogmatics – the hallmark of law – susceptible to ideological deformity. In practice this is the case whenever legal dogmatics, other sciences as well as many other approaches to legal phenomena appear to be impenetrable. Sociologically, this is strengthened even more by the fact that the character of the jurist as a jurist including that of the legal student who emulates the jurist, is held responsible for ideological deformation. Statistical analyses prove that figures were manipulated in the Federal Republic of Germany during a survey conducted to determine how many children of jurists were created judges.[21]

The fact that legal science is a closed system of knowledge is traceable to a very old tradition. At the time when pretensions to perfect the Civil Code were made, the position that legal science was a unity could already be found to exist. This position was held by the exegetical school which formed part of continental thought that was dominant between 1804 and 1880. Such unity and perfection allowed for only one mode of expression and expansion, namely, *application*. Thought in terms of application remains dominant in every legal position which takes its point of departure from *legal dogmatics*. The latter is deemed to be an autonomous unit within the wider legal discourse. However, thought in terms of application is Platonic in character. The crucial point to grasp here is that one must acknowledge the *independent* existence of rules in the noumenal and accept that such rules must be applied in reality – the phenomenal sphere – in order to warrant the operation of law. In 1857 the Dean of the Law Faculty in Paris stated that:

> Toute la loi, dans son esprit aussi bien que dans sa lettre, avec une large application de ses principes et le plus complet développement des conséquences qui en découlent, mais rien que la loi, telle a été la devise des professeurs du Code Napoléon.

The above citation appears, justifiably, in the first pages of Chaim Perelman's *Logique Juridique.*[22] Thus there is a legal scientific tradition which may be found not only in France but also in Germany albeit with some differences in form. Against the background of the strictly closed character of legal science, the central position of legal dogmatics and the equally rigorous application-mentality law and statute have become identical. Only the brave will dare to tamper with this sacred shrine of knowledge for their profane action will undoubtedly be visited with a banning order!

The German tradition may be identified by reference to the term *Begriffsjurisprudenz*. The term is closely associated with the name of Puchta. The latter is widely regarded as the father of mid-nineteenth century legal thought. Like Kant, he also spoke in terms of the architecture of concepts. By this he meant complete systematisation with its own peculiar or characteristic logical structure. Such a structure, pyramidally constructed, would be the foundation for the objective interpretation of the text and rule application.[23] Facts are facts. They constitute the foundation for the positivity of legal facts. On this basis both law and state are deemed to be positive concepts.

Nowadays the idea that legal science is a closed system of knowledge, even the legal positivism of Hans Kelsen, is widely contested. However, a legalism which is tied to both positivism and the exegetical school forms the point of departure for every excogitation on legal dogmatics as well as for any other object of legal theory. This may be found, for instance, in the analytical legal philosophy of Hart who speaks about the 'open texture' of the law.[24] The same observation applies to that German legal theory which presents itself as *topische Jurisprudenz* (Viehweg, Struck). In this category arguments may be found which are pertinent to the problem of legal dogmatics. The manner in which *arguments* are used enjoys much wider acceptance and importance than the manner in which *concepts* are used. A similar kind of awareness lies at the base of 'functional legal dogmatics'. According to this viewpoint, the place-and-time-bound function of law in the sphere of social relations must be accorded primacy over the closed systematic character of legal dogmatics (Scholten, Esser).

All the above trends hardly clarify the position with regard to the precise relationship that holds between legal dogmatics, legal theory and the philosophy of law. Is it perhaps assumed that it is the task of legal dogmatics to extricate itself out of the entangling morass of dogmatism, ideological captivity and inaccessibility? Or is it perhaps the task of legal theory, as some authors maintain, to develop a meta-theory as a way out of the morass already described? Yet another view could be that legal philosophy is best suited to perform the task because it is willy-nilly constantly present in whatever the legal practitioner says or does.

Inasmuch as the speech acts and the image of man of the jurist remain captive to legal discourse so it is with regard to the theoretical question raised above. This hardly cancels out the fact that exactly what the whole of legal science will turn out to be depends upon an answer to our question. Yet the answer is not forthcoming neither is the problem posed in clear and precise terms. Therefore, the presuppositions already alluded to continue to do their work. Whoever is capable of understanding that anthropology is a concealed discourse should also be in a position to draw the necessary distinctions and thence proceed to focus on the relationship between the three aspects of legal science.

First and foremost legal dogmatics must be viewed, so to speak, as a unity of juridical articles of faith. These latter provide for their own credibility which is drawn from the inner logic of the closed system of knowledge. Alternatively, their credibility is derived from the authority of the teacher (this category includes Roman jurists, great modern and contemporary teachers of law, custom and tradition). In principle legal dogmatics traverses the whole field of legal science and legal practice. Questions relative to the interpretation and application of certain parts of positive law are continually dealt with in terms of legal dogmatics merely by reference to specific aspects thereof. In brass tacks therefore, the main issue revolves around drawing inferences in law; the study of the preamble, the preparatory work or surrounding circumstances relative to an acceptable interpretation or application; analyses intended to arrive at what is called the intention of the legislature; the expression of generally recognised values and judgments. On this basis legal dogmatics is also the source of law. According to Esser this represents a kind of juridical economy: legal dogmatics is a device contrived to save the judge the trouble of thinking through on his own the values, purposes and the foundations of principles that he applies in order to arrive at specific decision. It would appear that in the absence of this juridical economy the judge would never attempt to do the task himself because it would be difficult and he would also not have the time. That which at first sight appears to be a time-saving, reasonable practice and a sound professional etiquette does in fact turn out to be a prohibition. The dominant dogma ensures that the foundations are not called into question; it creates and establishes a secure *silence*. Esser describes this as an offence. He sees it as an authoritarian dogma obscuring values and purposes; it prescribes valuation schemes and maintains that elementary concepts must be deemed to be self-evident. Accordingly, thus Esser concludes, it is an obstacle to development and a hindrance to the qualitative improvement of our law.[25] This observation has received wide acceptance but only to the extent that it could lead to re-excogitation still within legal dogmatics!

There is the need for a more flexible interpretation cf vague legal concepts. Similarly, it is necessary to have much clearer guidelines for the application of legal rules. There is also the inescapable requirement to direct thought upon the internal construction of the law. Despite this the jurist is bent upon enhancing the effectiveness of law. He considers that alongside the perfection of law there will be an increase in justice. Furthermore, he assumes that the criticism on legal dogmatics can be met by an improvement in the modalities of application. Thus all these concerns could be removed as soon as people tread *outside* the boundaries of legal dogmatics. Within the confines of legal dogmatics the relationship between legal theory and legal philosophy is pre-eminently a thetical division of tasks. Tradition has it that not infrequently, *legal theory* is a mixture of philosophical and scientific answers to questions that have been posed by positive law. The answers provided fulfil the task, especially through case law, albeit indirectly of being the source of law.

Thus Esser's criticism retains its validity. The reason for this is that traditional legal theory is still concerned with the internal economy of law in the sphere of the legal enterprise. Legal dogmatics still operates securely within its boundaries and it can freely extend its own horizons. For this reason it is generally accepted that the legal theoretician is a jurist who adjudicates upon theoretical and philosophical questions from the standpoint of legal dogmatics. Karl Larenz' widely quoted expression is an apt description of this attitude: the jurist is concerned with '*Reflexion auf eigenes Tun*'. At the fringes of the jurist's reflection there is an inchoate emergence of all that falls outside the scope of legal dogmatics. The latter may be described as general legal theory or legal philosophy. Whether or not the first or the second concept will be accentuated depends exclusively upon the origin and the scholastic training of the one concerned. Thus jurists take the former whereas philosophers take the latter for their consideration.

It is of the utmost importance to provide lucid portrayals of whatever else falls outside the boundaries of legal dogmatics. Otherwise, the boundary of legal science itself will be obscured and in that way the task and function of law in society will also be dimmed. A dogmatic and ideological attitude has the tendency of pursuing the path of obscurity just described and as it treads along it affects terrains which in the first place it should not have touched. All too often one hears the complaint that legal thought and law have a rather excessive and extensive range relative to the problems of social life. The unsupervised quantity of legislative activities as well as the random but tireless turning of the legislative machine must surely be taken as an important warning in this connection.

Somewhat programmatically, it must therefore be stated that *legal theory is the theory of legal science*. This formulation has, at least, the following implications:

(1) The object of study in legal theory is not identical to that of legal dogmatics. Legal theory deals especially with questions that impinge upon legal dogmatics. Moreover, the position and the particularity of legal science relative to other sciences are also the object of legal theory. Thus legal theory considers scientific theoretical questions and the approaches thereto. The dogmatician deals with legal theory by way of extrapolation from legal dogmatics. But this approach to legal theory places the dogmatician in a position in which he simply finds himself incompetent to deal with legal theory.

(2) The study of legal theory focuses constantly upon the question of the theoretical character of legal science. It is not simply a matter of pure theory (theory for its own sake) but it is also an issue of the utmost practical importance. Clearly, one would not expect any science, at least in principle, to yield any other result than that relative to the material injected into it. Thus the theoretical form of any science is precisely – consciously or unconsciously – that which is pegged on to it. On this showing, knowledge of the material provides an insight into the effect as well as the scope of legal science as a social science. But if such knowledge is left to dogmatics, the vagaries of chance or intuition, then neither the effect nor the social range of legal science would be determined.

The question of the theoretical character of law may be subdivided into manifold questions:

– What is the kind of theory formulation that generally takes place in law? The answer must be, *grosso modo*, that a theory which is still tied down to and determined by the philosophy of Descartes is characteristic of law. For this reason contemporary legal theory raises the pertinent problem concerning the possible character of *post-Cartesian legal theory*. Such a theory must also include a post-Cartesian anthropology. Questions like these can come to the fore only if legal theory is no longer assumed to be part of legal dogmatics or an extrapolation thereof. Such questions could, on an experimental basis, provide legal theory with the possibility to excogitate *an alternative legal thought* without necessarily having to discard currently operative law.

– What is the significance of the fact that the theoretical character of legal science is greatly determined by the assumptions of the legal practitioner concerning legal science itself? The orientation of the legal practitioner may be characterised as application-thought. It is by preference immediately at home with the casuistry peculiar to it. In its operation the thought of the legal practitioner is closely interested in legal dogmatics as such. From the viewpoint of the legal practitioner, legal theory and philosophy of law are nothing more than an academic exercise. Accordingly, the legal practitioner regards neither legal theory nor philosophy of law as spheres within which his concept of law can be based. The collection and systematisation of jurisprudence together with other practice-oriented data provide adequate theoretical weight. This conviction leads immediately to a concealed positivism which is beyond the reach of theory formulation. The theoretical concern of the legal practitioner is confined to the concrete legal fact. Therefore, it would be quite out of character for him to extend his theoretical concern to cover legal regulation that is determined by time and place. But he fails to perceive that the latter already implies a more general and quite another legal concept than the one determined by the concrete legal fact. A similar shift is made whenever questions concerning legal dogmatics as a specimen of a theory of science are raised. In this connection a certain positivist-analytical legal concept is in function. Every legal practitioner would be apt to define the latter as a philosophical concept although the philosopher would disagree.

– What is the relationship between the *necessary unity* of legal science and the *interdisciplinary* character of legal theory? At present, legal arguments are being studied from the viewpoint of linguistic philosophy and rhetorics. The question 'what are the "objective facts" with which the jurist deals' is considered from the standpoint of cognitive and scientific theory. Communication and systems theories study the subdivisions of law within legal science and dogmatics as legal mechanisms within the state. On the other hand the psychology of human relations considers the social structure of the juridical man-to-man relations as its object of study. This short list of the package of interdisciplinarity can easily be further multiplied! Legal theoretical investigation does not compromise the necessity for the unity and dogmatic character of legal science. On the contrary, it studies the latter in an attempt to comprehend its principles of justification including their social effects. In this manner legal theory develops an emancipatory attitude towards law in our social life.

– The question concerning the *frontiers as well as the delimitation* of legal theory is also raised persistently. Far from being a matter of scientific or philosophic pedantry, this question is raised precisely because an answer to it determines the scientific character of law and accordingly brings legal science into dialogue with other sciences. Very often the legal dogmatician reveals great indifference towards the scientific character of law. Nevertheless, he is very much disposed to borrow from other sciences those methods and techniques which he considers useful for the secure preservation of the limits and operation of legal dogmatics. The coercive character of his dogmatic enterprise provides the ease as well as the security that is useful for his activity. It is precisely this that the dogmatician regards as his specific area of competence. Thus the question of the scope and the delimitation of legal theory strikes him rather as a critique on law and ideology. On this view, the question falls outside the sphere of legal dogmatics and thus derives importance only from the point of view of theory.

(3) The *specific legal form of thought* constitutes the third element of contemporary legal theory. This relates to the manner in which the jurist thinks. However, it does occasionally also refer to the statesman and to the political and legal philosophers. The thought-form involves a more encompassing structure whose profile must always be present in legal theory. Accordingly, theological legal thought, social contract thought, civil-individualistic legal thought and socialist legal thought must as a whole be regarded as thought-*forms*. The suggestion here is that ultimately such thought-forms lead to the existence of theory. Of course, neither the social-contract nor the civil-individualistic thinking are the only legal thought-forms. Qualitatively similar thought-forms operative within legal dogmatics deserve to be mentioned here. Thus for example the already mentioned application orientation emerges in diverse forms as a moment in legal dogmatics. It is clear that in the absence of such an orientation many jurists would find themselves unable to explain their application of rules to facts. Neither would they be able to describe their activity. Even here the observation still holds that *legal theoretical* thought about something other than the actual legal activity could prove to be both illuminating and emancipatory. Another example of a legal thought-form may be found in the widely prevalent pragmatic-instrumentalist attitude. The question: 'how can I adjudicate upon this argument, this fact, this situation, this knowledge of the state of affairs arising from the conflict of interests between the parties' is so dominant that even language and text, the very presence of a fellow human being and the world of facts must, without exception, be considered from the standpoint of pragmatic instrumentalism. This leads to an all-objectifying and instrumentalist mode of thought. Ultimately, this touches upon thought itself. Thus, as von Ihering and Marx state, knowledge and law become transformed into power. Accordingly, the study of the legal thought-form is the study of epistemology. It goes without saying that once on this path then we are treading on a terrain

which is entirely outside the range of positive law. The issues considered in this context cannot, therefore, form part of the *sources* of law.

From the foregoing it would appear that even at the level of legal theory it is possible to make a contribution to the theme 'law and anthropology'. The dogma of human thought which is manifest in legal dogmatics as a whole is expanded by *the specific legal mode of human thought*. Legal man is brought about by the legal thought-form. Thus legal pragmatics is simultaneously anthropological pragmatics. The latter forms the background for legal self-interpretation. The character and purposes of law, its characterisation by rules, its system of organisation as well as its coercive character give form to the legal man.

On the basis of the preceding outline of legal theory, it is possible to determine what is *legal philosophy* in terms of the same trend of thought. *Legal philosophy is understood as the philosophy of the theory of legal science*. At first sight, this characterisation would appear to be rather strange as it includes without further ado two traditional attitudes: (1) legal philosophy is often regarded as the clarification of principles such as law and justice; (2) legal philosophy as a conceptualisation of the foundations of legal theory remains up to the present concealed under legal dogmatics or legal theory. The latter is clearly an extrapolation from the former.

As a counter to these two attitudes it must be mentioned that they interpret legal philosophy in terms of a fixed thought-form, namely, Platonism. As soon as legal philosophy is conceived of in terms of the clarification of principles such as justice, then we are once more brought face to face with the opposition between the noumenal and the phenomenal on the one hand and the application-schema including its consequences on the other. If legal philosophy must excogitate the principles of theory within the limits of the operative legal dogmatics then philosophy is thereby brought under the power of dogma and the enforceable regulative order. Thus legal philosophy would be brought under the sanction of an ideologically coloured relationship between theory and praxis.

From this perspective it is relatively easy to understand why modern legal theory regards classical natural law as a subtle ideology which has persisted through the ages. The same natural law identifies legal theory with the philosophy of law. By so doing it has brought philosophy under the power of legal dogmatics and the corresponding enforceable regulative order. Such identification has brought about misunderstanding with regard to the particularity of legal philosophy. Accordingly, legal philosophy was not regarded as an independent theoretical model. Neither was it viewed as a distinct legal mode of thought nor a possible legal theory. Consequently, classical natural law claimed to be the only possible foundation of positive law. Thus in this latter sphere questions of legal philosophy purporting to be either specific thought-forms regarding the foundations of law or an independent theory were to be excluded. This may be illustrated by reference to contemporary legal philosophy which after Hegel and Marx may be viewed as the critical moment relative to legal theory.

A clear perception of these emphases leads to the observation that (a) the problem of individuality as a basic value of law characterises legal anthropology. This legal anthropological character of law functions as a stepping-stone towards anthropology and thence to legal practice. Taking the cue from this one (b) could regard the problem of causality as a moment of legal theoretical reflection. This same moment provides the gateway from legal theory to legal practice. In conclusion, it is evident therefore that (c) legal philosophy brings to light in concrete legal practice the problem of equilibrium and its attendant philosophical as well as metaphysical background.

In the first case one encounters *legal man*. Here the word 'of' is used in its double sense: law as the work *of* man and man as the work *of* law. In the second case the issue revolves around *the law of legal science*, its internal structure and function as a dogmatic entity. In the third case we find legal *values* such as justice. In this connection the *meaning and purpose* of law in the life of man come into question. Cumulatively, the three cases mean that anthropology, legal theory and the philosophy of law form one whole.

From the foregoing the following may be inferred:

(1) the view that dogmatic and non-dogmatic concepts of legal science are used to specify both the legal subject and object and the effect of the law on both, is confirmed. That which was thought to be implied is now affirmed. In effect: (a) every legal subjectivity remains founded in the dualistic subject-object relationship; (b) every legal subject as a unit is placed in a situation of manifold legal acts in which the subject functions as a bearer of rights and duties. This leads to two results. One is that the Cartesian dualistic position of closed consciousness is juridically affirmed. The other is that the practice of legal dogmatics imposes the model of closed consciousness upon legal subjects through the application of rules. Thus legal man is brought into existence.

(2) It is clear that human conduct conceived of in terms of legal rules and legal order constitute the background to legal dogmatics. In terms of juridical relations, objective law becomes a matter of rules and legal regulation. This implies the differentiation between legal subject and the sub-ject of (i.e.,

someone *under*) the law. This brings to the fore the 'dual character' of a legal rule. Law is a collection of *valid* rules. In law validity has got two meanings. The one meaning refers to legal rules that are *actually being followed* while the other denotes rules that *ought to be* followed. However, if it were simply a matter of following rules then custom and law would be synonymous.

The manner in which legal dogmatics develops the idea of a legal subject forms the foundation for the legitimation of law in its democratic garb. This once more provides the jurist with the opportunity to interpret rules of behaviour in terms of legal rules existing in a legal order. The legal order is itself the kind of ordering within which every subject must submit to legal rules. In exchange for their submission the participants in the legal order enjoy the appropriate conditions to engage in various forms of mutual dealings. In terms of legal dogmatics this means that law provides the necessary conditions for the exercise of rights and the necessary security for the enjoyment of rights. This, in fact, is the way in which law penetrates deeply into the *core* of social life. Social life is then viewed as 'intersubjectivity' but then it is the inter-*subject*-ivity of legal subjects! The undeniable presence of law in the core of social life is thus an event which (a) considers itself to be a process of regulation, (b) creates the social relations of specific legal subjects into elements of juristic relations. Thus the dogma of the jurist first creates its own elements and thence conceives of social life as the intercourse of such elements which only the jurist has the competence to interpret and control. The force of the legal metaphor is much greater than people generally believe.

The above outline of legal dogmatics and methodology in law makes it plain that dogma is through and through purposive and that law necessarily depends upon the category of subjectivity for its very existence.

According to dogmatic tradition the concept of subjective law is related to that of objective law. The idea of legal subject is not only formulated within the confines of subjective law but it also functions therein. Here the concept of subjective law is tied to the idea of legal subject. This procedure accordingly clarifies how the hierarchical determination of position through dogma relates at the same time to the idea of legal subject. On the other hand, according to objective law the individual of subjective law is a *legal subject*. This same individual is the 'bearer of rights and duties'. Clearly, he is not this 'by nature'. Instead, he is the result of a legal transformation of anthropological reality. Hence, as the word *persona* suggests, the human person under cover of a mask finds his mirror image in a legal situation. In this context the same individual is then invited to become a bearer of rights and duties. Once the invitation is accepted then the individual can enjoy his freedom for as long as he keeps on wearing the juridical mask. On this basis legal dogmatics can present the 'exercise of own rights' which is obviously coupled with the teaching on legal capacity. Such are the dogmatic reasons for the recognition of the individual as someone capable of being a bearer of rights and duties. There might be little suspicion, though justifiable, that all this is coloured with a wide anthropological perspective. On this same basis the jurist posits the 'being-in-itself' of the legal subject and holds that thus defined, the legal subject must realise itself in state and society. Legal subjectivity as the dogmatic self-interpretation of the jurist provides us with an image of law which could prove to be *emancipatory*. Thus for every natural person the enjoyment of subjective rights constitutes the first necessity for individual self-realisation. But alas! the 'self' which could possibly emerge from the self-realisation juridically mapped out lies buried in the dark dungeon of silence! Accordingly, in law anthropology subsists as a concealed discourse.

Katholieke Universiteit Leuven

NOTES

[1] J. M. Broekman, *Recht en Antropologie*, Serie Rechtstheorie, Standaard W. U. 1982 (2nd edition).

[2] A recent example concerning the possibility for a theory of legal argumentation is found in: A. Aarnio, R. Alexy, and A. Peczenik, 'The Foundation of Legal Reasoning', in: *Rechtstheorie* **12** (1981), nos. 2, 3 and 4, 133–136.

[3] J. M. Broekman, *Recht en Antropologie, op. cit.*, 199–200.

[4] I. Jenkins, *Social Order and the Limits of Law*, Princeton, New Jersey 1980, 314.

[5] M. Miaille, *Une Introduction Critique au Droit*, Paris 1977, 67.

[6] J. M. Broekman, 'Sprechakt und Intersubjektivität', in *Phänomenologie und Marxismus*, Vol. III (B. Waldenfels, Jan M. Broekman and A. Pazanin, eds.), Frankfurt 1978, 66–115.

[7] K. Lüderssen, *Erfahrung als Rechtsquelle*, Frankfurt 1972. Lüderssen uses techniques to investigate how a legal system and concrete social relations come into being. He applies his investigation to cartel penal law and finds that to a very large extent the concretisation and the validity of legal norms depend upon the recognition of norms by the enterprises and their subsequent adjustment of economic behaviour to conform to the norms. The recognition as such becomes the source of law. At the same time the ambivalence becomes apparent when legal dogmatics begins to extend itself into the sphere of economic reality. This then gives rise to some thoughts concerning the possibility of conditions under which legal theory may claim to be necessary for practical purposes.

[8] J. M. Broekman, 'Recht en Strukturalisme', Preadvies voor de Nederlandse Vereniging voor de Wijsbegeerte des Rechts, 1973, in *R & R*, 1973, 181; 'Juristischer Diskurs und Rechtstheorie', in *Rechtstheorie* **11** (1980), no. 1.

[9] J. M. Broekman, *Recht en Taal*, Preadvies Koninklijke notariëele Broederschap, Kluwer, Deventer 1979.

[10] J. M. Broekman, 'Betere taal is beter recht. De rechtskundige significa van Jacob Israel de Haan', in *Wijsgerig Perspectief*, 1979/80, no. 2, 48–56.

[11] J. M. Broekman, *Recht en Antropologie, op. cit.*, 186 ff.

[12] On transformations in law especially with regard to the logic of norms and legal argumentation see: Aarnio, Alexy and Peczenik, 'The Foundations of Legal Reasoning', *Rechtstheorie* **12** (1981), 133 ff; A. Peczenik, 'Legal Errata', in *Deontic Logic, Computational Linguistics and Legal Information Systems*, A. A. Martino, ed., Vol. 2, Amsterdam 1982, pp. 102–125; *id.*, 'Rationality of Legal Justification', in *ARSP* **LXVIII** (1982), 2, 137–163.

[13] J. M. Broekman, *Recht en Antropologie, op. cit.*, 199 ff.; for an extensive discussion of name, domicile, residence and patrimony see: de la Pradelle, *L'Homme Juridique*, Grenoble/Paris 1979, 117 ff.; see also I. Jenkins: 'The human person and the legal person', in *Equality and Freedom*. Proceedings of the 10th World Congress of IVR, New York and Leiden 1977, 117–125.

[14] The problem of *transsexuality* illustrates the kind of problem that arises once the giving of a name has been completed. See: J. M. Broekman, *Recht en Antropologie, op. cit.*, 80–95.

[15] A. J. Arnaud, *Essai d'analyse structurale du Code civil français*, Paris 1973, 50 ff. "Comme toute législation, le Code civil est un monument de la PEUR . . . Mais il est le Code d'une peur très particulière, celle du petit-bourgeois qui a vu ses aspirations individualistes comblées, et veut se prémunir contre le risque qu'il court, de perdre les avantages acquis" (55).

[16] A. Baruzzi, *Europäisches 'Menschenbild' und das Grundgesetz für die Bundesrepublik Deutschland*, Alber-Verlag, Freiburg 1979, 86 ff.

[17] W. Weischedel, *Recht und Ethik. Zur Anwendung ethischer Prinzipien in der Rechtsprechung des Bundesgerichtshofes*, Karlsruhe 1956.

[18] J. M. Broekman, *Recht en Antropologie, op. cit.*, 49 ff. and 115–151.

[19] E. Denninger, *Einführung in das Staatsrecht*, Hamburg 1973.

[20] Baruzzi, *Europäisches Menschenbild, op. cit.*, 112.

[21] W. Maihofer (ed.): *Ideologie und Recht*, Frankfurt/M. 1969. See the contributions of Maihofer, Viehweg, König and Kaupen.

[22] C. Perelman, *Logique Juridique*, Paris 1976, 23.

[23] K. Larenz, *Methodenlehre der Rechtswissenschaft*, Berlin 1969, 17 ff.; W. Fikentscher, *Methoden des Rechts*, Vol. III, Tübingen 1976, 87–94, 692–696.

[24] For a discussion of this theme, see J. M. Broekman, *Recht en Antropologie, op. cit.*, 38 ff.

[25] J. Esser, 'Möglichkeiten und Grenzen des dogmatischen Denkens im modernen Zivilrecht', *Archiv für die civilistische Praxis*, 1972, 97 ff.; W. Fikentscher, *op. cit.*, 357 ff.

JOHN B. OAKLEY

SOCIOBIOLOGY AND THE LAW

Lawyers' interest in anthropology is generally confined to social anthropology, which is the historical and comparative study of human culture. But the science of anthropology also embraces physical anthropology, which is the study of the biological evolution of the human species. I happen to have a spouse who is a physical anthropologist, and for that reason I attend more closely than most lawyers to the insights physical anthropology has to offer about the human condition. I cannot claim professional expertise in the field, but I think I have a sufficiently informed awareness of what physical anthropologists are thinking and saying to defend my thesis that their work has relevance to problems of law and justice. My emphasis is on the relatively novel theory of sociobiology.[1] I begin with an overview of sociobiology's relation to physical anthropology and consideration of some of its broader ramifications. I conclude by referring to legal rights of access to adoption records as an example of how evaluation of the justice of particular legal norms may be swayed by due consideration of the biological constitution of the human beings whose social behavior the law seeks to guide and to govern.

Physical anthropology is a discipline defined not by its methods but by its focus on the evolutionary origins of man. The methods used by physical anthropologists are drawn from a melange of related but more general schools of science, principally geology, paleontology, genetics and biology. Geology and paleontology, the study of the earth and of fossils, permit anthropologists to find and analyze the fossil record of human evolution, and thus to reconstruct its history. Genetics and biology, the study of genetic replication and of the physical organisms which genes have produced, are enlisted by anthropologists to explore the physical processes which constitute us as living human beings, and which constituted the organisms from which we evolved. My principal topic today, sociobiology, is that branch of biology which deals specifically with the biological bases of social behavior, including sexual reproduction and parent-child relations.[2]

I should note at the outset that I accept as fact the standard features of the theory of biological evolution which Charles Darwin, among others, introduced into scientific thought in the 19th century. By this theory man

E. Bulygin et al. (eds.), Man, Law and Modern Forms of Life, 43–54.

and all other organisms have evolved from a common ancestor by a process of genetic mutation and natural selection which has extended over several hundred million years.

Although human social behavior is the most complex and labile of any organism,[3] millions of other species exhibit social behavior and in many cases depend for survival upon intricate schemes of social organization. Sociobiological theory draws on the work of many sorts of zoologists, but much of the momentum for constituting it as a distinct branch of biology has come from entomologists and their studies of insect societies.[4] Entomologists were puzzled by certain features of insect societies which seemed anomalous within conventional evolutionary theory. Most puzzling was the common phenomenon of altruistic behavior, that is, behavior harmful to the actor but beneficial to other organisms.

We must remember that here, and indeed throughout sociobiological jargon, there is a bit of metaphor at play.[5] In conventional usage the term "altruism" connotes an act of conscious selflessness, rather than an unconscious act or conscious submission to compulsion. We would agree that the passenger on a sinking ship who voluntarily yields the last place in the last lifeboat to another person is acting altruistically. We would not typically view this act as altruistic if it occurred only at the point of a gun. But of course insects don't act at all, in any cognitive sense; they exhibit the characteristics of their genes, and they react to their environment as their genes dictate. Their existence is a drama of compulsion and chance directed by the caprice of natural selection.

Altruistic insect behavior thus presented a paradox: how can behavior which is by definition disadvantageous to the actor, be behavior which has evolved through natural selection? Genetic mutation might produce some insects that will respond altruistically to threats to their societies, the way termites confronted by a predator will cluster at its mouth, allowing themselves to be easily eaten while the rest of the population retreats before the predator is in a position to close off their escape.[6] But since the altruists will have been eaten, and the non-altruists will have escaped to breed more non-altruists, altruism should genetically extinguish itself.

This paradox has been resolved by a significant revision in evolutionary theory which more or less marked the birth of sociobiology. Investigation of insect social behavior led to the development of kinship theory, which explains altruism by discarding the idea that the fitness of individual organisms is crucial to the evolution of species, and emphasizing instead the fitness of particular genes and the degree of kinship or genetic similarity shared by social groups within a species. It holds that altruism can survive by inheritance alone, unblessed by culture or ethics, as long as the population benefitted by the altruism shares a sufficient degree of kinship with the altruists.[7]

Sociobiologists have been quick, a bit too quick in my opinion, to generalize from insect social behavior to human social behavior. Among the more grandiose suggestions of sociobiologists is that it blazes the future path of all philosophy, because the elements of any philosophy – such as the concepts of mind, of self, of beauty, of truth – are concepts made possible only by the evolution of our brains, and their meaning is necessarily tied to the biological structure of brains shaped by the caprice of inheritance and the ultimate causal course of evolution. I am skeptical that the undeniable truth of sociobiology's account of insect social behavior, even as elaborated in other fields of zoology, establishes sociobiology as the gospel for understanding all human social behavior.[8] Nevertheless, I think sociobiology does have relevance to human affairs. Provided we recognize that the study of the influence of biology on human social behavior is only an avenue of inquiry, still at a pre-theoretical stage and inherently speculative,[9] I think that sociobiology poses useful questions for those who care about why humans act as they do, and for those who seek through law to influence such actions.

Sociobiology is a politically controversial subject, at least in the arena of human rather than insect conduct, for the obvious reason that it draws attention to the primal machinery of genetic replication and to the way in which our present beings have been genetically constituted by prehistoric conditions of nature.[10] The idea of biologically determined behavior is particularly difficult for lawyers and social philosophers to accept. Law seeks to guide and control social behavior through culture, and social philosophy deals largely with the justice of the constraints we culturally impose on ourselves in the name of social order. To talk of social behavior as instinctual rather than culturally learned and ethically guided seems to debase our conception of human nature as distinct from other forms of animal life precisely in the primacy of psychological free will and the capacity of culture to bend that will in service of the good.[11]

We do not deny that our minds exist in bodies with primitive needs which manifest themselves through psychological desires, but we insist, quite properly, that primitive selfishness be constrained by observance of ethical and legal norms of social behavior. The claim that someone is "acting like an animal" is generally meant pejoratively, with reference to behavior which fails to heed the limits culture places on biological autonomy. Because sociobiology takes seriously the degree to which human social behavior, like animal social behavior, proceeds from the biological constitution of an organism, it is often spoken of pejoratively too. Those who share my ideals of human equality and free will are discomfited by talk of biological determinism which seems to give laws of nature primacy over the laws of men and the ethical standards by which we judge the justice of our laws.[12] I cannot deny the potential of sociobiological rhetoric for abuse by demagogues who hope to legitimate social inequality and human oppression through appeal to the panoply of myth and prejudice by which humans have historically exaggerated the degree of their genetic variation, used physical difference to justify political oppression, and generally committed moral wrongs under the blasphemous banner of natural rights.[13] But before we put sociobiologists to the political sword, we must be careful that we are not murdering the messenger because we don't like the message.

We all acknowledge that it is silly to punish the innocent bearer of bad news. Of course, if the bad tidings turn out to be false, the innocence of the messenger is suspect. This seems to be the attitude of political critics of sociobiology. But we must take care to distinguish false messages from discomfiting truths. Critics of sociobiology decry it as a pseudo-science used to legitimate racial, sexual and economic inequalities, diverting our attention from the problem of achieving just laws by postulating bogus laws of nature from which our treasured human institutions of culture and ethics offer no escape.[14] Such claims deserve to be put to the torch, but my reading of the sociobiological literature reveals them to be claims of straw constructed by the critics themselves, in reaction to the basic proposition of sociobiologists that since biology dominates the social behavior of every other form of animal, it must play some role in the social behavior of humans as well.[15] This may be distasteful to acknowledge, and it may lead to incautious claims that sociobiology sets the future agenda for all philosophy, but if we overcome our distaste and discount the exaggerations of others, can we deny the truth of the proposition that human social behavior is at least influenced by our biological heritage? I think not.[16]

I also think that we need not fear that this concession commits us to a painful slide down some slippery slope toward biological determinism. Sociobiology does not dismiss consideration of culture in explaining human social behavior; it seeks only to place the capacity for culture in a biological perspective.[17] It acknowledges that the social transmission of behavioral traits is the hallmark of human evolution, allowing humans to adapt to and exploit an ever-changing environment with the speed and power that makes human invention the only foreseeable threat to human existence at least within the lifespan of the solar system. The fragility of existence of non-intelligent species stems from the eons of evolution necessary to encode genetically a sufficient population with patterns of behavior adaptive to some specific ecological niche. It is the ultimate irony of human evolution that we have evolved a capacity for culture which not only allows us to adapt rapidly to environmental change, but also allows us to change our environment even more rapidly and drastically, so that the ability to act in cohesive social groups which established human dominance may yet lead to a holocaust which will be the human doom.

Sociobiology thus does not discount the significance of culture in determining human social behavior. What sociobiology adds to the nature versus nurture debate is a heightened awareness that biology and culture may pull in different directions because human culture is so much more malleable and adaptive than human biology. Sociology certainly does not argue that these conflicts should be resolved in favor of biological tendencies. For example, sociobiologists generally acknowledge that a biological adaptation which began evolving in precursors to the human species millenia before the comparatively recent capacity for culture has left human beings with an innate tendency for aggressive behavior which, given the awesome destructive power of modern human culture, is now a distinctively disadvantageous behavioral trait.[18] If biology has its way, it may result in the extinction of the human species, just as it has resulted in the extinction of many millions of other species which became unfit for the world in which they had to live. By identifying the biological bases for aggressive behavior, sociobiology does not argue against the cultural control of aggression. It argues instead, with all the passion of a drowning man, that we need to understand our biology well enough for our culture to succeed in controlling it.

I want to illustrate this point by reference to a more mundane problem than the spectre of war, and one more demonstrably subject to legal control. The degree of confidentiality which the law should maintain regarding the identities of the "birth" parents of adopted children is an issue of lively current debate, at least in the United States.[19] The problem of confidentiality rarely arises in an "open" adoption, where the fact of adoption is freely acknowledged and the parties concerned make their own arrangements concerning the relations, if any, to be maintained between the birth parents and the adopted child.[20] In a "closed" adoption, whether arranged privately or through an adoption agency, conflicts are more likely to arise among the concerned parties as to the appropriate degree of secrecy concerning the fact of adoption and the identities of both sets of parents.[21]

The "adoption triangle" consists of the birth parents, the adoptee, and the adoptive parents. Theoretically the two sets of parents have mutual control over the terms of the adoption, including whether it is to be "open" or "closed", although I suspect as a practical matter that where an adoption agency is involved its policies are generally acquiesced in by both sets of parents.[22] Most jurisdictions give official blessing to closed adoptions by legally "sealing" the adoption records and issuing amended birth certificates in the name of the adoptive family. Some jurisdictions, including Finland, qualify closed adoptions by granting adult adoptees the right to discover the identities of their birth parents from their adoption records. The predominant legal posture, however, is to maintain the secrecy of sealed adoption records even after the children involved have come of age and requested disclosure.[23]

In recent years organizations of adoptees have sought to reform the law of a number of American states to provide to adult adoptees a legal right of access to their sealed adoption records.[24] These efforts have not met with immediate success.[25] Opposition to reform has come chiefly from adoptive parents and adoption agencies.[26] The adoptive parents fear alienation of the affection of their children if they are assisted by the law in discovering the identities of their birth parents.[27] Adoption agencies, despite generally counseling that the fact of adoption be disclosed to adoptees at an early age, assert that adoptee access to sealed adoption records might frustrate the expectations of birth parents should their adopted children pursue potentially embarrassing reunions.[28] For their part, the adoptees support the call for reform with extensive evidence that adoptees denied knowledge of their biological parentage suffer the psychological pain of "genealogical bewilderment."[29] They juxtapose the evidence that this pain is real and substantial with evidence that the adoptive parents' fears of alienation are empirically unfounded,[30] that the adoptees' major interest is in learning about rather than meeting their birth parents,[31] and that birth parents are generally supportive of opening adoption records to adult adoptees.[32]

Before discussing the relevance of sociobiology to this interesting question of social justice, I want to make clear that I have no personal stake in the issue. Neither I, my wife, my parents nor my children are adopted. I am not, however, a neutral observer, and I hope that what I have to say will not offend those whom the issue does touch personally. I think justice demands the reform the adoptees seek.

In part this is because I am skeptical that the arguments offered in opposition to reform are fully explanatory of the current content of the law and the resistance to its reform. I suspect that the predominant legal posture, in the United States at least, reflects a stereotypical conception of the personal virtue of the respective parties, particularly in view of the clerical affiliations of many adoption agencies.[33] The birth parents are seen as morally blameworthy, either for forsaking their child or for conceiving it in circumstances which compelled consigning it to the care of others.[34] The adoptive parents are seen as either saintly, for having altruistically assumed the burden of raising a homeless child, or at least as the innocent victims of the sterility which prevented them from conceiving a child of their own.[35] The adopted children are seen as the lucky beneficiaries of their adoptive parents' altruism or biological misfortune, and their interest in ascertaining the identities of their birth parents is seen as a perversely rebellious expression of ingratitude.[36] The law is accordingly protective of the jealous interests of the adoptive parents, and rather callous in its disregard of the interests of adoptees.

Having disclosed my skepticism of the moral beliefs which underlie the debate, I want to discuss the relevance of sociobiological theory, and how it contributes to my support of the adoptees' position by lending credence to the claim that permanently sealed adoption records cause adoptees significant psychological suffering. The phenomenon known as "genealogical bewilderment" was once thought to indicate a deviant psychological adjustment to the fact of adoption.[37] The current trend of thought is to regard it as both normal and natural, a "deep-felt need" arising out of the innate psychological process of forming a personal identity.[38] It seems to me that sociobiological theory provides an explanatory link between the empirical evidence of the innate basis for genealogical bewilderment and the evolutionary biology which must account for any biologically based behavioral tendency.

I suspect that the principal evolutionary benefit of the desire to ascertain one's ancestry stems from exogamy and the avoidance of incest. Inbreeding reduces genetic fitness, and natural selection has accordingly favored the development of exogamous mating patterns in many species.[39] Although cultural incest taboos are probably the principal cause of the prevalence of exogamy among humans,[40] there is evidence of innate behavioral tendencies in humans which promote exogamy independently of culture. For instance, unrelated children raised on kibbutzim in daily proximity of a sort generally found only between siblings display a virtually total lack of mutual erotic interest despite the absence of any cultural pressure against kibbutz-mate marriages or sex-play.[41] This suggests that genealogical bewilderment may similarly have evolved out of natural selection for exogamy and incest avoidance.

In addition to having enhanced the probability of avoiding incestuous mating by providing the information necessary for the cultural overlay of incest taboos to operate effectively, innate human behavior patterns which tend to maximize knowledge of ancestry may have developed through natural selection by having increased the probability that altruism would benefit relatives of the altruists. Certainly common knowledge suggests that there is more than a random degree of relatedness between orphans and their foster or adoptive parents. The possible relation between genealogical bewilderment and altruism is especially interesting in view of the evidence that the desire for knowledge of the identities of natural parents is more acute among females than males,[42] becomes particularly intense among female adoptees who are beginning their own families,[43] and is paralleled by a desire among female birth parents to communicate information about themselves to their relinquished children.[44]

If my hypothesis is correct, sociobiology counsels that the pain which adoptees seek to redress is both genuine and grave; justice accordingly demands that it be taken seriously, and that the law not exacerbate it without appropriately serious justification. If humans do innately desire to know their ancestry, it follows that the frustration of this desire will cause suffering which cannot be cured by counseling or any other form of cultural mediation other than outright dishonesty about the adoptive status of a child. Our calculations of justice must therefore accept that the denial of access to sealed adoption records will inevitably and irreducably inflict pain on adoptees, which by almost any conception of justice can be justified only by the avoidance of greater pain to others, or by some important contribution to the general welfare.

Is this standard of justification met by the laws which the adoptees seek to reform? Certainly there is much room for disagreement about the the nature and moral weight of the interests of the various parties to the adoption triangle, and of the public interest in avoiding disruption to adoptive families during the children's infancy and adolesence, even if one credits my sociobiological hypothesis. For me the twin limitations of the adoptees' proposed reform to laws sealing adoption records, restricting access to adoptees, and only after they have become adults, are of decisive importance in avoiding conflict between the adoptees' interests and the public interest in stable childhood environments. Since both fact and theory indicate that adult adoptee access to sealed adoption records does not conflict with the interests of most birth parents, the crucial issue of justice becomes the proper balance to be drawn between the interests of adult adoptees and the interests of those adoptive parents who would prefer their children to suffer genealogical bewilderment rather than discover the identities of their birth parents.

I find this issue simplified by the lack of any empirical or theoretical reason to suspect that the interests of adoptive parents, like the conflicting interests of their children, are based on biological tendencies. I do not doubt that maternal and paternal solicitude for the welfare of the children one nurtures has a biological component triggered by proximity rather than bloodlines, in the same way that a mating aversion operates among kibbutz children regardless of actual sibling status. But because of the general advantage of having others contribute to the nurturing of one's own offspring, it would be bizarre to find any innate basis for an inhibition against having others love one's child as their own. Such possessiveness is more likely rooted in the cultural attitude, by no means unique to adoptive parents, that children are chattels whose loyalty the law should guarantee to those who hold legal title over them.[45] The fears of adoptive parents that the law reform sought by adult adoptees will lead to a loss of the love which adoptive parents are due can and should be allayed by counseling that such fears are neither empirically corroborated nor morally worthy.

Although I have expressed my own view on the ultimate issue of justice posed by the issue of adult adoptee access to sealed adoption records, I want to emphasize in conclusion that sociobiology plays only an advisory role in my thinking. As I earlier cautioned, the application of sociobiological theory to human affairs is inherently speculative. Since I am not professionally trained as either an anthropologist or a biologist, my theory of the evolutionary benefit of genealogical bewilderment is particularly speculative, and should certainly be elaborated by a suitably trained investigator before it is considered authoritative. But justice is speculative too; we can only do our best.

My discussion of adult adoptee access to sealed adoption records is, after all, intended to illustrate only that sociobiology can be relevant to mundane and practical problems in the critical evaluation of the law. I claim that an understanding of the biological tendencies at play in human social behavior is informative of our calculations of justice, not dispositive, even when the speculativeness of that understanding has been reduced as much as science will allow. Society is a creation of man, but man is a creature of nature. In shaping society through law justice demands no more than that we keep this in mind. Justice also demands no less.[46]

University of California, Davis

NOTES

[1] See G. B. Kolata, 'Sociobiology (I): Models of Social Behavior', *Science* 187 (1975), 50.

[2] G. B. Kolata, 'Sociobiology (II): The Evolution of Social Systems', *Science* 187 (1975), 156. See generally E. O. Wilson, *Sociobiology: The New Synthesis*, Cambridge and London 1975. See also C. Lumsden and E. O. Wilson, *Genes, Mind and Culture*, Cambridge and London 1981; E. O. Wilson, *On Human Nature*, Cambridge and London 1978.

[3] See D. Barash, 'Some Evolutionary Aspects of Parental Behavior in Animals and Man', *American Journal of Psychology* 195 (1976), 215.

[4] The final chapter of E. O. Wilson, *The Insect Societies*, Cambridge and London 1975, is clearly the precursor to *Sociobiology: The New Synthesis* (1975). Richard Alexander is another prominent sociobiologist with an entomological background. See R. Alexander, *Darwinism and Human Affairs*, 1980. See also S. Benzer 'From the Gene to Behavior', *Journal of the American Medical Association* 218 (1975), 1015 (explaining that fruit flies are useful models for studying the hereditability of social behavior because their biological complexity is intermediate between that of humans and that of bacteria).

[5] See D. Barash (1976), 196 and n. 1.

[6] See E. O. Wilson (1971), 321.

[7] D. Barash, *Sociobiology and Behavior* xi, 309 (1977), 84–85. E. O. Wilson, 'The Social Instinct', *Bulletin of the American Academy of Arts and Sciences* 11 (1976), 22–24. See also A. Rosenberg, *Sociobiology and the Preemption of Social Science*, (1980), 176–179.

[8] See A. Rosenberg (1980), 176–179.

[9] See D. Barash (1977), 277; A. Rosenberg (1980), 177–178, 186, 195; R. Boyd and P. J. Richardson, 'A Simple Dual Inheritance Model of the Conflict Between Social and Biological Evolution', *Zygon* 11 (1976), 254, 255.

[10] See N. Wade, 'Sociobiology: Troubled Birth of a New Discipline', *Science* 191 (1976), 1151.

[11] See Sociobiology Study Group of Science for the People, 'Sociobiology – Another Biological Determinism', *Bioscience* 26 (1976), 182.

[12] See C. Geertz, 'Sex and Sociobiology: Sociosexology', *New York Review of Books* Jan. 24 (1980), 3 (reviewing D. Symons, *The Evolution of Human Sexuality*).

[13] See Sociobiology Study Group of Science for the People (1976), 11. See generally, S. Shields, 'Functionalism, Darwinism, and the Psychology of Women: A Study in Social Myth', *American Psychologist* (1975), 753. See also R. C. Lewontin, 'The Liberation of Biology: The Corpse in the Elevator', *New York Review of Books* Jan. 20 (1983), 34.

[14] Sociobiology Study Group of Science for the People (1976).

[15] See N. Wade (1976), 1152–1155; E. O. Wilson, 'Academic Vigilantism and the Political Significance of Sociobiology', *Bioscience* 26 (1976), 183.

[16] See. G. E. Hutchinson, 'A Speculative Consideration of Certain Possible Forms of Sexual Selection in Man', *American Naturalist* 93 (1959), 81, 84. See generally R. Dawkins, *The Selfish Gene*, New York 1976.
[17] See D. Barash (1977), 319–324. See also W. Etkin, 'Social Behavior and the Evolution of Man's Mental Faculties', *American Naturalist* 93 (1954), 129.
[18] See, e.g., D. Barash (1977), 321; N. Wade (1976), 1154.
[19] C. Anderson, 'The Sealed Record in Adoption Controversy', *Social Science Review* 51 (1977), 141. See generally A. Sorosky, A. Baran and R. Pannor, *The Adoption Triangle: The Effects of the Sealed Record on Adoptees, Birth Parents and Adoptive Parents*, New York 1978. See also B. Lifton, 'The Search', *New York Times Magazine* Jan. 24 (1976), 15.

The term "birth parents" has come into general use in deference to the feelings of adoptive parents, who sometimes resent references to the biological parents of their child as its "real" or "natural" parents. See A. Baran, A. Sorosky and R. Pannor, 'The Dilemma of Our Adoptees', *Psychology Today* Dec. (1975), 38, 96.
[20] See generally A. Baran, R. Pannor and A. Sorosky, 'Open Adoption', *Social Work* 21 (1976), 97.
[21] See A. Sorosky, A. Baran and R. Pannor, 'The Effects of the Sealed Record in Adoption', *American Journal of Psychiatry* 133 (1976), 900–901.
[22] In the case of adoption at birth, neither the birth mother nor the expectant adoptive family are in a strong bargaining position. Adoption agencies may favor closed adoptions in order "to allow the adoption to materialize like the birth of a natural child." C. Anderson (1977), 149.
[23] See Sorosky *et al.* (1976).

"The adult adoptee has the legal recourse to petition the original court that handled the adoption and ask for the records to be unsealed. The courts are generally conservative regarding such matters and will open the records in unusual cases where matters of health, property inheritance or other such practical issues are at stake." R. Pannor, A. Sorosky and A. Baran, 'Opening the Sealed Record in Adoption – The Human Need for Continuity', *Journal of Jewish Communal Service* 51 (1974), 188, 190–191.
[24] See R. Pannor, *et al.* (1974), 190–191; A. Sorosky, A. Baran and R. Pannor, 'The Reunion of Adoptees and Birth Relatives', *Journal of Youth and Adolescence* 3 (1974), 195, 197. See generally C. Anderson (1977).
[25] See L. Jurgens, 'The Emotional Struggle Over Adoptees' "Right to Know" ', *California Journal* Aug. (1978), 262.
[26] A. Baran, R. Pannor and A. Sorosky, 'Adoptive Parents and the Sealed Record Controversy', *Social Casework* 55 (1974), 531. See also A. Baran *et al.* (1975), 38; L. Jurgens (1978), 263.

Some adoptive parents are supportive of the adoptees' reform movement. See J. Freedman, 'An Adoptee in Search of Identity (Notes for Practice)', *Social Work* 22 (1977), 227; B. Lifton (1976), 22.
[27] A. Sorosky *et al.* (1976), 901.
[28] On the schizophrenic aspects of adoption agency policy toward adoptee awareness of biological parentage, see C. Anderson (1977), 144; A. Baran *et al.* (1974), 536; A. Sorosky *et al.* (1976), 902.
[29] See A. Sorosky *et al.* (1976), 901, 902–903. See also C. Anderson (1977), 901.
[30] A. Sorosky *et al.* (1976), 901.

31 A. Sorosky *et al.* (1976), 902.

32 A. Sorosky *et al.* (1974), 205. See generally A. Baran, R. Pannor and A. Sorosky, 'The Lingering Pain of Surrendering a Child', *Psychology Today* June (1977), 58. See also J. Freedman (1977), 227.

33 *Cf.* B. Lifton, *Twice Born: Memoirs of an Adopted Daughter*, New York 1975 (Jewish agency); M. Howard, 'An Adoptee's Personal Search for Her Natural Parents', *Psychology Today* Dec. (1975), 33 (Roman Catholic agency).

34 See, e.g., R. Pannor *et al.* (1974), 33; A. Baran *et al.* (1976), 98.

35 *Cf.* A. Baran *et al.* (1976), 97 (questioning lack of "critical evaluation" of shift in adoption patterns from ancient practice of "open adoption" which served "as a means of protecting young children who lacked parents to nurture them" toward the "closed adoption" which "fulfills childless couples' lives and gives them a tight family unit that conceals their infertility and denies the existence of another set of parents. What was originally seen as a great need for the child is now viewed, perhaps, as a greater need for the parents.").

36 See A. Baran *et al.* (1975), 96; A. Baran *et al.* (1974), 532; M. Howard (1975), 33; B. Lifton (1976), 15.

37 See A. Baran *et al.* (1975), 38; B. Lifton (1976), 15.

38 'Adopted Children and Their Search for Roots', *Business Week* Feb. 6 (1978), 85. See C. Anderson (1977), 144–145; A. Sorosky *et al.* (1974), 197, 205.

39 See, e.g., R. Dawkins (1976), 107.

40 See D. Barash (1977), 290.

41 J. Shepher, 'Mate Selection Among Second Generation Kibbutz Adolescents and Adults: Incest Avoidance and Negative Imprinting', *Archives of Sexual Behavior* 1 (1971), 293.

42 'Adoptees Unite', *Newsweek* April 28 (1975), 86; A. Baran *et al.* (1975), 38.

43 See B. Lifton (1976), 17, 18; A. Sorosky *et al.* (1976), 902; A. Sorosky *et al.* (1974), 204.

44 See A. Baran *et al.* (1977), 60; R. Pannor *et al.* (1974), 192.

45 "If we as adopted adults are required by law to respect a contract made over our bodies, at a time when we were unable to give our consent, then we have indeed been bought and sold on the open market." F. Fischer, speaking as President of The Adoptee's Liberty Movement Association, quoted in J. Freedman (1977), 229. See also P. Aries, *Centuries of Childhood*, London 1962, 353–356, 398–415 (modern European conception of childhood historically linked to post-medieval subordination of women; emergence of the family as the major unit of social organization led, first among the wealthy and then throughout society, to "an obsessive love" for children "which was to dominate society from the eighteenth century on," introducing into home-life an emphasis on insularity). "It is not individualism which triumphed, but the family . . . The modern family satisfied a desire for privacy and also a craving for identity: the members of the family were united by feeling, habit and their way of life." P. Aries (1962), 406, 413.

46 I am indebted to my wife, Fredericka B. Oakley, and to Professor Peter S. Rodman of the Department of Anthropology, University of California, Davis, for their insights and encouragement. The research and conclusions presented here are my own, and I bear sole responsibility for any errors.

ANDREW OLDENQUIST

GROUP EGOISM, ALIENATION, AND PROSOCIAL MOTIVATION

Someone who said he would like being alienated wouldn't understand the idea of alienation: It is intrinsically critical, writers almost invariably making society or the political system the object of their criticism. If it were just a descriptive notion we should be able to pick out alienated people by differences in the ways they feel, behave, and in what causes their feelings and behavior. But I don't think we can. For example, a worker may *feel*, "I just work here", and have no sense of fulfillment or loyalty, but because he chose the wrong kind of job or is mentally ill. This isn't alienation, or at least, not the sort I wish to explore. The feelings Melvin Seeman has listed as characteristic of alienation – powerlessness, meaninglessness, social isolation, and the others – while evidence for alienation, can exist without it, as when I am a refugee, or stranded in a strange city, or in prison.[1]

A worker may *behave* carelessly and be frequently drunk or absent, not because he is alienated but because he was never socialized to be careful and responsible, or because he wants to hurt the company for a personal or political reason. I am not necessarily alienated when I have no loyalty to my job or neighborhood because I am enslaved, sick, if it's full of cobras and tsetse flies, if I am regularly shot at, or if in certain objective ways the job or neighborhood is simply no good.

We could define "alienation" in terms of objective, descriptive conditions (and leave implicit the judgment that the conditions ought to be changed by political action). I may sell my labor under working conditions accepted by Western labor unions and make a product whose price, quality, and distribution are determined not by me but by external market forces. This would satisfy one Marxist conception of alienation, or of what is sometimes called "reification"[2]. The inferiority of the Marxist idea lies in its abstractness, its failure to insist upon an empirical connection with what satisfies and dissatisfies us: Workers are alienated if certain theoretical conditions obtain, regardless whether or not their work is poor or they are dissatisfied: a worker might be efficient, well paid, secure, happy in his work, and alienated. When workers or citizens are alienated we should mean that something has *gone wrong*, that something hurts or doesn't work right; otherwise we only have a piece of jargon and not a usable concept for social diagnosis and criticism.

E. Bulygin et al. (eds.), Man, Law and Modern Forms of Life, 55–63.

On the other hand, we have seen that just appealing to feelings and behavior inadequately identifies cases of alienation. The solution I suggest assumes and depends on a particular theory of human nature, one for which there is growing anthropological and evolutionary evidence: Humans evolved to be innately social animals; on this view we are tribal ceatures, group egoists who are emotionally dependent on group membership and are discontented and function poorly in environments that are too individualistic. The theory depends on evidence of what social living was like for the million years during which what we may call our Pleistocene emotional legacy evolved; it implies testable hypotheses about which social structures and institutions tend to make us secure, or instead insecure and hostile. Such a theory is collectivist in the sense of communitarian (and is as well a form of historical materialism – Darwin merely having pushed back history a few million more years than Marx did). It counts as an "essentialist" theory of alienation, and I wish to argue that attending to human nature, in a scientific rather than an ideological sense, will redress an imbalance in our thinking about modern urban society.

Given this, I define alienation as missing community: *A person is alienated from his workplace, company, neighborhood, or school, if, in a situation in which it is expected of him to view it as "his" and have a sense of community, he does not.* I am alienated if I never show willingness to sacrifice for the good of my community, if I vandalize it, never express pride or shame over its condition, reject all solicitations for my time or money, respond to serious community problems by moving away, and so on. Now, for such behavior really to evidence alienation, we have to understand when – in the deliberately ambiguous phrase I chose – committed labor and good citizenship is "to be expected of someone".

I'm not expected to feel commitment to Chicago if I just visit the city; in Moscow I felt alien, not alienated. In neither case do we "expect" group loyalty, as we might from a life long resident, and just because of that we do not claim I am alienated from Chicago or Moscow. We do not *expect* commitment from residents who are uneducated and unemployable, mentally retarded, or so totally engrossed in their work, or in drinking, that they care about nothing else. Nonetheless, while in some cases we may not *expect* it we may at the same time feel it *is expected of them*. For this reason construing alienation as a false expectation of good citizenship doesn't get us very far.

The main problem with defining alienation in terms of what we expect from a person is that *whenever* someone cares nothing about his community there is an explanation, and if we know it we no more expect civic loyalty than we do from an infant. So if we conclude Jones is alienated our judgment is just a product of our ignorance. This is a familiar deterministic argument, which makes the difference between the alien and the alienated depend only on whether we know what makes them behave as they do. Saying criminals are not responsible when we can give psychiatric or sociological causes of their behavior, and that otherwise they are responsible, confronts the same argument: The distinction seems indefensible if the only difference lies in us, not in the criminals, insofar as we blame criminals when we are ignorant of what causes their behavior and we excuse them when we think we know what caused them to act as they did.

The point is that slovenly, uncaring or hostile behavior counts as alienation only in normal and "appropriate" people, not in visitors, aliens, the retarded, professional criminals, dedicated political enemies, people who would have serious character defects in any society, and others. The teachers and students in school *A* can be alienated from school *A*, but not the pigeons on the roof, a Naga tribesman, or the teachers and students from school *B*. The same is true of our workplaces and societies. Behavior counts as alienation only among people who belong, and saying that only those who belong can be alienated is understandable because of the *demands* a school, job, or society can make on its own people but not on Nagas or on the pigeons on the roof.

Even to qualify for alienation you must in some sense belong to the workplace or community. Behind the importance we attach to belonging is the idea that citizens *ought* to be committed and cooperative, and that when they don't and are alienated something has gone wrong *with them*; unless what makes them poor workers or poor citizens is, so to speak, *too good a reason*, and we say instead that they are sick and excused; or simply alien and we have no claim on them; or they are disloyal or predators, and are our enemies.

In everyday use "alienation" often implies criticism of the alienated individual: Something is wrong that reflects poorly on you if you are alienated from your job, family, or neighborhood. Most writers on alienation, on the other hand, consider the individual 100 percent a victim and if criticisms are implied the blame is put entirely on society. Two reasons for this are contemporary social scientists' inclinations to blame society and not individuals for crime and for failings of any kind, and Marxists' use of "alienation" as an overall criticism of non-Marxist political/economic systems. The "pure victim" theory of alienation distorts our understanding of particular alienating policies and effective remedies as they bear on individuals, whether in the mixed economies of Western Europe and the U.S. or in socialist countries. For example, on the "pure victim" view it will be more difficult to appreciate the alienating effects of value-free, non-judgmental processing of juvenile delinquents, and the importance of announced personal accountability to society as a de-alienation strategy.

When we speak of citizens or young people being alienated we usually imply a failure of loyalty or commitment, an individualist pulling back from collective involvement, a retreat from "us" to "me". There is overall a tone of moral failing, not in the sense of gross violation of duty or principle, but of default on one's owed emotional contribution to a collective enterprise. Alienated people are not just victims. Healthy societies *demand* loyalty from members who are adult, sane, and normal in certain other respects: The uncaring businessperson and the barfly *ought* to care about their community; they lack the generally accepted kinds of excuses that apply to infants, the retarded, aliens, and the socially ostracized.

But in calling people alienated we are at the same time saying something has gone wrong with the causal machinery that we think it both desirable and possible should operate in our society: It is not a predatory, evil will but a failure in their socialization or social environment. It is vitally important that we be able to distinguish alienated people – and therefore the criminal acts including vandalism and hooliganism that can be traced to alienation – from predatory criminals, whose overt behavior sometimes is indistinguishable from that of the alienated. We need to search for social policies that will manipulate social causes and reduce alienation. But what will eliminate alienation need not have the slightest effect on the predatory criminal.

We lay varying degrees of responsibility on those we call alienated and who care nothing for – or harm – their own schools, towns, neighborhoods, or countries, and *also* admit that there are identifiable causes of why they behave the way they do. It is part of the good society that it contain citizens who care, and we try to discover what changes will make individuals care and no longer be bad citizens. It is not different in the case of crime: It would be mad to deny that crime has causes and equally mad to deny that sane, adult criminals are personally responsible for their crimes.

There are important differences between the Marxist view of alienation as a necessary failing of a political system and alienation as an avoidable *malaise* that is found here and there in a mixed economy (as well as here and there in socialist societies). On the Marxist view alienated individuals are 100 percent victims. Second, those who are interested in piecemeal de-alienation think of alienating social practices and policies as deviations from attainable normal functioning, whereas alienating causes according to the Marxist criticism of capitalism are essential to the system. Third, alienation as a necessary consequence of capitalism tends to be independent of psychology and non-empirical, whereas localized, contingent alienation is immediately and painfully evident.

"Practical" American social planners have largely ignored alienation and focused only on what is "useful": good sewer lines, highways, and welfare checks delivered on time. What is useful people accept, but it does not create the sense of possession and commitment on which society depends. We are all too often anti-historical, boring, utilitarians who think that ritual, ceremony and symbol, even a sense of style, are useless nonsense best left to strutting dictators and New Guinea tribes. So we offer each other nourishing cold porridge. We actually think of *mailing* diplomas to college graduates, and General Motors would never dream of making its employees dance (nor would the United Auto Workers look kindly on the idea). But the New Guinea tribe makes its "employees" dance, the Japanese corporation makes them sing, and each reaps a much deeper commitment.

We have forgotten, in our cities and in our factories, how essential to collective commitment is the "useless" – the ornaments, the rituals and ceremonies, attention to the past, and the things which are expensive and relatively functionless but grand. We alienate delinquents and misbehaving students by not holding them personally responsible to society: for that is a way of telling them that they do not belong, that they are things, like viruses, or as alien to us as Nagas. We alienate by dispensing with formal solemnity in juvenile justice proceedings. We alienate the young by teaching them a relation between the individual and society that is as wary, commercial, and cold as our relation to a gas station. In all these respects street gangs and New Guinea tribes are wiser about which practices alienate and which de-alienate than a great many educators and juvenile justice professionals. We need to look for clues to what, in modern urban society, is structurally analogous to prehistoric, intimately social, tribal life, and hence is likely to create in us a sense of belonging and communal value. When we translate ignorance of our history – our evolutionary history, not just our recent political history – into social policies, the result is insecure, alienated, hostile, people who don't care about anything, often not even about themselves.

Surely, it will be objected, alienation is caused by poverty, powerlessness, and racial discrimination and is at best marginally related to ceremonies and park statuary: If someone is deprived of the basic protections and opportunities of his society he will reject it; he will be alienated and it will be unreasonable to expect good citizenship. I shall attempt to pin down when this rejection response comes. But there is ample evidence that poverty, political despotism, and insecurity have little to do with it. History is replete with groups and subgroups who have lived with far less freedom and prosperity than the residents of the worst urban slums and who yet are relatively law abiding because of a strong sense of community and group identity. Conversely, wealth and political representation are by no means a guarantee of good citizenship.

Someone who thinks he is not getting a fair share of whatever benefits his society has to offer is not to be counted on for law-abiding citizenship. We can call him "radically alienated"; but how do we distinguish him from a social predator? I wish to try an analogy. Compare badly off slum dwellers with people in a movie line (waiting for a benefit, the movie), with an eye to finding a way to predict when each will "give up on the system". Each is being asked to pay a certain price: The slum dweller (minimally) to obey the law, the movie-goer to wait his turn in the line. Assume, at least for the sake of argument, that moral psychology and elementary game theory will tell us that a person who follows the rules and does his share – who stays in line – is *second* best off: He is *best* off if he is a free-rider within a cooperative system, and *worse* off if he lives in a world in which everyone tries to be a free-rider and no one restrains self interest.

Most of us are willing to wait in line even if we know we would be better off jumping the line (assume that the other people in line will merely grouch at us, if they even notice). *Why do we stay in line*, assuming that pure selfishness tells us not to? Sense of fairness is one reason: other people wait their turn and we are no different from them. We may add childhood socialization that reinforces, or even helps create, our sense of fairness. We know we are better off in a world of wait-your-turn than in a world of push-and-shove; but this awareness does not give us a *selfish* reason to wait our turn, it only gives us a reason of fairness, because we know we could be free-riders in the world of wait-your-turn.

What happens when we see people cutting in ahead of us? We are indignant, which is the natural response of a moral community toward members who receive its benefits without paying their share, but most of us remain in the line unless the free-riders become too numerous. *What is "too numerous?"* At what point, in the gradual corruption of an orderly movie line by line jumpers up ahead, do you quit the line and join the game of push-and-shove? The answer I suggest is that we quit when "it doesn't pay", when "we might as well push and shove with the others or forget the movie". This answer is not as obvious as it first appears. We obviously quit if so many parasites are cutting in that we don't move forward at all.

But there is another point, short of this, at which we decide waiting in the line "doesn't pay". It is when we feel we are not better off waiting in the line than we are likely to be in the game of push-and-shove. In other words, we are willing to make sacrifices as members of a rule-guided social system – for example, we don't join a small number of line jumpers – but we expect as a result to be better off than we would be in a world of line jumpers. This is the pay-off that will be insisted on. We do not insist that rules of fairness and restraint make us *best* off, like the free-rider is; but we do insist that they make us *better off* than we would be in a world without rules of fairness, cooperation, and restraint.

This is the grain of truth in the individualist, social contractarian conception of society. Members of a moral community are willing to pay a real price but they expect to receive the benefits of civilization in return: To be better off than they would be in a world in which nobody paid that price. I most emphatically am saying that slum youths have the same obligations not to be egoists and free-riders as do the rest of us. But if someone sees himself in society as he would in a movie line in which he doesn't get a ticket more easily and safely than he would if everyone were pushing and shoving, he is no more likely to feel obliged to follow that society's rules than to wait in such a line. There is little doubt that many street youths in slums *believe* they personally are not better off in the world of mutual concession than they would be in the world of push-and-shove.

If youths in slums are minimally socialized, or not socialized at all, they are doubly lost. For if they *believe* they are not better off obeying the rules than living in the "state of nature", they are radically alienated. If they are not socialized they will be unsuited to live anywhere but the slum, if even there: They will lack the social morality and personal virtues that enable one to flourish in society, and will lack the group loyalties that motivate one to obey the rules – which means their belief that they are not better off will be true, although not for the reasons they think.

The eighteenth century moral psychologist Joseph Butler said that rational selfishness does not create or motivate the social ethics of citizens, but it does, when certain limits are reached, exercise a veto power over it.[3] Civilized society depends on most people following rules which require small to moderate sacrifices of self-interest. If the demands become too large, the great mass of the citizenry cannot be counted on: Social morality cannot be made too expensive or self-interest will exercise its veto. So too regarding our model for predicting radical alienation: Society asks its members to be willing to restrain self-interest, follow rules, and hence be "second best off".

This we are willing to do; but we will not make this sacrifice unless we sense that we *are* second best off, that is, better off on the whole than we would be in a world of dog-eat-dog. Beyond this point rational selfishness exercises the veto: we will follow the rules and not take unfair advantage, but we will not wait in pointless lines.

I began by arguing that particular social institutions and policies can alienate citizens by ruining sense of community, in turn diminishing their tendency to follow the rules and respect the common good. In addition, I have described a felt situation in which a person accuses society of false advertising: he *isn't* better off than he would be in a Hobbesian state of nature. So he becomes *radically alienated* and either has no tribal identity whatever, which will make him miserable and unpredictable, or he joins a street gang whose rules, he hopes, do *not* constitute false advertising. It is difficult, however, to see how we can actually apply the idea of radical alienation. This is because it is very difficult, in particular cases, to distinguish someone who is radically alienated from a predator.

Sissela Bok has noticed the distinction between predators and people I call radically alienated. Speaking of liars, she says,

> At times, liars operate as if they believed that such a free-rider status is theirs and that it excuses them. At other times, on the contrary, it is the very fact that others *do* lie that excuses their deceptive stance in their own eyes. It is crucial to see the distinction between the free-loading liar and the liar whose deception is a strategy for survival in a corrupt society . . . . While different, the two are closely linked. If enough persons adopt the free-rider strategy for lying, the time will come when all will feel pressed to lie to survive.[4]

The theoretical distinction is clear: Predators know they are better off in a world in which people follow a social ethics than in a world in which they do not. They just want to be best off, not second best off. The predator elects to be a piranha in a tank of guppies, whereas the person who is radically alienated thinks that he might as well be a piranha since he is not better off than he would be if the tank were full of piranhas. This is a different, although related, sense of alienation from the one I began with and more closely linked to the traditional notion of the alienated as social victims.

But which of these persons is Mr. Jones, who has just robbed a gas station? It of course is in the interest of people who do not believe in criminal responsibility to label him "alienated" instead of "predator", since it appears to provide an excuse. My suggestion is that we react to the idea of radical alienation only on the level of large scale social and economic policy and not on the level of how one treats individual criminals. For if it is true that the integrity of a moral community requires holding its delinquents personally responsible for what they do, true that radical alienation destroys a society's shared common good, and true in any case that we cannot easily tell predators from the alienated, the only rational option is to punish criminals and enact policies that minimize alienation.

Ohio State University

NOTES

[1] Melvin Seeman, 'On the Meaning of Alienation', *American Sociological Review* 24 (1959), 783–91.
[2] Cf. Joachim Israel, 'Alienation and Reification', in: R. Felix Geyer and David R. Schweitzer (eds.), *Theories of Alienation*, Leiden 1976, 41–57.
[3] Joseph Butler, Sermon Eleven from *Fifteen Sermons Preached at the Rolls Chapel.*
[4] Sissela Bok, *Lying: Moral Choice in Public and Private Life*, New York 1978, 23.

PETER G. SACK

HOMOSEXUALITY, EARTHQUAKES AND HART'S CONCEPT OF 'PRIMITIVE LAW'

I

Whereas 'primitive law' has a natural place in (modern, Western) historical jurisprudence, and whereas it ought to have such a place in comparative law, the same cannot be said about 'natural law' or 'positivism'.[1] Yet, there are exceptions, and H. A. L. Hart's liberal brand of 'naturalised' positivism is one of them.

Hart proclaims that he did not have to invoke 'primitive law' to demonstrate the inadequacies of "the simple model of law as the sovereign's coercive orders" (*The Concept of Law*, Oxford 1961, 77).[2] Nevertheless, 'primitive law' plays a central role in his counter-proposal according to which 'law' is "the union of primary and secondary rules" (*ibid.*). Although Hart's concept of 'primitive law' is, essentially, an analytical construction, it is incorporated into a model of 'legal' evolution: 'primitive law' is characterised by the absence of "secondary rules", whose introduction was "a step forward as important to society as the invention of the wheel" (*ibid.*, 41). But, 'primitive law' has also a positive side: it consists (exclusively) of a set of "primary rules". Hence the social universe of man, whether 'legal' or 'pre-legal', always was and always will be rule-governed. However – in contrast to 'modern law' – 'primitive law' has three fundamental defects, namely its uncertainty, its static character and its inefficiency (*ibid.*, 90–91).

This is all the preparation required for the construction of Hart's own scheme. Secondary rules, in the shape of the "rules of recognition", the "rules of change" and the "rules of adjudication", provide the necessary and sufficient remedy for each of these defects, turning the scheme at the same time into a self-supporting structure, which defines the strengths of 'law' by the weaknesses of 'primitive law' and *vice versa*.

How does this approach differ from that attacked by Hart in his disputation with Lord Devlin – whom he offered

> the alternative of supplementing his contentions with evidence, or accepting that his statements (. . .) were not empirical statements at all but were disguised tautologies or necessary truths (. . .) (*The University of Chicago Law Review*, vol. 35, 3)?

E. Bulygin et al. (eds.), Man, Law and Modern Forms of Life, 65–77.

More particularly, is Hart's concept of 'primitive law' – to use his own comparison – entitled to any more respect than Emperor Justinian's claim that homosexuality was the cause of earthquakes (see *Law, Liberty and Morality*, London 1963, 50)?

To appreciate the scope of this question we must stay a little longer with Justinian; for, despite appearances, his claim was not chosen by Hart as a 'disguised tautology'. Rather, it was selected as the epitome of all statements that are patently untrue.

Moreover, irrespective of its factual truth, Justinian's claim can be seen to be methodologically dishonest, because it presents a subjective value judgement in the form of an objective causal connection, because it gives an ideological statement a pseudo-scientific form, because it wants to further dubious political ends in an objectively deceitful manner. Instead of disclosing his real reasons for condemning homosexuality, Justinian is hiding behind a screen of fictitious facts – which in turn seems to justify us in condemning Justinian without having to consider his real reasons – a highly questionable result.

Fortunately this need not worry us, as it is sufficient for present purposes to realise that the question Hart put to Devlin and which is here – *mutatis mutandis* – applied to himself goes far beyond an inquiry into whether Hart has verified or would be able to verify the factual propositions on which his concept of 'primitive law' rests. Instead, it aims at discovering if Hart's concept of 'primitive law' – like Devlin's statements about the necessity of a common morality for the existence of society, according to Hart – is the product of ideological preference rather than 'natural necessities'.

I agree with Hart that there are theoretical statements about 'law' which apart from being untrue are also objectively evil, in the moral and political sense. But this is where our roads part, for Hart believes that such evils will cease to exist if ideology is finally banned from the realm of jurisprudence. As this is, in my view, neither possible nor desirable, I neither wish to attack Hart's ideological position, nor do I want to prove the superiority of my own by pointing to flaws in his argument. I merely want to demonstrate that he is sitting in the same boat as Devlin and the rest of us and that calling an ideological spade a tautology does not help us, even if it is true, to steer 'law' in the right direction, whichever that may be.

II

Hart develops his concept of 'primitive law' in four steps. The first asserts that it is possible to imagine a society "without a legislature, courts or officials of any kind" (*Concept*, 89). The second claims that this possibility has in fact been realised (*ibid.*). The third step contends that the 'law' of these societies consists exclusively of "primary rules of obligations" (*ibid.*). According to the fourth, the minimal content of these rules can be deduced from a few "obvious truisms about human nature and the world we live in" (*ibid.*).

1. On the face of it the first step is superfluous. What, could be asked, is the point of claiming that something is imaginable if it actually exists? Yet, from Hart's perspective it is essential, because he believes that human imagination rather than empirical knowledge defines the limits of reality. This is not as fanciful as it may seem since 'imagination', for Hart, is not a matter of intuition but of rational analysis to be contrasted sharply with "fantasy" – its negative counterpart.[3] The significance of the first step therefore lies in its implied message: "It is, of course, possible to imagine a society without a legislature, courts or officials of any kind" – but: it would be fantastic to suggest that there ever was or ever could be a society without "primary rules of obligations".

2. Under these circumstances it is Hart's second step that lacks weight. Still, it is surprising just how lightly he takes it.

While maintaining in the text that there are *many* studies of (presumably different) primitive communities "without a legislature" etc. (*ibid.*, 89, emphasis added), he happily admits in an explanatory note that "[f]ew societies have existed in which legislative and adjudicative organs and centrally organised sanctions were entirely lacking" (*ibid.*, 244, emphasis added).[4] And, instead of referring to at least one of them, Hart is satisfied to point – in general terms – to studies of the "nearest approximations". This is to say, Hart does not bother to produce one shred of evidence to substantiate his proposition.

His low opinion of anthropological evidence comes through even more clearly in the following note, where he refers in all innocence to an Evans-Pritchard quotation in Gluckman (incidentally reproducing the wrong page reference given by the latter), satisfied that there is no need to see his only evidence for himself in its original context. But why does Hart not name Gluckman himself as a witness, whose comments on the Evans-Pritchard quotation would seem – with their stress on 'rules' – strongly to support his own position?[5] Did Hart manage to read on and realise that the 'rules' Gluckman had in mind were, in content as well as in 'function', very different from his own conception?[6] Or did he object to Gluckman's view that "[o]ther approaches to the relation between custom, morality, and law . . .

[including the one he, Hart, intended to take? – my remark] have ended either in confusion or in mystique" (*ibid.*, 263–64)? In any case, Hart felt safer to use a moral philosopher as the authority for the historical reasons behind the "step from the pre-legal into the legal world" (see the next explanatory note in *Concept*, 244) – although others may feel that this authority crossed the line between the sublime and the ridiculous when suggesting that mankind stepped into the world of 'law' because 'customary' ways of dealing with offenders interfered with its food supply (see K. Baier, *The Moral Point of View*, Cornell University Press 1958, 128).

3. One can thus be forgiven for suspecting that Hart introduced the second step to conjure up a seemingly solid screen of anthropological evidence behind which he could proceed until he had reached the desired position. In the space of a few lines, he contends that 'primitive law' is identical with "social control", that it forms, at the same time, a "social structure", that a 'rule' is a certain type of "general attitude", that only 'rules' can create obligations and that there are no (imaginable) alternatives to "social control" by means of 'rules'.

Whatever one's attitudes towards any of these assumptions, it would seem well nigh impossible to forge them into a consistent argument without engaging in the kind of circular definition game Hart criticised in the case of Devlin.

However, Hart did not give anthropological evidence a central role in the form of his argument because he felt obliged to make a token genuflection before the altar of empiricism, but because he hoped that this would conceal the gradual shift from description to interpretation, from reality to theory and ideology. Although he recognises concepts, like 'rule', 'primitive law', or 'law' itself, as tools for talking and thinking about 'law', he refuses, for himself, to accept the lesson he is preaching. He refuses to admit that *The Concept of Law* is essentially an exposition of what 'law' in his opinion ought to be.

There would be nothing wrong with such an exposition if Hart did not insist on presenting it as a statement of fact. He denies that *The Concept of Law* is the product of his own preferences rather than of 'natural necessities' precisely because he wants it to become a statement of fact. He is forced into this paradoxical situation because he has been conditioned to believe that this wish is evil ideology. And he has been so conditioned because this is, according to the collective wisdom of his tradition, the best way of fulfilling it. Despite his awareness of the creative (performative, normative) role of 'legal' language, Hart must therefore masquerade as a "descriptive sociologist" (*ibid.*, vii) looking for historical and logical alibis.

Once this is understood, the status of Hart's concept of 'primitive law' changes dramatically. He can, at best, claim that it is possible to *interpret* the reality of 'primitive law' exclusively in terms of "primary rules". However, this interpretation can no longer be justified on the grounds that it depicts 'primitive law' as it is, but it must compete with other possible interpretations, proving itself by demonstrating its own superior explanatory capacity. In short, Hart's concept of 'primitive law' is in the same position as a concept which, for example, wants to interpret modern Western law in terms of magical powers.

4. It is not surprising that Hart felt, at this point, the need for a fresh start. This he achieves by identifying the content of 'primitive law' with "the minimum content of natural law" (*ibid.*, 189 ff).[7] The relevant 'rules' – and 'rules' they must be[8] – are determined by the same means: they follow from a few obvious truisms. Nonetheless Hart assures us:

> Such rules are in fact always found in the primitive societies of which we have knowledge (*ibid.*)[9].

As Hart treats the relevant questions in greater detail in the latter context, we will focus on that version.

Hart's starting point is the selection of a minimal aim of human society which he identifies as: survival.[10] He justifies this decision primarily on formal grounds:

> We are committed to it as something presupposed by the terms of the discussion; for our concern is with social arrangements for continued existence and not with those of a suicide club (*ibid.*, 188).

He then specifies his aim more clearly:

> We wish to know whether, among these *social arrangements*, there are some which may be *illuminatingly* ranked as *natural laws* discoverable by *reason* and what their *relation* is to human law and morality (*ibid.*, emphasis added).

One of these tasks is subsequently singled out for further treatment and thus given the key role.

> It is important to observe that in each case the facts [that is, the five truisms about human nature he wants to discuss – my remark] afford a *reason* why, given survival as an aim, law and morals should include a specific content (*ibid.*, 189).

Hart stresses the "distinctively rational connection between natural facts and the content of legal and moral rules", because he wants to distinguish them from what he calls "causal connexions" which are the province not of jurisprudence, but of the "still young sciences of psychology and sociology" (*ibid.*). The implications are obvious: such connections are not only different but – by definition – 'non-legal'. 'Law' is solely a rational enterprise which sees man as a (not always perfect) rational being.

Hart makes no attempt to justify this dramatic narrowing of the scope of 'law'. Nor does he reflect on the relations between 'extra-legal' causes and 'legal' effects. Are the former, for example, by themselves capable of creating ('legal') 'rules', 'rights' or 'duties'? To use his own example, is there in 'primitive law' a 'rule', according to which parents must feed their small children? Or, must a corresponding 'legal duty' on the part of the parents grow out of some additional 'reasonable' moral maxim? Can 'legal rules' only come into existence after the reasons behind them have actually been identified and articulated or are the "social arrangements", Hart refers to, themselves 'law'? And, should reasons be required, can they also be provided by the aim of survival itself? Does survival provide a reason for a 'legal rule' obliging parents to feed their small children? It seems not, since Hart is careful to classify survival as a mere condition for the existence of a 'legal system' (although it takes the shape of an aim and not a fact).

Even if we accept that survival is a necessary condition for the existence of 'law', it does not follow that it is also necessary, or at least illuminating, to assume that the aim of 'survival' has shaped the content of 'law'. On the contrary, human groups or societies must have solved the problem of survival long before they could start thinking about 'legal rules'; 'law' in the sense of a social organisation adequate for the purposes of survival predates the development of human rationality and even human language. 'Law', to put it bluntly, cannot, at least not initially, have been the product of human reasoning; 'law' must be historically older than 'rules'.[11] To ask what the law of the original human society would have looked like, if its members had appeared as fully rational beings out of the blue and had sat down to debate what 'rules' they would have to introduce to secure their survival – must result not only in 'imaginary' but also 'fantastic' history.

As the survival of human society must have been reasonably secure before a rational form of 'law' could develop, it is also unlikely that even this form of 'law' concentrated, when it developed, on the already solved problem of survival. Instead, it probably took survival for granted and concerned itself with problems for which the existing 'social instincts' did not yet provide solutions. In other words, in addition to "secondary rules" being, according to Hart, parasitic on "primary rules", "primary rules" are and must remain parasitic on 'social instincts', and Hart's approach, far from illuminating this relationship, makes it impossible to grasp it as a 'legal' issue.

Furthermore, if 'rules' were essential for the survival of human groups, would they then also be essential for the survival of groups of animals?[12] Do termites have a 'natural law'? If not, and if Hart is right in comparing the discovery of "secondary rules" with the invention of the wheel, should we then not compare the discovery of "primary rules" with the invention of fire? But would this justify the conclusion that people did not eat before the invention of fire or that they, henceforth, cooked all their food and must continue to do so until the Last (jurisprudential) Judgement?

Hart's explicit arguments in favour of his minimum content of natural law are barely more convincing. For example, he claims that the fact of human vulnerability (combined with the aim of survival) requires the provision: '*Thou shalt not kill*' (*ibid*., 190). He tries to prove this by showing it to be a mere 'truism' rather than a 'necessary truth':[13]

> for things might have been, and might one day be, otherwise. There are species of animals whose physical structure (including exoskeletons or a carapace) renders them virtually immune from attack by other members of their species and animals who have no organs enabling them to attack (*ibid*.).

It is perhaps more charitable to treat this not as an argument but as an attempt to deflect attention from the fact that species of animals whose physical structure is much closer to man have developed an instinct preventing them from killing each other. Is it, therefore, not the vulnerability of man which requires a 'rule' against killing other men but the lack of a 'pre-legal' instinct other animals possess? Besides, the lack of this instinct makes it improbable that such a rule could be at all necessary for the survival of man. On the contrary, at some stage a 'rule' requiring man to kill human enemies of his group as well as unwanted members became, if not necessary, at least advantageous to the survival of mankind.

Hart has similar difficulties with his argument in favour of the protection of property as a part of 'natural law'. He contends that this need follows from the truism that the resources man requires for his survival are limited and that:

> the simplest forms of property are to be seen in rules excluding persons generally or others than the 'owner' from entry on, or the use of land, or from taking or using material things (*ibid*., 192).

Would it not be more plausible to explain many of such 'rules' in political rather than economic terms, in the sense that groups are concerned to exclude potentially hostile outsiders from their territory instead of trying to monopolise its economic potential – quite apart from the role played by 'territorial' instincts etc? Also, may not the notion of 'property' have developed because people felt entitled to enjoy the fruits of their labour rather than because the materials used in producing the object in question were in limited supply?[14] And, if the mere fact that resources necessary for the survival of a group of men are limited gave rise to the institution of 'property', would the same not again apply to animals? Do packs of wolves have 'property laws' because their prey does not exist in limitless abundance? Conversely, are the food sharing 'customs' of groups of 'hunters and gatherers' which may prevent members from partaking in their own kill, 'unnatural' or are they instead another indication that 'primitive law' was, from the start, more concerned with social goals than physical survival?

III

So far our discussion has been concerned with the positive aspect of Hart's concept of 'primitive law', with his claim that 'primitive law' consists (exclusively) of "primary rules". We now turn to the negative aspect: his assertion that 'primitive law' lacks "secondary rules".

From Hart's point of view this lack is self-evident, and it is indeed a necessary truth that societies which have no "legislature, courts or officials of any kind" cannot have any 'rules' relating to these 'institutions'. However, this perspective ignores the crucial issue of how to define them. While Hart tried to overcome this problem in the case of "primary rules" by identifying 'primitive law' with a universal concept of 'natural law', this course of action is precluded in the case of "secondary rules" since they are supposed to be *not* universally necessary.

As far as 'primitive law' is concerned, the concept of "secondary rules" emerges directly form the defects 'primitive law' is said to possess and which are in turn seen as the product of the lack of such 'rules'.[15] Yet, even this approach cannot conceal the fact that "secondary rules" are not merely concerned with conferring specific legal powers for the purpose of dealing with specific legal defects, but with general questions of procedure and, ultimately, organisation. The "secondary rules" define 'law' as an operational system which is – in contrast to 'primitive law' – distinct from society (and happens to coincide with the 'legal' aspect of the State). Thus, if we really want to know whether 'primitive law' includes "secondary rules" we must ask how 'primitive' societies are organised.

As soon as the question is put in that way it becomes obvious that Hart's conception of 'primitive law' is inadequate and misleading. 'Primitive law' cannot merely consist of embryonic forms of criminal and property 'law' etc. Like any other forms of 'law', it must be primarily 'constitutional law'.[16] Its core is the organisation of society and not the specific obligations of its individual members.

Hart tries to play down this undeniable fact by describing it as: the knitting [!] together of 'primitive societies' "by ties [not 'rules'!] of kinship, common sentiment and belief" (*ibid*., 89). He persists in calling the "social structure" [!] of 'primitive' societies one of 'primary rules' (*ibid*., 90), because he would otherwise have to admit that his "secondary rules" are the 'primary rules' of human society instead of being an earthshaking modern discovery, that neither they nor the "primary rules" must take the form of 'rules' and that 'law' must not be – and perhaps, ought not to be – primarily concerned with the protection of individuals.

If these admissions are made, we are no longer confronted by a 'primitive law' that is defective because it consists only of "primary rules" and which is healed and enriched by the introduction of "secondary rules", invented for the purpose. Instead we observe the struggle between different organisational systems: we witness the take-over of 'law' by the state which reduces 'primitive law' artificially to a set of "primary rules" since they fit best into the new organisational system.

At first glance, it seems strange that lawyers should hail this bureaucratic revolution. Far from discovering the jurisprudential wheel, it merely tied 'law' to this particular mode of transport by 'outlawing' all other alternatives, such as walking, riding, flying or swimming. But lawyers themselves, as 'legal professionals', are a product of this revolution. It is they – not the 'law' – who are wedded to the notion of 'law' as a system of 'rules', because they know that this particular form of 'law' depends as much on them as they depend on it.

Those who picture themselves as the intellectual guardians of this 'legal system' understandably feel the urge to rewrite the history of 'law' so as to make its evolution appear to be necessary as well as desirable, since this justifies the task of system-maintenance in which they are engaged in terms of an objective duty rather than those of subjective preference.

The arrogance and hypocrisy this produces can be tolerated as long as 'the legal system' is capable of doing the tasks it is trying to monopolise. However, the more lasting, successful and ambitious the 'system' has been, the more serious the problems will be when it collapses; for the alternatives which must then be revived have been buried all the deeper under a self-reinforcing structure of selective techniques and ideas.

Hart's main contribution to that exercise begins with the concession that 'primitive law' is satisfactory as long as human groups remain small and their environment stable (*ibid.*, 89–90). But Hart is convinced that the 'destabilisation' of human groups (through an increase in their size) and their environment (for unidentified reasons) is for the better. Whatever he may say, Hart not only believes in the possibility of progress but sees the history of mankind as the actual manifestation of progress. Hence, it is the task of 'law' to accommodate and even to facilitate change and not to maintain a stable environment, small group sizes and common beliefs. There are no alternatives, no choices, not even compromises: if 'primitive law' is standing in the way of progress it has to go.

On the other hand, it is inconceivable for Hart that the new 'law' which replaced it may too become (or already has become) obsolete. It is inconceivable because the retrospective, self-fulfilling prophecy (which he calls history) has persuaded him that the limited technology of that particular form of 'law' is eternal.

This is why 'primitive law' must be a set of "primary rules", even if this creates the defects which the "secondary rules" are meant to heal.[17] Hart identifies such fictitious defects – rather than facing the real problems – because they are defects of 'rules' for which the introduction of more 'rules' can be claimed to be the only appropriate remedy – whereas a discussion of the real problems could well lead to the abolition of 'primary rules'. Hart proceeds that way because 'rules' are the only weapon in his 'legal' arsenal. It is, for him, no longer a matter of choice but of survival to present all defects of 'law' as defects of 'rules' – even if it means rewriting history, blocking out all other defects of 'law' and surrendering permanently all alternative remedies on which the future of 'law' may depend.

Hart's only consolation is that 'history' must somehow turn the increasingly smaller circles in which he is moving into a gloriously ascending spiral. He can be satisfied with maintaining the system, because it is bound to bring more freedom and wealth to individuals – and this is and always has been for him (despite the spiel about survival and morality) the real aim of mankind as well as 'law'.

Perhaps Hart does not want to appreciate that the achievements of mankind can become independent of the 'regime' under which they were made? Perhaps basic human rights (such as they are) can outlive liberal capitalism just as the 'King's Peace' outlived feudalism (or language, music, astronomy and the wheel outlived cannibalism)? Perhaps liberal capitalism as well as communism will become unable to maintain even the 'King's Peace'? Perhaps homosexuality does cause earthquakes? Perhaps the future of mankind was as dear to Justinian's heart as it is to Hart's heart? One thing at least seems certain: Hart's concept of 'primitive law' is not descriptive sociology.

The Australian National University

NOTES

[1] It is ironic that one of the few practical roles of 'natural law' in positive, modern, Western law concerned 'primitive law': it was used in colonial law, in particular by Britain, to limit the applicability of local 'primitive law' or to fill gaps in the colonial law as applied to 'primitive' peoples (see, for example, Bryce, *Studies in History and Jurisprudence* 2, 166–67 and 170–71, Oxford 1901).

[2] The volume of the literature on *The Concept of Law* is by now almost frightening. I have made no attempt to cover it systematically. It was, naturally, pleasing when I discovered that I was not alone in some of my criticisms. But by and large I found this a hindrance rather than a help. The perspectives were so different from mine, that where the views of others were similar they tended to distort the direction of my argument instead of advancing it. Nonetheless, I should at least mention that Cohen drew, almost immediately, attention to the central role of "secondary rules" in 'primitive law' (*Mind*, 71, 409), and that Summers, soon after, doubted the wisdom of Hart's attempt to reduce legal institutions to legal 'rules' (*Duke Law Journal*, 4, 643). In the recent literature, I found MacCormick's admission that it was probably misleading to assume that 'rules' played a prominent part in 'primitive law' most encouraging (*H. L. A. Hart*, London, 1981, 101). Yet MacCormick still criticises Hart within the framework of a shared tradition whereas I am concerned with the 'external aspect'.

[3] This contrast is particularly visible in *Law, Liberty and Morality* where the term "fantastic" is a favourite weapon for destroying factual propositions to which Hart objects (for example *ibid.*, 68, but see also *Concept*, 185).

[4] It is remarkable that a person putting so high a store on "inquiries into the meaning of words" as Hart (*ibid.*, vii) can move with such facility (or is it facilety?) from a "legislature" and "courts" to "legislative and adjudicative organs", not to mention the move from "officials" of any kind to "centrally organised sanctions".

[5] "[E]ven in a society where 'self-help' is the enforcing sanction, people judge situations of dispute in terms of rights and duties (. . .) Alleged wrongdoers justify their actions as reasonable and just in terms of common norms. Outsiders clearly give judgements and they do so in terms of a *corpus juris* of rules for rightdoing" (*The Judicial Process among the Barotse*, Manchester 1967, 263).

[6] "Nuer morality seems to be a set of general rules such as, respect your father, help your kin, observe your obligations, obey Nuer custom. These moral rules must inform the way in which people abide by custom" (*ibid.*).

[7] There are, of course, the by now familiar, though still irritating shifts in terminology. 'Rules' containing "in some form restrictions on the free use of violence, theft, and deception" (*ibid.*, 89), for example, become "rules respecting persons, property and promises" (*ibid.*, 193).

[8] Even at this crucial point Hart's terminology lacks firmness. When discussing the "open texture of law" (*ibid.*, 121 ff), his tune changes. While insisting that in 'primitive law' 'rules' are "the only [!] means of social control" (*ibid.*, 89), he now claims that in "any large [!] group general rules, standards and principles [!] must be the main [!] instrument [singular] of social control" (*ibid.*, 121). Also, instead of instantly collapsing if things were different, in such a group "nothing that we now recognise [!] as law could exist" (*ibid.*). And instead of being portrayed as the only possible source of obligations (*see ibid.*, 83), 'rules' become one form of "communicating [!] general standards of conduct" (*ibid.*, 121–22).

[9] The same claim is made for Hart's 'natural law' in the following terms: "Such rules do in fact constitute a common element in the law and conventional morality of all societies which have progressed to the point where these are distinguished as different forms of social control" (*ibid.*, 188). Whereas there is no reference to anthropological evidence in the former context, Hart bases his "empirical [!] version of natural law" on the most advanced results of comparative descriptive sociology, namely the accounts of Hobbes and Hume (*see ibid.*, 254).

[10] Hart is vague as to who is to survive: man as a chain of reproducing, rational individuals, mankind as a whole (as a zoological species) or the middle level of human groups. What Hart has in mind are certainly not concrete, historical societies but rather 'society' as a possibility which can be realised in different and changing forms. It is a pity that he did not adopt a similar attitude towards 'law'.

[11] This does not prevent us, of course, from rationalising the fact away by embarking on another circular definition game.

[12] Hart would be in a much better position if he were honest enough to argue instead that 'rules' are essential, if 'law' is to be a purely 'rational' enterprise, or for substantive 'legal' questions to be answerable by adopting his 'style' of jurisprudence.

[13] We must remember that "necessary truth" (like "fantasy") is a dirty word, whereas a truism on which Hart can exercise his imagination is manna. Nevertheless, it does not follow that something must be a truism because it is not a necessary truth. It remains pure imagination unless backed by positive evidence.

[14] How does the widespread protection of 'intellectual property' under 'primitive law' fit into Hart's scheme?

[15] Hart's concept of "secondary rules" changes conveniently, depending on the context in which it is applied (compare, for example, *ibid.*, 79 and 92). But we should not let ourselves be confused by this, since it does not prevent Hart himself from drawing firm and precise conclusions from any of the various versions.

[16] This does not only include 'primitive family law' but also the factors determining the assumption, exercise and loss of political power, the division and merger of groups etc. Different residence patterns, for example, can – without the need for 'rules' – have a much greater impact on the 'property law' of 'primitive' societies than all of Hart's truisms. It should also be remembered that where the principle of (unilineal) kinship dominates the socio/political organisation, not even the members of the nuclear family are all kinsmen (since either the father or the mother must be an 'outsider'). It is thus

most unlikely that even under this 'regime' kinship could be the only major principle of organisation. For the member of a 'primitive' society Hart's concept of 'primitive law' must look like an attempt to define a haystack in accordance with the needle that may be hidden inside.

[17] A "rule of recognition" only becomes necessary if 'law' must distinguish between 'rules' which are and those which are not to be enforced. In a society where dispute settlement is not geared to 'rule-enforcement', the problem of uncertainty, the "rule of recognition" is designed to solve, does not arise, or at least not in that form. Also: if obligations are defined by precise (and enforceable) 'rules', it may be necessary to devise "rules of change" to adjust them formally to changed circumstances, but if 'obligations' follow from general ideals, such as reciprocity, the "slow process of growth" may be quite adequate. And while "diffuse social pressure" may be an inefficient way of establishing whether a 'rule' has been violated, "rules of adjudication" may be unsuitable for maintaining community standards which are not 'rules'.

MICHAEL SALTMAN

ALTERNATIVES TO LEGAL POSITIVISM – AN ANTHROPOLOGICAL PERSPECTIVE

Many legal scholars appear to be quite distressed, when the sacred groves of their domain are perceived to be trampled upon by social scientists. Honoré accuses those sociologists, who have entered what he terms the "World Cup" game between the proponents of natural law and the legal positivists, of never having learned the rules of the game.[1] Auerbach takes the social scientists to task for having the temerity to look at such issues as the validity of laws,[2] and the accusatory list is yet longer. But social scientists have their own disciplinary rules and from the perspective of these rules may legitimately study any social phenomenon, which by definition also encompasses the polemics of legal philosophers. This holds true not only for the interactions between the protagonists but also for the substance of their debates.

This position derives in some measure from the present writer's own bias that the social sciences may make, although are not obligated to do so, critical assessments of social phenomena, under which rubric both the legal system and its practitioners become fair prey for critical evaluation. One can only concur with Ian Hamnett's concise and pointed statement that

> the specificity of the law then emerges as no more than the ideological charter of a particular professional group, and thus is subject to, rather than constitutive of the anthropologist's analysis.[3]

Firmly entrenched in their ideologies and their own perceptions of what constitutes law, and for whatever reasons, these practitioners, including some of their philosophers, function within and exert influence upon the network of social relationships within societies. By so doing, they create social facts that warrant critical study.

THE ARGUMENT

The main objective of this paper is to examine the process whereby concepts of social control become formalized into law-like propositions, potentially to become components of a system. If it can be established that this process of formalization is a general trend, then the plausibility of an evolutionary

E. Bulygin et al. (eds.), Man, Law and Modern Forms of Life, 79–84.

sequence might be argued. But assuming a universal common denominator of a transition from the non-formal to the formal does in no way imply either a unilinear evolutionary continuum or an inevitable guiding axiom that determines the nature of the formalization process. The points of reference on an evolutionary continuum would have to be sufficiently diverse in order to accommodate to the multi-directional trends that occur in a valid evolutionary model. The lessons to be learned from evolution are to be found both in the consequences of specialization and in the paying of attention to alternative viable forms.

The literature is replete with examples of polarities, between which lie implicit unilinear sequences – Maine's status to contract, Weber's formal irrational to formal rational. The broad historical scope of these studies raises a spectre of determinism, almost as if historical forces have created an inevitable end product. Recent studies of a more concise nature have also posed continua extending between such polarities as customary law to enacted law,[4] from order of custom to rule of law.[5] A basically similar dichotomy to that of Diamond's has been proposed by Cairns,[6] but for quite different reasons. Cairns' differentiation between the concepts of "power and order" becomes the theoretical point of departure for the present study. Cairns has differentiated between formal systems and speculative systems of law. "The limits of the legal order in the formal systems are defined in terms of power"; for the speculative systems, "the root idea is order, not power, and the ultimate postulate is the intelligibility of the world. In a word, the speculative systems are ontological in the traditional sense."[7]

An element of misnomer in Cairns' categorization is the apparent diametrical opposition between "formal" and "speculative", since this paper aims at demonstrating that speculative systems are also capable of undergoing formalization. The use of the word 'system' in itself implies some degree of formalization. The differentiation between these two types of system lies in the nature of the principle being formalized. While the true formal systems, in Cairns' sense, derive their logical rigour from an axiom concerning the uses of power and have committed their formalization to this direction, the speculative systems are concerned with different concepts relating to the social order, abstract concepts of justice and morality, ideological considerations or even psychological assumptions about man's nature. All or any one of these factors can serve as principles subject to formalization and there is no logical impediment to their systematization.

In many societies there is a parallel domain to the formal reality of lawyers' law. Moore has used the term "semi-autonomous fields" to describe this domain.[8] Within these fields are remedy agents that function within the wider setting. In all cases the wider setting is characterized by the formal legal system at the state level, which is usually a western model in one form or another. In her own study Moore looked at such disparate groupings, exemplifying semi-autonomous fields, such as the International Ladies' Garment Workers' Union and the traditional legal structure of the Chagga of Tanzania. These groupings have developed sets of rules that intimately evolve out of their own specific patterns of behaviour. In every society there are innumerable groups and institutions dispensing their own brands of justice on a daily basis – trade unions, cooperatives, disciplinary committees of institutions, ethics' committees of professional associations, traditional societies undergoing social change, voluntary associations that subscribe to a given ideology – a truly comprehensive list would be too long to enumerate here. The interactions and the independence of these parallel systems become the focal point of this paper. The basic question is why do these speculative systems, in Cairns' sense, become formalized. The answer is to be sought in the relationships holding between the semi-autonomous fields and the wider legal setting, and in particular the impingement of the formal legal system on its speculative counterpart. The resulting adaptations constitute the evolutionary process alluded to above.

THE EXAMPLES

The data used in this paper derive in large measure from the present writer's field studies on the customary law of the Kipsigis of S. W. Kenya[9] and on the formalization of rules in the Israeli *kibbutz* movement.[10] Additional comparative data has also been sought from bibliographical sources in order to demonstrate whether the trends demonstrated in the field studies may be further corroborated. These latter materials can be little more than inferential since their authors did not specifically address themselves to the problem of rule formalization.

The East African data indicated two specific trends in the formalization of indigenous principles of law. The Kipsigis, a traditionally pastoral group, have been transformed over recent years into a mixed farming community maintaining greatly reduced herds while at the same time growing staple crops and a limited number of cash crops. Within the context of a traditional pastoral economy and a long history of movement over huge expanses of territory the concept of landownership was alien to Kipsigis legal thought.

The advent of British colonial rule restricted the movement of the Kipsigis, introduced the factor of cultivation as a mode of livelihood and essentially forced the Kipsigis to face the reality of the alien concept of individual land holdings with all its ensuing problems. In facing this new situation the Kipsigis did not rely on extraneous legislation by the authorities for the purpose of resolving land disputes. Instead, they developed an indigenous principle of usufructuary right to cover the ever growing complexity of land ownership. This principle, in its pristine state, applied to the small plot of land in the immediate vicinity of man's residence. As long as he was actively using this plot for the cultivation of millet for the purpose of beer manufacture, others respected this right and were held liable for damages in the event that their cattle strayed onto this plot and caused damage. At the time that he ceased to cultivate this land for its defined purpose, it reverted to common land status. It was this principle that became developed, formalized and systematized in order to handle all contingencies of land ownership. An escalating scale of criteria from demonstrated intent of usage to actual everyday usage conferred on individuals lesser and greater rights for establishing ownership claims on plots of land. As claims and counterclaims became more complex, so did the scale become more finely calibrated to accommodate to the new situations.

The second factor enabling the traditional principles of customary law to apply to changing social conditions was the legislative decision of the colonial authorities to accept customary law practice in the state courts as long as this did not conflict with any state law or ordinance, or was not considered to be "repugnant to justice or morality". This accorded a new status to the traditional remedy agents who could now apply and adapt the customary law to new contexts with the full backing of the state's judicial authority. Whereas in the former absence of any centralized political authority, the Kipsigis legal system achieved remedies through compromises and arbitration, the new situation allowed for unilateral decision making and the establishment of precedent. But the proviso, enabling the application of customary law within the state court system, affords the potential development of an indigenous form of common law. The courts have to balance between state enacted laws on the one hand and the growing corpus of restated customary law on the other. The customary law, even in its restated form, can be clearly traced back to indigenous concepts of social order.

In examining the conditions under which *kibbutz* members hold rules to be "lawful", the historical point of departure in the research revealed a strong "anti-law" ideology. This has changed over time by transforming initial shared understandings into written, codified and formal sets of rules. The principle of the allocation of resources is seen as the central issue, and Marx's original precept of "from each according to his ability, to each according to his need" did not lend itself easily to the formulation of lawlike statements. But the introduction of qualifications to the precept, emanating from the reality of scarcity of certain resources, has facilitated the formulation of definitive norms of resource allocation. In addition, rules governing other spheres of life have also been formulated. The *kibbutz* General Assembly, acting in a judicial capacity, has not radically changed over the years. It uses a "whole man" concept in order to arrive at a decision, rather than acting solely on the facts of the case. In recognizing the semi-autonomous nature of the *kibbutz*, explanations for the phenomenon of rule making and systematization have to be sought in terms of the relationship between the *kibbutz* and the external wider society in Israel, essentially a capitalist society antithetical to the *kibbutz* way of life. The specific problems that have given rise to the plethora of rule making in the *kibbutz* movement derive from the significant number of members working outside the *kibbutz*, access to external sources of money and a number of national court decisions that challenge the very nature of the voluntary association. While there is no evidence to the effect that an incipient class structure is emerging within the *kibbutz*, which could possibly account for the emergence of rules, there is undoubtedly an ideological confrontation between the original concepts of collectivism and the growing phenomenon of individualism. The contention here is that there is a strong indication towards the fact that the formulation of the rules is an attempt to strengthen original shared understandings in the light of a waning ideological commitment, in turn engendered by the *kibbutz*'s external relations with the wider society. The *kibbutz* case exemplifies the way in which a semi-autonomous field has had to adapt to external conditions by means of systematizing its rules without jeopardizing its ideological commitment to a given social order.

A third example poses an entirely different question, yet nonetheless relevant. In examining two apparently disparate phenomena – land tenure in eleventh and twelfth century England and its counterpart in early twentieth century Uganda (as described in Fallers' work on the Busoga[11]) – some remarkable similarities emerge in terms of legal responses to problems deriving from the "feudal type" structure of both situations. In both cases, as political sovereignity shifts from the periphery to the centre, original sets of historical rights become preserved in a legal context, become reinterpreted by the courts and ultimately become integral parts of the common law. The question raised here is whether contemporary third world states do in fact possess a strong option for developing their own forms of common law as opposed to importing ready made "western" models that often have little or no relevance to the social, economic and political realities of these countries.

Why are these examples necessarily alternatives to legal positivism? In the first place, the rules are not sovereign commands. They have emerged from specific social contexts and their validity can only be construed in terms of their meaning. These contexts reflect shared understandings about principles of social order, which in turn are grounded in ideologies, prevailing moral attitudes or mutuality in social relationships. They do not constitute a closed system from which correct decisions are legally deduced. Second, these systems operate effectively within those contexts where political sovereignty is judiciously dispersed throughout different levels of the society. The viability of informal remedy agents, and their relative advantage over the formal systems, lie in their lack of specialization. This provides an adaptive potential to conditions of social change.

University of Haifa

NOTES

[1] A. M. Honoré, 'Groups, Law and Obedience', in: A. W. B. Simpson (ed.), *Oxford Essays in Jurisprudence, Second Series*, Oxford 1973.

[2] L. Auerbach, 'Legal Tasks for the Sociologists', *Law & Society Review*, 1966.

[3] I. Hamnett, Introduction, in: I. Hamnett (ed.), *Social Anthropology and Law*, ASA Monograph 14, Academic Press, London 1977.

[4] L. Fuller, 'Human Interaction and the Law', in: R. P. Wolff (ed.), *The Rule of Law*, Simon & Schuster 1971.

[5] S. Diamond, 'The Rule of Law versus the Rule of Custom', in *The Rule of Law*, *op. cit.*

[6] H. Cairns, 'The Community as the Legal Order', in: Carl J. Friedrich (ed.), *Community, Norms* II, N.Y. 1959.

[7] Cairns, *op. cit.*, 25.

[8] S. F. Moore, *Law as Process*, London 1973.

[9] M. Saltman, *The Kipsigis. A Case Study in Changing Customary Law*, Schenkman Publishing Co., Cambridge 1977.

[10] M. Saltman, 'Legality and Ideology in the Kibbutz Movement', *International Journal of the Sociology of Law* 9 (1981).

[11] L. Fallers, *Bantu Bureaucracy*, Chicago 1956; *Law Without Precedent*, Chicago 1969.

TIMOTHY STROUP

WESTERMARCK'S ETHICAL METHODOLOGY

I

T. D. Campbell has criticized those writers of "modern works in social science [who] spend too much time expounding their methodological approach and too little time doing anything significant with it."[1] Such a charge can scarcely be levelled against the Finnish philosopher and social scientist Edward Westermarck. In a lifetime dedicated to the study of three principal subjects – marriage, morality, and Morocco – Westermarck devoted only a few scattered pages out of a vast shelf of publications to considering the methods he employed in his researches.[2] Throughout the rest of his writings he was doing something with his method rather than merely analyzing it.

Partly as a result of this methodological self-effacement, Westermarck's writings have suffered from neglect and misinterpretation in the more than forty years since his death. When Westermarck was active as a writer (during the five decades from 1889 to 1939), he was almost universally respected, even by his opponents, as a researcher of massive erudition who expounded important and innovative doctrines which demanded serious attention. Today, however, he is scarcely even accorded his rightful place in the histories of philosophy and the social sciences, and the actual substance of his writings is little known or appreciated.

When Westermarck is remembered at all, it is usually for his alleged errors of method: he is variously viewed as a simplistic analyzer of moral language, an inconsistent relativist, an armchair comparativist, a naive evolutionist, and a biological reductionist. If these perceptions were accurate, Westermarck's writings could justifiably be relegated to oblivion. I want, however, to argue that this received view of Westermarck – or this hazy impression, since Westermarck is too little read nowadays to be received – is entirely incorrect. Westermarck's writings are worthy of attention from the standpoint of the history of ideas, for, as Claude Lévi-Strauss has observed, he "performed at the end of the 19th Century the same role for the social sciences that the Renaissance masters did for modern thought."[3] Further, and more important, Westermarck's writings have lasting value in their bearing on problems of moral and social philosophy that trouble us still. In the full version of this

E. Bulygin et al. (eds.), Man, Law and Modern Forms of Life, 85–95.
Revised and reprinted by permission of *Man* (N.S.) 19, No. 4 (December 1984), 575–592.

paper I have defended Westermarck by considering his work as both philosopher and social scientist.[4] In the version presented at the Congress and published here, constraints of time and space have forced me to concentrate my remarks on what I take to be Westermarck's major intellectual contribution, his moral philosophy, and thus to examine only the first two of the misinterpretations referred to above.

II

The main point to keep in mind about Westermarck's ethical theory is that it was based on the broadest possible empirical study he could make of the phenomena of moral behavior. Early in his career Westermarck gave a talk, at an international congress in Munich, on two types of ethics, normative and psychological. Normative ethics he held to be "the fruit of an illegitimate union between the theoretical search for truth and the practical need to erect norms for human conduct."[5] In contrast, he thought that the proper scope of ethics is that of a "science whose subject of investigation is the moral consciousness of mankind, its origin and nature."[6] In his emphasis on studying the empirical background of ethical practice, Westermarck paralleled developments in French sociology of the time: for Durkheim morality was a "system of realized facts" and Lévy-Bruhl advocated a science of customs that would explicate morality on a basis "comparable to mechanics and medicine" by relying on sociological and psychological laws.[7]

Westermarck's ethical methodology is firmly based on the conviction that any adequate metaethics must account for the descriptive facts of moral behavior, and he concluded that no other ethical theory, "whatever arguments have been adduced in support of it, has been subjected to an equally comprehensive test."[8] In developing his own theory, Westermarck combined his talents as philosopher and social scientist: the first half of his strategy was the negative, philosophical task of demolishing his objectivist rivals, to which he devoted the first two chapters of *Ethical Relativity;*[9] the second half drew on materials of social anthropology to provide a constructive, alternative explanation of moral behavior. Taken together, Westermarck's two approaches could show both why there are no objective moral facts and why we nevertheless behave as though there are. In particular, this latter explanandum was something that many relativists and subjectivists simply left dangling.

Yet when Westermarck's writings on moral philosophy have been considered at all in recent years, only the smallest, isolated bits of his comprehensive account have been selected for analysis. This results from the fact that often the perceptions of Westermarck's later philosophical critics have been limited by the blinders of ordinary language analysis. They have sought to locate in his work a simple formula that expresses "the moral judgment", and have then proceeded to deride the formula as absurdly simplistic. We find such examples as these:

To say that an action is reprehensible, according to Westermarck, is essentially to say: 'I have a tendency to feel moral disapproval toward the agents of all acts like this one.'[10]

[Westermarck defines] '*X* is good' as 'I feel moral retributive kindly emotion towards *X*.'[11]

[Westermarck held that] the proposition expressed by '*x* is right' is equivalent to that expressed by 'I have a tendency to feel required or compelled to do *x*, when fully informed, disinterested, etc.'[12]

But one can search in vain in Westermarck's mature writings for any such simple equations, for he was no ordinary language philosopher seeking linguistic reduction. On the contrary, there are explicit rejections of the very sort of view commonly ascribed to him: "To attribute a quality to something is not the same as to state the existence of a particular emotion or sensation in the mind that perceives it."[13]

When Westermarck treats the "language of morals", he does so in a much more sophisticated fashion than his critics have charged. He begins with a distinction between the logical structure of moral judgments and the psychological account of the origin of terms. Here the notion of "objectivizing" – a term that looks backwards to Hume[14] and anticipates the more developed account of J. L. Mackie[15] – is crucial to understanding Westermarck's view. Westermarck agrees with the objectivist that ordinary moral judgments do not merely express preferences, but rather claim to attribute objective properties to things and conduct. He disagrees with the objectivist by holding that such claims must fail, because there are no moral facts to which the judgments could correspond. He then seeks to analyze the derivation of the objectivity-claiming concepts in terms of their emotional origin. There is, thus, a clear demarcation between logical analysis via subject-predicate attribution and psychological explanation via objectivizing:

When we call an act good or bad, we do not *state* the existence of any emotional tendencies . . . : we refer the subject of the judgment to a class of phenomena which we are used to call good or bad. But we are used to call them so because they have evoked moral approval or disapproval in ourselves or in other persons from whom we have learned the use of those words.[16]

But the analysis of moral language is only one part of the wider inquiry into moral behavior, and consequently it is only one part of Westermarck's analysis of morality. I have elsewhere called Westermarck's view, taken as a whole, "soft subjectivism", and I would like to say a few words here in explanation of it.[17]

III

Westermarck's subjectivism is soft because it forgoes moral objectivism without embracing the sort of nihilistic subjectivism that refuses all coherence to moral distinctions or treats any and all moral claims, however bizarre, as equally worthy of respect. Insofar as Westermarck denies that there are any moral facts on which one could base an objective morality, his view looks merely skeptical; yet his inquiries into social anthropology, into the psychological motivations behind moral beliefs, and into the ultimate biological framework for moral behavior all work to soften this skepticism by substituting concrete empirical investigation for elusive moral justification. By replacing intuitive confidence in moral facts with inductive observation into facts about morality, Westermarck uses explanation as a tool to lessen ethical arbitrariness.

Let me illustrate this point by considering two quite different sorts of ethical relativism, which, with admitted oversimplification, I shall call "naive" and "constructive" relativisms.

Some early relativists, lacking the philosophical background of Westermarck, may have been unclear about the philosophical import of their anthropological researches and hence may have seemed somewhat naive. But the most naive form of relativism is the one created by opponents of the doctrine who then assume that the preposterous and ethically repugnant views they describe are typical of relativism generally. As John Ladd has pointed out, many of the definitions of "ethical relativism" have been framed by critics who find the doctrine "logically absurd and one that will more than likely also have morally objectionable consequences."[18]

"Naive relativism", which I use mostly as an illustrative straw-man, is the view that "chaotic diversity of opinion is the rule in the moral realm," as one of its more extreme critics has described it.[19] It builds on a thoroughgoing cultural relativism which emphasizes the irreducible variety of moral beliefs as they are actually exhibited throughout the world. In turn, this descriptive relativism may be an offshoot of a cultural determinism that attempts to settle the nature-nurture controversy by stressing customs rather than needs; thus some relativists seem to have engaged in field work precisely to verify preconceived notions of basic cultural differences, which their research, not surprisingly, then bore out.[20] To naive relativists, the link between descriptive and normative theses is often disarmingly simple: the mere facts of moral disagreement are taken to show that no single moral principle can be absolutely right, that all moral evaluation must be within a particular culture. This conclusion may lead naive relativists to embrace respect and tolerance for other societies as a moral imperative, a recommendation that many critics have seized upon as being inconsistent with any nonobjective view of morality.[21]

Constructive relativism, on the other hand, does not need to exaggerate the diversity of actual moral beliefs, because it rejects the simple jump from disagreement to subjectivity, or from agreement to objectivity. As Westermarck observed, even the scope of cultural disagreement can be reduced because much apparent moral controversy can be explained as resulting from cognitive causes:

> Insofar as differences of moral opinion depend on knowledge or ignorance of facts, on specific religious or superstitious beliefs, on different degrees of reflection, or on different conditions of life or other external circumstances, they do not clash with that universality which is implied in the notion of the objective validity of moral judgments.[22]

Of course, not all moral disagreements are rational in nature; there is an emotional component as well to moral beliefs. Yet here again Westermarck is not wedded to an extreme thesis about the diversity of emotions. He recognizes that basic regularities in human temperaments set broad limits to emotional dissimilarities; "certain cognitions inspire fear into nearly every breast."[23] Indeed, Westermarck's very emphasis on the process of objectivizing requires that there be substantial uniformity in the intellectual and emotional structure of human beings, for otherwise there would be no tendency to objectivize our feelings.[24]

Nevertheless there is room for variation, as displayed most notably by the sentiment of altruism. To use one of Westermarck's examples,[25] two members of different societies, assuming they have even a modicum of intelligence, will agree that a straight line is a shorter distance between two points than a crooked, meandering line. All that is necessary for the demonstration is a stick that can draw the respective patterns in the sand. But those same two persons may have fundamentally different views about the degree of kindness that should be accorded to strangers or to animals, because variations in the range of persons to whom moral rules apply result largely from different patterns of altruistic feelings and as such are not straightforwardly amenable to argument and demonstration. But the feeling of altruism itself is amenable to description and analysis, and Westermarck devotes an entire chapter in *The Origin and Development of the Moral Ideas* to its treatment.[26] Where the emotional pedigree of moral beliefs blocks their objective justification, the tools of social science can still take over the task of explaining their objective existence.

Westermarck does not make any easy transition from cultural diversity to ethical skepticism, but rather proceeds by offering the most plausible causal analysis of the various ways – both rational and emotional – in which differences in moral beliefs arise. By inquiring into the origin, development, and logical status of moral principles, he concludes that many of the moral problems we pose for ourselves cannot be settled by further observation or reflection because they exhibit a tenacity which discloses the varying emotional reactions that underlie moral beliefs. Furthermore, Westermarck's analysis of the emotional foundation of moral beliefs does not merely stand on its own, but rather is conjoined with the philosophical refutation of specific objectivist theories to produce an account in which the philosophical and social scientific conclusions are mutually supporting.

IV

Up to this point, Westermarck's relativism still looks largely negative, even though it is more sophisticated and more cautious than some of its relativistic rivals. But when I call his relativism "constructive", I do not mean simply to bestow a gratuitously honorific or euphemistically misleading description on it, but rather to call attention to some generally overlooked features of his writings that can contribute to a positive and hopeful way of looking at morality.

Westermarck can defend himself against typical charges that views like his are "fatal to the deepest spiritual convictions and to the highest spiritual aspirations of the human race," as Hastings Rashdall charged.[27] Of course, if the direst predictions of objectivist alarmists came true, that would be an unfortunate circumstance; but regrettable consequences could never of themselves disprove an otherwise established skepticism. As Westermarck put it, a theory would not be "invalidated by the mere fact that it is likely to cause mischief."[28] Nor is it plausible to assume that a philosophical demonstration of ethical skepticism would have any such results; thus Darwin ridiculed the idea that moral beliefs are "held by many people on so weak a tenure" that they could be overthrown by the latest scientific or philosophical findings.[29] Alarmists would do better to worry about objectivism itself, since so many of the moral horrors that have been and are being committed are fanatical extensions of dogmatic and cruel ethical objectivisms.

Even the effect of relativism on moral argument would be fairly modest. So much of ordinary moral controversy is centered not around ultimate moral facts but around ordinary, everyday facts: it is based on incomplete information, careless assumptions, false applications, and unconscious biases. Assume, however, that two Westermarckian relativists disagreed about some *fundamental* moral principle. They would both be using a standard moral vocabulary – one calling the principle right and another calling it wrong – for there are no other easily suitable terms. But if they are consistent, the speakers will not (unlike ordinary speakers) be attributing objective properties to the principle, but will merely be advancing their own preferences. On Westermarck's view, ordinary speakers objectivize, while soft subjectivists prescribe. How, then, is the dispute to be settled? The simple answer is that there is no further rational way to resolve the dispute, assuming it has *really* reached this stage, although there are always various nonrational methods of persuasion and compulsion; and sometimes the discussion will just have to be left at an impasse. But is the case so much different with objectivist disputants? At the lower, middle, and upper levels of ordinary and philosophical disputation are agreements radically easier on an objectivist account? "Each founder of a new theory," Westermarck said, "hopes that it is he who has discovered the unique jewel of moral truth,"[30] but still the disputes rage on. If only the real jewel could noncontroversially be identified, much effort would be saved!

At any rate, one of the implications of Westermarck's view is that such an impasse need not often be reached. Under a naive relativism, impasses would be frequent and inevitable, but Westermarck stressed "the similarity of the mental constitution of men" and the "comparatively uniform nature" of moral beliefs.[31] As a social scientist he sought to investigate the fundamental emotional urges to which we have been subjected by environmental and biological conditionings. According to Westermarck, there is variation in detail, but also considerable uniformity on the large scale, in the way people act and react. In the case of moral behavior, the specific emotions which give rise to moral beliefs can be isolated. These are retributive emotions, of either gratitude or resentment, which arise on an impartial and disinterested basis. We might expect, purely on grounds of self-preservation, that the moral codes built out of these emotions will exhibit a limited range in balancing selfishness and altruism, aggression and cooperation, or, to use the vocabulary of ethical theory, that individuals will exhibit varying, but not infinitely diverse, patterns of trading off their utilitarian or egoistic preferences for satisfying desires against their deontological pangs of conscience – various, but limited, methods of resolving the tension of competing emotions. The point of ultimate moral disputes, when they really exist, is to get you to shift your pattern to something more like mine, and if this cannot be done, then it cannot be done by the objectivist or by the relativist.[32]

One final defect of naive relativism is avoided by Westermarck's constructive relativism: this is the urge to tolerate the morally intolerable. If relativists think that the moral beliefs of any given society are right (for that society), then why should they be intolerant of what is right? But Westermarck is more nearly claiming that each society is *wrong* in objectivizing its claims about what is right, and once we recognize this there is no need to put up with whatever *feelings* others may have. Hence, extreme tolerance is neither a universally binding moral fact (which would be an inconsistency for any relativist) nor, for Westermarck, a personal preference:

> I do not even subscribe to that beautiful modern sophism which admits every man's conscience to be an infallible guide. If we had to recognise, or rather if we did recognise, as right everything which is held to be right by anybody . . . morality would really suffer a serious loss.[33]

But while extreme tolerance can be avoided, some ethical nondogmatism will inevitably creep in. On Westermarck's view, our moral judgments, instead of being complacent towards ourselves and critical of others, will through greater understanding become more critical of ourselves and more generous towards other persons and their circumstances. And unlike relativisms which make the individual the moral slave of society by basing all values on those which societies actually hold, Westermarck puts the individual at the center of the moral stage:

> Far above the vulgar idea that the right is a settled something to which everybody has to adjust his opinions, rises the conviction that it has its existence in each individual mind, capable of any expansion, proclaiming its own right to exist . . . .[34]

Thus Westermarck's relativism is constructive because it recognizes the continuing existence of moral emotions that will need reconstructed moral principles for their expression; it makes no hasty conclusion that mere disagreement proves relativism, but rather offers a sophisticated causal analysis to explain the apparent diversity of moral beliefs; it avoids a simplistic reduction of moral language to formulas about emotional states; it strikes a plausible balance between selective tolerance and the forswearing of all moral criticism; it focuses on individual conscience rather than on received authority; and it goes beyond mere philosophical refutation of objectivist rivals to build a positive, social scientific account of the widest possible range of facts about human moral behavior.

V

My overall argument about Westermarck's ethical methodology is that it avoids linguistic reductionism and hasty relativism. Instead it attempts to bring together a variety of tools from different disciplines – sociology, anthropology, psychology, biology, history, and philosophy – making the best use of them that was possible at the time to propound a comprehensive social philosophy that explains the varieties of moral experience. But method, after all, is a means of achieving results, and in this respect Westermarck points us in a number of fruitful and provocative directions.

Viewed from the perspective of the history of ideas, he is a dominant figure in the early sociology of morals in England; later, he had a major influence on the sort of anthropological relativism that was prevalent between the wars; and, more recently, he anticipates the contemporary resurgence of relativism in such writers as J. L. Mackie, John Ladd, and Kai Nielsen.

But the substance of Westermarck's moral philosophy is also worthy of respect, for it is complex and sophisticated in analysis, powerful and persuasive as an explanation of the facts of moral behavior, and hopeful, rather than nihilistic, in its normative implications. As Ronald Fletcher has asked:

> Where is the study of the elements of men's moral consciousness which is more wide-ranging, contains a clearer theoretical basis, and brings together more empirical evidence, and more satisfactorily, than this? Let the question be answered.[35]

ACKNOWLEDGMENTS

Grants from the Academy of Finland and the PSC/CUNY Research Program provided assistance at various stages of the research, and a grant from the American Council of Learned Societies funded travel to the Congress.

John Jay College, The City University of New York

NOTES

[1] T. D. Campbell, *Adam Smith's Science of Morals*, London 1971, 238.
[2] See Edward Westermarck, *The History of Human Marriage*, 5th ed., 3 vols., London 1921, 1:1–25; 'Sociology as a University Study', London 1908; *Memories of My Life*, transl. Anna Barwell, London 1929; and 'Methods in Social Anthropology', *Journal of the Royal Anthropological Institute* 66 (1936), 223–48.
[3] Claude Lévi-Strauss, 'The Work of Edward Westermarck', in: Timothy Stroup (ed.), *Edward Westermarck: Essays on His Life and Works*, Helsinki 1982a, 181.
[4] Timothy Stroup, 'Edward Westermarck: A Reappraisal', *Man*.
[5] Westermarck, 'Normative und psychologische Ethik', Westermarck Archives, Åbo Akademi, Turku/Åbo, Finland, Addenda, 1.
[6] *Ibid.*, 9.
[7] Émile Durkheim, *De la division du travail social*, 2nd ed., Paris 1902, xli, and Lucien Lévy-Bruhl, *La morale et la science des moeurs*, 5th ed., Paris 1913, 256.
[8] Westermarck, *Ethical Relativity*, London 1932, 177.
[9] *Ibid.*, 3–61.
[10] Richard Brandt, *Ethical Theory: The Problems of Normative and Critical Ethics*, Englewood Cliffs 1959, 166.
[11] Erik Stenius, 'Definitions of the Concept "Value-Judgment"', *Theoria* 21 (1955), 131–45.
[12] David A. J. Richards, *A Theory of Reasons for Action*, Oxford 1971, 63.
[13] Westermarck (1932), 114.
[14] See Stroup, 'Westermarck's Debt to Hume', in: Krister Segerberg (ed.), *Wright and Wrong: Mini Essays in Honor of G. H. von Wright*, Turku/Åbo 1976, 73–82, and *Westermarck's Ethics*, Turku/Åbo 1982b, 134–46.
[15] J. L. Mackie, *Ethics: Inventing Right and Wrong*, Harmondsworth 1977.
[16] Westermarck (1932), 114–15.
[17] Stroup, 'Soft Subjectivism', in Stroup (1982a), 99–121.
[18] John Ladd, 'The Poverty of Absolutism', in Stroup (1982a), 161.
[19] Stuart Lee Penn, 'The Ethical Relativism of Edward Westermarck: A Critique', Ph.D. diss., Yale University, 1977, 2.
[20] Derek Freeman has levelled such a charge against Margaret Mead in his *Margaret Mead and Samoa: The Making and Unmaking of an Anthropological Myth*, Cambridge, Mass. 1983.
[21] For example, see B. A. O. Williams, *Morality: An Introduction to Ethics*, New York 1972, 20–21.
[22] Westermarck (1932), 196.
[23] Westermarck, *The Origin and Development of the Moral Ideas*, 2 vols., London 1906–8, 1:11.
[24] *Ibid.*, 1:8.
[25] Westermarck, 'Normative und psychologische Ethik', 6.
[26] Westermarck (1906–8), 2:186–228.
[27] Hastings Rashdall, *Is Conscience an Emotion? Three Lectures on Recent Ethical Theories*, London 1914, 200.
[28] Westermarck (1932), 58.
[29] Charles Darwin, *The Descent of Man and Selection in Relation to Sex*, new ed., London 1901, 152.
[30] Westermarck (1932), 4.

[30] Westermarck (1932), 4.
[31] Westermarck (1906–8), 1:8–9.
[32] Admittedly, if it can be done the objectivists may have an easier time of it, because their arsenal of moral rhetoric includes the "opium" of moral truth.
[33] Westermarck (1906–8), 1:19.
[34] *Ibid.*, 1:20.
[35] Fletcher, 'On the Contribution', in Stroup (1982a), 209–10.

TIMO AIRAKSINEN

WESTERMARCK, MACKIE, STROUP, AND HARRISON

I

The main motive behind Professor Stroup's large and ambitious Westermarck-project is to show, first, that Westermarck was, and still is, seriously misunderstood; and, secondly, that Westermarck's sociological and philosophical views really are close to the truth.[1] It is quite evident that Stroup has reached his first goal: Westermarck had been misinterpreted in outrageously varied ways. As to Stroup's second goal, it is more difficult to take a stand on it. Subjective and cultural relativism is an ancient tradition in moral and legal philosophy; whether Westermarck has made a substantial contribution to it may still be taken to be an open question. Anyway, Stroup has pointed out that at least Westermarck is a respectable thinker who deserves to be taken seriously.

In this commentary I shall focus on three points: *First*, I shall try to reinforce the feeling that Westermarck's ideas are acceptable by pointing out their reappearance in John Mackie's ethics. But I shall *also* show that in spite of the new respectability of Westermarck's views, there is little hope that they will not be misinterpreted in the future. Jonathan Harrison's Mackie-criticism shows that the tradition of interpretation Stroup is interested in is still alive and well. *Finally*, I shall suggest that subjectivist relativism in ethics is such a radical position that its advocates can hardly expect a better fate when they meet their audience.

II

I think it is a very interesting observation indeed that John Mackie's famous 'error theory of ethics' is so clearly and straightforwardly anticipated by Westermarck's ideas.[2] As Stroup writes,

> Westermarck agrees with the objectivist that ordinary moral judgments are not mere expressions of preference, but rather claim to attribute objective properties to things and conduct. He disagrees with the objectivist by holding that such claims must fail, because there are no moral facts to which the judgments could correspond (p. 87).

This is exactly what Mackie says. How does Stroup try to convince us that

E. Bulygin et al. (eds.), Man, Law and Modern Forms of Life, 97–101.

this is also what Westermarck says? Stroup gives a reference to pages 114–5 of *Ethical Relativity* and quotes the following sentences:

When we call an act good or bad, we do not *state* the existence of any emotional tendencies, . . . ; we refer the subject of the judgment to a class of phenomena which we are used to call good or bad.

Well, this does not show any *exact* identity between the views of Westermarck and Mackie, although there certainly exists a plausible way of supplementing Westermarck's theory so that the result will fit Mackie's error theory. Whether this operation can be done so that it will impress a critic of Westermarck, who says that his theory is very vague, is another thing. Especially the latter part of Stroup's Westermarck-quotation is tricky. Westermarck mentions there some kind of implicit moral *conventions*, and not any Mackie-style ordinary-fact-like prescriptive but objective entities. Westermarck speaks at least in the present context about our normatively relevant customs, and not about our common tendency to postulate reified moral facts. Perhaps this indicates a weak point in Stroup's argumentation. However, I must admit that a Mackie-style reconstruction of Westermarck's relativism fits its new frame quite nicely. A perfect fit is only a dream anyway.

III

Jonathan Harrison's recent paper 'Mackie's moral "scepticism"'[3] is a perfect example of how a competent philosopher may fail to give a fair analysis of his colleague's ideas. To show what I mean, I shall offer a simple example of inconsistency from Harrison's paper. He writes both that

Mackie believes that moral statements are neither true nor false (p. 174),

and

Indeed, Mackie describes his theory as an error theory, which implies that moral judgments are capable of being true or false, *for if they were not capable of being true or false, they could not be false; error concerning them would then be impossible* (p. 175). (my italics.)

Is Mackie really confused in the manner indicated by Harrison?

Notice that the part of Harrison's argument which I have emphasized above is clearly *false*: If agent *A* believes that his normative statement *S* is true, when it is neither-true-nor-false (or, exemplifies a truth-value gap), *S* commits an error, just as *S* commits a (slightly different) error when he claims that S is true, when it is in fact false. In general, we need to think only that the error theory says that it is a mistake to believe in objective prescriptive facts.[4]

The real question concerning the interpretation of the meaning of 'error' in Mackie's ethics is not whether the (empirical) truth that no moral facts exist makes statement S false or neither-true-nor-false. Harrison notices that in his book *Ethics* Mackie himself is not quite clear about this, but Harrison does not see that this point is of no consequence to the essence of Mackie's moral theory. Let us see next what this means.

Harrison argues as follows: Look at the following propositions,

(1) It is true that random killing is wrong.

If (1) is *false*, as Mackie's error theory seems to say all like statements are, it follows that

(2) It is not true that random killing is wrong, or
(3) It is false that random killing is wrong.

So, it seems that the error theory allows us to infer that the contradiction of a moral statement is *true*. But, according to the error theory, (3) must be false too.

From Mackie's Westermarckian perspective it is easy to answer Harrison. One says, simply, that (1) and (3) do not have truth values at all. They are both neither-true-nor-false. We already saw that this proposal can be accepted. However, Harrison's argument teaches us one important thing: Mackie's recurring insistence that statements like (1) and (3) are false is really too strong: if S is false, its contradiction S' must be true; and yet no moral statement can be true. Another possible line of comment concerning the present issue of truth is the following: If (1) and (3) are both false, they are not contradictories, presumably because of some relevant violations of their presupposition-requirements. The problem, however, is that this idea demands a semantic theory which Mackie does not supply. Yet, it is quite possible to pursue this line of argument, saying that because (1) and (3) presuppose the existence of objective moral facts in order to be true or false, and no such facts exist, they are false, but not mutually contradictory. I think it is simpler to maintain that (1) and (3) are both neither-true-nor-false. But this implies that Mackie's theory is at least incomplete.

Nevertheless, it does not follow that "(i)f Mackie is right, then talking about morality would, if people were rational, be a completely pointless business," as Harrison claims (p. 177). As Stroup has shown, this type of 'counterargument' was directed also against Westermarck; therefore, let us take a closer look at it.

First, Mackie can answer by remarking that either (1) or (3) would be true if moral facts existed. This counterfactual proposition is certainly a sensible one and it shows that Mackie's error theory is not inconsistent in any obvious way. Ethics might be a *useful* fiction. Secondly, if people are merely logically rational, so that they do not recognize any norms of *practical* rationality, they may indeed infer from the contradiction between (1) and (3), if it is taken to exist (does it?), that ethics is nonsense. But maybe Mackie is right and they are both practically rational and willing to forget their ideas of objective values after their invention of some substitutes for the falsely objectivist moral codes. Those people need not panic. Harrison's accusations are too hasty.

IV

Why is subjectivist ethics such an infuriating topic? Perhaps the main reason can be found in its very radical nature. Once we reject the idea that objective moral values exist we must return to the view that ethics consists of fitting together people's beliefs and feelings of what is right and what is wrong. And because this process is *not* grounded in any subject-independent and non-relative way, there will be no guarantee that in every situation at least some kind of ideal, theoretical solution to our practical disputes can be found. Morality is then essentially an open-ended affair. Moreover, it has no one uniform characterization. If we miss all objective grounds for moral decisions, we shall also lack the basis for deciding what morality really is. Indeed, to say that morality is subjective is to say hardly anything. All this leaves room for social power, coercion, manipulation, indoctrination and even violence as practical conflict-resolution methods.

This explosion of moralities without any common denominator is what many thinkers seem to be afraid of. They feel that any suggestion of a subjective inclination is more or less immoral. And they are not really consoled by the Westermarckian idea, echoed by Mackie, that objectivism leads to moral rigorism and fanaticism. Stroup seems to buy exactly this argument but most philosophers seem to think that the problems caused by rigorism and fanaticism are more tractable than that caused by subjectivism, namely, the diversity of *all* opinions. And I do not see much hope that any *sociobiological* thesis could convince those who are worried about the existence of moral standards. Biology can promise only that people are in a certain measure developing in one direction and that they are in a certain measure similar so that their emerging moral systems can give some bite to their decisions and actions. But biology does not offer any help in one's struggle with one's personal moral dilemmas at a given time and place.

On this basis, I cannot believe that the fight over subjectivism could be won by either side. Subjectivism is too radical a view, but yet it must be taken seriously, simply because no one has been able to make sense of what *moral truth* means.

University of Helsinki

NOTES

[1] See his book, T. Stroup, *Westermarck's Ethics*, Åbo 1982.

[2] Mackie sketched his theory as early as 1941, and published it in *Australasian Journal of Psychology and Philosophy* 24 (1946), 77–90. See also J. L. Mackie, *Ethics, Inventing Right and Wrong*, Harmondsworth 1977, 241.

[3] J. Harrison, 'Mackie's Moral "Scepticism"', *Philosophy* 57 (182), 173–191.

[4] See Mackie (1977), 35.

TIMOTHY STROUP

REPLY TO PROFESSOR AIRAKSINEN

Professor Airaksinen agrees with what I take to be my main theses: that Westermarck's writings in moral philosophy have often been misinterpreted and that when they are suitably understood they are worthy of serious consideration. These are theses of an exegetical and exhortatory nature, and they may now seem fairly noncontroversial. But they have not always seemed so. I have come across nearly a dozen cases, and I cite three in my paper, of noted philosophers ascribing to Westermarck views that have neither much plausibility on their own nor textual support in his writings. Too often Westermarck has been cited cursorily by critics more interested in refutation than exegetical accuracy; hence the first step is to be clear about what he really said.

This is none too easy on its own, for, as I have argued in an earlier paper, "There are three possible positions on the question of the truth-value of moral judgments, which correspond to differing views about their meaning and nature, and Westermarck seems at times to have held all three, despite the fact that they are mutually contradictory."[1]

One of these theses is that moral judgments are all false, which is the error theory made popular by John Mackie and which is cited in that form by Professor Airaksinen. As Westermarck puts it, "If, as I maintain, the objective validity of all moral valuation is an illusion, and the proposition 'this is good' is meant to imply such validity, it must always be false."[2]

I would not presume to speak for John Mackie, although he himself recognized, both in print and in conversation, his indebtedness to Westermarck. I have argued elsewhere that we need to be aware of the variety of things that go on in moral discourse: ethical language has imperative, persuasive, interjective, expressive, ceremonial, reportive, prescriptive, and purportedly objective uses. Thus error theory would apply to one common, indeed central, use of moral language – the use in which moral *judgments* make claims about what is *really* right or wrong.

What does seem fairly clear to me, though, is that no argument of the sort that Harrison offers could be decisive against error theory understood in this limited sense. Harrison's perplexities arise because he has difficulty shedding his objectivist ways of looking at things. The error theorist either

E. Bulygin et al. (eds.), Man, Law and Modern Forms of Life, 103–105.

can think of seemingly contradictory moral pronouncements as contraries or can maintain that they embody false presuppositions which make any ordinary assessment of their truth value problematic. One need only recall the controversies surrounding such statements as "The present King of France is bald" to realize that there are suggested methods of resolving problems of reference without having to admit that there is a present King of France. Of course, we would begin to wonder if there were endless discussions about the putative properties of nonexistent individuals, but the case of moral argument is quite different in this respect: there are good reasons – of sociological, psychological, and biological sorts – why people would think of morality objectively even if no objective morality existed. Here the closer analogy would be between seemingly contradictory theological pronouncements, which all fail if there is no God, yet which have an underlying religious impulse behind them that can be explained empirically.

In concluding my reply, I want to propose two thought experiments. First, let us assume that moral objectivism is correct. For it also to be effective we must be able to demonstrate which normative moral theory is the true one. We could then dismiss all the other "false stones" and be satisfied in the possession of our jewel; we could replace moral argument with moral instruction. Unfortunately, as Professor Airaksinen concedes, "no one has been able to make sense of what *moral truth* means."

Now let us assume that there is no objective moral truth. What then follows? Surely not the "explosion of moralities without any common denominator" that Professor Airaksinen says the objectivists so fear. Quite the opposite, the actual explosion of moralities that we see all about us has been an explosion of objectivist moralities all convinced of their own rightness, and their apparent contradictoriness seems to rule out any common denominator among them. What follows instead, if there is no objective moral truth, is that we would have to pay more attention to moral rhetoric and to the "similarity of the mental constitution of men", as Westermarck puts it, in order to get anywhere.[3] We would not rush to embrace moral nihilism, but would rather seek to soften our subjectivism to allow for continued moral discourse. We would try to identify inconsistencies and unrecognized entailments in the views of opponents, sort out the factual questions that so easily get mixed up with moral questions, and then determine to what extent genuinely ultimate moral principles are based on irreconcilable feelings. It is only here that biology may give some consolation by holding out the hope that feelings at this very basic level may not be so chaotic as the objectivist fears. The moral skeptic does not maintain that we consult biology in answering particular normative questions – there are other devices for this – but only that biology may play a useful part in *explaining* why we act the way we do morally, even if we are not aware of the underlying causes of our behavior.

But this is a subject more appropriately addressed elsewhere. My chief object in my paper – although this reply may seem to indicate otherwise – has not been to launch a general defense of what I call "soft subjectivism" or of particular sociobiological theses, but rather to show that Westermarck's writings pose problems that can interest us still. The seriousness and vitality of Professor Airaksinen's comment are proof enough of that.

John Jay College, The City University of New York

NOTES

[1] Stroup, 'In Defense of Westermarck', *Journal of the History of Philosophy* 19 (1981), 219.
[2] Westermarck (1932), 142.
[3] Westermarck (1906–8), 1:8.

II

SCHOOLS AND PERSPECTIVES IN LEGAL THEORY

JOHN H. CRABB

HISTORICAL CAUSATION AND THE INDEPENDENCE OF WESTERN LAW

I. INTRODUCTION

What can be called "western law" has evolved into an essentially universal or world law. The genesis of this traces back to the Roman origins of legal system, which entered into the bloodstream of general Roman civilization. Law as the Romans evolved it had a unique quality of independence which is not found in any other known system of law. This means law as a social institution independent most significantly of both religion and governmental administration.[1] It is this independence of law which unifies this edifice of western law. Independence was part of the strain of the law which Roman civilization transmitted to the European states which succeeded the Roman Empire, and thence by them to essentially the rest of the world as a result of their implantation of their law wherever they established sovereignty and of the adoption of their legal concepts in the few areas of the world that have never known European sovereignty.

If this independence of law is traced to Roman origins, it does not thereby mean that this "western law" is "Roman law" in the historical or comparative law sense. Indeed, the western law which is unified by the criterion of independence includes the legal comparatists' principal distinct families of Anglo-American law and civil (or Romano-Germanic) law. Marxist theory clearly denies all independence to law, but in a sense Marxist law can be included with western law for purposes of this discussion. This has to do with the wholly European historical origins of Marxism and with its notion of "socialist legality", whereby Marxist states continue to utilize many aspects of the legal systems of their predecessor regimes. This is recognized as an expedient derogation from ideology while awaiting the Marxist millenium of the "withering away" of the law, along with the state.[2]

The assertion of essential universality of the western law does not ignore the present existence of other legal systems, of which the most important are Islamic, Hindu and African customary laws. However, such legal systems, with minor exceptions, function inside of or subordinate to national legal systems of western law. Aspects of the current scene suggest possible recrudescence of non-subordinate Islamic law, not necessarily limited to the extraordinary case

E. Bulygin et al. (eds.), Man, Law and Modern Forms of Life, 109–117.

of Iran. However that may be, such events are too recent and unsettled to provide adequate historical perspective for this discussion.

The Roman law which generated this concept of independent law showed its first permanent institutionalized facet to history with the Twelve Tables of the Law around 450 B.C. This can be used as a reasonable and convenient event from which to trace the historical evolution of the notion of the independence of law, as originally generated by the Romans. This involves showing the development of the institutions of the Roman legal system and how they endowed the law with its quality of independence.[3] This paper is intended as a kind of sequel to such a supposed investigation,[4] and to suggest implications for legal philosophy from the legal historian's explanation of the evolution of this western law through his presentation of the chain of historical causation.

II. HISTORICAL CAUSATION

Perhaps there is no notion of more general interest and concern than that of causation. Indeed, perhaps causation could be offered as a way of putting what philosophy is all about.[5] But if causation represents a unified general notion, it is nevertheless treated in myriad different ways, in accordance with the discipline or purpose involved.

The law has an extremely limited concept of causation, at least as applied to judicial proof. This is "proximate" (or "legal") cause, which typically involves only a short chain of events that will be considered legally causative of the event at issue.[6] It is of course recognized that an infinite number of causes combined to produce any event, but those that are not christened "proximate" are only "causes in fact" which do not entail legal consequences. Judges have stated that they can accompany philosophers only a short distance in seeking the full causative explanation, even within human limitations, behind any event. Figuratively speaking, there is no logical stopping point in this process of regression short of Adam and Eve.[7]

The task of the historian has been described as that of placing himself mentally in the time and place of the past which he is investigating and then reporting his findings in a manner which is coherent and relevant to his contemporaries.[8] His research will reveal to him a prodigious mass of facts or events among which he must choose as being pertinent and productive for inclusion in his particular historical account. His criterion for selection is in effect whether the event being considered is a link in the chain of causation relevant to his task.

A simple illustration of this process would be the statement of a historian that "Columbus discovered America", as an indispensable event in the chain of causations that he is presenting. It would take its place between the antecedent events leading up to it and the subsequent events to which it gave rise. But the historian could properly ignore the fact that some five centuries previously Leif Ericson had come to North America, and had even established settlements lasting a generation or so. For these exploits of Leif Ericson had only temporary and capsulated consequences, even for his Scandinavian community of origin, which reacted to them mainly merely by mentioning them uncertainly in the mists of various Norse legends or sagas. Since these events did not cause subsequent events of consequence for history, they need not be reported by the historian dealing with the chain of significant events of history. Or, Leif Ericson's presence in America was not a "discovery" for the historian's purpose.

But the historian can explain the cause of events only in terms of their having been produced in fact out of the complex of antecedent events. It is not his essential function to explain why these antecedents produced the results that they did in fact rather than a different result. Events may succeed each other in an expectable way in a sort of flow of history. If the course of history takes a surprising turn, such as the victory of the Scots over the English at Bannockburn, it will have been because the causes were not apparent, even though in existence at the time and only revealed by hindsight. The historian's commentary and analysis as to the *why* of events may be a particularly illuminating part of his presentation. This may include references for illustrative purposes of how matters might plausibly have gone otherwise, although generally the historian must refrain from venturing very far into history's outer space of the might-have-been. But the essence of history remains the explaining of events through causation by prior events.

Thus there is ample explanation in terms of prior events or circumstances to show why Leif Ericson's activities did not serve to "discover" America while those of Columbus centuries later did. Briefly, the European society of Leif Ericson's time had no interests to which his exploits responded, so they remained unimportant and for long essentially unknown. They "caused" nothing. But five centuries later the situation was vastly different, and Columbus' exploit evoked the liveliest response in Europe, as is evidenced by the rapidity of the exploration and colonization of the Americas which ensued. By hindsight it is clear that the Europeans were on the verge of making contact with the unknown Americas, regardless of Columbus or any other particular actors. Indeed, the evolution of European interests and activities had been such as possibly to stimulate querry as to the reasons ("causes") why Europeans had not "discovered" America considerably earlier than Columbus in fact did.

History can convincingly explain why the consequences of these two apparently similar exploits in navigational pioneering were so radically different, by analyzing the antecedent events and surrounding circumstances of each. But such method cannot answer the question as to *why* those respective events and circumstances existed as they did. Explanation in terms of endless regression through the same methodology of showing prior causations can never answer the ultimate or original *why*. Such are necessarily the limits of the province of history.

III. THE TWELVE TABLES OF THE LAW AND LEGAL HISTORY

Legal history is of course not law, but one of the limitless specializations of history. We have posited the Twelve Tables of the Law as a plausible starting point for legal history as it evolved with the Romans and continued with their successors, with our interest focused on the uniquely independent quality of this law. From this can be constructed the causal chain in accordance with the historical method as an explanation of this independence.

The Twelve Tables are significant in being the first written code of law in the primitive society of Rome to be permanently maintained and transmitted, and hence to enter into history.[9] This permanent recording, as opposed to oral or informal transmission of enacted law, lent stability to law and made it appear as an ongoing thing less subject to re-creation or oblivion at the whim of successive governmental administrations. It is not difficult to see in this the seed of independence of law as a social institution. The seed proved to fall on fertile historical soil, as it was fostered by the institutions of law that accompanied the development and spread of the Roman Empire and then by the successors of Roman civilization.[10]

However, the Twelve Tables are far from being the first permanent written code known to history, which reports of others in earlier Antiquity, the celebrated first of which being the Babylonian code of Hammurabi over fifteen centuries prior to the Twelve Tables. There is no claim that the Romans' code had an impelling superiority over the others of Antiquity whereby only it over all the others could have been expected to spawn a legal system destined to encompass the world. Indeed, a comparative examination of the respective circumstances of Hammurabi's code and of the Twelve Tables would suggest a far more promising future or progeny for the former.

Hamurrabi's code was promulgated by an already burgeoning and powerful empire of the time. Its text was by far more complete, or at least more voluminous, than that of the Twelve Tables and seemingly was not inferior to them in terms of quality or effectiveness. The Babylonian empire lasted many centuries thereafter before finally disappearing by absorption into the Persian empire. By contrast, the Twelve Tables were the creation of a still obscure community of central Italy struggling for survival among quarrelsome neighbors. Indeed, the Twelve Tables were only some fifty years old when the city of Rome, except for the Capitol, was captured and pillaged by the Gauls, who treated most of Rome's neighbors similarly. We know now, of course, that this catastrophe was but one of various setbacks that Rome surmounted among many vicissitudes in the long course of becoming a so-called "universal" empire. Still, the Roman Empire, like the Babylonian, ultimately disappeared. But unlike the Babylonian case (as one example among many possible), Rome's concepts and institutions of law continued with a life of their own after the demise of their parent society as a political entity. This figures as evidence of the unique independence of the law historically generated by the Twelve Tables, which in turn furnishes a thesis for explaining the singular permanence and universality of this law.

The historical method of presenting a continuous chain of causative events explains these contrasting results without mystery. It is analogous to the historian's conclusion that Columbus rather than Leif Ericson "discovered" America. The historian thereby finishes his tasks. He answers the *why* objectively in terms of antecedent causes, beyond which any further questions do not concern history.

IV. VIEWS FROM LEGAL PHILOSOPHY

The above hypothesized completed task of the legal historian could be grist for the legal philosopher's mill. The philosopher could accept, at least for discussion, the correctness of the historian's findings as to "western law": its universality, its independence and its decendency in these respects from the seed of the Twelve Tables. There might well be as many views as there would be legal philosophers that might care to comment. Here we will limit outselves to presenting supposed comments distilled from general notions of the historical school of legal philosophy and from the Aristotelian-Thomistic axis of natural law philosophy.

Historical legal philosophy says that the legal historian's findings explain not only what happened in fact but also what the nature of the law itself is.

Law is what it has been and has become. In the process the law reflects and is imbued with a certain mystique of the society which produced it, in a manner analogous to the way in which a given society evolves its own language in terms of the particularities of its experiences.[11] If the legal historian is correct that western law has become essentially universal and that it has had a quality of independence that contributed to its spread, then such is the present nature of this western law. However, just as history in no way purports to predict the future, so does legal historical philosophy abstain from ascribing permanence or universality to characteristics of the law as they may be reflected in any given time or place. The factors that produced this identified western law may or may not in the future continue to produce this character of independence. Moreover, its universality may fragment in the future, whereupon any distinct legal system so resulting would bear the philosophical stamp of its then total historical experience.

Indeed, the establishment, in countries hitherto of western law, of Marxism, whose fundamental tenets involve the suppression of the independence of law pending the disappearance of law itself, is arguably a case in point. Those of the historical school could contend that, if Marxist law to any extent or for any purpose is to be considered as still part of western law, it appears that the asserted independence of western law was but a prolonged passing phase of it, without being an inherent or permanent characteristic. This argument would also supposedly deny the existence of "western law" if independence is imposed as a necessary identifying feature of it.

The nineteenth century German legal scholar Savigny is considered to be the originator of the historical school of legal philosophy.[12] His career was before the macro-law approach which has come to characterize comparative law with its treating of large "legal families". He considered that each national legal system was to be treated separately in accordance with its own particular historical experiences as to law. Hence he was not concerned to seek any general characteristics or nature of law that would have universal validity. Although also of the historical school, Sir Henry Maine of England did seek to distill universal concepts of law overriding national compartmentalizations, and for that purpose conducted a sort of legal anthropological investigation.[13]

Historical legal philosophy has affinities with other developed schools of thought. One is the sort of existentialist line of philosophy which ascribes the basic nature of things to the unending process of movement and becoming.[14] Another is the legal sociological school,[15] which is distinguished from the historical primarily in different emphasis on the time dimension.

Other related approaches might be mentioned, all of which have a common orientation in positivism. In terms of the present discussion, they could agree that the ultimate explanation of things lies in the coherent presentation of a historical chain of causative events. The regression in the presentation of causes can never arrive at the first cause, which necessarily lies outside the domain of the empirical, which is the ultimate limit of man's capacity. If a logically presumed first cause is outside man's possibility of discovery, man has no reason to concern himself with it and should limit himself to what lies within his capacities. Kelsen's *Grundnorm* is a vivid, though invisible, representation of this notion. It is the ultimate cause, so to speak, but it lies beyond man's uttermost capacities to concretize or to identify objectively.[16] The *Grundnorm* is nevertheless there, but must remain permanently as a formless abstraction.

As to those of the most traditional natural law persuasion, they could see in the evolution of western law toward independence and universality a tendency toward the application or fulfillment of their premises. Their basic position is that justice exists as a universal value which man did not create, but toward the realization of which man is oriented by his nature. Man's rational capacity, even though limited, permits him ideally to see what is just in any given material situation, and to orient the positive law which he creates toward what he objectively finds to be just.[17]

A legal system which approaches universality suggests that it tends to adhere to the natural law's ideal of justice as a human constant. That is to say, it could be that the cause of the universality is some inherent superior capacity of such legal system to create positive law which satisfies the craving for justice common to all human societies. This does not mean an identity of western law with natural law, as each solution offered by western positive law is subject to being examined for its compatability with justice under the circumstances.

Institutional independence of law is favorable to the accomplishment of the law's mission of finding justice. If it is in subordination to governmental administration, religion or other authoritative institutions of society, interests extraneous to the pursuit of justice will adulterate or impede the proper functioning of the law. Independent law will thus be more likely to be satisfying to society in terms of securing justice and hence is more likely to endure. Its independence of other institutions means that it is better able to survive the turbulence of political and social upheavals of a society. Such law by not being inherently tied to the cultural and ideological idioms of particular societies can appeal to human nature generally and spread indefinitely from its place of origin.

This linkage between independence of law and the pursuit of justice would appear to the natural law philosopher as a desirable institutional feature of western law tending to encourage the infusion of positive law with the natural law's ideal of justice to be concretely determined in operative circumstances. This receptivity of western law to principles of natural law would be viewed as a wholesome orientation of the law, and this relative superiority would expectably produce the most durable and widespread system of law in the long run. Its independence suggests itself as an essential cause of the manner in which western law evolved historically, a hypothesis on which the historian's evidence can be brought to bear.

Ferney-Voltaire, France

NOTES

1 Pound, *Introduction to the Philosophy of Law*, 1921, chapter 1.
2 Kerimov, 'La Conception Marxiste du Droit', *66 Problèmes du Monde Contemporain*, Moscow 1979, 13–15.
3 Jolowicz, *Historical Introduction to Roman Law*, 1939, 86.
4 A schematic effort at this is my paper presented at the IVR meeting in Basle, 'Le Droit Occidental comme Justice Mondiale', 1979.
5 Dunham, 'Platonism', in: Ferm (ed.), *A History of Philosophical Systems*', New York 1950, 93, chapter 8.
6 Prosser, *Law of Torts* (3d ed.), St. Paul (Minnesota, USA), 1964, 282.
7 Atlantic Coast Line R. Co. v. Daniels, 8 Georgia App. 775, 70 S. E. 203 (1911, American judicial decision): "But to make such a standard (that, if the cause had not existed, the effect would not have occurred) the basis of legal responsability would soon prove very unsatisfactory; for a reduction ad absurdum may be promptly established by calling to mind that, if the injured person had never been born, the injury would not have happened. So the courts ask another question: Was the wrongful act the proximate cause?"
8 Collingwood, *The Idea of History*, New York 1956, 282–302.
9 Villey, *Le Droit Romain*, Paris 1964, 15–16.
10 See Vinogradoff, *Roman Law in Medieval Europe*, 1929.
11 Kantorowicz, 'Savigny and the Historical School', *L. Q. Rev.* (1937) 53, 326.
12 See Savigny (tr. Hayward), *The Vocation of Our Age for Legislation and Jurisprudence*, 1831.
13 See Maine, *Ancient Law*, 1861 (with subsequent English and American editions).
14 Kantorowicz, *The Definition of Law*, Cambridge 1958, chapter 1.
15 See Pound, *op. cit.* note 1. A 65 page résumé of Pound's prolific writings as a leading figure of the sociological school of jurisprudence is his *Law Finding through Experience and Reason*, Athens (Georgia, USA) 1960.
16 Kelsen, 'The Pure Theory of Law', *Harvard Law Review* 55 (1942), 44.

[17] This proposition is offered as one of many possible of synthesizing the many expressions by a host of writers of the legal side of the *philosophia perennis* and related concepts, as to the essence of the theory of natural law.

MIKAEL M. KARLSSON

LEGAL PHILOSOPHY IN ICELAND*

I am pleased to be offered this opportunity to say a few words about legal philosophy in Iceland. Actually, my talk might more accurately have been entitled 'An Ontological Proof for the Existence of Iceland'. By way of explaining this point, I shall describe how it is that I came to be addressing you at this Congress.

I might mention first of all that I am a naturalized Icelander. And so – like a typical convert to a cause – I may have reacted overzealously when I received the Congress program and saw that there was to be a plenary session entitled 'Legal Philosophy in the Nordic Countries', with representatives from Norway, Denmark, Sweden, and Finland – but none from my adopted home country; so that as it stood, a more fitting title for the session would have been: 'Legal Philosophy in the Nordic Countries – Except Iceland'.

Anyway, I wrote to the Program Committee, who very kindly invited me to join this session in order to represent the fifth of the independent Nordic Nations.[1]

What I have to give you is by no means a scholarly survey. Indeed, as the Program Committee may well have suspected in the first place, there is not all that much to say about legal philosophy in Iceland, though what there is may be of some interest.

But before I go into my presentation such as it is, I would like to express my thanks to our Finnish hosts for organizing this very fine and impressive congress. There are certain special forms of kinship – some of them not very well known – between the Finns and the Icelanders: Finland and Iceland constitute, first of all, the eastern and western boundaries of the Nordic world. Both the Icelanders and the Finns (that is, the vast majority of Finns) speak languages which few of their Scandinavian colleagues can understand,

* *Author's note to the reader*: As will be plain from both its style and content, this talk was not originally intended for publication. However, quite a few participants in the world Congress requested copies, so I cheerfully made available a virtually unrevised version of my manuscript, which was photocopied and circulated in Helsinki. The Congress organizers have now arranged to publish it, and I have consequently revised it a bit and added notes. Nevertheless, the reader is kindly asked to keep in mind the purpose for which, and the conditions under which, this piece was drafted.

E. Bulygin et al. (eds.), Man, Law and Modern Forms of Life, 119–124.

although Icelandic is the not-very-remote ancestor of the Scandinavian languages, while Finnish is – as far as is known – an entirely unrelated language, which does not even belong to the Indo-European language group. By coincidence, however, Icelandic and Finnish sound rather alike – at least to the untrained ear – a result of which is that Icelanders are often mistaken for Finns in bars and nightclubs in Scandinavia. So, despite Iceland's rather close and long-standing ties with Scandinavia, we have these special sympathies with our Finnish cousins, to whom I say in their own language: *kiitos*.

What there is to be said about legal philosophy in Iceland is of quite a different sort than that which has been recounted here by the other speakers at the Plenary Session on Philosophy of Law in the Nordic Countries. For there is no appreciable Icelandic literature in the area of legal philosophy. We do not have a Hägerström, or a Ross, or an Olivecrona, or a Westermarck. This lack is, indeed, only a symptom of the more general lack of Icelandic philosophical literature.[2]

Our single university – the University of Iceland – is a young one. It was not established until 1911.[3] And philosophy as a degree subject is only ten years old.[4] It will therefore not surprise you to learn that until recently only a few Icelanders had ever received philosophical training, and even fewer had undertaken philosophical writing.

Naturally, in such circumstances, no independent philosophical tradition has taken root; nor can there even be said to be an Icelandic branch of any foreign school of philosophical thought.

Contemporary Icelandic law and jurisprudence are, to be sure, influenced by legal positivism, the natural law tradition, and also so-called "Scandinavian Realism"; but there is nothing in this remarkable enough to be worthy of special discussion.

What *does* Iceland have, then, to offer legal philosophy? What it has, I think, are raw materials, which may lead to interesting developments in the future.

First, Iceland has its *language*. This language, Icelandic, is in most important respects identical with Old Norse, the language spoken by the Norwegians who settled Iceland in (as we think) the 10th century.

Icelandic has been successfully preserved by the Icelanders for more than 1000 years. But it has never been developed as a philosophical language; or rather, its development as such is currently in the very early stages. If this enterprise should succeed, as I believe it will, it could lead to philosophical innovations.

For if you believe along with me that philosophy can be characterized (albeit oversimply) as an attempt to create ways in which to talk about matters which, in the absence of such creations, must remain mysterious, then you are bound to believe that the development of philosophical thought in a given language will inevitably affect the historical development of that language. At the same time, the language in which philosophy is conducted is bound to influence the direction of philosophical development. Thus, the exploration of a language previously untried as a vehicle for philosophy offers the distinct possibility that philosophical inventions may result.

Neither the Scandinavian languages, nor Finnish, have been successfully developed as independent philosophical languages, which may be one reason why Nordic philosophy, though conducted expertly, and to a high standard, has tended overall to be derivative. In general, Nordic philosophy has adopted its philosophical vocabulary, and indeed much of its philosophical language, from abroad.

In Iceland, however, the path which has thus far been followed elsewhere in the Nordic world has not been taken. Rather, Icelandic philosophy, whatever other influences it may import, is being deliberately, systematically, and conscientiously developed in an Icelandic idiom, although at present, as I mentioned, this idiom barely exists.

But, why, it may be asked, should Iceland differ in this way? Perhaps the most striking point to be made is that Icelandic culture is, and has been since the 10th century, centrally and fundamentally a *literary* culture, and a powerful one at that. After the settlement (thought to have begun circa 874), the court poets of Norway were, for example, almost exclusively imported from Iceland. One of the recognized great literatures of the world, generously referred to as the "Norse Sagas", was written almost wholly by Icelanders writing in Iceland (principally in the 12th century). And the greatest Nordic writer of the medieval period – one of the greatest writers, incidentally, of all time – was the Icelander Snorri Sturluson (1179–1241).

It is these, and other writings in Icelandic, which form the principal anchor-point of Iceland's life and culture, even today in this so-called "Information Age". And probably because the Icelandic language has, from very early times, served as the significant fulcrum of Icelandic culture, the tendency to preserve it – to resist loan words, foreign idioms, and, in short non-Icelandic forms of expression – has remained strong.

Thus we may predict that the exploitation of Icelandic as an independent philosophical language will occur. It is indeed underway at present in the hands of a new generation of academically-trained Icelandic philosophers.

And this may well lead to substantive innovations in philosophy, including, of course, the philosophy of law.

In the second place, beside its language Iceland has a relatively unique, highly interesting, legal tradition, which has been little explored from the philosophical point of view. It is widely supposed that the history of Icelandic law forms a sort of uninteresting appendix to the history of Scandinavian (and, more generally, Germanic) law; but this supposition is vastly exaggerated. For example, the law of the Icelandic Free State (early 10th to mid-13th century), the codified form of which is known in Iceland as *Grágás* ("grey goose"), has many important parts and provisions which are not known anywhere outside of Iceland. Tradition says that this law was formulated for Iceland by Icelanders who were sent to Norway for the raw materials. But even if that is so, much of what stands in *Grágás* is not traceable to further sources, if indeed such ever existed. Moreover, although *Grágás* was later replaced by other law codes imposed upon Iceland after the nation was brought under the throne of Norway in the mid-13th century, these later codes incorporated native provisions which had stood in *Grágás* and were not found elsewhere. *Grágás* has, in fact, not entirely lost its influence on the contemporary law of Iceland.

This native, and, as I said, relatively unique legal tradition is preserved in medieval manuscripts, both in law books and in Icelandic literature. One of the most extensive descriptions of Icelandic legal practices in the Free-State Period is actually to be found in the greatest of the Icelandic sagas, the *Saga of Njáll*. There, the importance of their law to the Icelanders is indicated in a famous motto: *Med lögum skal land byggja*, which may be freely translated, "In law is our preservation"[5] (and, Njáll adds, "in lawlessness, our destruction"). This motto stands today in the hearts of the Icelanders, and on every Icelandic police car.

In any case, because the Icelandic legal tradition has fortunately been so well preserved, it has been – and continues to be – rather well studied *historically*, largely by Icelandic legal historians.[6] Unlike philosophical writing, historical writing is an Icelandic tradition of long standing, dating back to the 12th century when it was established by the historians Ari the Learned (1067–1148) and Snorri Sturluson (mentioned earlier).

Because philosophy depends so heavily upon the examples with which it deals – and, as Wittgenstein reminded us, can become stale if we stick always to the same diet of examples – what is unique in the Icelandic legal tradition has at least the *potential* to serve as a refreshing source for legal philosophy; and no doubt it is principally Icelandic philosophers who will be concerned to exploit it.

Third, and last: There is now a degree program in philosophy at the University of Iceland; and this will provide, for the first time, a continuing supply of Icelanders trained in philosophy, a growing philosophical literature in Icelandic (that is, in an Icelandic idiom, as I called it), and, in short, the means for utilizing that which Iceland *may* have uniquely to offer philosophy.

As regards philosophical jurisprudence: courses in legal philosophy have, in the past few years, been introduced in both our law and arts faculties.[7] Thus far, these have, for the most part, been historically oriented, being designed to give our students a good grounding in the more important traditions of philosophical jurisprudence: the Natural Law tradition (where they read, for example, St. Thomas Aquinas), the tradition of Legal Positivism (where they read, among others, John Austin), and more contemporary movements such as that of Scandinavian Legal realism, about which we have heard in such detail at this session. Recent writings are also discussed, though to a lesser degree. Our hope is to train up a generation of students with the background to appreciate, and participate in, the debates in legal philosophy which belong to our own times.

University of Iceland

NOTES

[1] I was not, however, the only Icelandic representative at the Congress. My colleague, Gardar Gíslason, also attended.

[2] The largest work is *Saga mannsandans* (History of the Human Spirit), by Ágúst H. Bjarnason, and historical survey of philosophy which first appeared in four volumes in the years 1906–1915, and was later expanded into a five-volume work. Ágúst H. Bjarnason was the first professor of philosophy at the University of Iceland, serving from 1911–1945.

[3] Instruction at the university level actually began somewhat earlier. A theological school was established in 1847, a medical school in 1876, and a law school in 1908. These became the theological, medical, and law faculties of the University in 1911, and a faculty of arts was added at that time.

[4] Previously, philosophy was taught only in the form of a general *philosophicum* – a philosophical introduction to the arts and sciences, presented as a single course. The *philosophicum* is still taught.

[5] This motto does not originate with *Njáls Saga*, but was, and is, famous throughout the Nordic world. In medieval sources, it is found in the Danish Jutland Laws, the Swedish Uppland and Helsinge law codes, and the Norwegian law code of Frostathing, as well as in *Njáls Saga* (ch. LXXI).

[6] There is probably little point in mentioning Icelandic works here. In English, Jón Jóhanneson's *History of the Old Icelandic Commonwealth* (Manitoba, 1974) contains

a detailed chapter on the constitutional law of the Free-State period. *Grágás* is being translated into English by Andrew Dennis, Peter Foote, and Richard Perkins: The first part has already been published under the title *Laws of Early Iceland: Grágás I* (Manitoba, 1980) and includes a short introduction on the laws of Iceland in the Free-State period. A useful article on *Jónsbók*, a later medieval Icelandic law code of considerable interest, is 'The Law Book of the Icelanders', published in Sigurdur Nordal (ed.), *Monumenta Typographica Islandica III* (Copenhagen, 1934). This article is a translation of 'Lögbók Íslendinga', by Ólafur Lárusson, which appears in the same volume. For those who read German, the classic works by Konrad Maurer may be of interest. These include: *Die Entstehung des isländischen Staats und seiner Verfassung* (Munich, 1852), *Island von seiner ersten Entdeckung bis zum Untergang des Freistaats* (Munich, 1874), and *Vorlesungen über altnordische Rechtsgeschichte*, in 5 volumes (1907–1910).

[7] There is a *philosophicum* for first-year law students directed by the professor of philosophy, Dr. Páll Skúlason, and taught by Prof. Skúlason, Gardar Gíslason, and myself. Gardar is municipal court judge in Reykjavik and an instructor in the Faculty of Law. He and I teach an optional course in legal philosophy for fifth-year law students; and I also teach a course in the philosophy of law in the Faculty of Arts.

ROBERTA KEVELSON

PEIRCE'S PHILOSOPHY OF SIGNS AND LEGAL HERMENEUTICS

There is no direct communion between the minds of men; whatever thoughts, emotions, conceptions, ideas of delight or sufference we feel urged to impart to other individuals, we cannot obtain our object without resorting to the outward manifestation of that which moves us inwardly, that is, to signs . . . (Lieber 1839, 2–3).

This contention by Lieber prefaces his now classic exposition on Legal Hermeneutics; it appeared in 1839, the year of Charles Peirce's birth, and anticipates in significant ways, with especial reference to law, the method of inquiry of Semiotics – that new field of investigation in which Peirce rightly regarded himself as a frontiersman.

Peirce's prolific writings, most of which are yet unpublished, which he continually rethought and revised throughout his long and thankless career, are rarely referred to by our seasoned jurisprudes and legal philosophers today, despite the fact that direct reference to legal practice and reasoning are significantly found in all stages of his work, and in relation to nearly all the major topics of semiotics which deeply concerned him.[1] Not only does the law serve Peirce as prototypical of social institutions, but the legal argument, as Toulmin has pointed out (1958) is assumed as the prototype of ordinary argument; thus the skeletal structures of modes of thought are those logics which terms and propositions flesh out. All of logic, according to Peirce, should be regarded as Semiotic. The impact of Peirce's thought until only recently has been greatest, in the study of law, upon some of the great revolutionaries in jurisprudence both in the United States and on the Continent, namely on Oliver Wendell Holmes and on Francois Gény. Although Robert Summers places scant emphasis on Peirce's significant and direct contribution to Instrumentalism, Legal Realism, Legal Pragmatism, etc. (1982), the application of Peirce's semiotic to law logic, or a-logic where the term 'Logic' is used for example by Holmes to refer to traditional and inadequate logics is unmistakeable in the thought of those who, like Jerome Frank, Karl Llewellyn, Roscoe Pound, and others, insist that the Law be responsive not only to its own codified authority but to the changing values and wishes of society – the new authority of The People.[2]

Thus it is in the context of an emergent social conscience that legal consciousness of correctible social inequity develops, e.g., in Bentham's

E. Bulygin et al. (eds.), Man, Law and Modern Forms of Life, 125–135.

Utilitarianism, in Mill's social and economic justice, etc., which stimulates, directly and indirectly, the formulation of laws of juridical interpretation throughout the world – both in so-called civil law countries and in common law countries.[3]

While the ideas of the need for rules for legal interpretation were in the air, so to speak, since at least the first quarter of the 19th century, it is Peirce who contends that hermeneutics is not merely a theory and method of the exegesis of special texts – sacred, on one end of the spectrum, and profane, on the other – but should be regarded as the "method of methods" of Semiotics in order to ascertain not only how each field inquires into the objects of its special concern, but how the separate institutions of human, social value communicate with one another and, therefore, how such communication between systems results in the emergence of new values and new meaning in human intercourse, i.e., in new signs and sign-systems.[4]

Throughout his writings Peirce is careful to distinguish between the theoretical and the speculative sciences, linking the most speculative with the most abstract modes of developing an idea, i.e. the mathematical sciences, and the most practical with the applied sciences such as law and economics. Semiotics is viewed as applying the principles of mathematical inquiry, for its purposes, to account for the structure and use of thought, in order to serve as referential model for those institutions which more directly interact with persons in society, such as the law. Thus Semiotics mediates between speculative and practical acts. A legal system can be said to represent, or be a sign of, that particular semiotic process most appropriate to it; by the same token, each mode, or style of a semiotic process or event – an occasion of inquiry – is a representation, or interpretative sign, of a more abstract process of discovery, which in turn, takes its cues from the world of experience and observation and forms its hypotheses as abstracted from the actual, practical world.[5] Therefore, the actual practice of law, among other practices, is resourceful of the basic material upon which more theoretical investigations are developed.[6] In this sense, the higher the level of abstraction the more authoritative the referent system so characterized, and the whole of semiotics is concerned with how one level may be translated into a different level or method of inquiry. Peirce asks, "What does it mean to speak of the 'interpretation of a sign?' Interpretation is merely another word for translation . . . " (MS 282, 100).

Understood in this manner, the legal system *interprets* its referent, which is to say that a particular structure of thought – a logical pattern – is a referent sign or Authority which as Type becomes that upon which the Legal Acts of any given legal system is predicated, as Tokens of that Type.

Pragmatism, or Pragmaticism as Peirce redefines and distinguishes his concept of Semiotics from other, then prevailing notions of pragmatism, refers to a *method* of inquiry. Semiotics is characterized by the pragmatic method precisely because the role of logic is, as a whole, heuristic; the main agency in this logical role is to present a structure of procedure – a sign-structure showing the process by which any idea, itself a sign, develops from one stage of interpretation to the next, according to rules for interpretation which are integral with the appropriately selected mode of reasoning. Peirce's expanded logic is subdivided into three parts: the first is Speculative Grammar, and this consists of the levels of syntax, semantics, and pragmatics as they concern linguistic structures; the second is Critic, or what had been traditionally understood as Formal Logic, and which consists of three modes of formal reasoning; abductive (or hypothetical), deductive, and inductive; the third and highest division of his expanded logic, or Semiotic, is Methodology, used synonymously by Peirce with the terms Speculative Rhetoric and Methodeutic.

Most of the literature on Legal Methodology to date has centered on the ambiguity of the term, Methodology, itself. E.g., does Methodology in Law refer to a descriptive process, or to a prescriptive process, or to both? An interesting and comprehensive discussion on this issue may be found in Horovitz (1972). Space does not permit discussion on Horovitz' distinctions here, but, rather, provides an opportunity to reject both alternatives as characterizing the ultimate purpose of Methodology, from a semiotic perspective, which is, as mentioned above, neither prescriptive nor descriptive in its main thrust, but heuristic. Thus Peirce's expanded logic, or Semiotics, is not intended, as a whole, to reiterate no more in its conclusions than is given in its premises, but rather to invent, to discover, and to create new meaning, new meaningful signs which, as provisional judgments, may act as subjects for continuing and even endless inquiry.

Elsewhere Kevelson writes in more detail on the relation between authority and freedom, which as a relationship characterizes all of creative activity, the purpose of which is to make new meaning out of old and to realize that which is felt to be potentially valuable. In this context the concept of continuity is reexamined; the continuum of law is presumed here to be an aspect of the continuum of thought in general. According to Peirce, Semiotics, as this expanded Logic, serves in the creating of new values and value-systems. In this process, Peirce says, Aesthetics, considered as the science of values, is related to Logic through the mediation of Ethics. Peirce speaks of the "ethics" of right thinking, for example in MS 313, 13:

What is the use of thinking? . . . it is the argument alone that is the subject of logical goodness and badness . . . [and further, in this passage,] . . . an argument is sound if it necessarily must predict facts in the measure in which it promises to do so . . . . All this is entirely contrary to the doctrines of leading logicians of today. I make the soundness of an argument to consist in its conformity to the law of the facts. (13, 15)

An important paper on Peirce's influence on Oliver Wendell Holmes and the "Prediction Theory" in law is by Max Fisch, whose recognition of Peirce's impact on jurisprudence and the philosophy of law has been a key factor in bringing into prominance for continuing inquiry the relationship between Peirce's semiotic theory of interpretation and Legal Hermeneutics (Fisch 1942, 85–97).

Yet as early as the period between 1865 and 1867, Peirce writes in the "logic notebooks" that the phrase 'the burden of proof' belongs in the courtroom,

and has no place in speculative science where indefinite suspension of judgment is permissible. However, since several of the important questions of philosophy are matters of practical interest, it may be allowed to speak of a burden of proof in their practical reference (MS 337).

In passing we want to recall Justice Story's dilemma which briefly stated confronted him with a commitment to an ethical position in deciding on changing values with respect to slavery and related questions of property and civil rights which strongly leaned to greater liberty for all, against traditional, established discriminatory practice in 19th century United States. The tools of reasoning with which he had to structure his liberal views on slavery cases, for example, were "formalistic" and thus incongruous with his judgment. According to Gilmore, Story was "driven" to present and justify his decisions in a "formalism" which was entirely foreign to the content of his convictions and liberal ideas, and to the principles he had firmly stood for during his career (cf. Gilmore 1917, Kevelson 1981).

Story, as famous for his work on the codification of law as Lieber is for his work on Legal Hermeneutics and Political Ethics, were close colleagues during the especially turbulent period in post-Civil War legal thought, both in the United States and abroad. Peirce, as a matter of fact, selects both Story and Lieber to represent the "great men of the 19th century," in law (MS 1123, 25).

Gilmore points out that "formalism" permitted Story an acceptable and political mode of deciding cases "according to the letter of a statute or of an established rule of law, without further inquiry," but, it must be noted, that such resort severely compromised what Peirce would call Story's ethics in reasoning.

In having to choose between a mode of interpretation which would accord either with that of Legal Interpretation or of Doctrinal Interpretation, Story chose the former, and thus postponed for a later date well into the 20th century the role of the activist judge in his role as Legal Hermeneutist.

Story wrote during a period in the development of new juridical values when rules for interpretation had not yet become canonized and made an integral part of statutory law. Indeed, it was not until 1896 that the revised notion of the Cardinal Rules of Legal Interpretation was summarized, as in Beal (1896), Gény (1899), Ross (1912) and others. Certainly Savigny must be acknowledged as one of the forerunners of the modern concept of Legal Hermeneutics, bringing forward a tradition of interpretation in law which dates back at least as far as early Roman law, and indeed, includes hermeneutic exegesis of sacred texts, such as the Talmud. Regarding, for a moment, the hermeneutics of sacred texts only – which until recently represented hermeneutics as a whole – we want to stress that much of the current literature on hermeneutics in the writings of Apel, Habermas, Gadamer, Ricoeur and others seem not to be concerned with the fact that the traditional purpose of hermeneutic, or interpretive examination of sacred texts, was primarily to clarify sacred law. Among contemporary hermeneuticists in this vein perhaps only Betti has maintained the link between sacred and profane interpretation. If we grant that the problems of theological interpretation are taken up by metaphysical inquiry, then Peirce's concern with explicating the relation between authority and liberty, and causation in continua, within the context of pragmatic method in Semiotics, can be readily understood. His views on these matters are taken up more fully elsewhere. In passing, recall his comment on the subject:

> . . . logic ought not to be founded on metaphysics; but on the contrary metaphysics ought to be founded on the science of logic. Logic ought to rest directly on those phenomena of life which nobody doubts. (MS 313, 18)

But that which nobody doubts is precisely that which has become established in some system of belief as a sign of Truth, an assumption of Truth, a referent judgment or law-like representation of reality which members of any given community have come to accept and defer to as binding, and as such becomes represented and codified in institutionalized, written law.

But Peirce's contention is that the truth is not a property of a law any more than what we interpret as real is a property of the phenomenon in question – the object of our inquiry. Peirce does not deny that what exists is, indeed, real. But what we know to be true of existents we know because of the effects of their acts upon us. And further, we know what these acts mean to us by interpreting them, by inferring meaning in a cumulative manner with regard to the thing in question until we have settled doubts and achieve, through reason, some sense of certainty, which we hold and use as true. A judgment – whether it presume to make or discover law – is, both in law as well as in ordinary life, a symbol of such truth. And a symbol, together with an index (such as a system of classification) and an icon (such as a pattern of thought or a procedure capable of being diagrammed) is the third of these coordinate, co-functions of all signs. The dominance of one function over the other two depends primarily on context and purpose.

Thus, in conclusion, this most condensed discussion of Peirce's semiotic notion of interpretation as it affects or relates to Legal Hermeneutics, is brought to a point of view which necessarily stands in opposition to the traditional juristic principle of hermeneutics which holds that *In claris non fit interpretation*, or "When the text is clear there is no room for interpretation."

Regardless of whether we speak of Usual or Authentic Interpretation, both of which Savigny tells us is implied by the term Legal Interpretation (1867, 167–68), or of Doctrinal Interpretation which calls upon, in the absence of rules for interpretation in the system of law which prevails, the ability of the judge to make decisions by employing a kind of free legislative and law-creative activity, Semiotics in Peirce's sense must insist that even the laws and rules for interpretation, in any given system of law, must themselves be regarded as provisional only and so subject to reinterpretation.

If, ultimately, as Peirce argues, all observation is in error and all fact is the result of a process of inference and is, itself, a generalization of two or more observations – if ever a single observation could be isolated and defined – then all our premises in reasoning are at bottom hypothetical and not true, that is, not absolutely true, statements. And if, as Peirce maintains, every interpretation of a law-like rule increases the meaning of that referent rule or statute the interpretation, or sign, which evolves is not a duplication of its referent, but a new sign the structure and internal relation and organization of which is the representation of a complex system of thought constituents which are not inherent in the referent, but which come into being – which *become* – through the creative process of interpretation.

In Plucknett's words,

The more one examines the historical processes by which the judicature interprets the written and the unwritten laws, the laws that are enacted and the laws that are unenacted, the more clearly one sees that the office *ius dicere*, to interpret law, involves also the office *ius dare*, to make law. (1922, vii.)

Thus Tedeschi's (1967) concern that Ascarelli's "anarchic" view of "free interpretation" in law will "lead to the elimination from the world of law of anything that is not a concrete, immediate relevant order" will not hold, when we introduce into this absolute freedom in interpretation the authority of those rules of the system which indicate procedure.

For, as Gény points out, the interpreter is constrained by rules for discovery and interpretation, "the best defined of which come from the formal sources of positive law," ((1899) 1963, 565).

Gény goes on to say that the main one of the acknowledged constraints on the interpreter is the written law, and this exerts the primary authoritative source when it exists: "Statute as such is the expression of the authority of a man or a group of men, commensurate with their intelligence." (Gény (1899) 1963, 565.) In other words, even though a statute carries forward the intention of its authors, and the situations which it was presumed to govern, and therefore no statute "becomes an independent entity separate from the thought of its author," the process of Legal Hermeneutics must be regarded as a continuation of an idea, a human thought, a question, posed in the form of a statement, or indication, by the expresser to a respondent. Thus a statute represents a *general*, a *quality*, or vague – in degrees of vagueness – judgment; every reply in the form of interpretation of such question, or statute, assumes the structure of dialogue, an ongoing and continuous dialogue on some point in law.

In Peirce dialogue is the basic structure of all sign-interpretation and hence of Semiotics as a whole.

Peirce asks,

What are signs for, anyhow? They are to communicate ideas, are they not? Even the imaginary signs called thoughts convey ideas from the mind of yesterday to the mind of tommorrow into which yesterday has grown . . . But why should this idea-potentiality be so poured from one vessel into another unceasingly. Is it a mere exercise of the World-Spirit's Spiel-trieb – mere amusement? . . . it is a part, perhaps we may say the chief part, of a process of the Creation of the World. (MS 282, 101.)

Thus I conclude that Legal Hermeneutics, as other interpretive processes, derives its impetus and takes its authority from that which the poet Schiller spoke of as the transformation of values in the fusing of rule with liberty, in the free-play of the imagination together with the inhibitory power of self-control in thinking. In Peirce's sense, boundaries link possibility with forms of thought which permit us to evolve our vague notions into consequential judgments, from which acts in the world proceed. Understood in this manner, we see the domain of ethics governed by aesthetics, and governing in turn what we call, variously, logic. The choice of an appropriate, or ethical mode of thinking, of interpreting *vis-à-vis* law and legal systems depends, ultimately, on those values predicted to be realized through interpretation. In this sense all Legal Hermeneutics is teleological, where the term 'teleological', in the Peircean sense, refers to the influence of future goals on the here-and-now, as a kind of precedential authority totally different from that notion of precedent so strongly criticized by the great Legal Realist, Llewellyn. Thus modality, especially all degrees of the possible, becomes in Legal Hermeneutics the life of the law.

The Pennsylvania State University, Berks

NOTES

[1] See Fisch (1942), 85–97; see also Fisch's papers on the reciprocation between Peirce and prominent lawyers of the 19th century (1964, 3–32) and also in the forthcoming Introduction to the third volume of the new edition of the Writings of Charles S. Peirce which Professor Fisch was kind enough to share with me, in draft.

[2] See Kevelson (1981a, 1981b, 1981c, 1982a, 1982b). In these papers, especially, is discussed Peirce as foundational for Legal Semiotics, and in *Peirce's Method of Methods* (forthcoming in 1985) shown the correlation between Legal Hermeneutics and Peirce's concept of the Interpretant in Semiotics.

For discussion of the sovereignty of The People see Francis Lieber's *Hermeneutics of Law and Politics* ((1839) 1880, Hammond Edition), especially 206–227, 312–331.

[3] Compare, for example, Britto (1927), Betti (1948) with Plucknett (1922) on Legal Interpretation with respect to Civil Law countries on the one hand, and England's Common Law tradition on the other hand.

[4] Peirce's 'method of methods' is intended to interpret the method of inquiry which characterizes a specific science or discipline, into the mode of communication of other disciplined inquiries; Semiotics is seen to be the mediating process in intersystemic communication. See Kevelson's *Peirce's Method of Methods* (1985) and also *Inlaws/Outlaws* (1977).

[5] See Peirce's MS 605 on the classification of the sciences. See also MS 852 on Semiotic Philosophy as heuristic of categorical truths.

[6] The actual practice of law corresponds with the notion of "experience" in Peirce, which, he says, is the basis for our investigations. Experience is predominantly contradictory and oppositional in its representational sign structure, according to Peirce, and thus corresponds with the typical factive sign. Note also, in this respect, Holmes' insistence that the law is primarily concerned with factive relations ((1881), 1963); see

also 'The Path of the Law' (1897) and Summers' commentary on Holmes' fact/prediction relation in legal interpretation (1982, 116–135).

[7] See Gilmore's account of Story's applying the "wrong" logic to the "right" law ((1917) 1977, especially pages 27, 38, 48, 50). In a similar sense Lieber criticizes Locke for his inappropriate use of axiomatic reasoning, e.g., in the *Political Ethics* (1839) at pages 67–68; and again, more specifically in *Civil Liberty and Self-Government* (1853) pages 211–12.

SELECTED BIBLIOGRAPHY

Beal, Edward: 1896, *Cardinal Rules of Legal Interpretation*, Stevens & Sons Ltd., London.

Betti, Emilio: 1948, *Le Categories Civilistiche Dell' Interpretazione*, Dott, A. Giuffre, Milano.

Britto, Antonio R. C.: 1927, *Systema de Hermeneutica Juridica*, Livraria Francisco Alves, Rio de Janeiro.

Bübner, Rudiger, Cramer, Konrad, Wieh, Rainer (eds.): 1970, *Hermeneutik und Dialektik*, J. C. B. Mohr (Paul Siebeck), Tübingen.

Bübner, Rudiger: 1976, 'Is Transcendental Hermeneutics Possible?' in: J. Manninen and R. Tuomela (eds.), *Essays in Explanation and Understanding*, D. Reidel, Dordrecht, pp. 59–77.

Campbell, John: 1980, 'Locke on Qualities,' *Canadian Journal of Philosophy* **X**, 4, 567–586.

Cohen, Morris R.: 1954, 'Legal Thought,' Ch. VI in: *American Thought: A Critical Sketch*, The Free Press, Glencoe, Ill., pp. 135–180.

Dewey, John: 1938, *Logic. The Theory of Inquiry*, Holt, Rinehart & Winston, New York.

Dietze, Gottfried: 1964, 'The Limited Rationality of Law,' in: W. Friedrich (ed.), *Rational Decision*, Atherton Press, New York, pp. 63–88.

Fisch, Max H.: 1983, Introduction to Volume Three, New Edition, *The Writings of Charles S. Peirce*, manuscript.

Fisch, Max H.: 1964, 'Was There a Metaphysical Club in Cambridge?' in: E. C. Moore and R. S. Robin (eds.), *Studies in the Philosophy of Charles S. Peirce*, University of Massachusetts Press, Amherst, pp. 3–32.

Fisch, Max H.: 1942, 'Justice Holmes, the Prediction Theory of Law, and Pragmatism,' *Journal of Philosophy* 39, 12, 85–97.

Folsom, Gwendolyn B.: 1972, *Legislative History: Research for the Interpretation of Laws*, University Press of Virginia, Charlottesville.

Frank, Jerome: (1930) 1967, *Law and the Modern Mind*, Doubleday & Co., New York.

Gény, Francois: (1899, 1954) 1963, *Methode d'interpretation et sources en droit prive positif* (Paris), Engl. Transl. J. Mayda, St. Paul, Minn.

Gilmore, Grant: 1977, *The Ages of American Law*, Yale University Press, New Haven.

Grimke, Frederick: (1848) 1968, *The Nature and Tendency of Free Institutions*, J. Ward (ed.), The Belknap Press, Harvard University Press, Cambridge, Mass.

Holmes, Oliver Wendell: (1881) 1963, *The Common Law*, M. D. Howe (ed.), Little, Brown Co., Boston.

Holmes, Oliver Wendell: 1952, *Collected Legal Papers*, New York University Press, New York.

Horovitz, Joseph: 1972, *Law and Logic*, Springer Verlag, Wien and New York.

Howe, Mark De W.: 1957, *Justice Holmes: The Shaping Years 1841–1870*, Vol. 1, Belknap Press, Harvard University Press, Cambridge, Mass.

Kahneman, D., Lovic, Paul, Twersky, Amos (eds.): 1982, *Judgment under Uncertainty: Heuristics and Biases*, Cambridge University Press, Cambridge and London (especially 'Variants of Uncertainty,' 509–520).

Kant, Immanuel: (1781) 1956, *Critique of Pure Reason*, transl. M. Muller, Doubleday Anchor, New York.

Kant, Immanuel: (1788) 1958, *Critique of Practical Reason*, transl. L. B. Beck, Bobbs-Merrill Co., Indianapolis.

Ketner, K. L. and Cook, J. E. (eds.): 1975, 1978, 1979, *Charles Sanders Peirce: Contributions to The Nation*, Parts One, Two, Three, 1869–1908, Institute for Studies in Pragmaticism, Lubbock.

Kevelson, Roberta: 1977, *Inlaws/Outlaws: A Semiotics of Legal Systems*, Center for Language and Semiotic Studies with the Peter de Rider Press, Bloomington.

Kevelson, Roberta: 1981a, 'Semiotics and Structures of Law,' *Semiotica* **31**, 1/2, 183–192.

Kevelson, Roberta: 1981b, 'Semiotics and Law,' in: *Encyclopedic Dictionary of Law*, R. Sebeok and J. Umiker-Sebeok (eds.), DeGruyter, in press.

Kevelson, Roberta: 1981c, 'Peirce as Catalyst in Modern Legal Science,' *Semiotics* **80**, J. Deely and M. Lenhart (eds.), Plenum, New York.

Kevelson, Roberta: 1982a, 'Francis Lieber and the Semiotics of Law and Politics,' in *Semiotics 81*, J. Deely and M. Lenhart (eds.), Plenum, New York, in press.

Kevelson, Roberta: 1982b, 'Comparative Legal Cultures and Semiotics: An Introduction,' *American Journal of Semiotics* **I**, 4, 63–84.

Kevelson, Roberta: 1983, *Charles S. Peirce's Method of Methods*, to appear in 1985.

Kretzman, Norman: 1982, *Infinity and Continuity in Ancient and Medieval Thought*, Cornell University Press, Ithaca.

Laski, Harold: (1919) 1968, *Authority in the Modern State*, Archon Books, Cambridge Mass.

Lieber, Francis: (1839) 1963, *Legal and Political Hermeneutics*, Hammond Edition, Press of G. I. Jones & Co., St. Louis, originally published by Little, Brown, Boston.

Lieber, Francis: (1839) 1911, *Manual of Political Ethics*, Vols. I–II, 2nd ed., T. D. Woolsey (ed.), J. B. Lippincott Co., Philadelphia and London.

Lieber, Francis: 1853, *On Civil Liberty and Self-Government*, J. B. Lippincott and Co., Philadelphia.

Lieber, Francis: Special Collections of Lieber mss. housed in The Huntington Library (San Marino) and Library of Congress (Washington, D. C.).

Merryman, John Henry: 1969, *The Civil Law Tradition*, Stanford University Press, California.

Nelson, William E.: 1975, *Americanization of the Common Law: The Impact of Legal Change on Massachusetts Society 1760–1830*, Harvard University Press, Cambridge, Mass.

Nisbet, Robert: 1975, *Twilight of Authority*, Oxford University Press, New York.

Peirce, Charles S.: 1869–1908, *Charles Sanders Peirce: Contributions to the Nation*, three volumes, K. L. Ketner *et al.* (eds.), Center for Studies in Pragmaticism, Lubbock (N).

Peirce, Charles S.: 1931–35, 1958, *Collected Papers*, 8 volumes, P. Weiss, C. Hartshorne, A. Burks (eds.), Harvard University Press, Cambridge (CP).

Peirce, Charles S.: 1982, *Writings of Charles S. Peirce*, Vol. I, 1857–1866, Max Fisch (General Editor), Indiana Press, Bloomington.

Peirce, Charles S.: 1849–1914, Microfilm Collection, 30 reels of Peirce mss., with Richard Robin's *Annotated Catalogue of the Papers of Charles S. Peirce* (1967), University of Massachusetts Press (MS).

Pound, Roscoe: (1922) 1956, *An Introduction to the Philosophy of Law*, Yale University Press, New Haven.

Plucknett, Theodore, F. T.: 1922, *Statutes and their Interpretation in the First Half of the Fourteenth Century*, Pref. H. D. Hazeltine, Cambridge University Press, Cambridge.

Presser, Stephen B. and J. S. Zainaldin: 1980, *Law and American History: Cases and Materials*, West Publishing Co., St. Paul.

Reichenbach, Hans: 1947, *Elements of Symbolic Logic*, Macmillan Co., Toronto and New York (especially pages 336–444).

Ross, Robert E.: 1912, *The Laws of Discovery*, Butterworth & Co., London and A. C. Forster Boulton, Toronto.

von Savigny, Friedrich Carl: 1867, *System of the Modern Roman Law*, Vol. I, trans. Wm. Holloway, Hyperion Press, Inc., Westport, Conn. (especially Ch. IV, 'Interpretation of Written Laws,' 166–268).

Summers, Robert S.: 1982, *Instrumentalism and American Legal Theory*, Cornell University Press, Ithaca.

Tedeschi, G.: 1967, 'Insufficiency of the Legal Norm and Loyalty of the 'Interpreter,'' in: *Proceedings of the Israel Academy of Sciences and Humanities* 1, 3, 1–19.

Tsune-chi Yu: 1927, *The Interpretation of Treaties*, Columbia University Press, New York.

Vaihinger, Hans: (1924) 1966, *The Philosophy of 'As If'*, transl. C. K. Ogden, Barnes and Noble Inc., New York (especially Ch. VIII on 'heuristic fictions,' 39–42).

Whewell, William: 1845, *Elements of Morality*, Vols. I–II, Harper & Bros., New York (especially Vol. II, Book V, on Politics, Authority, Facts, and Social Contract, 181–382).

HANNU TAPANI KLAMI

LEGAL PHILOSOPHY IN FINLAND

Trends in Past and Present

I

Legal philosophy reflects the relationship between *law and society* at each particular time.[1] It is also a kind of response to trends in general scientific discussion. But legal philosophy should not be seen as *determined* by society as a whole or by its scientific superstructure. For example, it is not always so that obsolete law inevitably creates an attitude alien to legal positivism. Moreover, even if lawyers often are concerned about the scientific nature of their profession, they do not always blindly adopt patterns of scientific activity, that is, models developed for other sciences. Nevertheless we cannot understand the development of legal philosophy in a certain country without taking its social and scientific background into consideration.

The main problem of legal philosophy is the allegedly *autonomous nature of law.*[2] Law is a dualistic phenomenon. It consists of norms and behaviour, which reflect each other. Law-making *is* behaviour (of legislators, courts, and so on), but law is a *model* of behaviour as well. On the other hand, legal norms are used when human behaviour is interpreted. It is asked whether this or that action is legal or illegal. Norms are concretized by these acts of interpretation.

It is characteristic of legal positivism that norms are justified by *authoritative arguments* referring to the behaviour of authorities or power organs: legislators, courts, even professors of law. But, *vice versa*, behaviour is justified by legal norms. Adherence to legal norms is considered a sufficient or at least a necessary condition for the justifiability of behaviour. But it is not clear that the above-sketched idea of the autonomous justification of law – a justification "from within" by its own elements, as it were – is sufficient. It is in my opinion necessary to take the *social impact* of norms and behaviour into consideration and evaluate its role. What is then required is that law is justified by a *teleological* rationality. This I propose to call the *finalistic* approach.

The dialectic between norm-rationality and goal-rationality is an ever-present problem in law-making. This dialectic is also reflected in different legal philosophies. Whereas in "pure" legal positivism the role of evaluations

E. Bulygin et al. (eds.), Man, Law and Modern Forms of Life, 137–159.

is rather residual, extreme finalism tries to reduce the problem of the relevance of norms and authoritative arguments to a problem of evaluations only. There are several intermediate positions between these extremes; it should perhaps be added that I am personally inclined to adopt a *broadly* understood finalistic way of thinking.[3]

II [4]

Finland had been a part of Sweden for seven centuries when it was conquered by Russia in the war of 1808–1809. But Tsar Alexander I adopted in Finland the role of a parliamentary monarch, similar to that of the King of Sweden. Finland was given an "autonomous" position: Swedish laws were to remain in force unless they were changed in due course, a procedure which involved the cooperation of the monarch – in Finland called the Grand Duke – and the Finnish Diet consisting of four Estates.

The Swedish legislation was relatively modern. The Code of the year 1734 was based upon a reception of Roman Law, even if the code was written in a very simple and popular fashion. The sources-of-law doctrine had become entirely "nationalized". Roman Law and foreign doctrine were rarely used. The protagonist of Finnish legal science was Professor Matthias Calonius (1737–1817).[5] He was an adherent of legal positivism, even if there were in his writings numerous attempts at justifying valid law by arguments of Natural Law theory. He was not interested in legal philosophy: his main scholarly achievements pertain to legal history and methodology.

Until his last years Calonius remained the sole representative of academic legal learning in Finland. The Faculty of Law of the Academy of Turku consisted of his professorial chair only.[6] But as time went on, legal science slowly began to expand its position. The successors of Calonius – such as W. G. Lagus (1786–1859), J. J. Nordström (1801–1874) and K. E. Ekelund (1791–1843) – were mainly interested in legal history. This is not to say that they would have been particularly influenced by the Historical School. Their interest in legal history was rather an expression of Scandinavian Romanticism. The memories of the lost union with Sweden were still cherished. On the other hand, there were also practical reasons for the historical interpretation of law. The Finnish Diet was not convoked until 1863. The Code of the year 1734 remained in force. Historical analysis would perhaps have revealed the possibilities of a dynamic interpretation of law, typical of the Historical School. But this line of inquiry was not followed.

Until the end of the nineteenth century interest in matters of legal philosophy remained relatively slight. It soon became fashionable to quote phrases from Hegelian philosophical jargon. J. J. Nordström became acquainted with Hegelian thinking at his mature scholar age. Although he thereafter made use of Hegelian slogans, his historical method was not much affected by Hegelian philosophy. To take another example: the *Treatise on Law* by J. Ph. Palmén (1811–1896) begins with a methodological introduction [7] which is completely eclectic. There are some Hegelian features in it, but Palmén declares human reason to be the ultimate source of law. Even if he apparently was not directly influenced by the Exegetic school, his attitude toward Natural Law much resembles French legal positivism. Natural Law was a kind of *ultima ratio* – as a justification of valid law it was a *deus ex machina*.

Palmén dominated the Finnish legal science of his time. His response to the stagnation of legislative activities was straightforward: he advocated a strict, grammatical adherence to the Code of the year 1734. To understand the Code in a correct manner, studies of legal history were needed. The reasons for adopting this kind of methodology were mainly political. The Russians had refused to convoke the Finnish Diet. Instead, there were attempts at changing Finnish legislation by cooperation between the Finnish bureaucratic élite and the Russians. Palmén had himself participated in an attempt to thwart back a Russian "codification plan" which the imperial authorities had intended to accomplish without the consent of the Diet. The political course of Finnish lawyers soon became clear: domestic legislation, even an obsolete one, was better than reforms dictated by the Russians. Palmén remained a stern legalist even after becoming a leading member of the bureaucratic élite. It was thought that law and legality were the most important political weapons of a small people.

Philosophical problems were more or less ignored. There was in Finland, however, an insightful Hegelian philosopher, J. V. Snellman (1806–1881), who also became one of the central ideological spokesmen of the emerging Finnish national consciousness. Snellman was a nationalist; for him the economic, cultural and political position of the Finnish-speaking majority of the people was a decisive matter. As a Hegelian he belonged to the "moderate left wing": he was inclined to regard the present state of development as optimal, but this rationality was not tantamount to the maintenance of the *status quo*. Snellman also wrote extensively on legal philosophy, but in spite of his great political eminence he won only a few followers among the lawyers. Mention should be made of Robert Lagus (1827–1863). He earnestly sought to employ the Hegelian holistic method: his attempts resemble modern structural explanations.[8] But he died rather young and created no school.

Slowly but surely legal philosophy began to become an integral part of legal thinking. However, for some time to come the philosophical culture of Finnish lawyers remained rather superficial. This was the situation when the disciples of Palmén started adopting the doctrines of the German "jurisprudence of concepts" (*Begriffsjurisprudenz*). An interesting thing is that one of them, R. A. Montgomery (1821–1890), began his *scholarly* activities soon after the revival of Finnish *legislative* activities in 1863. But the pace of legislative reforms remained rather slow. Law was also – to a certain extent – developed through *judicial practice* and *scientific construction*. The publication of *precedents* began.[9] The creative aspect of the "conceptual" school was rather pronounced in Finland. However, at the same time *teleological* considerations were banished from legal science. In the beginning they were ignored, in the first place. Later on, R. F. Hermanson (1846–1928) made a sharp distinction between *legal philosophy* – which involved the teleological justification of law – and *legal science* where *quasi-causal relationships* between legal facts and their legal consequences are treated.[10] It is easy to see that this conception is influenced by such German authors as Wundt and Zitelmann: a positivistic model of science was applied in law. Hermanson was the founder of Finnish public law research – but even if he clearly represented the contemporaneous *legal positivism*, he could not solve the problem of legal validity without resorting to God. Legal order also had to be a divine order. (Only in very exceptional circumstances was this quality denied to present law.)

Modern trends of the nineteenth century in scientific thought – such as Darwinism and positivism – did not much affect Finnish legal science. Toward the end of the century Finnish legal science became more and more involved in the Finnish fight to uphold the law and lawfulness. Finnish legal science was well equipped in view of resisting the Russian attempts to abolish the autonomous legislation of Finland.

In private law the systematics and also important principles of the German *Begriffsjurisprudenz* were adopted.[11] The *systematic argument* played an important part in legal reasoning, even if the system in question was no longer a universally-valid structural pattern of legal thinking but rather a system of *present* law. In spite of this "nationalization" of systematical thinking, German patterns were followed. They were in fact not so very alien to Finnish law: the Code of the year 1734 relied heavily upon Pandect law. One could discuss the problems of subjective vs. objective interpretation of law;

but irrespective of the position adopted, a large part of legislation was so obsolete that it was totally impossible to pay attention to the intentions of its originators – assumed that these in principle could be revealed by means of historical analysis. Hence the interpretation practice mostly followed an "objective" course, here and there supplemented with historical and/or comparative aspects.

Judicial practice did not much contribute to legal regulation. Legal decisions were extremely laconically formulated, as they still tend to be even today, and only in some cases attempts were made at formulating an abstract *ratio decidendi*. It took a relatively long time for jurist's law to be recognized as a source of binding customary law. In Finland the tendency was rather to stress the immediate relevance of the people's legal consciousness. This was in a way understandable. The Finnish Supreme Court was not an independent tribunal but a Department of the Senate: its members were nominated by the Tsar, who could also dismiss them. It was considered dangerous to recognize the abstract law-making powers of an organ which could any time become Russianized.

The methodological choices in Finnish public law were largely guided by more or less conscious *political considerations*. The political problem was the autonomy of Finland. There were in Russia more or less chauvinistic tendencies which considered the autonomous status of Finland as inexpedient, even humiliating to the Russian Empire. It was at the juristic level that the Finns gave their retort: Finland was a State, a juridical person. The juridical constructions of Gerber, Laband and other scholars concerning the German *Reich* provided a clear background here. The Russian counter-argument ran along similar lines of thought: sovereignty was a matter of the Empire, not of its provinces. Sovereignty, as the Russians claimed, was indivisible and unquestionable. Therefore the self-imposed limitations of Russian sovereignty, as far as Finland was concerned, could at any time be removed.

It is not particularly interesting – at least not from a philosophical point of view – to follow the scientific and political discussion between Finnish and Russian lawyers towards the end of the nineteenth and the beginning of the twentieth century. But the impact of this situation upon Finnish legal philosophy was clear: the Finns could not themselves afford to be legal *realists*. Until the end of World War I the Finnish situation at times resembled the aftermath of a successful *coup d'ètat*. To be a realist would then have been equivalent to admitting that the privileged position of Finland in the Russian Empire had ceased to exist – the validity of constitutions presupposes at least some political realities.

In short, the development of Finnish legal philosophy at that time was clearly delayed by external conditions. The main line of thought was a stern *conceptual normativism*: no room was left for considerations of interests or empirical viewpoints. Paradoxically enough, at the same time the Finnish sociologist and philosopher Edward Westermarck (1862–1939) was laying down the sociological foundations of an analysis of human morality, publishing most of his work abroad.

There were only certain exceptions to the general trend. F. O. Lilius (1862–1934) criticized the defects of *Begriffsjurisprudenz*. Even if his arguments clearly resembled those of von Ihering, neither he nor any other notable Finnish legal scientist can be labelled a herald of *Interessenjurisprudenz.*[12] On ther other hand, there were several good legal historians. Mention should be made here of J. K. Paasikivi (1870–1956), who after World War II became the President of the Finnish Republic and the founder of our "new" foreign policy. Profound historical analysis had taught him that Finno-Russian relations are by their nature strategic and political, not legal questions.

There were no chairs for legal philosophy. When this subject was apportioned to the chair of a recently appointed professor, F. W. Ekström (1871–1920), an unusual combination was created: legal encyclopedics plus Roman and international private law. Nor were any significant treatises on legal theory published. The *Naturrecht* of H. Ahrens was used almost until the end of the nineteenth century. It was replaced by the introductory chapters of the Private Law treatises of Montgomery and Ekström. This is a fairly good overall description of the whole situation. Every scholar was expected to know something about legal philosophy, but it was considered that a kind of preliminary, encyclopedic knowledge was enough for scholarly purposes.

III[13]

When Finland became independent during World War I, the Russian problem seemed to vanish: over several decades it had given an extra colouring to any political or legal problem. But legalistic thinking as such did not disappear. On the contrary: when Finland proclaimed herself independent, this was not considered a revolutionary act but rather a necessary juridical step occasioned by the fact that the Romanovs had abdicated. Consequently, it was deemed that a new King should be elected. (The German Prince sought up for this purpose did not come to Finland because of the collapse of the German

Empire, and Finland became a republic after all.) In independent Finland, legalism became a method for consolidating the social *status quo*.

But it soon became apparent that Finland's independence had not much affected matters. The problem of the attitudes to and relations with Russia – now a Soviet state – still existed. Also the far-reaching ignorance in matters of legal philosophy continued to exert its influence. A rather blind legalism was followed, unfortunately in political questions as well.

Only very slowly did new trends begin to be noticed by the Finns. This revival of interest was in my opinion partly due to the interaction with the Scandinavian countries, even if Swedish-Finnish relations were for a long time hampered by the embarrassing struggle between the Finnish and Swedish lingual interest groups in Finland.

Professor Elieser Kaila (1885–1938) was the first Finnish "professional" legal philosopher.[14] He wrote a doctoral dissertation on "legal logic" in 1924. In this he tried to develop a kind of "volitional logic", based on German inspirations. The fact that a modern reader may find the book rather uninteresting is partly due to Kaila's unhappy terminological innovations. There was admittedly no established terminology of legal philosophy in Finnish scientific language; but creating this far exceeded the limits of Kaila's talent.

In the 1930's there were already certain signs of a breakthrough of new ideas. I would say that at the scientific level this was due to the impact of *logical empiricism*. But what about the *social* aspect of the phenomenon?

The direct influence of Axel Hägerström and *early* Scandinavian realism was insignificant. It was not until after World War II that the thought of Alf Ross became widely known in Finland. It should be noticed that Ross has really been the only protagonist of Scandinavian realism who has been widely read in Finland. Only a handful of specialists have become acquainted with Hägerström. Vilhelm Lundstedt's reflections have been practically ignored by Finnish private law specialists. Karl Olivecrona has been somewhat better known.[15]

This situation is rather surprising because the cooperation and intercourse with Scandinavian countries was of considerable importance for the renewal of legal philosophy in Finland. The fact was that in Sweden, Norway and Denmark legislation had been used for important *social reforms*. It had become a commonplace there to say that legislation gave an expression to conflicting *interests*. Legal science had taken on the task of examining and discussing these interests. The method for this it had learned from the German "genetic" or "productive" *Interessenjurisprudenz* and also from "legislator" of the country, whose powers were often held by Social Democrats.

The traditional function of law is to *solve conflicts between individuals.*[16] Legal norms have of old been used to *legitimate structures of social power.* But if law is used as an *instrument for intentional social "engineering"*, the ideologies and the methods pertaining to the old functions of law soon prove inadequate. Quasi-impartial normative legalism is at least to some degree unable to cope with the new problems of law-making. In Finland the social aspect of legal science was recognized somewhat later that in other Scandinavian countries. The approach of *Interessenjurisprudenz* was never adopted; it should be borne in mind that social and political development in Finland was somewhat slower than that in Sweden, Norway and Denmark. In Finland there had been a civil war in 1917–1918: the political left was defeated and was to remain almost isolated for nearly twenty years. The pace of social legislation was slower than in Scandinavia: the conceptual circles of the learned lawyers were not disturbed by any pressure towards reforms.

In the 1930's, several lawyers however realized that a methodological change was bound to come. Already in 1929 Viljo Sainio had committed himself to Scandinavian realism in a dissertation on environmental law. There were some Swedish-speaking lawyers who apparently were familiar with the ideas of their Swedish colleagues (Erik af Hällström, i.a.). But the beginning of the new era is particularly marked by two names, Otto Brusiin (1906–1973) and Paavo Kastari (1907–), even if their approaches to these problems were somewhat different. Brusiin was a legal philosopher *par excellence*, whereas the purely theoretical part in Kastari's work has remained relatively modest. Kastari has, however, exerted a great influence upon Finnish Constitutional law through his own writings and by raising a whole generation of empirically oriented scholars of public law.

With the growth of the scholarly achievements of Finnish legal philosophy, it becomes impossible to give an overall survey of the thinking of all relevant writers. A brief outline of the general development may suffice here. Certain admittedly original thinkers will be omitted. For instance, I shall largely leave aside Finnish Kelsenians. Kelsen's Pure Theory of Law has exerted a considerable influence upon Finnish legal science. But this influence has been more or less indirect: several scholars were "compelled" to discuss Kelsen's thoughts (no legal philosopher of our century can ignore them), but his views were not so much adopted. This may in large part be due to the fact that Kelsen's Pure Theory of Law is the culmination of the mighty *Rechtsstaat* tradition in which the role of law is mainly *static*. Kelsen's theory became known in Finland in the late 1930's. A significant point is that Paavo Kastari, who was the first one to introduce Kelsen's ideas to the Finnish audience, in fact sought to integrate legal science with sociological and politological approaches rather than to adopt the idea of an autonomous legal science advocated by Kelsen.[17] There has been only one notable Kelsenian philosopher of law in Finland: B. C. Carlson (1890–1966). This district-court judge, who eventually became an honorary LL. D., was even more orthodox than Kelsen. He claimed that Kelsen's normativism was not pure enough.[18]

Otto Brusiin was the first internationally renowned Finnish legal philosopher.[19] It is somewhat difficult to briefly characterize him as a thinker – even for me, one of his last disciples.[20] Brusiin had read immensely, absorbing everything through his versatile and "multidimensional" mind. He had a notable mathematical and musical talent as well. He did not create any school around him. He understood that legal philosophy has many different aspects. He himself used to emphasize the trichotomy of logical, sociological and axiological approaches to legal theory. His own approach was that of a legal sociologist. But for him legal sociology was not a mere observational study of legal behaviour in society. It included into itself the history of legal culture, comparative law, in the last instance all aspects of humanity.

Brusiin's methodological programme is already apparent in his doctoral dissertation on the discretion of the judge in gap situations (1938, in Finnish). He stressed the social aspect of the judge's behaviour: the judge neither could nor should ignore his *cognitive* and *evaluative* cultural background. But how should all these elements be methodically controlled? Brusiin's answer reveals the influence of François Gény and his "libre recherche scientifique" as the method of law-finding. The rules of law-finding cannot be established in advance, but law-finding is not a process of free creation either.

I have got the impression that international audiences usually label Brusiin as an exponent of Scandinavian realism.[21] To my mind this is an oversimplification. Brusiin was deeply interested in the complex interconnections between the various "elements" or "levels" of the human mind. His approach was here influenced by Edmund Husserl and Max Scheler as well. To Brusiin it would have been completely inadequate to think that the impression of validity in the human mind was due to a false myth or that legal obligations could be traced back to the magic of the Roman *fides*. The iconoclastic idiosyncrasy of a Hägerström, Lundstedt or even a Ross was no inspiration to him.

Brusiin's scholarly achievements were interrupted by World War II and by a short-lived political engagement in the late-1940's turmoil circumstances as the chief of the Security Police. The antipathy and discrimination toward Brusiin and his work in Finnish academic circles over the following years can be seen partly as an unhappy consequence of his political engagement. In any case, Brusiin soon disengaged himself from every kind of political activity. In his *Über die Objektivität der Rechtssprechung* (1949) and *Über das juristische Denken* (1951) he developed the central themes of his doctoral dissertation further.[22] But he soon also became interested in problems of comparative law, which for him was closely bound up with legal sociology and legal theory. Legal phenomena were to be studied *irrespective of time and place*: this could aptly be called a *general, universal theory of law*. Such was his programme in *Zur Ehescheidungsproblem* (1959) and *Zum Problem des immateriellen Schadens* (1963).

After World War II a great methodological breakthrough of *logical empiricism* took place in Finnish legal science. In Finland this resulted in the emergence of the *analytical school* which took a lively interest in the logical analysis of legal language. This sort of analyticism of course has not much in common with Jeremy Bentham and John Austin.

The doctrinal background of the Finnish analytical school was the logical empiricism represented in Finland by Eino Kaila (1890–1958), and it soon also acquired inspirations from the analytical philosophy of ordinary language represented in Finland first of all by Georg Henrik von Wright (1916–). The empiricist tradition had slowly but surely acquired a firm standing in the behavioral and social sciences in Finland. In the post-war situation its influence was strengthened by a brisk American empiricism in the social sciences. The U.S. replaced Germany as the country of supreme scientific authority. The problem of the social factors in the background of the analytical school is far more complicated. We shall return to it; to begin with, it should be noticed that Finnish statutory law at that time was developing at a rapid pace. The pressure that the involved social forces exerted on the established systematics and principles of (the jurist's) law was growing. In private law there was a need for more clearly argued and articulated decisions. This was now more important than the creation and establishment of new regulations by means of legal systematics and construction. The *Begriffsjurisprudenz* had established and manifested itself in Finnish legal practice and to some extent in legislation as well (a major part of the legislation in independent Finland was based upon its systematic background).

Construction had in earlier days been a method of legal *dynamics.*[23] Now it had turned into a *conservative*, even reactionary element. An often effective way of shaking up established judicial practice is to question or even "prove" false its methodological background assumptions. This was something that the Finnish analytical school now set about to do as well.

Logical empiricism provided the methodological tools for this task. But there was one crucial problem (which even today permeates the situation in Finnish legal science): the lack of empirical knowledge. In short, there was (and still is) no powerful tradition of Finnish sociology of law. It was thus understandable that the Finnish analytical school became *logically* rather than empirically oriented. In this respect there was a profound difference from the thinking of Brusiin. This was the more remarkable, because Brusiin was always very sympathetic towards the analytical school which he considered to be progressive. He even tutored a number of analytically-minded younger colleagues, even though in the beginning of the 1950's he had himself not managed to climb higher on the academic ladder than the post of docent.

Simo Zitting (1915–) presented his doctoral dissertation on the transfer of ownership (in Finnish) in 1951. This comprehensive work (Finnish dissertations correspond to German *Habilitationsschriften*) has remained his *magnum opus* even if he afterwards has written extensively on various topics.[24] His starting-point was similar to the viewpoints of the Scandinavian realists Östen Unden and Alf Ross. Zitting maintained that the concept of ownership had no extensional counterpart in reality. It was a *syntactic expression for certain legal relations*. Therefore it was impossible to speak about such things as "transfer of ownership". The legal position of the so-called owner was subject to change: but this change *depended solely on the content of the applicable legal norms*, not on the alleged "essence" of the concept of ownership. But Zitting's purpose was not only to criticize the "material" concept of ownership based ultimately upon the Natural Law tradition. He also tried to *resystematize* the norms concerning ownership. The starting point was the legally protected right of the owner to use the object. This corresponded to the concepts "claim" and "privilege" in the scheme of Hohfeld. But beside the right of *conduct* there was a *competence* granted by law (to sell, to pledge, and so on). This recalls the Hohfeldian concepts of power and immunity. Zitting pointed out that it was possible to speak of a *static* and a *dynamic* protection of the owner.[25]

It was relatively easy to criticize the methodological policies of the *Begriffsjurisprudenz* by pointing out that their manifestations in Finnish legal science were not based upon legal norms. They were in fact often adopted from German law and doctrine. Moreover, several of the concepts employed had no straightforward empirical reference. This seemed to call for a logical analysis of the legal discourse in order to *improve* legal language (and the decision involved).

The analytical school soon gained a firm standing and became dominant in many branches of law (with the exception of criminal law and procedural law). There was no viable alternative school of legal philosophy, because the situation up to that time had been rather impervious to philosophy. Differences of opinion naturally turned up between analyticists and more traditionally oriented scholars; sometimes the gravity of differences also gave rise to short-sighted and even intolerant attitudes of the analytical school. However, the most important question is the contribution of the analytical school to *problems of legal reasoning*.

The main issue at stake is the standpoint taken by the analytical school in questions of *argumentation*. Was the analytical school a variant of legal positivism? Or was it something else? It should be noticed that the links between logico-philosophical positivism and legal positivism are notoriously complicated. Legal positivism is an attitude toward the problems of *justification of law*. In this sense, even Roman lawyers were legal positivists although they were certainly not "positivists" or "empiricists" in the philosophical sense.[26] On the other hand, positivistic models of justification can be used for different, even contradictory patterns of legal methodology. It can be argued that because values are not cognizable, legal science should itself refrain from presenting evaluative statements and restrict itself to study either legal *rules* or legal *behaviour* as they actually appear (or, rather, *legal rules as understood in legal behaviour*). A standpoint opposite to this would be: Let us study the *actual social impact of law*. But even if we cannot probably reach unanimity in axiological questions, we should be content with a *systematically relativized evaluation* of the social impact of law.

It is clear that the Finnish analytical school indeed sought to modernize juristic argumentation. Its aim was to show that many currently used types of argument were mostly delusive. Arguments pertaining to man-made legal constructions were to be replaced by a *realistic weighting* of the different pro's and con's. *Analysis as such would give no answers to legal problems.* The answers depended on law and (acceptable) argumentation. The main task of theoretical analysis was therefore to reveal the true nature of the argumentation problems involved. At this stage the legal scientist would take off his cloak of objectivity. He would then say: "This-and-this problem is a question of legal policy – it involves evaluations. Now I am not speaking as an analyst but rather as a citizen with a certain professional knowledge (and ideology). Let us now weigh up the arguments. Let us make the decision". This is a free interpretation of the methodology used and advocated by Aulis Aarnio (1937–) in his doctoral dissertation on the legal position of the heir (1968, in Finnish). But Aarnio soon realized the additional problems involved. The main question of course is that *empirical knowledge* is required in order to weigh up arguments of legal policy. It is not enough to speak about *values. The thing to be evaluated is the real or conceivable social impact of different decision alternatives.*

This was the insurmountable problem faced by the Finnish analytical school. The available empirical knowledge largely consisted of commonsense conjectures – which more often than not were completely misleading. But it was not only Aarnio who faced this problem. It had become evident to every representative of the analytical school; but only in the late 1960's there began to appear criticisms of the (alleged) social *laissez-faire* attitude of the analytical school. This critique (Antero Jyränki, Antti Kivivuori, Hannu Tapani Klami, Juha Tolonen, to mention only the most representative names[27]) probably contributed to the change in Aarnio's position. This was the more remarkable as Aarnio was commonly considered the most brilliant protagonist of the analytical school.

But what had happened to the analytical school in the meantime? It should be observed that its critique of the conceptual legalism prevalent in Finnish judicial practice and legal science was not as profound as it may have seen at first sight. If one was able to abolish certain types of arguments but unable to present new and more plausible ones, progress could not be expected to be very dramatic. At this point, the methodological programme of empiricism contributed a peculiar feature by way of its emphasis on *observational* knowledge. It was easy to say that the thing to be observed was *legal language* (or, if the thesis of Ross[28] about legal theory as metascience was adopted, the language of legal science). The *facts* of observational knowledge in this sort of empiricism dealt with the factual use of legal language – not only in legislation but also in *judicial practice*. The observation of judicial practice was thus the empirical foundation of legal science. Judicial practice was an acceptable fact whereas the facts presented by empirical studies concerning the social impact of law were either entirely absent or at the most speculatively established.

In this manner the analytical school remained a "paradigm articulation" of legal positivism, as Aulis Aarnio has expressed it.[29] A new paradigm was not created. However, it would be futile to lay the blame for this on Finnish legal sociologists' neglect to work out the empirical foundations needed to transform the paradigm of legal positivism into, say, a finalistic one. There have been many extremely powerful representatives of a sociological legal theory in Finland. We have already mentioned Brusiin. Another important scholar was Osvi Lahtinen (1908–1966).[30] He was a Member of the Finnish Supreme Court. He published in 1950 a splendid dissertation on the foundations of legal theory (in German). He began in the footsteps of Theodor Geiger's functional theory of legal validity; but as years passed by, he became more and more interested in the problems of everyday language and in Wittgenstein's later philosophy. His last publication, the extremely lucid essay 'Von konstruierten Denkschemas und von der Sprache' appeared in a volume dedicated to Otto Brusiin on his 60th anniversary, *Ius humanum* (1966). There he analysed the ability of the human mind to create new schemes of thought. This constituted a clear critique of the extreme form of empiricism.

Empirical studies on law in society have not been *totally* non-existent in Finland, either. In criminology Inkeri Anttila (1916–) has made a notable career.[31] However, comprehensive general expositions of sociology of law in Finland are still lacking, and the first academic textbook of this discipline, by Finnish authors, has appeared only very recently. Generally speaking there has not been much material for empirical legal argumentation either. As I have said, the "empiricism" of the Finnish analytical school mainly consisted of "observing" legal language. This has resulted in what I would call "*case-positivism*".[32] Judicial practice is considered to be the factual basis of legal science. Such a legal science is doomed to more or less remain at a *descriptive* level. It will tell us how cases have been solved. However, I do not wish to blame the legal philosophical starting points of the analytical school for this triviality. A similar development has in my opinion taken place in Swedish legal science where the realistic element of legal science is more pronounced.

IV

The present situation in Finnish legal philosophy can be understood as a kind of reaction against the *reluctance of the analytical school* to *discuss arguments* (at least earnestly). The present Finnish legal theory takes a wide interest in argumentation theory, and this is not only a reflection of current international trends. On the other hand it is claimed that the analytical school has ignored the social impact of law, as legal positivism in general seems to have done also elsewhere. The interdependence of law and society, however, has been examined from other viewpoints. There is in Finland a rather heterogenous "school" of talented Marxist legal philosophers such as Eero Backman (1945–) and Lars D. Eriksson (1938–).

The number of legal philosophers in Finland is not particularly great – the country is small and there are only three law faculties[33] – but there are several different traditions and tendencies represented among these few scholars. This many-sidedness makes it impossible to give here a detailed account of present-day Finnish legal philosophy. But I will try to depict the general background, show some common features, and give a sketchy analysis of the different tendencies.

Brusiin was already in his fifties when he at last became a full professor in the new Law Faculty at the University of Turku. There he mostly studied the history of legal studies in Finland. To his pupils he stressed that every young scholar should choose the philosophical outlook that best corresponded to his mind and research interests; on the other hand, as a result of his influence, a strong interest in the relevance of legal history for present-day problems developed. Today one can say that the Faculty of Law at the University of Turku consists in large part of legal-historically oriented scholars representing different disciplines within the science of law. I shall only mention Eero Backman, Lars Björne, Antero Jyränki, Martti Kairinen, Heikki Kulla and Jukka Urpo.[34]

Another noteworthy feature is the interest shown in *legal systematics*. Even if Brusiin tended to stress the social dimension of legal thinking, he also emphazised that it was legal systematics that provides us with relatively independent doctrinary explanations of law and the activities of lawyers. The interest in such questions is manifested in several monographs both in Helsinki and in Turku. Erkki Aurejärvi has studied the contract of tender; Martti Kairinen has written a monograph on the contract of employment. Juha Tolonen has examined general problems of private law ("allgemeine Lehren") whereas Lars Björne has written a historical treatise of the development of legal systematics.[35]

But from a philosophical point of view these features only belong to the background of development, even though they express a keen interest in the *dynamic and functional coherence of law*. It is easy to observe that the "atomistic" positions of logical empiricism are no longer embraced. However, the *justification* of law and justification in legal science still are the main theoretical issues.

In 1965 Kaarle Makkonen (1923–) published his widely acclaimed doctoral dissertation *Zur Problematik der juridischen Entscheidung – eine strukturanalytische Studie*. In this book Makkonen sought to show the discrepancies between the semi-officially accepted patterns of justification (such as the so-called syllogistic justification) and actual legal heuristics. Makkonen was influenced by Wittgenstein's later ordinary-language philosophy as well as by the Oxford school.[36] Makkonen also showed how evaluations are concealed behind the humpty-dumpty phrases of the courts. But even if Makkonen's analysis stressed the *openness of argumentation*, he after all had not much to say about the criteria of weighting up different arguments. In spite of its considerable merits Makkonen's book in the first place pointed out relevant problems of argumentation rather than contributed to their solution. It should also be added that Makkonen's book has not been widely read by Finnish lawyers.

In the late 1960's the critics of the analytical school became rather vociferous. One of them, Antti Kivivuori (1940–), expressed considerable scepticism about legal argumentation as an object of legal science: arguments, as a rule, seemed to be incommensurable and could not be added up so as to produce sound statements about valid Finnish law.[37] In Kivivuori's opinion, the important thing was to examine legislative and judicial behaviour with the help of a scheme of *intentional* explanation of individual acts. For Kivivuori, law was a political issue (he later became a high official in the Ministry of Justice).[38] Juha Tolonen (1941–) has taken up the *rationality of law* as an important research issue. In his doctoral dissertation, *Der allgemeine Erklärungshintergrund der wirtschaftlichen Ordnung und seine Anwendung auf das Aktiengesellschaftsrecht* (1974), he examines legal development as a dialectical process between "theory" and "practice". He wanted to reconstruct the rational grounds for the different regulations on joint stock company, using them as a kind of *tertium comparationis*. In his later works Tolonen has stressed that we still have much to learn from the classics of legal theory, particularly from Natural Law.[39]

There are other critics of the analytical school as well – including myself. In the beginning of the 1970's the leading exponent of the analytical school, Aulis Aarnio, began himself to modify his methodological outlook. He developed an approach which he has called *analytical hermeneutics*, drawing much inspiration e.g. from von Wright's theory of action and from the New Rhetoric. Aarnio's approach is a highly original contribution to international discussion.

Aarnio's starting point was quite similar to that of the New Rhetoric: justification of legal decisions and propositions of legal science is *audience-relativized*. But one of Aarnio's original contributions was the analysis of the relationship between the person who asserts something and his audience. Justification does not depend solely on the reactions of the audience. In argumentative discourse there prevails a certain kind of overall coherence, even if Aarnio admits that the ultimate arguments are "arational". The uniting element is the structure of the argumentative *language*. It is inter-subjectively valid because behind it there is something like a Wittgensteinian *Lebensform*. Different types of legal reasoning Aarnio conceives as "language games": they are neither commensurable nor interreducible but rather belong to the same "family". This Wittgensteinian idea of a family resemblance Aarnio uses in an interesting manner when he claims that certain weakly normative rules follow from the structure of the *language* of legal argumentation: If you wish your proposition to become accepted by a certain audience, you must act in a certain manner.

It is not possible to give here a comprehensive detailed account of Aarnio's legal theory which he has developed in several books: *On Legal Reasoning* (1977), *Denkweisen der Rechtswissenschaft* (1979), *Philosophical Perspectives in Jurisprudence* (a collection of essays, 1983), and *Rational as Reasonable* (forthcoming in 1986). Aarnio has created a school among present-day Finnish legal scholars – not only in legal theory but also in private law which was in fact the starting-point domain in his own theoretical research. Some of Aarnio's close colleagues have already attained their full professoriates: Thomas Wilhelmsson (1949–), who has written much on the problems of the freedom of contract, and Ahti Saarenpää (1946–), whose specialty is the law of inheritance. But there are other talented disciples of his as well. Urpo Kangas (1951–) has written, among other things, a monograph on Brusiin. Juha Pöyhönen (1953–) has together with Aarnio and other authors worked on a study of scientific progress in legal science; Pöyhönen has also published a monograph of his own on the nature of theories in the science of law.[40] Scholars more or less loosely connected with Aarnio's circle are Markku Helin, Sami Mahkonen and Matti Niemivuo: Helin is a theoretician, Mahkonen a historian whereas Niemivuo has written extensively on public law. All this also shows the width of Aarnio's own interests. Also Matti Mikkola (1945–), who writes on labour law and social security legislation, and Heikki Mattila (1947–), who writes on comparative law, belong to the community of scholars around Aarnio.[41]

Several present-day scholars in the Law Faculty of the University of Turku were Otto Brusiin's pupils when he taught in Turku. Juha Tolonen has already been mentioned: at the present time he is particularly interested in the discussion in legal and social philosophy from the Middle Ages onwards on the relationship between law and state. Kauko Wikström (1943–) has been influenced by hermeneutical tendencies of thought but he has adopted a rather different interpretation of hermeneutics if compared to Aarnio's linguistically accentuated theory. For Wikström the testing ground of legal scientific propositions is *judicial practice*. This shows that he has adopted one of the central theses of legal realism. But he sees legal practice as *kommunikatives Handeln* in the Habermasian sense: There is a constant dialectic between norms and facts, and the meaning of legal norms is established in this interpretative activity. This is the central argument in Wikström's doctoral dissertation on the interpretation of legal practice (in Finnish, 1978).[42] He is at his best in his critique of other legal theories – he has sharply criticized the use of the so-called practical syllogism in the explanation of judicial behaviour. As far as my own legal theoretical work is concerned, I feel unable to summarize its key tenets in a manner similar to the accounts given here of the ideas of other Finnish philosophers of law.[43] The basic idea in my theory is the finalistic, instrumental nature of law – this is also reflected in the accounts I have given about justification and heuristics.

The role of Marxist theory of law in Finland has been relatively modest. However, as I have said, there are at least two significant Marxist scholars of law. Eero Backman[44] is a notable legal historian and professor of criminal law. Lars D. Eriksson has written a number of sparkling essays on different topics in legal theory, and his witty style has brought him the nickname "master of legal lyric". His doctoral dissertation on Marxist theory and legal science consists of a collection of articles plus a general survey in book form.[45] Eriksson does not think that the economic basis of society in an unmediated way determines law. It only creates the set of possible *alternatives* in legal development. The interdependence between law and the economy is a very complicated one because the economy influences the law through the *political* system. But Eriksson's most interesting contribution to the methodological discussion has been his attempt at developing a Marxist method for interpreting law in bourgeois society. It starting point is a finalistic value system where the key notion is the *objective needs* of the people. Bourgeois law is partly built upon the interests of production and exchange, but there are in it also "interventionistic" features, *i.e.*, norms meant to prevent or correct dysfunctions of the production system. It is now a strategic and tactical problem whether a Marxist lawyer falls back on his own goals and values when interpreting bourgeois law. It is equally possible for him to resort to the classical *syllogistic* model of legal reasoning: in this case, formal justice and legal certainty will be emphasized.

Even if the number of vowedly Marxist scholars is not great (and even they are often rather unorthodox, as Eriksson), many Finnish legal philosophers have been influenced by Marx in some way or another. Marx as a classical social theorist has, at least up to some degree, inspired those scholars who belong to Aarnio's circle as well. But they have managed to integrate their social criticism and the crucial thesis of the New Rhetoric: argumentation is *in ultima analysi* a social phenomenon – its paradigms are socially conditioned and therefore also subject to political criticism.

It is perhaps fitting to conclude this brief presentation of Finnish legal philosophy by mentioning the work of Professor Seppo Laakso (1945–). Much of his work is inspired by Miguel Reale's theory of the three-dimensionality of law and legal thinking, and Laakso has also written extensive studies of Hans Kelsen's pure theory of law.[46]

To sum up: The Finnish analytical school is still dominant in the methodology of legal science, even if its basic thoughts sometimes have tended to become more or less a commonplace, a justification for a simple "case-positivism". But in legal philosophy there are no longer active representatives of the "pure" form of this school, with the possible exception of Makkonen. But if the analytical school is the *de cujus*, there remains the question: who are its heirs? This question is far from being settled. The hermeneutical trend seems to be its nearest relative, but its relationship with Marxism is still very unclear. Legal sociology would be needed to give substance to legal methodology; but powerful contributions of legal sociology are still lacking. How is it possible to exert critical influence upon law, unless there is sufficient knowledge about the social impact of law? It seems to me that an increasing drifting away of the Marxists from the hermeneutical school is imminent, even if this is just a conjecture. What will the non-Marxist answer be? Should we expect to see a return to Natural Law, a tradition which has not been exercised in Finland for two hundred years? Or will there emerge new sorts of syntheses of different traditions? In any case, Finnish legal philosophers nowadays have far more contacts and interaction with their foreign colleagues than before. In view of this fact, there is no acute need to be afraid that the lively interest in questions of legal philosophy would disappear and give way to superficial learning and eclecticism. The possibility of giving interesting and fruitful contributions to international discussion will hopefully remain one of the foremost motive forces upholding legal philosophical research and learning in Finland in the future.

University of Turku

NOTES

(For the reader's information, the Finnish titles of books and essays are here also given in English.)

[1] See Hannu Tapani Klami, *Länsimaisen oikeusfilosofian historia* (History of Western Legal Philosophy), Turku 1980, 1 ff.

[2] I have discussed the philosophical background of this problem e.g. in Hannu Tapani Klami, 'Dualism of Law', in *Objektivierung des Rechtsdenkens. Gedächtnisschrift für Ilmar Tammelo*, Berlin (W) 1983, pp. 471–80.

[3] Hannu Tapani Klami, *Anti-Legalism: Five Essays in the Finalistic Theory of Law*, Turku 1980.

[4] This section is to a great extent based on Hannu Tapani Klami, *The Legalists: Finnish Legal Science in the Period of Autonomy 1809–1917*, Helsinki 1981 (appeared in somewhat longer version in 1977 in Finnish, *Oikeustaistelijat, Suomen oikeustiede Venäjän vallan aikana*).

[5] On Calonius see R. A. Wrede, *Matthias Calonius*, Helsingfors 1917, *passim*; Wilhelm Chydenius, *Matthias Calonius såsom civilrättslärare: Akademisk inbjudningsskrift*, I–II, 1909–1910. Both works are rather descriptive. The lectures of Calonius on private law have been published (by W. Chydenius and V. Nordström), but not until 1907: *Praelectiones jurisprudentiae civilis*. (A Finnish translation appeared in 1948, transl. E. Linkomies).

[6] In the original Academy of Turku (founded in 1640) there was from the very beginning a Faculty of Law, i.e. one chair in Jurisprudence. The first professors, Johannes Olai Dalekarlus (ennobled: Stiernhöök) and Michael Wexionius (-Gyldenstolpe) were scholars of distinguished merit. Academic activities in Turku were, however, interrupted by war in 1709. When the Academy again began its work in 1722, it was impossible to find a competent professor of law. Legal science was laid waste until Calonius – a self-educated scholar without any academic degree – was appointed professor in 1778. See Hannu Tapani Klami, *Suomen oikeustiede Ruotsin vallan aikana*, I (Finnish Legal Science during the Swedish Period, I), Turku 1981, *passim*.

[7] J. Ph. Palmén, *Juridisk handbok för medborgerlig bildning*, Helsinfors 1859.

[8] See his *Om oäkta barns rättsförhållande till familjen* (On the Legal Relationship between the Natural Child and the Family), Helsingfors 1858.

[9] The first legal periodical in Finland, the *Juridiskt Album*, was founded by Robert Lagus in 1861 but it expired when its editor died young. In 1865 the society "Juridiska Föreningen" began to publish a periodical, *Tidskrift utgiven af Juridiska Föreningen i Finland* (*JFT*), in which precedents were also published and commented on. The periodical is thriving and lively even today.

[10] Hermanson's most important theoretical work was his dissertation *Om lagstiftningen* (On Legislation), Helsingfors 1881.

[11] On the reception of German doctrines and systematics see Lars Björne, *Siviilioikeuden yleiset opit* (The General Doctrines of Private Law), Turku 1977, *passim*.

[12] F. O. Lilius, 'Katsaus päävirtauksiin 19. vuosisadan oikeustieteessä" (A Survey of the Main Currents of Nineteenth-Century Legal Science), *Lakimies* 2 (1904), 81–93.

[13] This section is an overview of main tendencies of thought in the first half of the 20th century. There are also several other comprehensive presentations of Finnish legal

philosophy in our century. See Aulis Aarnio, *Philosophical Perspectives in Jurisprudence*, Helsinki 1983, chapter 1; Kaarle Makkonen, 'Der Stand der finnischen Rechtstheorie', *Rechtstheorie* 1 (1970), 96–106; Wolfgang Mincke, *Die finnische Rechtstheorie unter dem Einfluss der analytischen Philosophie*, Berlin 1979; Juha Tolonen, 'Grundzüge der finnischen Rechtstheorie', *Rechtstheorie*, Beiheft 2, Berlin 1981. See also Hannu Tapani Klami, *Suomen oikeustiedettä 1900-luvulla* (with an English summary), Turku 1981.

14 On Kaila, see Ilkka Patoluoto, 'On the Logic of Norms in El. Kaila', in: A. Peczenik and J. Uusitalo (eds.), *Reasoning on Legal Reasoning*, Vammala 1979, pp. 207–218. My opinion of Kaila's scientific merit is rather more sceptical than Patoluoto's. Kaila was even worse as a scholar of Roman Law than he was in legal logic.

15 The treatises of Tore Strömberg and Karl Olivecrona have also been used as course-books in the law faculties. Olivecrona's *Rättsordningen* (in English version known as *Law as Fact*) is still used in my Faculty. It has, however, proved rather difficult for students.

16 On this problem see Hannu Tapani Klami, *Luentoja suomalaisesta oikeussosiologiasta* (Lectures on Finnish Sociology of Law), Turku 1981, 10 ff.

17 'Eräitä Hans Kelsenin oikeusteoriaa koskevia näkökohtia' (Aspects of Hans Kelsen's Legal Theory), *Lakimies* 34 (1936), 80–100.

18 See B. C. Carlson, 'Strenger Normativismus', *ARSP* 42 (1956), 329–350. He also published a collection of essays, *Rätten. Ett rättsteoretiskt försök* (On Law. An Essay in Legal Theory), Helsingfors 1954.

19 On Brusiin see Urpo Kangas, *Piirteitä Otto Brusiinin ajatusmaailmasta* (Features of the Thinking of Otto Brusiin), Helsinki 1976. Kangas has succeeded admirably well in penetrating in the thought of Brusiin whom he did not know personally.

20 For Brusiin's sixtieth birthday a collection of essays was published entitled *Ius Humanum – Studia in honorem Otto Brusiin*, Turku 1966. The book includes also a bibliography of Brusiin's writings and of the reviews of his works. After 1966 Brusiin did not publish much on legal philosophy; he wrote instead a number of small books and articles on the history of Finnish legal science and legal philosophy.

21 See, e.g., Luis Legaz y Lacambra, *Rechtsphilosophie*, Neuwied 1957, 225. It is significant that Brusiin had become acquainted with the manuscript and had helped Legaz to get the German translation published (see *op. cit.*, Preface, 6).

22 Both books have been translated into Spanish: *El pensamiento juridico*, transl. by Jose Puig Brutau, Buenos Aires 1959; *De la objetividad de la jurisdiccion*, transl. by E. Carzon Valdes, Cordoba 1966.

23 Cf. Franz Wieacker, *Industriegesellschaft und Privatrechtsordnung*, Stuttgart 1973, 12 ff. Cf. also Björne, *Siviilioikeuden yleiset opit*, 209 ff.

24 Zitting has also published some articles in international languages: 'An Attempt to Analyse the Owner's Legal Position', *Scandinavian Studies in Law* 3 (1959); 'Über den Unterschied des Sachenrechts und des Obligationenrechts', in *Ius Humanum* (see note 20), p. 148 ff.

25 Simo Zitting, 'Omistajan oikeuksista ja velvollisuuksista' (On the Rights and Duties of the Owner), *Lakimies* 50 (1952), 387–401 and 501–531.

26 This opinion I have expressed in Hannu Tapani Klami, *Sacerdotes iustitiae*, Turku 1978.

27 See, e.g., Antero Jyränki, 'Teesejä juridiikasta ja juristeista' (Theses on Lawyers and Legal Science), *Lakimies* 67 (1969), 880–892; Antti Kivivuori, 'Suomalaisen

oikeustieteen virheet' (The Vices of Finnish Legal Science), *Lakimies* 68 (1970), 422–429 and 929–940; Hannu Tapani Klami, 'Oikeustieteen empiirinen kriisi' (The Empirical Crisis of Legal Science), *Suomalainen Suomi*, 1968; Juha Tolonen, 'Muutamia näkökohtia oikeustieteen nykytilasta' (Aspects of the Present State of Legal Science), *Lakimies* 68 (1970), 138–154.

28 See Alf Ross, *On Law and Justice*, London 1958, 24.

29 Aulis Aarnio, 'On the Paradigm Articulation in Legal Science', in: I. Tammelo and A. Aarnio (eds.), *The Advancement of Theory and Technique in Law and Ethics, Rechtstheorie* Beiheft 3, Berlin (W) 1981, pp. 45–56. (Reprinted in Aarnio, *Philosophical Perspectives in Jurisprudence*, Helsinki 1983, as chapter 10.)

30 In Finland Lahtinen was better known for his brilliant analyses of the conceptual problems of positive law than for his writings in legal philosophy. His only monograph was the dissertation *Zum Aufbau der rechtlichen Grundlagen*, Helsinki 1951. On Lahtinen's thought, see the short article by Kauko Wikström, 'Filosofian ja oikeusteorian välisestä suhteesta Osvi Lahtisen ajattelussa' (On the Relation between Philosophy and Legal Theory in Osvi Lahtinen's Thinking), *Oikeus* 4 (1975), 19–22.

31 Anttila has published a number of her essays in English, also in the series of the Research Institute of Legal Policy whose founder and first Director she was. See, e.g., 'Current Scandinavian Criminology and Crime Control' (1974); *Papers on Crime Control 1977–1978* (1978).

32 Cf. Martti Kairinen, *Perussuhdeteoriasta Suomen työoikeuden yleisten oppien osana*, Vammala 1978, 54–5, where Finnish legal science is criticized for excessive "compliance" toward the authority of cases.

33 The law faculties are in Helsinki University (founded in Turku in 1640, transferred to Helsinki in 1828), in University of Turku (founded in 1960) and in University of Lapland at Rovaniemi (founded in 1979). There are no professorial chairs for legal theory exclusively. In Helsinki and in Turku legal theory is paired with private international law (in Helsinki Professor Makkonen has, however, a personal chair in jurisprudence). In Rovaniemi there is no professorship as yet, only an associate professor in legal theory and legal history (a similar associate's chair exists in Turku). For the basic law degree, the candidate of law (corresponding to the English LL.B), two courses in legal theory are obligatory, one at the beginning of the studies (an introductory course), another in the last year. As to the textbooks and treatises used, there are differences between the faculties. Books by Aarnio, Makkonen and myself are used, but the students must be acquainted with some of the classics of legal theory as well. For instance in Turku they must read parts of Kelsen's *Reine Rechtslehre* (which have been translated into Finnish). The history of legal ideas is particularly emphasized.

34 A short history of the Faculty of Law in the University of Turku is presented by the author: Hannu Tapani Klami, *Juridiikkaa Suomen Turussa 1960–1980* (Legal Science in Turku 1960–1980), Turku 1984.

35 This book by Professor Björne is particularly interesting. It appeared in 1979: *Oikeusjärjestelmän kehityksestä* (On the Development of Legal Systematics). A new edition in German has appeared: *Deutsche Rechtssysteme im 18. und 19. Jahrhundert*, Ekelsbach am Main 1984.

36 In the present essay I will not deal with the development of academic professional philosophy in Finland. It should be noted, however, that Finnish philosophy, especially the work of G. H. von Wright has greatly inspired out theoretically-minded jurists –

even if Finnish legal philosophers do not show any particular interest in legal logic (in spite of von Wright's great merit as an innovator in this branch of logic). The Finnish interest in Wittgenstein is partly due to the influence of von Wright who was his successor at Cambridge in the 1950's.

37 See Antti Kivivuori, *Suomen vahingonkorvauslainsäädännön kehitys*, I (The Development of the Finnish Legislation on Torts, I), Joensuu 1969, 24.

38 See his *Politische Rechtswissenschaft*, Helsinki 1971. Kivivuori is presently the Director of the Department of Legislation in the Finnish Ministry of Justice. I do not know whether he still thinks that legislation can be explained by individual intentional models.

39 Cf. Juha Tolonen, 'Das Recht und die wirtschaftlichen Theorien', in *Rechtstheorie* Beiheft 3 (see note 29), p. 95 ff. There is no established Natural Law tradition in Finland. Professor Aatos Alanen (1896–1974) admittedly represented a Christian philosophy of law; but although his *Jurisprudence* (2nd ed. 1965, in Finnish) was relatively long-lived as an academic treatise, his influence on legal science and legal theory was minimal.

40 A. Aarnio, J. Pöyhönen *et alii, Paradigms, Change and Progress in Legal Dogmatics* (in English), forthcoming; J. Pöyhönen, *Juridisista teorioista*, Helsinki 1981, key ideas are presented in his article in A. Aarnio, I. Niiniluoto and J. Uusitalo (eds.), *Methodologie und Erkenntnistheorie der juristischen Argumentation, Rechtstheorie* Beiheft 2, Berlin (W) 1981, pp. 127–136.

41 Their dissertations are also theoretically interesting: Mikkola, *Työttömyysturvan ehdoista* (The Conditions of Unemployment Security; English summary), Vammala 1979; Mattila, *Les successions agricoles et la structure de la société*, Helsinki 1979.

42 There is a German summary in Wikström's dissertation *Oikeuskäytännön tulkinnasta* (On Interpretation of Legal Practice), Vammala 1978. See also his essays 'The Problem of Truth and Propositions in Legal Dogmatics', in *Rechtstheorie* Beiheft 2 (see note 40), pp. 85–89, and 'The Theoretical Nature of Propositions in Legal Dogmatics', in *Rechtstheorie* Beiheft 3 (see note 29), p. 181 ff.

43 A short list of my own works on legal theory: *Oikeudellisen säätelyn yleinen teoria* (A General Theory of Legal Regulation), Turku 1977; *Johdatus oikeusteoriaan* (Introduction to Legal Theory), Turku 1981; *Sääntö ja käyttäytyminen* (Norm and Behaviour), Turku 1979; *Finalistinen oikeusteoria* (The Finalistic Theory of Law), Turku 1979; *Anti-Legalism*, Turku 1980; *Comparative Law and Legal Concepts*, Turku 1981; *Ihmisen säännöt* (The Rules of Man), Turku 1983 (an English version of the book has appeared in *Oikeustiede-Jurisprudentia* 1984).

44 Backman's main work so far is his doctoral dissertation *Rikoslaki ja yhteiskunta* (Criminal Law and Society), Vammala 1975, but he is presently writing a comprehensive book on the relationship between criminal law and legal theory.

45 See his *Marxistisk teori och rättsvetenskap*, I–II (Marxist Theory and Legal Science), Helsingfors 1980.

46 See Laakso, *Über die Dreidimensionalität des Rechts und des juristischen Denkens*, Tampere 1980; his essay on the same theme in A. Peczenik and J. Uusitalo (eds.), *Reasoning on Legal Reasoning*, Vammala 1979; 'Puhtaan oikeusopin problematiikkaa' (Problems of the Pure Theory of Law), in *Oikeustiede-Jurisprudentia*, vol. 13, Vammala 1980, pp. 91–183 (German summary); and *Oikeuden systeeminyhteydestä Hans Kelsenin puhtaassa oikeusopissa* (Systemic Coherence of Law in Kelsen's Pure Theory), Tampere 1980.

KAZIMIERZ OPAŁEK

PROBLEMS OF SCHOOLS IN LEGAL THEORY

1. INTRODUCTORY REMARKS

In present-day discussions in science studies, quite a lot of attention is paid to the problem of schools in science. It is traditionally an important subject of research in the history and sociology of science, the latter being often supplemented by the psychology of scientific activity. It has been noticed also that many problems of scientific schools belong to the philosophy and methodology of science. There exists nowadays an extensive literature on this subject matter, including several Polish contributions.[1]

Studies on schools in science fall into two basic categories: studies on particular schools in various fields of science, undertaken mostly by historians of science, and considerations of the general problems of scientific schools. The latter concentrate on the concept of the scientific school, the role of schools in the development of science, and on further perspectives of such schools – together with the question if the existence of scientific schools, generally speaking, is desirable and should be in some way or another promoted or not.

In all these general problems we encounter far-reaching differences of views. Various authors entertain different concepts of a scientific school. The role of schools in science is evaluated positively, negatively, or positively in some aspects while negatively in others. Admittedly, negative evaluations often tend to prevail: as to the desirability and development of schools, the answers are on the whole determined by standpoints in the preceding topic. The controversies around all these general problems induce the authors of monographic studies on particular schools to make their own attempts at answering such general questions.

There are monographic studies on some schools in legal theory as well. Even though these studies do not always explicitly mention "schools" as their subject matter, they do in fact contribute to the investigation of schools. On the other hand, much attention has not been paid to general problems, that is to say, to the question what things are common to and specific of the schools in legal theory in relation to scientific schools in other fields as well as to the question of the role of legal theoretical schools, and of their

E. Bulygin et al. (eds.), Man, Law and Modern Forms of Life, 161–173.

further perspectives. These problems seem to be important and apt to be easily overlooked in detailed historical studies on particular schools. The problematics of particular schools in legal theory will be not discussed systematically in this paper. It deals only with the general problems characterized above. For obvious reasons, the term 'school in legal theory' is meant to cover also what some authors call 'schools in legal philosophy' or 'schools in jurisprudence'.[2]

In the following sections I shall discuss some essential traits and aspects of schools in science and try to show how these general traits and aspects manifest themselves in legal theoretical schools. I also try to point out what things are specific to the latter. In view of the controversies mentioned above, I will also try to elaborate my own standpoint in the question of the concept of the scientific school – in a way intended to overcome some of the existing theoretical difficulties. My standpoint, however, certainly cannot be devoid of some arbitrariness.

2. SCHOOLS AND TRENDS OF THOUGHT IN SCIENCE

In the present author's opinion, schools in science as social phenomena which to a great extent have the character of social *groups*, should be distinguished from *trends* or *currents* in science. This distinction is intended to avoid the loose and often misleading use of the term 'school' to cover also researchers' scientific constructions, based on the similarities of views of scholars in the scientific field under study, irrespective of their real connections (contacts, ties, influences). This loose usage of the term is carried to an extreme in the concept of 'schools in typological sense'.[3] This usage of the term has given rise to notions such as "the Marxist school" or "the functionalist school" in sociology, which blurs the important difference between school as a phenomenon and school as a typological construction. One should rather speak of e.g. Marxist and functionalist *trends* or *currents* in sociology into which various "real" schools can be included.

We frequently meet this misunderstanding in considerations of schools in legal theory. E.g., some authors speak in a loose sense of the "natural law school", which in fact is a current or trend, in fact a group of currents or trends, to which different schools can be said to belong (e.g. the Spanish school of the 16th century, the German schools of the 17th and 18th centuries). Even Continental legal positivism of the 19th century, in view of its dispersion, ought to be qualified as a trend (current), not as a school. Within legal positivism one can discern various schools connected with different eminent scholars and marked by orientations characteristically related with the main branches of the study of law (private or public law).[4]

3. SCIENTIFIC SCHOOL AS A HISTORICAL PHENOMENON

A scientific school is obviously a historical phenomenon, coming into being, functioning and decaying in determined circumstances of time and place. The lifetime of schools can be longer or shorter, depending on various factors (stability or early decline of the school's organizational form, if there was one, long persistence of given conceptions, or their short-lived character). Schools that at an earlier time had passed away can have their revival or recurrence (e.g. the Neo-Kantian schools and schools of "revived" natural law). It seems to be a historical regularity that the period of duration of scientific schools in modern times tends to be relatively short, by virtue of (a) the increasing rate of the development of scientific thought and (b) the progress in communication processes, contributing to the overcoming of particularist tendencies. However, the extra-rational attractiveness of the conceptions of the school (mostly in humanities and social sciences) on one hand, and its openness to various conceptions on the other, is apt to generate some breaches in this regularity. One should also add that schools are essentially *static* phenomena in view of scientific development, since they tend to preserve some given views and to resist their changes.

One cannot say that legal theoretical schools were particularly long-lived as compared with schools in other fields of science. It can be observed, though, that schools more apt to assimilate new attainments relevant for legal theory have a longer duration that schools that show a "closed" and "fighting" attitude (e.g. the still existing British school of analytical jurisprudence on one hand, and such decayed schools as that of Uppsala, or that connected with the psychological theory of L. Petrazycki on the other). It seems, however, remarkable that while the schools in legal theory decline and are replaced by new ones, they are marked by the recurrence of three tendencies in particular: that of the axiology of the "just law", that of legal formalism, and that of legal realism. New schools are to some extent new variants of the previously existing schools. This does not signify any lack of progress in legal theory, but the general way of this progress is complicated and only seldom revealing relevant innovations. The processes under discussion find their most distinct expression in schools proclaiming the revival of the views of thinkers and schools of the past. In legal theory, which, as

Kelsen put it, is a discipline "abounding with mistakes", there frequently arises the question,

(...) if a thinker before ages has not resolved a given problem better than the contemporary, and if one could not learn something from the former?

Hence we are dealing in this field with

(...) a great debating parliament, in which on the same benches sit the ever-alive and vigorous thinkers of various epochs together with young assistants of our universities of today.[5]

Another important thing is that the coming into existence and decaying of schools in legal theory is to a particularly great extent determined by factors other than those of the inner development of the discipline – by those connected with legal practice, and social-political ones. For instance, the German historical school had its roots in the feudal reaction against the penetration of progressive changes from France, and it decayed when resistance against codification turned out to be contrary to vital national interests. The schools of legal positivism came into being in the conditions of the stabilization of the social-political system, they became impaired in the time of rapid social change at the beginning of the 20th century, and discredited when accused of their ancillary role in Fascist regimes. The crisis of social systems paves as a rule the way to natural law schools on one hand, and to realist schools of an "unmasking" character (e.g., *Freirechtsschule*) on the other.

4. SPATIAL DIMENSIONS OF SCIENTIFIC SCHOOLS

A scientific school has also spatial dimensions, which are particularly distinct when it has an established organizational framework. They are not so distinct when the school is but a spiritual community of scholars who share some ideas or ways of approach to certain problems. These differences are to some extent relative; well-organized schools usually have also outside adherents, and even an informal community, in spite of its dispersion, has always some main or initial centre. Roughly speaking, it seems to be a regularity that a school gradually transcends its initial scope connected with a concrete place. This tendency is limited by historically conditioned particularisms especially strong in some countries, or by difficulties in scientific communication (e.g., the school publishes its contributions in a language which is not widely accessible).

Among schools in legal theory we find both "organized schools" (e.g., German historical school and the normativist school of Vienna) and schools showing the traits of a spiritual community only (e.g. *Freirechtsschule*, the school of sociological jurisprudence around Roscoe Pound, and the school of American legal realism).[6]

Schools in legal theory, however, seem to be frequently confined to national or regional limits, and they often have difficulties in overcoming the existing spatial barriers. The particularisms are here much greater than in case of schools in other humanistic-social disciplines and in philosophy, not to mention natural and formal sciences. Many schools in legal theory, even in not very distant countries, are only known to singular scholars with encyclopedic interests, or to those acquainted with these views by chance. This may be so even in spite of these schools' interesting contributions and efforts at propagating them. To some extent this is certainly due to the differences between legal systems and their study in various countries, these differences shaping up also tendencies of thought in legal theory but at the same time occasioning national or regional limitations of scientific interests in the field.

It is striking, for instance, that in the period before the Second World War the psychological school of L. Petrazycki and even the school of Uppsala exerted but a very limited influence. Also the school of analytical jurisprudence was – with few exceptions such as F. Somlo – unknown on the European continent. Neither did the schools of the Continent arouse noteworthy interest in Britain. The same thing happened even with the newer legal theoretical schools of USA. "The American legal realist movement", writes H. L. A. Hart, "has found little echo and approval in Britain: and with few exceptions the renaissance of ethical and natural law philosophy in the United States has evoked scant enthusiasm in Oxford, Cambridge and London".[7] All this was frequently connected also with such factors as cultural isolationism and conservatism, or – in some cases – with linguistic barriers. It is true that after the Second World War the achievements of various schools have became wider known and the communication between the schools in different regions of the world has improved. However, the mentioned barriers are still far from being removed.

5. ELEMENTS OF CONSCIOUS CREATION AND SPONTANEOUS FORMATION IN SCIENTIFIC SCHOOLS

A scientific school can either come into existence as result of some conscious measures (although fully planning the school in advance and "decreeing" it seems hardly possible), or it can be formed spontaneously. In the latter case it is retrospectively qualified as a "school" by its adherents themselves and/or by outside observers (e.g. by other researchers of the same field, or by historians of science). The difference, however, is but relative. The conscious measures are as a rule preceded by some spontaneous activities (e.g., achievements of a scholar, gaining adherents; convergent ideas of several parallelly working scholars; initially loose contacts of some scholars working on the same problems). On the other hand, when a school is originated as a result of some conscious organizatory measures, it tends later to surpass spontaneously the initial designs. For instance, a team organized to work on a research project may later give rise to a wider "movement" inspired by conceptions elaborated by the team. Also, an organization originally designed to serve didactic purposes or the training of beginners for scholarly work, may later give rise to serious and scholarly scientific activities.

In the above respects, schools in legal theory do not seem to greatly differ from schools in other fields of science. "Academic" schools seem to show more elements of conscious creation than schools that come into existence as a result of strivings outside the established scholarly-academic tradition and involve efforts of non-conformist scholars and practitioners (e.g., the German historical school and the British school of historical jurisprudence, as opposed to *Freirechtsschule* and American legal realism). However, retrospective evaluations of the degree of spontaneity involved in the emergence of schools of the latter type are not always reliable. Characteristically enough, one of the founders of legal realism, Karl Llewellyn, claimed that "there is no school of realists", but at the same time mentioned the following traits shared by realists:

> First, (. . .) certain points of departure are common to them all. Second, (. . .) a cross-relevance, a complementing, an interlocking of their varied results, as if they were guided by an invisible hand. A third thing may be mentioned in passing: a fighting faith in their methods of attack on legal problems.[8]

Such traits do seem to constitute a school, contrary to Llewellyn's opinion.

6. INTERPERSONAL RELATIONSHIPS

Characteristic of most scientific schools is the relationship between the "master" (or "masters") and the disciples or adherents. This relationship can be either that of a direct contact, or that of recognizing somebody's "mastership" in more distant circumstances of time and place. In the latter case we often deal with activities of intermediaries between the "master" and his followers and further audience. These intermediaries – especially in social sciences, humanities, and philosophy – are persons fascinated by the "master", having direct contacts with him, faithful to his views, safeguarding their "purity", and defying deviations from them. Other important persons in the life of schools are the "opponents", either directly attacking the "master", or silently moving away from his views.

There is hardly a need to separately mention the numerous "masters" of the schools in legal theory. It is psychologically interesting that they often seem to be persons as if predestined for this role and early conscious of their "vocation". A striking example is Friedrich von Savigny, about whom we learn the following:

> His plan to be the reformer of jurisprudence, the Kant of the science of law, is a great one, one worth being pursued by outstanding men: it is not an effort of some years only, but the whole existence and the realization of this plan is meant to be the main objective of his life.[9]

Legal theoretical schools have also their intermediaries, as for instance Dupont de Nemours in relation to Quesnay as the founder of the physiocratic natural law doctrine, Puchta in the German historical school, Lundstedt in relation to Hägerström in the school of Uppsala, or Lande in relation to Petrazycki and his theory. As far as the opponents – often "loud" ones indeed – are concerned, a good example is F. Sander in relation to Kelsen. Alf Ross, on the other hand, is an example of a scholar who liberates himself, step by step, from the master Hägerström's views.

7. MAIN TYPES OF SCHOOLS IN SCIENCE

An association serving research or didactic purposes is not yet a scientific school, but can be a prerequisite of it. Among scientific schools we can distinguish "specialistic" schools of thought from "theoretical" schools. Characteristic of the former are specialization in some field of research plus research methods and techniques as well as a certain style of presenting results, characteristic of some group of scholars.[10] Characteristic of the theoretical school is adherence to certain hypotheses and/or theories which can be either more or less unprovable or genuinely empirical ones. There is an essential difference between these two sorts of theory, but it would be far too rigid to hold on to the positivistic view that the empirical hypotheses and/or theories are fully verifiable or falsifiable so that some of them could be definitely eliminated while others necessarily accepted. Consequently, one cannot speak of a once-and-for-all acceptability of given hypotheses and/or theories. What is at issue is the *degree* of acceptability and acceptance of various hypotheses and/or theories.[11] It is, however, not possible to elaborate this point here. Anyway, a rigidly positivistic idea of acceptability is not adequate in view of the study of the cognitive behaviour of scientific schools.

Analytical schools can be said to belong to the specialistic schools of though in legal theory. In analytical schools, hypotheses and/or theories about the nature, origin, and functions of law are either not advanced or play a secondary role, while much stress is laid on the way of analysis of legal texts and reasonings. Similar features can also turn up in some realistic schools in their "embryonal" stage, that is to say, before the formulation of commonly recognized hypotheses and/or theories (e.g., American legal realism in its early stage).

It is striking that in legal theory we also meet several theoretical schools adhering to unprovable hypotheses and/or theories. In the main, these are schools with axiological tinge, mostly accepting strong ontological assumptions of the idealist philosophy (natural law theory, the phenomenological theory of law, *et al.*). Schools advancing empirical hypotheses and/or theories can be found among realistic schools, but some of them adopt theses of a mixed character – partly empirical and partly unprovable ones (e.g., the sociological jurisprudence of Pound, or the policy-oriented jurisprudence of Lasswell and McDougall).

8. THE PROBLEM OF EMOTIONAL COMMITMENTS IN SCIENTIFIC SCHOOLS

At first sight, one could presume that the irrationality of emotional commitments is to be traced back to unprovable hypotheses and/or theories, professed by certain theoretical schools. One can observe, however, that such commitments are characteristic of schools of all categories – however, perhaps to a somewhat smaller extent of the specialistic schools of thought. Decisive here seems to be the very fact of "staying together", a conviction of the rightness of the chosen course and of the value of own achievements, solidarity in defending them and in attacking the positions of the scientific adversaries. Even members of a research team, which is not yet a school, will be conscious of their distinctness and of the importance of the tasks they are accomplishing. If necessary, they will defend the existence and assets of their scientific community. All this indeed seems to be true of the schools in legal theory as well. The realistic schools, such as those marked by empirical-rational attitudes, typically display at the same time aggressiveness and strong emotional commitment. That was the case with *Freirechtsschule* and American legal realism. Drastic words also have been used by some spokesmen of the school of Uppsala or of the psychological school of Petrazycki. The force of emotions is at its strongest, for instance, when Hägerström is presented as the "Copernicus of social sciences", or when "the Copernican turn in legal science" is ascribed to Petrazycki.[12]

Emotional commitments are just as strong in schools adhering to unprovable hypotheses and/or theories, as for instance in natural law schools. However, the way of building up preferences for the schools' own views is here different; it is more impersonal. It consists in referring not as much to the scholars' subjective inventiveness as to the objective, simple truths, which error and prejudice veil from general public, scientific adversaries included. For instance, Grotius calls the principles of natural law "irrefutable", "in itself intelligible and evident", and we learn the same thing from Pufendorf.[13] In this connection the following characterization of physiocrats is also highly suggestive: "They were boring, sectarian, pompous, and speaking in such a way as if they were owners of some eternal truth".[14]

9. CONNECTIONS WITH OTHER LEGAL AND EXTRA-LEGAL DISCIPLINES

It is a peculiarity of legal theoretical schools that they were always inspired, in a decisive manner, by developments in other, legal or extra-legal disciplines. This feature is so distinct that one can make a division of schools with legal dogmatic, legal historical, philosophical, sociological, and psychological origin.

The schools with legal dogmatic origin include analytical jurisprudence, several schools going under the heading of legal positivism (the German ones, the French *école d'èxegèse*, and so on), normativism and various new analytical schools. Initially, they have only generalized the results of legal dogmatics in the fields of the analysis of legal texts, legal interpretation, and juristic reasonings. Later they also have started making resort to modern logic, linguistics, and philosophy of language. The most important schools which came into existence under the influence of legal history were the German historical school and the British historical jurisprudence. Most legal theoretical schools have strong connections with philosophy. In the first place this holds for the natural law schools, and also for the schools inspired by such "maximalist" philosophical trends as Kantianism, Hegelianism, philosophy of culture, phenomenology, existentialism, and so on, in contradistinction to the philosophical "minimalism" of the more recent analytical schools. Philosophical minimalism, or even a-philosophical attitudes which go back to positivism, are also characteristic of those realistic schools that are influenced by sociology, psychology, or both. Schools of this sort are the *Freirechtsschule*, American legal realism, the school of Uppsala, that of Petrazycki, sociological jurisprudence, experimental jurisprudence and policy-oriented jurisprudence, to mention the most important specimens. (I must add that some of these schools are not purely empirical-realistic ones; cf. above section 7 *in fine*).

The question now arises as to why several legal theoretical schools have sought after inspirations from outside rather than from the inner development of legal theory itself. One should point out, first, that legal theory (legal philosophy, jurisprudence) is a discipline of a general character, and as such makes use of legal data explored by other disciplines (legal dogmatics, legal history, sociology and psychology). On the other hand, the philosophical framework of legal theory may be important in the integration of these findings. All in all, the choice of the sources of inspiration is conditioned by the very "composition" of law itself: "There is vastly more to law than any rules", as Llewellyn put it,[15] and, as it is nowadays more precisely stated, law is a "multi-plane" phenomenon of its character, containing such aspects as the logical-linguistic one, that of psychological experiences, that of "legal behaviour" (the sociological dimension), and the axiological one.[16] The role of philosophy in legal theory, admittedly, cannot be reduced to the aid philosophy can give in dealing with axiological problems, as there arise also the ontological and epistemological ones. The upshot of my argument thus is that the disciplines mentioned above clearly exert an influence on legal theoretical schools, first, in virtue of the character of their subject matter, and secondly, via the general way legal theory seeks to integrate all the findings.

10. THE ROLE OF SCHOOLS IN LEGAL THEORY AND THEIR FUTURE PERSPECTIVES

The role of schools in natural sciences is sometimes negatively evaluated, and there is a great deal of scepticism about their perspectives, except for the different specializations of particular groups of scientists.[17] This view is to be traced back to the thesis of the possibility of full verification or falsification of empirical hypotheses and/or theories, which, if it were true, would leave no room for the reasons for existence of different schools. Having called in question this thesis (cf. section 7 above), we are not inclined to accept the view that there were no place for schools and their variegated perspectives in natural sciences, but we will not develop this point here. Such a view is usually not even advanced in the case of humanities and social sciences, unless it is thought that empirical social sciences develop according to patterns of natural sciences. As to the schools in legal theory, one has to remark that they had and still have some inevitably negative, i.e. less desirable, traits of any scientific schools, such as the dogmatization of some theses and resistance as far as their revision is concerned. On the other hand, the multiplicity of legal theoretical schools tends to favour, first, the increasing specialization in research of various aspects of the law (cf. section 9 above), and secondly, the competition of various views, which contributes to scientific progress.

Specialization has its drawbacks when it consists in recognizing some chosen aspects of law as exclusively capable of supplying the explanation for any possible legal problem. At the same time, however, specialization makes possible deeper insights into some given aspect. Analytical schools, especially in the past, were guilty of neglecting the study of "law as fact" and isolating the study of law from humanities and social sciences. On the other hand, especially in present times, analytical schools have contributed to analyses of the logical-semantic properties of the legal and juristic language, to the construction of systems of logic of norms and deontic logic as applied to law, and to the deepened study of the peculiarities of legal reasonings, while making use of topics and argumentation theory. The realistic schools (including their precursors like the historical schools of the 19th century), have often adopted – especially in our century – a militant attitude against "legal formalism", not devoid of oversimplifications, and tending towards legal nihilism. On the other hand, these schools have contributed to the study of law as psycho-social phenomenon and to the integration of the study of law with social sciences. The schools of philosophical origin may be criticized for advancing unprovable hypotheses and/or theories, but they do contribute to the investigation of the fundamental ontological and epistemological problems of law. When considering axiological problems, these schools achieve important insights into the criteria of the valuation of positive law and into the problematics of *de lege ferenda*.

As to the future perspectives of schools in legal theory, two points should be stressed. First, as far as the specialization is concerned, the continuing existence of these schools seems to be as indisputable as that of schools in other disciplines. Secondly, the acceptability of different hypotheses and/or theories is in our discipline much more optional. One should also notice that the acceptance of unprovable hypotheses and/or theories by quite a number of schools has grounds which are extrascientific but the more enduring, and that these schools have an important role in keeping the focus on "great philosophical problems" of the law. That is why the schools in legal theory are likely to have also in the future a wide field of activity. Thus I conclude that legal theoretical schools will continue to exist, notwithstanding the contrary postulates, and that there are important reasons, if not for promoting, at least for not blocking the activity of schools in legal theory.

Jagellonian University of Kraków

NOTES

[1] *Szkoły w nauce* (Schools in Science), several authors, Wrocław 1980, with an extensive survey of literature.

[2] Cf. H. L. A. Hart, 'Philosophy of Law, Problems of', in P. Edwards (ed.), *The Encyclopedia of Philosophy*, vol. 6, New York and London 1972, p. 264; K. Opałek, 'Der Begriff der Rechtsphilosophie', *Österreichische Zeitschrift für Offentliches Recht* **29** (1978), 236 ff.

[3] J. Szacki, 'O szkołach naukowych – zarys problematyki' (On Scientific Schools – Outline of Problems), in *Szkoły w nauce, op. cit.*, p. 16 ff.

[4] K. Opałek and J. Wróblewski, 'Pozytywizm prawniczy' (Legal Positivism), *Państwo i Prawo* (1954), 1.

[5] J. Lande, *Studia z filozofii prawa* (Studies in Legal Philosophy), Warszawa 1959, 414.

[6] On *Freirechtsschule*, cf. K. Larenz, *Methodenlehre der Rechtswissenschaft*, Berlin 1960, part I, ch. 3; on legal realism and sociological jurisprudence cf. K. Opałek and J. Wróblewski, *Współczesna teoria i socjologia prawa w U.S.A.* (Contemporary Theory and Sociology of Law in USA), Warszawa 1963, ch. 3.

[7] H. L. A. Hart, 'Philosophy of Law and Jurisprudence in Britain (1945–1952)', *American Journal of Comparative Law* **2** (1954), 456.

[8] K. N. Llewellyn, 'Some Realism about Realism – Responding to Dean Pound', *Harvard Law Review* **44**, 1233.

[9] A. Stoll, *Friedrich Karl von Savigny. Ein Bild seines Lebens mit einer Sammlung seiner Briefe*, Berlin 1939, vol. I, 54.

[10] Cf. S. Ossowski, *O osobliwościach nauk społecznych* (On the Peculiarities of Social Sciences), Warszawa 1962, 171.

[11] A. Siemianowski, 'Zagadnienie szkoł naukowych a zagadnienie sprawdzalności teorii'

(The Problem of Scientific Schools and the Problem of Provability of Theories), in *Szkoły w nauce, op. cit.*, 55, 57.

[12] Cf. V. A. Lundstedt, *Legal Thinking Revised*, Stokholm 1956, 7; J. Lande, *op. cit.*, 813.

[13] H. Grotius, *De iure belli ac pacis, Libri tres*, curavit B. J. A. De Kanter-Van Hettinga, Tromp, Lugduni Batavorum 1939, 20 and also 34 ff.; S. Pufendorf, *De iure naturae et gentium, Libri octo* (photographic reproduction of the edition of 1688), V. 1, London 1934, esp. Book II, ch. III. 13, 138 ff.

[14] C. Gide, C. Rist, *Histoire des doctrines economiques*, V. 1 (Polish edition, Warszawa 1919), 4.

[15] K. N. Llewellyn, 'Law and Social Sciences – Especially Sociology', *Harvard Law Review* 62 (1949). Reprinted in K. N. Llewellyn, *Jurisprudence. Realism in Theory and Practice*, Chicago 1962, 354.

[16] Cf. J. Wróblewski, 'Zagadnienie przedmiotu i metody teorii państwa i prawa' (Problems of the Subject Matter and Method in Theory of State and Law), *Państwo i Prawo* (1961), 11.

[17] Szacki, *op. cit.*, 29.

MIHÁLY SAMU

POWER AND LAW: A HISTORICAL MATERIALIST APPROACH

Surveying the development of legal theory very abstractly, the following can be laid down as a fact: different kinds of theoretical approaches usually emphasize one essential (or less essential) feature as the key element in the notion of law. They underline *differentia specifica* such as: law as a cluster of *norms*, law as a *social fact*, law as a *social-spiritual* factor, law as *legal intuition*, law as *will*, law as *interest*, law as *state command, class will, decision of power*, and so on.[1]

The fundamental aim of Marxist legal theory is to critically integrate the "rational core" and the positive theoretical insights of the above mentioned views into a comprehensive conceptual framework. Marxian historical materialism seeks to determine the essential elements of law in the society as a whole.

According to the Marxist approach in legal theory, law is a social-historical phenomenon. It has a specific regulative function in society as a whole. Law is inseparably bound up with the characteristic features of the given social system and is ultimately determined by the economic conditions. This starting point should be emphasized because Marxist legal theory is sometimes considered a basically one-sided economical or political world view (*Weltanschauung*).[2] These considerations, however, seem to distort the essence of Marxist theory into a strawman. The fundamental requirement of Marxist analysis is the *totality* viewpoint. That is to say, law can and should be apprehended in the historical process of whole social movement.

There often occur evaluations, in Western literature, to the effect that Socialist law and legal theory tend to overemphasize the power and politics elements in law. On this opinion, Socialist law is an instrument of power and politics, and legal theory, in its turn, provides the political justification of law, serving as its ideological legitimation. Besides, there can be found an approach in Socialist legal theory itself which underlines one-sidedly the power-political character of law and sees the law primarily as will of the state. In view of these opinions, it is necessary to discuss the power-political character of law theoretically. I would like to contribute to this discussion by way of a macro-social approach analysing the interplay of power and law. By way of introduction, I emphasize that I wish to couch my study in terms of a macro-social, not a micro-social approach.

E. Bulygin et al. (eds.), Man, Law and Modern Forms of Life, 175–183.

I

1. The power character of law is discussed in juridical literature mainly in connection with the analysis of the interdependency of state and law.

Extreme views can often be encountered in studies of the relationship of state and law. *Etatism* conceptualizes law as a state command; *pan-jurism*, on the other hand, emphasizes the primacy of law as an institution.

Some adherents of Socialist legal theory hold that law has the character of a state institution. They are inclined to consider the state primary in relation to law.[3] The argument for this is that state has the decisive role since laws are made, administered and enforced by state organs.[4] This answer is, however, somewhat superficial since it leaves the question of the relevant characteristics of law unanswered.

It seems fruitful to start from the principle that state and law are both particular manifestations of power: this would then entail that the relationship between state and law can be more closely determined within the frame of the power system.

2. In Socialist thought and legal theory, something like a vulgar-materialistic approach sometimes is advocated as a simplifying explanation for the state-law relationship. This vulgar-materialistic viewpoint claims to take into consideration the historical reality and the theoretical achievements of historical materialism. The classics of Marxism, however, saw state and law as separate social institutions which are connected with each other within the society *as a whole*. It was in terms of this "viewpoint of totality" that they discussed several characteristic features of power, authority, politics and political power, state and law. The classics made distinctions between different kinds of power and examined the role of the various sorts of power-political factors (the army, the executive power, the parties, the Church, political struggles) as well as the connections between society and state, constitution and law, the political role of law, etc., within the historical development of bourgeois-capitalist society. (It should be noticed that there are illuminating references to power-political conditions in the social theory of Marx and Engels, even though they did not work out a particular theory of the inner characteristics, functions and autonomous role of power, politics, state and law.)

An uncritical identification of power and policy or state is equally illicit as their rigid *detachment* from one another. Their mutual dependence, inseparable connection and historical determination, however, makes sense only if we also notice that power as a social phenomenon can exist also irrespective of and prior to politics, state and law.

To better understand this relationship, one should first briefly touch upon the development of power, politics, state and law. It is a historical fact that the relations of power manifest themselves even in the elementary communal organization of primitive societies. However, there are not yet here any political relationships, let alone law or state. The social forms of class societies give rise to specific systems of power (besides economic and ideological systems), and state and law emerge in the course of this development. Finally, the historical perspective of communism assumes that the "political sphere", the state and the legal power wither away, which will be followed by a humanization of social power. The overall structure of this historical frame also assumes that these phenomena have particular characteristics peculiar to each social form.[5]

3. *Historicity* as the principal special quality of power should be pointed out: in diverse historical conditions the relations of power can take on manifold forms. To illustrate this diversity, some extreme effects of power can be mentioned. There are negative utmost verges such as wrong and harmful anti-human activities and the abuse of power in general. Consequently the exercise of power is often considered to be evil and inhuman as such (in literary fiction mainly emphases of this aspect are encountered).[6] But the exercise of power has also its positive sides as it serves social development or displays activities creating and realizing values which contribute to the development of the culture of public life and the stabilization of the achievements of mankind. The historically variable content of power is an indisputable fact. Nevertheless, a feature common to all power-wielding can be pointed out. It manifests itself constantly in different kinds of systems of power: The integrative function of power is to guarantee the inner unity and order of human community.[7] This function of power is in compliance with the historical basis of social development. Power preserves the unity of a community or of the whole society, it protects the social order, and it prevents society (or community) from relapsing into anarchy. It is a historical fact that those communities, nations, peoples and states that are not able to preserve unity and prevent anarchy, rapidly disappear from the stage of history.

Engels has an important observation about the integrating role of power. He remarks that as society is divided into antagonistic classes, class struggle threatens to upset the whole society unless this is prevented by a separate organization of power which keeps class struggle within certain bounds.[8]

4. Power is institutionalized in the course of historical development and assumes thereby specific forms. The social power relations manifest themselves primarily in the relationships between subordinators and those being

subordinated (in class society, in the separation and interdependence of ruling classes and oppressed classes), as well as in the various possible forms of coercion.[9] The exercise of power, in the first place, means that specific forms of guidance, decision and control are attached to the organization and regulation of power. It should be pointed out that the organizing activity is performed mainly by the state, whereas regulation is performed by law in class societies. This observation, however, should not lead to the simplified view that only the state and law exist as institutions of power. There are also other institutions performing organization and regulation, being dependent on the historical basis of society.

Also another oversimplification about power as a social phenomenon is sometimes found. Some theorists hold the view that only the ruling class has power in class societies. Against this view it can be, however, maintained that besides the different sorts of power means and institutions of the ruling class, also the suppressed classes have their specific forms of power-wielding. Moreover, different social strata, ethnic communities, territorial unities, tribal and clan communities, associations, business corporations, communities of production and profession, cultural and scientific societies and various kinds of official or voluntary unions manifest themselves as agents of power. A basic point in the dialectics of social development is that the "struggle of the opposites" between progressive and regressive forces, classes and other interest groups, strata and associations in society manifests itself within the system of power as well. The fundamental function of the system of power is to uphold the unity of the opposites in this process.

5. Historical experience shows us that the system of power also seeks to protect its *own stability*. In addition to its function of social integration, it safeguards its own survival. The exercise of power has several dimensions, such as political activity, legal activity and the activity of the state. These different sorts of activities posit specific forms of institutionalization and implementation.

This structural differentiation means that the statics and dynamics of the system of power manifest themselves in different sorts of activities, such as the functioning of political, state and legal organs. However, the primary form of activity is the political struggle.

It is generally conceded that the primary factors of change within the system of power are political activity, political struggles, political alliances, political interests and values. This is the reason why Marxist social theory advocates the thesis about the primacy of politics.[10]

Political activity and the dynamics of political conditions manifest themselves first of all in the state activity. For this reason, the day-to-day struggles in political life are framed mainly within state activity. Political achievements are expressed and protected by way of state measures and find also their legal expression within state frames. Law is influenced by the political struggles and events as well. The achievements of political struggles are built into the stable system of law. The prevailing political practice seeks to express its own efforts also in a legal form and to enforce them by legal means: for instance, important political achievements are legally fixed in the constitution.

Historical experience also shows us that the stabilizing role of the law enforced by the state is not in the foreground in certain systems of power. In these systems, it is mainly the changing political endeavours that are given a legal expression. This is due to the fact that the basic character of the system of power is always reflected in law: legal institutions and decisions manifest themselves in different ways in democratic *vis-à-vis* dictatorial systems.

The relations of power in a given country are not the only factor determining the peculiarity of law and the legal system. The *international* constellations of power influence the inner characteristics of law in a given country as well. It should be also emphasized that in international law, the international power relations (struggles, agreements, compromises) very much influence the legal regulation of international coexistence and the development of international law, its stabilization and degree of effectiveness.

The previous analysis suggests that law exists as a special social phenomenon within a social class system of power. Law is closely connected to political and state activity but has also its autonomous role, first of all in safeguarding the stability of the power system.

II

1. The basic thesis of Marxist social theory, as we have seen, is that law has its own function within society and the system of the interaction of social phenomena. This means that law has its own social goals, specific functions and forms of activity which have a distinct influence on society.

In historical development, the determining role of economy in relation to law is mediated by the system of power. Law has its relations to different social, economic and cultural factors, and it has an influence on the system of power. But it is not only in connection with the power of the ruling class and political power but in connection with the whole system of power that law plays its specific role as a part of the social totality. Law has an important role in organizing social intercourse and coexistence, and it protects the stability of the all-embracing system of power.

The regulative function of law has its positive role in the organization of different systems of power, such as the legal defence of the political establishment, the economic management system and the ideal-educational system of ideological power.

2. It is an essential thesis of the Marxist social theory that law does not have an independent history.[11] However, this does not mean that law has no independent social influence and activity. The basic thesis only says that law exists and functions in its dependence on the concrete historical circumstances and conditions and is bound up with the development of the society as a whole. Historical evidence shows that legislative power, military power and judicial power are centralized in primitive systems of power (such as the Asian despotisms), where the position and independence of law are uncertain and vacillating. On the other hand, in modern systems of power a differentiated organizational structure and distribution of power can be found. Law has a significant, autonomous social role in these systems.

Law contributes as a specific factor of power to social integration and displays a regulative activity, depending on the nature of the system of power and the given historical circumstances. Since law is dependent on the demands of the system of power, the role it plays in social development can be positive or negative. Law produces conservative effects or promotes the realization of the values underlying the exercise of power. The realization of these values is confirmed in law in virtue of special legal values such as legal security.[12]

I have already emphasized that law promotes the stabilization of the relations of power. In addition to this, it displays an activity which is connected to the dynamics of power relations. The context of this activity is the dialectics of stability and change in legal development. It is here that the self-movement and self-development of law are particularly relevant.

The power-character of law is formulated in the socialist legal theory in terms of the two *functions* of law: its class function and its normative function. First of all, law serves the leading role and the interests of the ruling class through its regulative activity. The other field of activity is based on the normative function of law: law promotes social integration, social reproduction and public security. In addition to these, law maintains public order, solves conflicts and promotes the development of social intercourse.

3. Several peculiarities of law depend, to a great extent, on the social basis of *legal activity* and concrete legal decisions. The positive or negative character, the progressive or conservative tendency of a given system of power influence also the trends of juridical activity. The significance of non-professional legal activity depends, in the first place, on the system of power and the political establishment. Also the role and reputation of professional legal activity and the choice and recruitment of the legal profession reflect the power-political conditions.

The peculiar features of law are basically connected to the system of the division of labour in society. The autonomous position and effects of law can be explained by the fact that a particular group of people takes over the tasks related to the legal regulation of a given social system. This differentiation and emergence of the legal and juristic profession forms the starting point for the development of the organs of the administration of justice. Important characteristics ensuing from this are the structure and the distribution of the administration of justice, the connection between the official and non-professional administration of justice, the structure and the mutual relation of the institutions of law-making as well as application of law. No analysis of law in its social setting can ignore these.

The institutionalization of legal activity may historically take on various forms. The institutionalization in a typical modern system of power leads to the emergence of legislative organs for the legislation, courts for the application of law, and executive bodies (e.g., prisons). An important problem in connection with this is the question of the primariness of state in the state-law-relation. Does the state determine the law? We can conclude on the basis of historical evidence that the organs of legal activity do not necessarily manifest themselves as state organs. Legislation may be performed e.g. by ecclesiastical authorities, military organs, ruling parties in modern societies, or military cliques and governments. Under their guidance certain organs (military organs, administratives, ecclesiastical authorities, party organizations, party courts, *ad hoc* established courts) then attend to the application and administration of law. This shows us that to attribute legislation and enforcement to state organs only would be a simplification of the problem. Besides, state organs as legislators and enforcers of law display legal activity essentially as specific organs of power (for instance, there are state organs for administering cultural, social or economic activities). In view of the interplay of legal organs/power organs, a very interesting problem is the coexistence and sometimes persistence of the communal, the traditional (e.g. tribal, ethnic, religious) forms of the administration of justice. All in all,

I conclude that we should reject the thesis that law is essentially of state character. Recall here what Russell has written: Law

(. . .) as an effective force, depends upon opinion and sentiment even more than upon the powers of police.[13]

4. Important peculiarities of law in its relation to conditions of power result from the *regulative order* of a given social system, that is, from the interrelationship and hierarchy of various norms. The specific social role and place of law depend on its place in the system of norms. Central issues here are: which system of norms is put into prominence; which one is preferred; and which one is put uppermost in the hierarchy of regulative order. These states of affairs are influenced by the practice of the governing system. This explains why such historical examples can be met where law is replaced by a religious or a military norm system or loses its importance and political-organizational norms assume the decisive role in the hierarchy of regulation.

The specific social role of law manifests itself in historical situations where social conditions (mainly the constellation of power) make legal activity possible and necessary. Legal activity as a part of the system of division of labour promotes the effectiveness of legal regulation in a special way, and it is influenced by the ruling ideology of society.

The question of ideology deserves particular attention in the study of legal activity. Legal theory has relatively little discussed the problem of legal ideology and its practical influence. Legal ideologies naturally do not exist in a vacuum. Emphasis should be laid on the effects of the power-ideological and cultural elements which determine the peculiar content of legal ideologies, viewpoints and tendencies of thought. The ideological requirements of the legal profession are essential components in all legal activity. In particular, environmental factors (intellectual and social) determine the character of tasks to be performed by lawyers, legislators and judges, and they also determine the requirement of the realization of power-related, political and legal values. It depends on the particular social situation whether the realization of legal values is emphasized or lawyers are expected to support the biased interests of power with legal means and thereby ignore some traditional legal values. This of course is related to the ubiquitous and perennial question what the role of law is in the development of society.[14]

The social determination of law manifests itself not only in the wielding of power in society but also in the economic and cultural conditions of this activity and in the influence of the international conditions as well. The upshot of our study is that law is a specific and complex social phenomenon which has its autonomous role in society. It affects the system of social interrelationships, the social totality as a whole. However, law cannot be studied in isolation, as it exists only through its social determinations in concrete circumstances.

Finally, I would like to emphasize that the stress on the interplay of power and law is likely to safeguard legal theory against one-sided approaches which simple-mindedly overemphasize the effect of power upon law or the power-character of law. Marxist social and legal theory studies law in its social totality and social environment and analyses its autonomous position and social influence as connected with the historical development of societal forms.

Eötvös Loránd University, Budapest

NOTES

[1] See Lord Lloyd of Hampstead, *Introduction to Jurisprudence*, London 1972.
[2] Imre Szabó, *Jogelmélet* (Theory of Law, Hungarian ed.), Budapest 1977, 74 and 91.
[3] Vilmos Peschka, *A modern jogfilozófia alapproblémái* (The Basic Problems of Modern Philosophy of Law), Budapest 1972, 354.
[4] M. Posch, 'Zum Widerspruch zwischen Form und Inhalt des Rechts', *Staat und Recht* (1957), Heft 6, 612.
[5] See Mihály Samu, *Hatalom és állam* (Power and State), Budapest 1982.
[6] See for instance Stefan Zweig, *Fouché*, Budapest 1968; Heinrich Mann, *Az alattvaló* (Subjected), Budapest 1974.
[7] B. Russell, *Power. A New Social Analysis*, London 1938, 16.
[8] Marx-Engels, *Selected Works*, Vol. 2 (Hungarian ed.), Budapest 1963, 287.
[9] A. Gramsci, *Az új fejedelem* (The New Prince), Budapest 1977, 287.
[10] Lenin, *Works*, Vol. 32 (Hungarian ed.), Budapest 1955, 74.
[11] "It should not be forgotten that law has not, any more than religion, an independent history." K. Marx, *German Ideology*, in K. Marx, *Selected Writings in Sociology and Social Philosophy*, London 1961, 229.
[12] E. Bodenheimer, *Jurisprudence*, Cambridge, Mass. 1962, 238.
[13] B. Russell, *op. cit.*, 38.
[14] See W. Friedman, *Law in Changing Society*, London 1972.

III

IS AND OUGHT: PRESENT ISSUES IN ARGUMENTATION AND LEGAL THINKING

JUNICHI AOMI

PERSUASIVE DEFINITIONS IN SOCIAL SCIENCES AND SOCIAL THOUGHT

The concept of "persuasive definition" was introduced by C. L. Stevenson in the 1930's. Stevenson's theory may be paraphrased as follows: A persuasive definition is a definition of a word that changes – *mala fide* or *bona fide* – the listeners' or readers' emotional attitude, by giving a new meaning to the word. A persuasive definition is effective, when (1) the word has strong emotive connotations (good or bad, laudatory or derogatory, and so on), which Stevenson calls "emotive meaning" (a phrase coined by Ogden and Richards in their *The Meaning of Meaning*, 1923); (2) the word is vague and ambiguous enough, in respect to its "descriptive meaning", for purposes of semantical manipulation; (3) the changes of meaning by means of redefinition have to proceed unnoticed by naive listeners and readers so that they remain unaware of the fact that their emotional attitudes are actually affected as a result of manipulation; and (4) the *emotive* meaning of the word remains unaltered (normally this is *bound* to be the case, because our emotive reactions depend on the phylogenetically older parts of our brain).

I hope that the paraphrase given above is not a gross misinterpretation of Stevenson's views. I would specify two additional conditions that tend to enhance the efficacy ('force', 'convincing power', and so on) of a persuasive definition: (1) additional use of esoteric, profound-sounding expressions, which are in reality highly vague, ambiguous, and devoid of content (e.g., "*das wahre Wesen von* x", etc.); (2) (in connection with the above) additional use of styles of argumentation which sound or look very impressive but which are so confusing and obscure that they hardly lend themselves to rationally controlled validation or refutation.

Understood in this way, Stevenson's theory of persuasive definition turns out to be a very important tool in analyzing and criticizing "profound" theories in philosophy, social sciences, and social thought.

In philosophy, I will cite as one of the most important examples the Hegelian doctrine or notion of "freedom", a notion which has been so often exploited for purposes of ideological manipulation by the Frankfurt school of social theory, Harold Laski, and others. Hegel's contention that freedom is "self-determination" is, as such, understandable and acceptable.

E. Bulygin et al. (eds.), Man, Law and Modern Forms of Life, 187–190.

However, with the aid of mystifying expressions like "der allgemeine Wille" (which is certainly even more nebulous than Rousseau's *volonté générale*), and of his favourite distinction of *die Vernunft*, a higher form or source of knowledge, often hypostatized, from what he calls *das blosse und platte Verstandesdenken*, he succeeds in insinuating a totally different emotional attitude into the hearts of naive and unsuspecting believers.

In the fields of social sciences and social thought, one may cite the Marxian doctrine widely known as "the labour theory of value". To put it briefly, the central issue here is the *logical status* of this "theory". If we borrow C. G. Hempel's framework from his theory of definition, there are at least three possibilities of interpretation here. The Marxian theory can be interpreted: (1) as a definition (which means nominal definition); (2) as an empirical statement; or (3) as a "meaning analysis" (an analytic explanation of the meaning of a word). The third possibility is likely to be rejected by orthodox Marxians as being "trivial". On the other hand, it is difficult, for simply logical reasons (apart from non-logical considerations), to consider the labour theory of value as an empirical statement, because, first of all, the meaning of the term "value" has to be clear (that is, precise and unambiguous), either by established unanimous usage or by careful redefinition (which is obviously not the case).

For these and many other reasons, I am inclined to regard the labour theory of value as a definition. My standpoint here finds support in works of many scholars, including Bertrand Russell (who shows incredible insight and foresight already in his first publication, *German Social Democracy*, 1896, written when the author was twenty-three years old) and Joan Robinson (e.g., in her *An Essay on Marxian Economics*).

If you regard the Marxian theory as a definition, however, the consequences are disastrous, simply on logical grounds. First, a definition is nothing more or less than a decision (a stipulation, an agreement, etc.) to give a certain meaning to a word or to use it in a certain way.[1] Definitions are often important and sometimes even necessary. As such, however, they are devoid of empirical content and do not have a truth value. Secondly, a sentence which is derived from a definition alone is also devoid of content (though it may have a truth value), unless an empirical statement is used as an additional premise in conjunction with the definition. For instance, it is logically valid to deduce from Marxian theory of value sentences such as "Only labour is capable of producing value"; "Capital as such is incapable of producing value, although it may be helpful in an indirect way by enhancing the productivity of labour", and so on. Such sentences *are true*, but do not provide us with any empirical information. They are true only in the same sense in which the sentence "All bachelors are unmarried" is true.

For the sake of fairness, I hasten to add that it *is* possible to reinterpret the Marxian theory as a kind of set of empirical statements. In that case, however, the theory turns into an empirical hypothesis, which is only approximately true, and only under a number of specified conditions. As such, it is also subject to refutation. In fact, some of the theories of value proposed by Marx's predecessors, especially by Ricardo, were theories of this type.

This interpretation will not satisfy orthodox Marxians, either. They will contend that the Marxian theory of value has a status and content which are much more profound, important, and "essential". They will say that Marx succeeded in unveiling "the true nature and essence of value" which had remained concealed from his predecessors. From the viewpoint of modern theories of definition (propounded by Dubislav, Carnap, Hempel, and others) a statement of the form: "*A* (or *A, B, C* and so on) is *das Wesen von x*", is highly ambiguous – to say the least, from logical points of view. Karl Popper, too, has dwelt on this question, which he discusses in connection with his criticism of what he calls "essentialism", though his standpoint differs from those of Carnap and others in that he is reluctant to admit the importance of definitions.

In this paper, let me simply point out that I am basically in agreement with the scholars whose names I have just mentioned. From this point of view, it is clear that the Marxian theory of value is one of the most important achievements (if you like, an achievement of "world-historical importance") in the history of ideas. In the eyes of those who admired Marx, the theory constituted the central part of his system of economics (or, more broadly, of his social thought), because it makes it possible for them to prove *in a scientific way* that capitalism is a regime of exploitation. It is interesting to note that Marx, Engels and their followers believed *bona fide* that they provided a *scientific foundation* for their moral resentment (which I sincerely share) against the class society that they observed in the latter half of the 19th century. It is this combination of scientism and moralism that made them proud, criticizing other socialists as being "mere Utopians". (Incidentally, it is to be noted in passing that Marx's meta-ethical position was one of a naturalist, though not always consistent.)

I have discussed the Marxian theory of value, in order to show that Stevenson's theory of persuasive definition, dating back to the 1930's, may still be regarded as a very useful analytic tool in social sciences and social thought, for purposes of *Ideologiekritik*. This is so especially if we combine this theory with the modern theories of definition, the Popperian criticism of essentialism, Ernst Topitsch's theories concerning what he calls *Leerformeln*, the critique of "mythical models in epistemology", and so on.

The University of Tokyo

NOTE

[1] The traditional theory that there is another (and much more important) kind of definition called "real definition" is, in my opinion, untenable, although I do not deny that there are some elements in the traditional doctrine that deserve attention. The obscure notion of "real definition" was clarified and rationally reconstructed by Carnap's theory of "explication".

RISTO HILPINEN

NORMATIVE CONFLICTS AND LEGAL REASONING

I

Much of the recent research on the logic of norms (deontic logic) has been based on the view that the normative concepts of *obligation, permission*, and *prohibition* are analogous to the modal concepts (alethic modalities) *necessity, possibility*, and *impossibility*, and that the logic of norms can be regarded as a branch of modal logic. This conception of the logic of norms may be termed "the standard modal approach to deontic logic".[1] It can be traced back (at least) to late medieval philosophy: several 14th-century philosophers and logicians observed the analogies between normative concepts and modal concepts and discussed the deontic counterparts of various laws of modal logic.[2] A simple deontic system of this kind, called the system *D*, is obtained by adding to propositional logic two deontic axioms (or axiom schemata), the *consistency principle*

(D) $OA \rightarrow \sim O \sim A$

and the *conjunction principle*

(C) $OA \,\&\, OB \leftrightarrow O(A \,\&\, B)$,

where '*O*' is the operator for "deontic (normative) necessity" or the obligation operator, and two rules,

(R1) From A, to infer OA

and

(R2) From $A \rightarrow B$, to infer $OA \rightarrow OB$.

(R1) is the deontic variant of the "rule of necessitation" of modal logic, and (R2) may be termed "the consequence principle". This system is often called "the standard system of deontic logic".[3] More generally, any deontic system which includes the system *D* may be termed a "standard system".

E. Bulygin et al. (eds.), Man, Law and Modern Forms of Life, 191–208.

II

Recently the standard approach and the systems of deontic logic based upon it have been criticized in several respects. I shall mention here two such criticisms.

First, some philosophers have argued that the standard approach exaggerates the analogies between deontic and alethic modalities and tends to ignore those features of normative concepts which distinguish them from other modalities. For example, Georg Henrik von Wright has observed that "fertile as the analogies between the alethic and the deontic modalities may be, they are also open to doubts".[4] Perhaps the most distinctive feature of deontic modalities is that unlike "natural necessities", moral necessities or obligations can (or at least can *seem* to) conflict with each other. The resolution of such normative conflicts forms an important part of moral discourse.[5]

According to this criticism, the concept of obligation does not satisfy the principle of normative consistency (*D*). This means that both OA and $O \sim A$, that is,

(1) $OA \,\&\, O \sim A$,

may hold in some situation. If (*D*) is rejected, the conjunction principle (*C*) must be rejected as well, since (1) and (*C*) entail

(2) $O(A \,\&\, {\sim}A)$,

which seems definitely unacceptable: a person may perhaps be under *conflicting* obligations, but he can hardly be subject to a self-contradictory (or impossible) obligation.[6] I assume here that the concept of obligation expressed by the *O*-operator satisfies a weak form of the Sollen-Können principle: genuine obligations cannot involve (logically) impossible or inconsistent acts or states of affairs.

The standard approach to deontic logic has also been criticized on the ground that the intended interpretation of the normative operators is often left unclear. Sentences containing the *O*-operator (the operator for deontic necessity) are variously interpreted as sentences about *obligations* or as sentences expressing what some agent *ought to do* (or about what *ought to be the case*) in a given situation, without any regard to the logical or semantic differences between these notions. For example, Bruce Vermazen has recently observed:

Where the writer is using '*O*' as the special deontic modal symbol, an expression like '*OF*(*a*)' may be rendered in one place as 'It ought to be the case that *F*(*a*)' or '*a* ought to *F*', in another as '*a* is obligated to *F*', in yet another as '*a* is obliged to *F*', and so on. Since it seems obvious that some pairs of these renderings have different truth-conditions, one wonders whether a theorem that seems intuitively valid when '*O*' is replaced by 'is obligated' will seem so when '*O*' is replaced by 'ought' and vice versa; often it will not.[7]

These two criticisms are related to each other. If the concept of obligation is distinguished from the concept of *ought*, the logical behaviour of the latter notion may be formalizable in terms of the standard system of deontic logic even though this does not hold for the former (or vice versa). But this depends on how ought-sentences and sentences about obligations are interpreted.

III

I shall assume here that a person's obligations are determined by various (moral and legal) rules and principles, and by the circumstances in which he acts. I assume that if a person has in a given situation an obligation to act in a certain way *A*, then some legal or moral rule or principle *requires A* in that situation, and if a person has an obligation to refrain from performing an act *A*, then some rule or principle *excludes A* in that situation. By an "act" I understand in the present context the *character* of a person's behaviour; thus acts are expressed by propositions, and the relationships of requirement and exclusion can be regarded as relations between propositions.[8]

A person is in every action situation subject to various requirements, according to which he should perform certain acts and avoid others. Normally he behaves in accordance with these requirements and fulfills them almost automatically without any deliberation. But when the requirements conflict with each other, i.e., when the agent is subject to several requirements which cannot be simultaneously satisfied, he has to deliberate and decide *what he ought to do*. In such a situation the same act is both required and excluded by the normative principles accepted by the agent. It is important to note that a system of norms need not be formally inconsistent to generate normative conflicts: the conflicts may depend on contingent circumstances – on the agent's past actions or on circumstances which are beyond the agent's control.[9] C. L. Hamblin has called systems of rules which do not generate normative conflicts "quandary-free" systems.[10] He distinguishes between several different senses of quandary-freedom. For example, a system is *legislatively* quandary-free if it cannot generate conflict-situations provided everyone obeys the rules of the system, and a system is *strategically* quandary-free if and only if it is possible for each person to find a strategy which does not violate the rules of the system and will keep him out of quandaries (conflict situations) regardless of what other persons do (provided they act legally). An even weaker requirement of consistency is that of *minimal* quandary-freedom: a set of norms is quandary-free in a minimal sense if it is not impossible that everyone's actions are always legal, that is, if it is possible for everyone to act (possibly in cooperation with others) in such a way that no quandaries arise.[11] The formal consistency of a normative system does not ensure more than minimal quandary-freedom. (It does not guarantee even this if the concept of possibility is interpreted as physical or human possibility and not as a logical possibility.)

IV

The characterization of normative conflicts given above concerns only conflicts between *mandatory* norms. Many legal philosophers assume that in addition to mandatory norms, a normative system may also contain *permissive* norms.[12] For example, Aleksander Peczenik has distinguished between two basic kinds of source-norms in the Swedish law: there are *mandatory* source-norms which tell which sources always must or should be used for the justification of judicial decisions, and non-mandatory norms concerning the materials which *may* be used as a basis of a decision. Norms of the latter kind are permissive source-norms.[13]

A situation in which the same act is both excluded (prohibited) and explicitly permitted by the norms of a certain system is without doubt a conflict-situation, even though an agent can *comply* with the norms of the system (i.e., avoid violating the norms of the system) simply by refraining from acting in the way indicated by the permissive norm. Here we have to observe a distinction which has no significance in the case of purely mandatory systems (systems of mandatory norms). To comply with a given system of norms, we need not act *in accordance with* or *conform* to every norm in the system. A person who does not act in conformity with a permissive norm does not thereby *violate* the norm. Failure to conform is a violation of the system only in the case of mandatory norms.

I shall say that an act *conforms* to a norm N whenever it fits the content of N – or has the characteristics specified by the content of N – regardless of whether N is a mandatory or a permissive norm. I propose to call the relation between a normative system and any act which is a necessary condition for the conformity to some norm in the system the relation of *support*:

a system *S* *supports* any act which is either required or explicitly permitted by some norm in *S*. Thus the relation of requirement is a special case of the relation of support: the acts supported by mandatory norms are *required* by the system.

Given the distinction between *support* and *requirement*, we can define three different types of normative conflict.[14]

Type 1. *S requires* in a situation *u* acts *A*, *B*, which cannot be performed together at *u*.

Type 2. *S supports* some act *A* which cannot be performed at *u* together with an act *B required* by *S*.

Type 3. *S supports* some act *A* which cannot be performed at *u* together with an act *B* which is also *supported* by *S*.

Since the concept of requirement is a special case of support, any conflict of type (1) is also of type (2) and (3), and a conflict of type (2) is also of type (3). Thus conflict-types (1)–(3) represent concepts of decreasing stringency: (1) is the strictest concept of normative conflict. This type of conflict was called above a *quandary*. If we assume that mandatory and permissive norms are distinguished by the fact that sanctions are assigned only to the nonconformity with mandatory norms, a quandary is a normative conflict in which the sanction is unavoidable. A conflict of the second type restricts the freedom of action of the agent in a way in which the third type of conflict does not: in a situation of the second type, an action which conforms to some norm *may* make the agent subject to a sanction, but this is not the case in situations of the third type. For this reason it seems inappropriate to apply the expression "normative conflict" to situations of the third type: only situations of type (1) and (2) are genuine conflicts. According to this view, permissive norms cannot conflict with each other.

Stephen Munzer has argued that even situations of the third type can sometimes be regarded as conflict situations.[15] He mentions two kinds of cases as examples of such situations. First, there are cases in which "the norm-subject acts on one permission and thereby fails to act on a different permission which is backed by a strong, intimately related pressure or policy". However, in cases of this kind the two acts are not merely *supported* by a system of norms: one of the acts is apparently also *required* by the pressure or policy mentioned by Munzer. Thus the appearance of a conflict is here due to the fact that the situation resembles a conflict situation of type (2). Examples of the second kind are cases in which conformity to two permissive norms *creates* a conflict situation of type (1) or type (2). But it is obvious that the permissions themselves do not conflict (in sense (3)), because it is possible to act in accordance with both in the same situation. In this paper I shall discuss only conflicts between mandatory norms, that is, conflicts of type (1).

V

I shall call an ought-statement which tells how an agent ought to act in a given situation a *practical ought-sentence* or a *practical directive*. If an agent has two mutually incompatible obligations, he cannot fulfill both, but it seems reasonable to assume that he ought to fulfill at least one of them. Practical ought-sentences or practical directives tell a person how he ought to resolve his normative conflicts. They can have this function only if they satisfy the principle of consistency and the conjunction principle. Thus I assume that unlike the concept of obligation (or requirement), the practical concept of ought satisfies the principles of standard deontic logic.[16]

The reasoning by which an agent infers from his obligations (or from the requirements pertaining to his conduct) what he ought to do in a given situation is a form of practical reasoning (or practical deliberation). This type of reasoning is formally analogous to the determination of an agent's intention to act (and hence of his actions) on the basis of his interests, objectives, and desires. The models of practical reasoning put forward in recent philosophy of action, for example, the models in which practical reasoning is presented in the form of a "practical syllogism", are unsatisfactory because they are not applicable to nontrivial situations in which the agent's interests and objectives conflict with each other.[17]

VI

How can conflicts of obligation and other normative conflicts be resolved? Many philosophers have suggested that moral rules and principles can be ordered according to their importance, and that obligations can be weighed on the basis of such an ordering: in the case of a conflict, the weightiest obligation prevails. A sophisticated form of this idea has been presented by Carlos Alchourrón and David Makinson in their recent paper 'Hierarchies of Regulations and their Logic'.[18] In some cases such an ordering is thought of as being determined by second-order rules which specify the relative importance of the first-order rules. The view that this solution is applicable to all normative conflicts implies that all conflicts of obligation are merely apparent, and result from an imperfect knowledge of the complete system of legal or moral rules and principles. A complete system of first-order and second-order rules should imply a unique solution to every (apparent) moral dilemma.

This conception of normative conflicts has been especially common in the philosophy of law. Many legal philosophers have assumed that conflicting laws cannot be valid, and that a complete system of laws must therefore contain second-order legal principles (such as *lex posterior derogat priori*), by means of which all possible conflicts between laws (or first-order rules) can be resolved in an unambiguous way.[19] However, the presence of second-order rules or principles in a normative system does not in itself guarantee complete quandary-freedom, because the second-order rules may also conflict with each other.

Even though such a method of resolution might be applicable to many apparent conflicts between legal rules – I shall return to this question later – it is far from obvious that *all* normative conflicts (for example, moral conflicts) can be resolved with the help of second-order rules. The philosophers who have argued that *genuine* moral conflicts are possible have in effect argued that *prima facie* conflicts cannot always be resolved by second-order rules or in terms of an ordering of the first-order rules.[20]

VII

Another possible way to resolve normative conflicts is to consider the *consequences* of the acts under consideration. I believe that this is the method we actually use in many situations.

What are the consequences of a given act? As was mentioned above, I take here acts to be (or to be expressible by) *propositions* of certain kind: the *identity* of an act is determined by an agent, an act-predicate which specifies the character of the act, and the situation in which the agent performs the act. The concept of requirement used in this paper can be regarded as a relation between propositions only if acts are understood in this way.

When an agent performs an act, he initiates a causal process and brings about various events. For example, by turning the steering wheel of a ship the steerman can cause the ship to turn. Such an event – or rather the fact that the agent causes the event – can often be redescribed as an act performed by the agent: when the steerman turns the steering wheel and thus causes the ship to turn, we say that he turns the ship by turning the wheel. Alvin Goldman calls such a relation between acts *causal generation*: the act of turning the wheel generates causally the act of turning the ship. More generally, whenever an agent does *B* by doing *A*, the act *A* is said to generate the act *B*. (All generation relations between acts are not instances of causal generation.)[21] Thus many consequences of an act *A* can be redescribed as acts generated by *A*, or as acts which the agent performs by performing *A*. We can say that the performance of *A* in a certain situation is also a performance of any act generated by *A*. It is important here to distinguish an act (in the sense intended here) from its performance. Logically speaking, the performance of an act in a certain situation can be regarded as an *individual* which exemplifies (or can be characterized in terms of) several different acts. The generation relation between acts is a special case of the possibility of viewing an individual thing from different perspectives or points of view and applying different descriptions to it.

VIII

Let us consider a normative conflict in which a certain moral principle *P* requires an act *A* and another principle *P'* requires *B*, and *A* and *B* are incompatible: the agent cannot do both. The agent is contemplating *A* and *B*; he has not yet performed *A* or *B*, and thus no acts have been generated by *A* or *B*. However, on the basis of his knowledge about the world the agent is in a position to regard certain possible consequences of *A* and *B* as *serious possibilities*, that is, as something which may reasonably be expected on the basis of *A* or *B*. These possible consequences can be redescribed as acts generated by *A* and *B*, in the way indicated above.

Let $A_1, A_2, \ldots, A_m$ be a sample of the possible consequences of *A* and let $B_1, B_2, \ldots, B_n$ be a sample of the possible consequences of *B*, redescribed as acts generated by *A* and *B*, respectively. If the agent chooses to do *A*, he may, as far as he knows, be performing any of the acts $A_1, \ldots, A_m$, and if he performs *B*, he may be performing any of the acts $B_1, \ldots, B_n$. These acts may also be regarded as (possible) characteristics of the performance of *A* and *B*, respectively.

When we judge or evaluate the actions of an agent in a given situation, the *object* of the evaluation is the agent's *behaviour* or his *performance* in that situation.[22] If the agent does *A*, then his behaviour can be described in terms of the consequences of *A* as well as by *A* itself, and therefore the agent's behaviour cannot be evaluated *retrospectively* (i.e., judged) without considering the consequences of *A* and the possible consequences of the acts which the agent could have performed instead of *A*, as well as the normative principles which may require or exclude these consequences. For this reason the traditional distinction between deontological and teleological (or consequentialist) approaches to ethics seems partly illusory: both approaches require the investigation of the (possible) consequences of our actions.[23] (In this paper I have adopted a (mainly) teleological conception of morality; cf. the beginning of Section III.) Practical directives or practical ought-sentences concern possible future acts; they evaluate actions *prospectively*, not retrospectively, but such a prospective evaluation should anticipate the future retrospective evaluation, which has the agent's actual behaviour or performance as its object.[24] Thus the resolution of a normative conflict involving two alternative acts, A and B, should be based on the investigation of the possible consequences of A and B, that is, on a study of the possible characteristics of the alternative actions open to the agent. Such an investigation yields the following method of resolving (or attempting to resolve) a moral dilemma involving A and B.

Let $C(A)$ be a sample of the possible consequences of A and $C(B)$ a sample of the possible consequences of B. All moral principles which *require* some act in $C(A)$ can be regarded as reasons for performing A – roughly in the way in which the verified consequences of some hypothesis are regarded as reasons for accepting the hypothesis – and the principles which exclude some act in $C(A)$ can be regarded as reasons for not performing A. (We might of course also say that the consequences supported or required by some principle are reasons for performing the act, and those excluded by some principle are reasons for not performing it.) Let the sets of these principles be $G(A)$ and $H(A)$, respectively: $G(A)$ may be termed the *normative ground* of A, and $H(A)$ the (normative) *counter-ground* of A. If we assume that the grounds and the counter-grounds of A and B can be compared with each other, it seems reasonable to say that the agent ought to perform A rather than B if its normative ground is in some sense weightier than that of B, but the counter-ground of A does not outweigh that of B – or if the counter-ground of B outweighs that of A, but the ground of B does not outweigh that of A. Let '$Z_1 > Z_2$' (where Z_1 and Z_2 are sets of moral principles) mean that Z_1 outweighs Z_2 and let '$Z_1 \geqslant Z_2$' mean that Z_1 and Z_2 are comparable but the latter does not outweigh the former. The analysis of the concept of practical ought suggested above can now be formulated as follows:

(D1) Ought (A, B) (the agent ought to perform A rather than B) if and only if (i) $G(A) > G(B)$ and $H(B) \geqslant H(A)$, or (ii) $G(A) \geqslant G(B)$ and $H(B) > H(A)$.

(D1) can be generalized in an obvious way to situations involving several conflicting acts:

(D2) Ought $(A, B_1, \ldots, B_m)$ if and only if, for every B_i $(i = 1, \ldots, m)$:
(i) $G(A) > G(B_i)$ and $H(B_i) \geqslant H(A)$, or
(ii) $G(A) \geqslant G(B_i)$ and $H(B_i) > H(A)$.

'Ought $(A, B_1, \ldots, B_m)$' may be read: "The agent ought to perform A rather than any of the acts $B_1, \ldots, B_m$".

This method need not always lead to an unambiguous resolution of a conflict situation: A and B may turn out to be incomparable (within a certain sample of their consequences). But there are also situations in which the comparison of the grounds and the counter-grounds of A and B seems to yield an unproblematic decision: for example, if $G(B)$ is a proper subset of $G(A)$, and $H(A) \subseteq H(B)$, A seems obviously preferable to B. Although the method need not always lead to an unproblematic result, it is a "rational" method of resolving normative conflicts in the sense that it is based on inquiry and argument.

Suppose that principles P_1 and P_2 (belonging to a normative system S) conflict with each other in a certain situation, and that an investigation of the possible consequences of the acts under consideration suggests that the agent should act in accordance with P_2. I have assumed here that this does *not* mean that the normative system is thereby revised by rejecting P_1: in this respect normative conflicts differ from conflicts among beliefs. However, if P_1 conflicts with various other principles on several occasions, and it always seems best to resolve the conflict by acting against P_1, it may be reasonable to revise P_1 or reject it altogether. The conflict situations show that P_1 does not "cohere" with the rest of the system; thus they "disconfirm" P_1 empirically. We have here a kind of (enthymematic) inference from "is" to "may". It is important to note that the incoherence of P_1 with the rest of the system S is relative to contingent empirical situations. Thus the present model of conflict resolution can also be regarded as a model of normative change: it shows how normative systems develop and become adjusted to concrete action situations.

IX

The model of resolution outlined above resembles that put forward by David Ross in his book *The Foundations of Ethics*. My concept of requirement corresponds to Ross's concept of *prima facie* obligation (or *prima facie* duty), and the concept of practical ought corresponds to Ross's concept of absolute obligation. Ross describes the resolution of a normative conflict (a conflict of *prima facie* obligations) in the following way:

Moral principles are not intuitions by the immediate application of which our duty in particular circumstances can be deduced. They state what I have elsewhere called *prima facie* obligations. This way of describing them is, I think, in two ways useful. In the first place, it brings out the fact that when we approach the question, what should I do in these particular circumstances, it is the fitness or unfitness of an imagined act in *certain respects* that first catches our attention. Any possible act has many sides to it which are relevant to its rightness or wrongness; it will bring pleasure to some people, pain to others, it will be the keeping of a promise to one person, at the cost of being the breach of confidence to another, and so on. We are quite incapable of pronouncing straight off on its rightness or wrongness in the totality of these aspects, it is only by recognizing these different features one by one that we can approach the forming of a judgment on the totality of its nature; our first look reveals these features in isolation, one by one; they are what appears *prima facie*. And secondly, they are, *prima facie, obligations*. It is easy to be so impressed by the rightness of an act in one respect that we suppose it to be therefore necessarily the act we are bound to do. But an act may be right in one respect and wrong in more important respects, and therefore not, in the totality of its aspects, the most right of the acts open to us, and then we are not obliged to do it; and another act may be wrong in some respect and yet in its totality the most right of all the acts open to us, and then we *are* bound to do it. *Prima facie* obligation depends on some one aspect of the act; obligation or disobligation attaches to it in virtue of the totality of its aspects.[25]

A more elaborate version of this account of the resolution of moral conflicts has recently been presented by Robert Nozick.[26]

Ross's terminology differs from that employed in the present paper. By an "act" he means what I have called a *performance* (that is, an individual action or an act-individual), and by the "aspects" of an act he means various *characterizations* of a given performance. I have assumed that such characterizations describe the performance (or the agent's behaviour) as exemplifying different *acts*. The "right-making" features of an act depend on what I have called above its *ground*, and its "wrong-making" features are determined by its *counter-ground.*[27]

Ross's characterization of moral conflicts must be clarified and completed in the following respect. As was pointed out above, some of the "properties" or "characteristics" of an individual action can be defined in terms of its consequences, and therefore they need not be immediately associated with the act (or with its performance), but may also be tied to it by complex causal processes. Different "right-making" and "wrong-making" features of an action are not related to it in the same way. We can speak here of the *distance* between the performance of an act and its consequences. In the prospective evaluation of a possible act this distance is a measure of uncertainty: the distant consequences of an act are less certain than its immediate consequences. For the purposes of prospective evaluation, the distance-factor can be expressed in terms of probability or by means of the concept of *degree of possibility.*[28] When we are considering two alternative actions, *A* and *B*, those moral rules and principles which require or exclude relatively distant consequences of *A* or *B* should clearly matter less in the weighing of their grounds and counter-grounds than the principles requiring their immediate or certain consequences. For this reason the weighing of the grounds of *A* and *B* cannot depend on any general ordering of moral rules or sets of moral rules, because a given rule or set of rules is not equally relevant to all moral conflicts. Moreover, the consequences of an act stretch indefinitely towards the future, and any individual action or performance can be viewed from indefinitely many different perspectives. An agent's knowledge of *what he does* in a given situation is necessarily incomplete. Thus it is not possible to compare actions on the basis of all their properties; it is possible to consider only a sample or a subclass of such properties. This holds for the retrospective or judgmental as well as the prospective evaluation of the agent's behaviour.

The distance-factor complicates the resolution of normative conflicts. For example, the inclusion relationships among the grounds and the counter-grounds of actions can be used for conflict resolution in the way suggested in section VIII only if the morally relevant consequences of the alternative actions are approximately equidistant from the action situation. In some theories of moral decision-making (for example, in some utilitarian theories) a measure of the moral relevance of the grounds and counter-grounds of an action is combined with the uncertainty-factor to yield a single measure of the *expected value* of an act. This procedure involves many simplifying assumptions which are not always (or even usually) satisfied in ordinary moral argumentation.

I have argued above that normative conflicts cannot be resolved in a straightforward fashion by an ordering of normative principles or sets of principles, because the relevance of a certain principle to a given dilemma depends on the specific features of the action situation. For example, Jean-Paul Sartre's well-known example of the young man who is torn between the obligation to stay with his mother and protect her, and the obligation to go to the war illustrates this difficulty:

[The young man] had the choice between going to England to join the Free French Forces or of staying near his mother and helping her to live. He fully realized that the woman lived only for him and that his disappearance – or perhaps his death – would plunge her into despair. He also realized that, concretely and in fact, every action he performed on his mother's behalf would be sure of effect in the sense of aiding her to live, whereas anything he did in order to go and fight would be an ambiguous action which might vanish like water into sand and serve no purpose.[29]

This example can be interpreted in different ways. One possibility is to understand the "ambiguity" of the latter action as the uncertainty of its intended effects, or, in the terminology employed here, as their distance from the situation in which the young man had to make his decision. According to Sartre, the young man

found himself confronted by two very different modes of action; the one *concrete, immediate*, but directed towards only one individual; the other an action addressed to an end infinitely greater, a national collectivity, but for that reason ambiguous – and it *might be frustrated on the way*. (Italics mine.)[30]

X

Above I assumed that the ground and the counter-ground of an act are determined by its possible consequences. By "possible consequences" I do not mean all theoretically possible consequences, but only *serious* possibilities, i.e. consequences which might be reasonably expected to follow from the act. New knowledge about the possible consequences may resolve a normative conflict, but it may also create new dilemmas, if an act required by some principle P is found to have a consequence which is excluded by another principle P' (or by the principle P itself). Scientific information about the world is often information about possibilities and not information about what is actually going to happen. For example, a few years ago it was suggested that high-altitude supersonic flights and aerosol sprays might (possibly) contribute to the destruction of the ozone layer around the earth – people were not aware of this possibility before research brought it into focus as a serious possibility. Thus information about the world and the society may resolve or create moral dilemmas, depending on how it affects our knowledge (or our beliefs) about the possible consequences and hence the grounds of various actions. It is often said that science enables us to understand the world; but we can also say that one task of science is to make it possible for us to understand what we do when we act.

The ought-statements determined by the grounds of acts depend on empirical information about the world in the same way as ordinary descriptive statements: they may be undermined or supported by new evidence; they are fallible and subject to doubt, and it is possible to have mistaken beliefs about them; it also seems natural to say that we can *know* that such a statement is true, e.g. if we have good reasons for believing that the ground of *A* is morally weightier than that of *B*, and this difference is not outbalanced by the counter-grounds of *A* and *B*. Ethical knowledge resembles in many respects empirical or scientific knowledge – and the acceptability or moral judgments depends on the available factual information. In this respect the model of moral reasoning outlined here is in agreement with Leonard Nelson's view that "we cannot determine a priori what the content of our duty is in a given case", but "to discover it we must undertake an empirical investigation".[31] However, according to the approach taken here practical ought-statements are always relative to the rules and principles which provide the grounds and counter-grounds for the actions under consideration.

XI

To conclude this paper I shall make a few observations on *legal* conflicts. As was mentioned above, many philosophers of law have assumed that valid laws or legal rules cannot conflict with each other. This classical view – or a view closely related to it – has recently been defended by Ronald Dworkin (among others). According to Dworkin,[32]

> [Legal] rules are applicable in an all-or-nothing fashion. If the facts a rule stipulates are given, then either the rule is valid, in which case the answer it supplies must be accepted, or it is not, in which case it contributes nothing to the decision.

This conception of legal rules presupposes that all *apparent* conflicts be resolved in an unambiguous way (e.g. by means of higher-order rules), and that *every instance* of an apparent conflict between two rules be resolved in the same way. In his paper 'Legal Principles and the Limits of Law' Joseph Raz has argued (seemingly against Dworkin) that laws or legal rules *can* conflict with each other.[33] However, Raz uses the expression "conflict" in a special way: he assumed that laws "conflict" if they "modify and qualify each other".[34] Legal rules can conflict in this sense if (for example) one of them expresses an *exception* to the other.[35] Conflicts of this type are resolved unambiguously within the legal system: they are merely apparent, not genuine normative conflicts.

If all legal conflicts were of this type, the general analysis of normative conflicts presented above in Sections VII–IX would not be relevant to legal conflicts, but the simple account suggested in section VI would be sufficient. According to this view, conflicts between laws are analogous to inconsistencies within belief systems. If two legal rules are found to be incompatible (or generate dilemmas), one (or both) of them must be rejected or revised, just as an inconsistency within a belief system is a sufficient reason for rejecting some of the beliefs belonging to the system. Earlier I have assumed that this does not hold generally for moral rules and principles: a conflict between principles is not always a sufficient ground for rejecting or revising them.

However, this view of legal conflicts seems oversimplified. Recently Ronald Dworkin has argued in several publications that the content of law is not exhausted by legal rules (in the strict sense of the word), but includes also what he calls *legal principles.*[36] According to Dworkin, the content of law may be regarded as analogous to the content of a novel or of a work of fiction.[37] The content of a work of fiction is not determined only by the sentences which the author of the work has written down, but also by various interpretative statements and principles, as well as by facts about the world, which the reader of the work must know in order to understand it.[38] In the same way, Dworkin assumes that legal obligations are not determined by the legal rules alone, but by legal rules together with various interpretative propositions, some of which he calls legal principles.

Legal principles are analogous to moral principles: according to Dworkin, it is in fact impossible to distinguish them from the latter, and therefore law has no sharp boundaries, but is seamlessly associated with other moral standards of the society. In the same way as moral principles, legal principles can conflict with each other, but need not be abandoned or revised on the basis of such conflicts. Thus conflicts between principles (unlike conflicts between legal rules) are genuine normative conflicts, and may be resolved in the way outlined in Sections VII–IX of this paper. According to this model, a legal decision can be redescribed in various ways in the light of different principles, and can therefore be regarded as a performance of several different acts. In the same way as in the case of other normative conflicts, these descriptions and the acts expressed by them may be partly determined by the possible consequences of the decision. This interpretation of legal conflicts is consistent with Dworkin's view that legal principles have relative weights which reflect their importance, but the weight of a principle depends on the circumstances in which the decision is made.[39]

The statement that valid legal rules cannot conflict with each other can be taken to mean that *if* such a conflict were to arise (or seem to arise) but could not be resolved within the system (e.g. by means of second-order rules), then at least one of the rules would have to be rejected or revised. The resolution of a normative conflict in this sense amounts to a revision of the system of rules. Such a revision should obviously be justified by considering the consequences of using the revised system as a basis of decision-making in various cases, that is, by the method described in Section VIII.

In his paper 'Justification of Legal Decisions' Jerzy Wróblewski[40] has distinguished three kinds of legal decisions: law-applying decisions, interpretative decisions and law-making decisions. I have suggested above that both law-applying decisions and interpretative decisions can be subject to genuine normative conflicts whose rational resolution requires an investigation of the possible consequences of the decision. The possibility of conflicts is even more evident in the case of law-making decisions, and in this case consequentialist considerations based on empirical information about the society are obviously essential for rational decision-making.[41]

ACKNOWLEDGEMENTS

This paper is based on research supported by the Finnish State Council for the Humanities. Part of an earlier version of this paper was presented in October 1982 at the First International Conference on the Philosophy of Law, La Plata, Argentina. I am indebted to Professor Jerzy Wróblewski for comments on the earlier version, and to Miss Riitta Lindholm for assistance in the preparation of the manuscript.

Florida State University

NOTES

[1] See Risto Hilpinen, ed., *Deontic Logic: Introductory and Systematic Readings*, Second Impression, D. Reidel, Dordrecht 1981, 'Introduction to the Second Impression', p. xi, and Dagfinn Føllesdal and Risto Hilpinen, 'Deontic Logic: An Introduction', in *Deontic Logic: Introductory and Systematic Readings*, pp. 8–15.

[2] Cf. Simo Knuuttila, 'The Emergence of Deontic Logic in the Fourteenth Century', in *New Studies in Deontic Logic: Norms, Actions, and the Foundations of Ethics*, ed. by Risto Hilpinen, D. Reidel, Dordrecht 1981, pp. 225–248.

[3] See Dagfinn Føllesdal and Risto Hilpinen, *op. cit.*, and Bengt Hansson, 'An Analysis of Some Deontic Logics', in *Deontic Logic: Introductory and Systematic Readings*, pp. 121–147; cf. especially pp. 122–128.

[4] 'On the Logic of Norms and Actions', in *New Studies in Deontic Logic*, p. 6.

[5] Cf. E. J. Lemmon, 'Moral Dilemmas', *The Philosophical Review* 71 (1962), 139–158; Bas C. van Fraassen, 'Values and the Heart's Command', *The Journal of Philosophy* 70 (1973), 5–19; Ruth Barcan Marcus, 'Moral Dilemmas and Consistency', *The Journal of Philosophy* 77 (1980), 121–136; Brian F. Chellas, *Modal Logic: An Introduction*,

Cambridge University Press, Cambridge 1980, pp. 200–202; Peter K. Schotch and Raymond E. Jennings, 'Non-Kripkean Deontic Logic', in *New Studies in Deontic Logic*, pp. 149–162, especially pp. 151–156.

6 Unlike (2), (1) does not entail that the agent is under an obligation to do the impossible. For a discussion of this point, see Bas C. van Fraassen, 'Values and the Heart's Command', 12–13.

7 'On the Logic of Practical 'Ought'-Sentences', *Philosophical Studies* **32** (1977), 1–72; see p. 1.

8 I have discussed this conception of action in greater detail in my paper 'On Normative Change', in *Ethics: Foundations, Problems, and Applications. Proceedings of the Fifth International Wittgenstein Symposium*, ed. by E. Morscher and R. Stranzinger, Vienna 1981, pp. 155–156.

9 Cf. Ruth Barcan Marcus, 'Moral Dilemmas and Consistency', 128–129.

10 C. L. Hamblin, 'Quandaries and the Logic of Rules', *Journal of Philosophical Logic* **1** (1972), 74–85; cf. pp. 79–81.

11 C. L. Hamblin, *op. cit.*, 80–81.

12 For the concept of a permissive norm, see Georg Henrik von Wright, *Norm and Action*, Routledge and Kegan Paul, London 1963, 85–92. See also Stephen Munzer, 'Validity and Legal Conflicts', *The Yale Law Journal* 82 (1973), 1140–1174, especially pp. 1141–2.

13 Aleksander Peczenik, *The Basis of Legal Justification*, Lund 1983, pp. 36–38.

14 The three types of conflict defined here correspond to the classification of legal conflicts given by Stephen Munzer in 'Validity and Legal Conflicts', 1141–1143.

15 Stephen Munzer, *op. cit.*, 1146.

16 I am assuming here that the logic of obligation can be systematized in the way suggested by Bas C. van Fraassen in 'Values and the Heart's Command', 16–18, or by what Brian F. Chellas calls "the minimal deontic logic": see his *Modal Logic: An Introduction*, p. 202. The distinction between requirements and practical directives (or practical oughts) is familiar from earlier literature on ethics, but different philosohers have expressed it differently. Many philosophers have described moral conflicts in terms of competing *oughts*; cf. Bernard Williams, 'Ethical Consistency', in *Problems of the Self*, Cambridge University Press, Cambridge 1973, pp. 166–186.

17 Cf. Georg Henrik von Wright, 'On So-called Practical Inference', in *Practical Reasoning*, ed. by Joseph Raz, Oxford University Press, Oxford 1978, pp. 46–62.

18 Carlos E. Alchourrón and David Makinson, 'Hierarchies of Regulations and their Logic', in *New Studies in Deontic Logic*, pp. 125–148. See also Carlos E. Alchourrón and Eugenio Bulygin, 'The Expressive Conception of Norms', *New Studies in Deontic Logic*, pp. 95–124.

19 Cf. Joseph Raz, 'Legal Principles and the Limits of Law', *The Yale Law Journal* **81** (1972), 823–854, especially p. 829.

20 See E. J. Lemmon, 'Moral Dilemmas'; Ruth Barcan Marcus, 'Moral Dilemmas and Consistency'; and Peter K. Schotch and Raymond Jennings, 'Non-Kripkean Deontic Logic' (cf. note 5).

21 Alvin I. Goldman, *A Theory of Human Action*, Englewood Cliffs, N.J. 1970, pp. 20–48.

22 This is only one possible way of evaluating actions. The evaluation might also concern the agent's *intentions*, but this possibility is disregarded here.

[23] For the distinction between deontological and teleological ethics, see C. D. Broad, *Five Types of Ethical Theory*, Routledge and Kegan Paul, London 1930, pp. 206–208. Andrew Oldenquist has presented a similar argument in his paper 'Rules and Consequences', *Mind* 75 (1966), 180–192. According to Oldenquist, the "traditional teleological-deontological distinction does not mark two fundamentally different theories about what is relevant to the rightness of an action, but instead only distinguishes two alternative ways of saying the same thing." (p. 180). I am indebted for this reference to Professor Robert Almeder.

[24] In his paper 'Deontic Logic as Founded on Tense Logic' (in *New Studies in Deontic Logic*, 165–176) Richmond Thomason has made a distinction between the judgmental and the *deliberative* use of ought-sentences, which corresponds to distinction between the retrospective and the prospective evaluation of action made here. See also Richmond Thomason, 'Deontic Logic and the Role of Freedom of Moral Deliberation', *New Studies in Deontic Logic*, 177–186; especially pp. 179–180.

[25] W. David Ross, *The Foundations of Ethics*, Clarendon Press, Oxford 1939, p. 84. The distinction between prima facie obligation and absolute obligation was introduced by Ross in his earlier work *The Right and the Good*, Clarendon Press, Oxford 1930, p. 19.

[26] Robert Nozick, 'Moral Complications and Moral Structures', *Natural Law Forum* **13** (1968), 1–50, and *Philosophical Explanations*, Clarendon Press, Oxford, pp. 474–504. I am indebted for the former reference to Professor Ingmar Pörn.

[27] Cf. Robert Nozick, *Philosophical Explanations*, 479.

[28] For an analysis of this notion, see my paper 'Some Epistemological Interpretations of Modal Logic', in *Logic and Philosophy*, ed. by G. H. von Wright, Martinus Nijhoff, The Hague 1980, pp. 19–29.

[29] Jean-Paul Sartre, *Existentialism and Humanism*, London 1948, pp. 35–36.

[30] Jean-Paul Sartre, *loc. cit.*

[31] Leonard Nelson, *System of Ethics*, Yale University Press, New Haven 1956, p. 95. I am indebted for this reference to Dr. Seppo Sajama.

[32] Ronald M. Dworkin, 'Is Law a System of Rules?', in *Essays in Legal Philosophy*, ed. by Robert S. Summers, Basil Blackwell, Oxford 1970, pp. 25–60; see p. 37.

[33] *The Yale Law Journal* **81** (1972), 823–854.

[34] *Op. cit.*, 832.

[35] Cf. Ronald M. Dworkin, *Taking Rights Seriously*, Harvard University Press, Cambridge, Mass. 1978, p. 74.

[36] 'Is Law a System of Rules?', *Essays in Legal Philosophy*, 34–41; *Taking Rights Seriously*, 22–28.

[37] See Ronald M. Dworkin, 'No Right Answer?', in *Law, Morality, and Society: Essays in Honour of H. L. A. Hart*, ed. by P. M. S. Hacker and J. Raz, Clarendon Press, Oxford, pp. 58–84.

[38] Cf. David Lewis, 'Truth in Fiction', *American Philosophical Quarterly* **15** (1978), 37–46, and Nicholas Wolterstorff, *Works and Worlds of Art*, Clarendon Press, Oxford 1980.

[39] See *Taking Rights Seriously*, 77–78.

[40] *Revue Internationale de Philosophie,* **127–128** (1979), 277–293.

[41] For a detailed discussion of consequentialist arguments in legal reasoning and justification, see Neil MacCormick, *Legal Reasoning and Legal Theory*, Clarendon Press, Oxford 1978, ch. VI.

JAAKKO HINTIKKA

LEGAL REASONING AND LEGAL SYSTEMS

It is often thought that the study of legal reasoning is a relatively recondite subject, connected much more closely with problems of epistemology and interpretation than with questions of the organization of the judicial system. However, I shall suggest in this paper that this impression is not entirely correct. What I shall do is the following: I shall first outline a new, wider conception of reasoning in general, wider than what is found in textbooks of formal logic or even in most discussions of legal reasoning.[1] Then I shall apply the new model to selected problems of legal thinking and argue that it is relevant to questions of legal systems, such as the completeness or incompleteness of a legal system; the alleged distinction between the investigative and deliberative aspects of a judicial process; the adversary method; the distinction between the functions of the prosecutor, the jury, and the judge; rules of evidence; and the role of precedents (special cases) in legal reasoning.

What is wrong with the usual deductive and inductive logics as models of human reasoning? What is not so much wrong as oversimplified about them is that reasoning is in them restricted to static, almost solipsistic situations. I shall in this paper call a rational agent who is engaged in knowledge-seeking an *Inquirer*. Using this term, I can say that in both deductive and inductive logic we are in effect considering an inquirer with a fixed store of information, and asking what the inquirer ought to believe or to do on the basis of that information, and that information only. The ways in which the inquirer can obtain further information are left out of the picture.

One of the symptoms of the inadequacies of all such static models is that in them we have to rely on the *totality* of information that the inquirer possesses. In the theory of inductive inference this problem is known as the problem of total evidence. The problem is that in order to use in the intended way some of the most important conceptual tools of inductive reasoning, we have to use literally this totality of what we know. One of these conceptual tools is the so-called Bayesian theory of statistical inference. Its reliance on the principle of total evidence is, for instance, one of the strongest objections to this important school of methodological thinking. I have argued elsewhere that there exists, on the traditional accounts of human reasoning, a similar problem of total deductive evidence.[2]

E. Bulygin et al. (eds.), Man, Law and Modern Forms of Life, 209–220.

In the study of legal reasoning, we find similar symptoms of problems. The applicability of traditional probabilistic methods to legal reasoning has recently been challenged among others by L. Jonathan Cohen.[3] In my opinion, the problem is not due to the use of probabilistic concepts, as Cohen thinks, but to the underlying static model of reasoning in general.

One further problem here is the following: In order to apply probabilistic concepts in the most straightforward way, that is, in the Bayesian way, one's total factual information is not enough. One must also have access to prior probabilities. And, as Cohen has pointed out, in legal reasoning the use of prior probabilities is often forbidden by accepted legal principles. Moreover, in legal reasoning, one often must disregard a part of one's actual knowledge, for instance if it is illegally obtained evidence. Inductive or deductive models do not tell us how such actual information can be disregarded in one's reasoning.

The new model of reasoning which I have proposed differs from the traditional one in one way, and one way only. Over and above the inferences the inquirer can make on the basis of the information he or she already possesses, the inquirer has access to a richer store of information. The inquirer does not have automatic access to this source of knowledge, however. What the inquirer can do is to direct a *question* to the source, and in certain circumstances expect to receive an answer. This answer the inquirer can then use as an additional premise for logical inferences in the traditional sense. In my model, these inferences are for the time being restricted to deductive ones, excluding inductive inferences. This is not an essential limitation, however. The inquirer's aim can be thought of either as a proof of a given conclusion *C* or as a proof of either *C* or of not-*C*, i.e., as providing an answer to the question, "*C* or not-*C*?". Different types of reasoning can be conceptualized by imposing different restrictions on the admissible questions and answers.

As a book-keeping method for these knowledge-seeking processes, which I shall call "games", we can conveniently use the well-known method of semantical *tableaux* of Beth.[4] The only difference is that at any one move, the Inquirer now has a choice. Instead of performing a usual step of *tableau*-construction ("deductive move"), the inquirer may address a question to a source of information ("interrogative move"). If the question can be answered, the answer is added to the left column of the sub-*tableau* with respect to which the move is made.

There must obviously be a separate *tableau* for each of the hoped-for conclusions *C* and not-*C*.

In typical cases, the initial *tableau* also contains one theoretical premise

T in its left column (i.e., as a premise). One of the uses of my model is to investigate how the prospects of the information-search by questioning depend on the properties of T.

Even at this crude level, it can already be seen that the new model offers better means of conceptualization for the study of legal reasoning than the old purely deductive model (or a purely deductive *and* inductive model, for that matter). For we can fit the concept of a precedent into the new model in a way which does better justice than the old one to the difference between codified law and precedents as bases of a judicial decision. Codified law can be compared to my theoretical premise T, whereas precedents are best thought of as answers to questions (of a certain kind). As such, they typically deal with particular cases, while codified law has an element of generality. A closer study of the logical situation shows how such precedents can, given a suitable T, add essentially to the consequences that can be established by means of the questioning "games" we are considering.

Such observations are also relevant to the much discussed idea of the completeness of a legal system. If precedents are playing a role, completeness cannot be understood in the same sense as in the case of the completeness of deductive systems.

What we have here is in fact a special case of a more general contrast. I have studied what happens when the question which the inquirer may ask are limited to yes-or-no questions concerning the simplest cases possible, logicians' "atomic sentences".[5] Then the best theory (read: legal system) is not necessarily what logicians call a *complete* theory, that is, a theory which either implies C or implies not-C for each proposition C formulated in the language of the legal system. Rather, the best theory (or legal system) is one which in each situation ("model") to which it is supposed to supply, implies each C or not-C expressed in the language of the legal system plus the model, provided that a finite number of answers to questions concerning atomic propositions concerning the model are allowed as additional premises. Logicians have a name for such theories, too. They are known as *model-complete* theories. It seems to me quite obvious that the kind of completeness legal systems can aspire to is model-completeness rather than completeness. In this sense, case law (i.e., incompletely codified law which relies on precedents) can in principle be as complete as a fully codified legal system. In more general terms, model-completeness as distinguished from completeness illustrates the kind of logic which is involved in legal reasoning and which is different from the logic represented in logic texts, not because this logic uses different intellectual tools, but because it uses them differently.

It is to be noted that model-completeness is a property of the initial theoretical premise *T*. This shows, when applied to legal reasoning, that the possibility of using precedents presupposes certain things about the codified legal system, which corresponds in the model to the theoretical premise *T*. For precedents are, I have suggested, rather like answers to questions concerning particular cases considered in the definition of model-completeness.

All this is perfectly straightforward, and perhaps not very exciting. You might perhaps suspect that such simple and perfectly natural ideas as I am putting forward here must be found somewhere in the earlier discussion. The answer is that they are not, at least not articulated on any satisfactory level of clarity and theoretical sophistication. The main reason is implicit in what I have said. One of the main ideas of my interrogative model of reasoning is that the Inquirer can guide the course of investigation by asking the right questions. Now this idea is useless unless we understand how they do this guiding, that is, how a question partly determines its answers. To understand this means understanding the crucial question-answer relation, that is, being able to answer the all-important "question of answerhood": Given a question *Q*, what counts as a statisfactory (conclusive) answer to this question? Rather surprisingly, there is no satisfactory answer to this question to be found in the earlier literature. In contrast, the cornerstone of my approach is precisely such an analysis of the question-answer relation.[6] I cannot try to reproduce the analysis here. Its upshot can be illustrated by a simple example. Given the question

(1) Who killed Roger Ackroyd?

a wide variety of responses is possible, e.g., "the village doctor", "a member of the medical profession", "the person who removed the tape recorder", "James Shepheard", or "the narrator". How can we find any reasonable condition which would govern such a messy set of candidates? The solution is easy. Whatever the response is, say "*d*", this response is a conclusive answer if and only if the questioner can truly say

(2) I know who *d* is.

It is indeed obvious that the reply "*d*" will not satisfy the questioner unless he or she can truly say (2). What is remarkable is not the condition (2) but (i) the fact that it results naturally and is indeed inevitable from my theory of questions and (ii) that it admits of a generalization to all other cases.

Notice, for instance, that we usually think of a proper name as the "real" answer to a "who" question. But if the person who asks (1) does not know who James Shepheard is, i.e. if the term "James Shepheard" does not satisfy (2), giving his proper name will not satisfy the questioner.

Now why hasn't this simple analysis of the question – answer (more properly, question – *conclusive* answer) relation been presented long ago? Because logicians, linguists, and philosophers have been committed to the deductive-inductive paradigm and hence have tried to deal with the question-answer relation in terms which do not (unlike (2)) involve a reference to the questioner's state of knowledge. They have for instance required that the criterion of answerhood should depend only on the logical and grammatical features of the question. But this rules out the informational state of the questioner, and hence is absolutely fatal to all real analysis of the question-answer relation, for the very purpose of asking a question is to change the questioner's epistemic state. Only by widening the basic model of reasoning can we thus hope to do justice to the logic of questions and answers.

Another important concept from the general theory of questions is the notion of the *presupposition* of a question. It is the statement to the effect that there is an answer available to the given question (apart from the purely epistemic situation). For instance, the presupposition of the question "Who killed Julius Caesar?" is the proposition "Someone killed Julius Caesar" and the presupposition of "Does Stig live in Sweden, Denmark or Norway?" is the proposition stating that Stig's domicile is in one of the three countries mentioned. The idea of presupposition is in practice familiar to everybody knowledgeable about the rules of crossexamination in the Anglo-Saxon legal tradition. Questions with nontrivial presuppositions are a species of leading questions. They are illustrated by the proverbial question, "When did you stop beating your wife?"

In my questioning model presuppositions naturally have to be taken into account. This can happen by requiring that a question may be asked by the inquirer only if its presupposition has already been established, i.e., occurs in the left column of the relevant *subtableau*.

But why do I claim that my questioning games can serve as a model of reasoning? Because much of what is colloquially called "reasoning" and even "deduction", "logic", or "inference" is best understood as question-answer sequences interspersed by logical inferences in the narrow sense of the word, just as in my interrogative games. Once again, I have argued for my point extensively elsewhere. Once again, I can best illustrate my point by reference to a homely example. One of the purest forms of reasoning or deduction in my extended sense are offered by the brilliant "deductions" of the likes of Sherlock Holmes or Nero Wolfe. (I have even proposed calling this wider notion of reasoning the "Sherlock Holmes sense" of "deduction" or "logic".) In brief, I am claiming that the solution of a typical Sherlock Holmes story can be presented as a question-answer series. If you don't believe this, here is an example in the form of one of the most famous Sherlockianisms, "the curious incident of the dog in the night-time". The background is this: The racing horse *Silver Blaze* has been stolen from its stable in the middle of the night and its trainer, the stablemaster, has been found killed out in the heath. Everybody is puzzled till Sherlock Holmes directs our attention "to the curious incident of the dog in the night-time." "The dog did nothing in the night-time." "That was the curious incident." What Sherlock is doing here is in the first place to ask a few well-chosen questions. Was there a watch-dog in the stable during the fateful night? Yes, we know that. Did the dog bark at the horse-thief? No, it did not. ("That was the curious incident.") Now who is it that a trained watch-dog is not likely to bark at in the night-time? Its master, the trainer, of course, who therefore must have stolen the horse himself. All that needs to be added here is, I suppose, "Elementary, my dear Watson."

It also turns out that there is a solid structural reason why Sherlock Holmes's "deductions" are so called. It turns out that the premise of each nontrivial deductive move in my games serves also as the presupposition of a question. If this question can be asked and answered, it serves the inquirer's purpose better (or at least as well) than the deductive move would serve it. Moreover, in so far as admissible and answerable questions are limited essentially only by their presuppositions, the quest of optimal questioning strategies is related extremely closely to the quest of optimal deductive strategies. Hence, even though my model widens immeasurably the scope of what can be accomplished by human reasoning, structurally and strategically it still employs the same tools as in ordinary logic. The "logic" of my model therefore still is in a way logic in the traditional sense.

What implications or suggestions does this wider model of reasoning have for legal thinking? I am convinced that this question deserves, and indeed needs, a much fuller answer than I can give to it here. Some of the more obvious suggestions can nevertheless be registered here. The very widening of our general conception of reasoning at once implies a similar widening in our idea of legal reasoning.

One of the first and foremost suggestions of the new model is an immediate consequence of the basic idea of the new model. In the new model, we cannot in principle separate legal decision-making from the process of ascertaining the facts of the case, i.e., separate the investigative and deliberative stages of the judicial process. For in terms of my model, interrogative moves can be compared to the establishment of the facts of a case and some of the deductive moves to judicial judgments, viz. those deductive moves which represent deductions from general legal principles. But in terms of the questioning model of reasoning different kinds of moves cannot always be separated from each other, in particular, interrogative moves cannot in general all be completed before the deductive ones. One reason for this is that some of interrogative moves requisite for the desired conclusion (or for obtaining an answer to the initial question) may depend for their admissibility on the products of earlier deductive moves. The simplest instance is a question whose presupposition is the output of an earlier deduction (step of *tableau* construction). Hence there is no general reason to believe that interrogative moves can always be made before deductive ones. In so far as my model applies to legal reasoning, the judicial fact-finding process cannot be separated from the decision-making one.

This impossibility is not an absolute one, however. Whether or not it is possible to order the different kinds of moves depends on the theoretical premise *T*, the question to be answered, and on restrictions imposed on admissible questions. For instance, if the admissible questions are restricted to concern simple matters of fact – in logicians' jargon, to questions concerning the truth or falsity of atomic sentences – then these questions can normally be asked before deductive steps.

The general situation can be illustrated by means of the partial analogy between interrogation and deduction explainer earlier. In the logical study of deduction known as proof theory, a central role is played by results usually known as normal form theorems.[7] What they are in turn based on is a number of results concerning the possibility of changing the order of different kinds of deductive rules. By repeated applications of such results, a given deduction can be transformed (on certain conditions) into a predetermined normal form. Different kinds of steps can be distinguished from each other in so far as such normal form theorems can be established.

I shall not touch the details of such normal form theorems, which are not directly relevant here. The point I am making here that the possibility of separating different kinds of steps of reasoning from each other is at best possible under conditions of considerable subtlety and complexity. It cannot be taken for granted. Hence my model strongly suggests that there exists no general guarantee that the fact-finding aspect of a judicial process can be separated from the deliberative one.

But what do these observations mean for legal reasoning in more concrete terms? One use of my interrogative model is that it provides a framework for discussing various questions of evidence and procedure. For instance, rules of evidence are from the standpoint represented here not just part of the context in which legal reasoning takes place. Rules of evidence are a constitutive element in the rules of legal reasoning. They are best thought of as limitations on the questions whose answers can be used as new premises in legal reasoning, i.e., limitations on interrogative steps. It is not hard to see in general that the nature of the reasoning that can be carried out in terms of my model depends essentially on the restrictions which are (or are not) imposed on admissible questions and answers.

An instructive example is offered by the rules of evidence governing cross-examination in a court of law. A comparison with the use of questions in an instructional process (teaching) is suggestive here.[8] The most useful questions a teacher can address to a student are, I have argued, the ones whose answers serve the same purpose as a deductive inference. In a court of law, they would be said to "call for an inference". Unlike a schoolroom, a court of law is no place for such questions; they are forbidden, and a judge will ask the jury to disregard their answers.

What this illustrates is (in more general terms) that in a legal process carried out in the Anglo-Saxon tradition there is a partial division of labor between, on the one hand, the attorneys and their witnesses and, on the other hand, the jury (and partly also the judge). The witnesses are supposed to supply the facts, but the jury is supposed to draw the conclusions. Only in their closing arguments are the attorneys allowed to provide a scenario to the jury as to how they should go about drawing their conclusions. The attorneys are also supposed to provide to the jury the relevant legal premises on the basis of which the jury must make their decision. The judge is supposed to see to it that the right legal rules are followed.

All this admits an unmistakable, albeit imperfect, formulation in terms of my interrogative model. The witnesses and the exhibits provide answers to questions. The attorneys provide (subject to the judge's rulings) the theoretical premise or premises *T*. Precedents evoked by the attorneys provide special premises ("answers to questions") of a different kind. The jury is supposed to carry out the deductive steps.

This scheme presupposes clearly that in a legal process, when conceptualized by means of my model, interrogative steps can all be performed before the deductive ones. What I have pointed out means that there does not seem to be any easy a priori guarantee that this presumption is satisfied, even though such a vindication can be forthcoming, at least for the typical cases that are most likely to come about. It may in fact be significant that in complex technical cases the jury system tends to be perceived as working less than perfectly. There is in actual legal practice apparently often a considerable tendency to have subtle technical cases tried before a judge rather than a jury. It may be that this is not merely a matter of clever lawyers' tactics, but a symptom of a conceptual limitation of the jury system. Another tacit recognition of the limitations of a strict separation of different elements is the recognition of a separate category of expert witnesses. Their role is not merely to provide answers to questions which cannot be answered by laymen. Unlike ordinary witnesses they are allowed to draw inferences, although only within their own area of special competence.

One subject which can be discussed by reference to my interrogative model of reasoning is the merits and weaknesses of the adversary system. For the purposes of this discussion, a general remark is in order. Since the traditional deductive and inductive models of reasoning assume a given fixed store of information, the only question that can be raised is basically the degree to which that information supports or justifies some desired conclusion. In a legal process, this conclusion may be the verdict "guilty" or "not guilty". The problems of justification, reliability and evaluation therefore become easily the be-all and end-all of the study of legal reasoning. In contrast, in my model the shoe is on the other foot. In my model, the emphasis is almost exclusively on finding out the truth, not on estimating how close we are likely to have come to it. This is admittedly an oversimplification which goes in an entirely different direction from the oversimplifications implicit in the customary models, and hence it helps to correct them. Eventually, this oversimplification of course must be corrected and my knowledge-seeking model combined with a model for evaluating what has apparently been found.

Meanwhile, the model can be used for a number of purposes, of which one is a discussion of the adversary system. For reasons just indicated, the earlier discussions of the adversary principle are characterized by an almost exclusive concentration on the problems of reliability and justification. If these were the main issues, much of the existing criticisms of the adversary method would carry considerable weight. As a good example of such earlier criticisms I can mention Janice Moulton's recent perceptive discussion.[9]

It seems to be that some of the most important issues concerning the adversary method nevertheless concern its role in discovering the truth rather than in justifying opinions already formed. And if this is the case, the situation looks rather different. First, as far as the logical situation is concerned, the adversary method means in terms of my model that each of the two adversaries is trying to establish one of the contradictory conclusions *C* and not-*C* each of which would answer the initial question. We can imagine each of them to have his or her own Beth *tableau* to construct. The question whether this adversary method is sound is essentially the question whether it is advantageous for the purpose of answering the initial question to keep the two *tableaux* separate and to let each adversary try to construct his or her own *tableau* (argument) independently of each other, or whether it is more advantageous for the purpose of finding out the truth to let some common direction guide both attempted *tableau* constructions. Even though I will spare you the details, a logical analysis unequivocally supports a separation of the two construction tasks, that is, supports the adversary principle in the form of its rational reconstruction within my model. For it can be shown that the optimal strategies of the two enterprises are not only independent of each other but opposed to each other. This is of course especially clear in so far as the desired conclusion (*C* or not-*C*, respectively) is relied on in the enterprise. Such reliance is a characteristic mark of the heuristic technique which was used by ancient Greek geometers and which they called the method of analysis.[10] This method has played an important part in the methodology of science, mathematics, and philosophy. Its importance highlights the point I am making here.

I want to emphasize strongly that my qualified defense of the adversary system is completely independent of Sir Karl Popper's well-known attempt to vindicate the adversary method. Popper's attempt is based on his idea that ability to withstand criticisms is a mark of a good theory or hypothesis. Popper's idea belongs on the side of evaluating, testing, and evidence, however, and not on the side of truth-seeking strategies, as is mine.

What I have said has to be understood in the right spirit. Needless to say, I am not maintaining that one can by means of logical analysis "prove" that one legal system (or one part of a legal system) is alone "correct" or better than another one. To maintain this would not only be mistaken but downright absurd. What one can try to show, and what I have sought to show, is that one kind of a legal system can serve its purpose without hitches due to the nature of legal reasoning whereas another one is either subject to certain limitations or else is free from these limitations only in certain special circumstances.

A comparison between the different things I have said serves to illustrate this. I have argued that the adversary principle does not involve any structural (logical) impediments to legal reasoning. The situation is different with the division of labor between the attorneys, the jury, and the judge which is built into the Anglo-Saxon court procedure and rules of evidence. This division of labor does involve a potential obstacle to legal reasoning, unless certain conditions are satisfied. More than this I cannot say, and don't want to say. What my conclusions may imply for the practical evaluation of different legal systems I shall leave for my audience to judge.

My model would be seriously defective if I could have exhausted its applications in one talk. Basically, all that I can hope to have accomplished here is to have illustrated its potentialities and thereby recommend it to you for your own uses.

ACKNOWLEDGEMENT

Work on this paper was supported by NSF Grant # IST – 8310936 (Information Sciences), Principal Investigators Jaakko Hintikka and C. J. B. Macmillan.

Florida State University

NOTES

[1] I am in the process of working out this new conception of inquiry and reasoning. An exposition of it will be published in a volume tentatively entitled *Verum Organum, or the True Logic of Scientific Discovery*. Some aspects of it are discussed in the following published or forthcoming papers of mine: 'Questioning as a Philosophical Method', in James H. Fetzer, ed., *The Principles of Philosophical Reasoning*, Rowman & Allanheld, Totowa, N.J. 1984; 'Rules, Utilities, and Strategies in Dialogical Games' in Lucia Vaina and Jaakko Hintikka, eds., *Cognitive Constraints on Communication*, D. Reidel, Dordrecht 1983; (with Merrill B. Hintikka) 'Sherlock Holmes Confronts Modern Logic: Towards a Theory of Information-Seeking by Questioning', in E. M. Barth & J. L. Martens, eds., *Argumentation: Approaches to Theory Formation*, John Benjamins, Amsterdam 1983; 'The Logic of Science as Model-Oriented Logic', in *PSA 1984*, vol. 1.
[2] See 'Sherlock Holmes Confronts Modern Logic' (with Merrill B. Hintikka), note 1 above.
[3] See L. Jonathan Cohen, *The Probable and the Provable*, Clarendon Press, Oxford 1977.
[4] Beth's own original paper still remains the liveliest (although not the most reliable) source. See E. W. Beth, 'Semantical Entailment and Formal Derivability', *Mededelingen van de Koninklijke Nederlandse Akademie van Wetenschappen, Afd. Letterkunde*, N. R., vol. 18, no. 13, Amsterdam 1955, 309–342.
[5] See 'The Logic of Science as Model-Oriented Logic' (note 1 above).
[6] For my theory of questions and answers, see *The Semantics of Questions and the Questions of Semantics*, North-Holland, Amsterdam 1976.

[7] See any exposition of proof theory, e.g., the one given in S. C. Kleene, *Mathematical Logic*, John Wiley & Sons, New York 1967, chapter VI, especially sec. 55.
[8] Cf. here my paper, 'A Dialogical Model of Teaching', *Synthese* **51** (1982), 39–59.
[9] Janice Moulton, 'A Paradigm of Philosophy: The Adversary Method', in Sandra Harding and Merrill B. Hintikka, eds., *Discovering Reality: Feminist Perspectives*, D. Reidel, Dordrecht 1983, pp. 149–164.
[10] Jaakko Hintikka and Unto Remes, *The Method of Analysis*, D. Reidel, Dordrecht 1974.

NIILO JÄÄSKINEN

EXTERNAL JUSTIFICATION OF PROPOSITIONS IN LEGAL SCIENCE

> First, it seems generally agreed among those philosophers who have discussed justification that if a person's belief is to be justified on the basis of some other belief, then the latter belief must itself be justified.
>
> Marshall Swain [1]

1. INTRODUCTION

According to Anthony Quinton sceptical challenges to some accepted variety of knowledge are in modern epistemology often based on a general theory of philosophical problems which derives its scepticism from the fact that knowledge of one kind rests exclusively on knowledge of another kind, but is logically distinct of it. Quinton mentions such pairs of objects of knowledge as laws of nature – particular events, material objects – sense-impressions, past events – present recollections, mental states – behaviour, theoretical entities of science – common observable material things and facts – values as instances of this dilemma. According to Quinton, "the list could be enlarged".[2]

An obvious addition to the list is the pair legal sources – the law. Knowledge about the law is evidenced by knowledge about legal sources but yet logically distinct from it and not reducible to it. When a legal scientist proceeds from propositions about the legal sources to propositions about the law there happens always an epistemological "jump" or a "transformation inside the law" because the relationship between these two kinds of knowledge is not analytical.[3]

An epistemological "jump" from evidence to beliefs about the object – e.g. from statements about the legal sources to an assertion about the content of valid legal order – must be justified with some philosophical theory. In modern legal theory the theory of legal reasoning or legal argumentation has had this transformative function. A step from legal sources to the law is justified if it is an inference which follows the accepted canons of legal reasoning or legal argumentation.

A common feature of different theories of legal argumentation is that a

E. Bulygin et al. (eds.), Man, Law and Modern Forms of Life, 221–231.

justified claim about the contents of legal order is required to be supported by reasons which themselves are justified in a legally relevant way. This view is based on a more general conception of rationality according to which every justified belief must be based on justified reasons.[4] Henceforth I call this view *the positive notion of justification*.

The aim of this paper is to contest the positive notion of justification in the field of legal justification. This because of two reasons, *viz*. the epistemological openness of legal systems and the possibility of rational disagreement in law.

Every scholar of the history of law and legal science is familiar with the fact that the conceptions about the contents of legal order have evolved because of changes in empirical knowledge and moral and political ideas. These factors have not only causally determined the legal ideology but they have as well been successfully forwarded as legally relevant reasons for legal solutions. Yet it is difficult to maintain that these reasons were before their embodiment into the legal ideology *legally justified* in any relevant sense of the concept. On the other hand the solutions which have been supported with them have often been understood as legally justified norm statements.[5] Thus the epistemological openness of law, i.e. *how legally justified conclusions can be inferred from legally unjustified premises*, is a reason to suspect the correctness of positive notion of justification in legal justification.

My second reason for the rejection of the positive notion of justification is the need to find a philosophically tenable explanation for the possibility of rational disagreement in law. I take it as granted that to many legal problems there exist two or more solutions which can be characterized as legally justified. The doctrine of one right solution only is to my mind inadequate both in its classical and Dworkinian forms. Disagreement can be rational only if it occurs *within a community which shares common standards of rationality*. Thus the second aim of this paper is to formulate a theory of legal justification which allows incompatible norm statements to be rationally justifiable in a legal community in which no radical differences concerning the standards of rationality occur.

By a norm statement (*NS*) I mean any proposition which refers to a valid legal norm. Depending on the nature of the speech act in which the *NS* is presented it can be characterized as a norm proposition, as a norm contention or as a norm recommendation.[6]

The most elementary requirement for a legal scientist to be justified in presenting a certain *NS* is that he or she believes in it.[7] He must in other words have a belief which corresponds to the *NS*. D. W. Hamlyn defines a belief as a state of mind in which propositions are taken to be true.[8] Because our definition allows also *NS*s which are norm contentions or norm recommendations, a belief corresponding to a certain *NS* can be a state of mind in which the *NS* is taken to be, if not true, then at least reasonable or otherwise worth of recommendation. Obviously a necessary condition for a certain *NS* to be justified is that corresponding belief is justified and legal justification is epistemologically justification of beliefs concerning the content of legal order.

It is quite common to distinguish between *internal* and *external* justification of a certain *NS*.[9] A *NS* is internally justified if it follows deductively or – more liberally – according to accepted rules of legal inference from the premises which are presented as warrants for it. External justification, on the other hand, concerns the justification of the premises and rules of inference which entail the *NS* in question. External justification is thus the vindication or demonstration of plausibility or validity of the material and formal premises of a legal inference.

Theories of legal argumentation seem to be based on the positive notion of justification, i.e. the idea that a certain *NS* must be supported by reasons (*R*) which make believing in it justifiable. Reasons can generally and vaguely be defined as propositions or sets of propositions in which the subject believes and because of which the subject believes in other propositions.

I find it obvious that the positive notion of justification is correct so far as the internal justification of *NS*s is concerned. It is doubtful that there could be *uninferred* justified legal knowledge, that is to say, that there would be justified legal beliefs without any reasons whatsoever. Even the most elementary *NS*s must be supported by such internally justifying reasons as the existence of norm formulations in authoritative texts and the meaning rules of the language. On the other hand, I think we have good reasons to reject the positive notion of justification in the context of external legal justification. This means that a *NS* can be justified solely due to the fact that it is internally justified with some reasons without these reasons being positively justified further reasons which count as legally justified in the legal community in question.

2. THE PROBLEM OF JUSTIFIED CONTRADICTORY NORM STATEMENTS

The problem of infinite regress in justification is by no means peculiar only to legal theory. On the contrary, it seems to be one of the central problems of the theory of knowledge and the theory of justification in general. Two principal kinds of solutions have been suggested for this problem in the theory of knowledge: foundations theories and coherence theories. According to the former there are epistemologically basic propositions which make up the foundations of all the rest of human knowledge. These basic propositions are "directly evident", "self-justifying", "incorrigible" or something like that. The chain of justification can be interrupted when the justification reaches these epistemologically privileged propositions.[10]

Coherence theories of justification and knowledge deny the very existence of epistemologically basic propositions. Knowledge does not have any foundations but a belief is justified if it either "coheres" with the subject's other beliefs (positive coherence theories) or is not in incoherence with them (negative coherence theories).[11]

If we accept the contention that in hard cases there may occur rationally justified contradictory *NS*s, we meet then some difficulties as far as the concept of external justification is concerned. Our concept of justification is to my mind based on two assumptions:

(1) (a) If NS_i^k is justified because of R^k, then R^k must also be justified; and
(b) If R^k is a justificatory reason for NS_i^k, then NS_i^k's contradiction cannot be justified because of R^k: R^k cannot be a reason for both NS_i^k and its contradiction ($\neg NS_i^k$).

If (1a) were not valid then we should reject the very notion of a reason because *NS*'s justifiability would be independent of its reasons: if it were unjustified to believe in R^k, it would *a fortiori* be unjustified to believe in any proposition because of R^k and consequently also unjustified to believe in NS_i^k because of R^k.

If (1b) were not valid, R^k would be a reason both for NS_i^k and its contradiction, i.e. for rejection of NS_i^k, which means that it would be justified to believe either in NS_i^k or in $\neg NS_i^k$ if one happens to believe in R^k. (To believe in proposition $NS_i^k \vee \neg NS_i^k$ is obviously always justifiable because that proposition is as a tautology necessarily true.)

If we accept the contention that in hard cases both NS_i^k and its contradiction should be legally justifiable we are compelled to conclude that the justificatory patterns $(R_n^k \vdash, \ldots, \vdash R_1^k) \vdash NS_i^k$ and $(R_n^j \vdash, \ldots, \vdash R_1^j) \vdash \neg NS_i^k$ should both count as externally justified patterns of legal reasoning in a certain legal community. This means that we must find a conception of justification which allows both R_n^k and R_n^j be justifiable without requiring justified reasons for them because such a further reason would according to the condition (1b) make either of them unjustified.

3. THE CONCEPT OF JUSTIFICATION

One can speak of justification in many senses. In the first place one can distinguish between subjective and objective justification. The subjective sense refers to the conditions under which a person is justified in believing in a certain proposition, the objective sense to the correct analysis of a given epistemic situation. The objective justification concerns in other words epistemically warranted propositions, the believing in which may, nevertheless, not be subjectively justified.[12] A judge, for example, is not subjectively justified in believing in a proposition presented to him as a testimony by a witness whom he knows to be unreliable even though the testimony would be correct, if he is not aware of other available evidence which also happens to support the testimony. In this case the proposition is warranted to the judge and believing in it is objectively justified but the judge is not subjectively justified in believing in it because he has no evidence which he himself would consider trustworthy.

The concept of justification is also connected to the concept of knowledge. The classical notion[13] defines knowledge as a justified belief which expresses a true proposition. In this context I do not take any standpoint concerning the truth of *NS*s. When I occasionally speak of legal knowledge or use the predicate 'true' attached to *NS*s, this refers only to legally justified *NS*s without other epistemological connotations.

A third way of understanding the concept of justification is to characterize it as argumentation,[14] i.e. as a process of persuasion which aims at convincing the audience about the justifiability of a certain proposition or of a certain standpoint. Justification as argumentation is conceptually dependent on the concepts of subjective and objective justification. This is so because obviously the only way to distinguish between rational argumentation and irrational (or "arational") persuasion is the epistemic attitude of the subject who presents his arguments. Persuasion (in pejorative sense) cannot be anything else than giving arguments which according to the standards of rationality adopted by the persuader should not count as rational. If the subject is of the conviction that his arguments are justifiable, his speech act is that of rational argumentation and not of persuasion, whatever his arguments might be from the point of view of a standard of rationality alien to him. Thus, for a subject to be justified in uttering a proposition, i.e. to argue for it, he must be subjectively justified in believing in it. In the same way, a proposition is rationally justifiable if it is warranted for the subject, that is, when the subject in his position is justified in believing in it and hence also justified in uttering it.

4. ALTERNATIVE EPISTEMOLOGICAL THEORIES AND LEGAL JUSTIFICATION

As already stated, the aim of this paper is to find a conception of legal justification which allows

(a) the introduction of new cognitive and ethical elements in the legal system as reasons for *NS*s without requiring these reasons to be previously legally justified, and
(b) that a *NS* and its contradiction can in some hard cases be legally justifiable.

It is obvious that no foundations theory of legal justification can fulfill this requirement. If there were foundations of legal knowledge which would give a justificatory basis for *NS*s, they could not give support for both a *NS* and its contradiction, because such basic statements of law would be reasons for *NS*s and, as indicated earlier, no proposition can be a reason for both a proposition and its contradiction (assumption (1b)). On the other hand, if there were basic statements which would support both a *NS* and its contradiction, the foundation of legal knowledge would be an inconsistent set of propositions and hence every possible *NS* would be justified. Thus we have to seek the solution for the problem of legal justification from some kind of coherence theory.

Aulis Aarnio and Neil MacCormick, for example, have proposed positive coherence theories of legal justification in recent discussion. Positive coherence theories, according to John L. Pollock, require that the believer actually has reasons for holding each of his beliefs.[15] This holds good e.g. for Aulis Aarnio's conception of the justification of interpretative propositions:

> (. . .) an interpretative proposition is true if and only if there is *coherence* between the justification materials (. . .) presented for the proposition, in other words, when the interpretative proposition is in harmony with everything that is otherwise believed.[16]

An argument against positive coherence theories of legal justification is that it may be possible to be justified in holding beliefs about the legal order without having any particular legally justified reasons for them. If we define a hard case as a case for which there are at least two equally plausible solutions, it is obvious that a legal scientist is justified in accepting either of them. He is certainly justified in believing in $NS_i^k \vee \neg NS_i^k$ because this is a tautology and almost as certainly unjustified in believing in $NS_i^k \ \& \ \neg NS_i^k$ because the legal order is supposed to be a consistent order of norms. But he is also justified *in choosing* either NS_i^k or its contradiction. On the other hand, incompatible *NS*s can often be in coherence with what is otherwise believed, i.e. in many cases contradictory opinions can be legally well-reasoned.

After rejecting foundationalist theories of justification and the positive version of coherence theory we have only one alternative left, *viz*. the *negative coherence* theory of justification. Negative coherence theories can generally be defined as theories which hold that all beliefs are automatically justified unless one has a reason for rejecting them. Reasons function according to these theories in a negative way: they are not required for the justified acquisition of a belief but they can lead to the rejection of beliefs. Inability to find reasons for a belief, if it is challenged, is a reason to reject this belief.[17] Negative coherence theories of justification thus consist of a twofold rejection: they reject both the claim that knowledge or justified beliefs do have foundations and that a justified belief must be based on justifying reasons.

5. A NEGATIVE COHERENCE THEORY OF LEGAL JUSTIFICATION

John L. Pollock has formulated a version of negative coherence theory of justification which can have some implications for the theory of legal justification, in following way:

(2) If *B* is *S*'s doxastic system and *P* belongs to *B*, *S* is subjectively justified in believing in *P* iff *B* does not also contain the proposition that *S* objectively should not believe *P*.[18]

A proposition which would make believing in a certain proposition unjustified can be defined as a defeater (*Df*) for the latter.[19] If we apply Pollock's definition to the justification of *NS*s we get the following definition:

(3) NS_i^k is justified iff the legal scientist who presents it
(a) can construe an internal justification for it;
(b) in fact does believe in NS_i^k; and
(c) does not believe in any Df_i^k which would make believing in NS_i^k objectively legally unjustified.

Negative coherence theory of legal justification can explain the possibility of two justified but incompatible *NS*s. It is apparently true that it is impossible to find conclusive rules which in every possible case would justify the transformation from legal sources into statements about the valid law. If one sticks to the positive notion of justification and requires every justified *NS* to be based on legally justified reasons, one has to postulate the existence of a conclusive set of the rules of interpretation, of the doctrine of the sources of law, of legal methodology, and also of rules which define their mutual preference order. On the other hand, one should also be able to justify these rules externally, which leads to an infinite regress. It can, however, safely be assumed that no such rules exist for other than relatively simple cases. And if they existed, they would according to our notion of a reason (assumption 1) lead to one right answer only.

According to the negative coherence theory of justification contradictory *NS*s can in a hard case be equally justified: if scholar *A* believes in internally justified NS_1^k and does not see any objectively valid defeaters for it, and scholar *B* believes in NS_2^k, internally justifies it, and does not consider it defeated, both of them are justified in holding their convictions. The (probable) possibility that they will not reach consensus concerning the matter at issue does not affect the justifiability of their standpoints. On the contrary, if there were a possibility of consensus, the case would obviously not be a hard one because there would be an objectively valid defeater for either of the *NS*s.[20] The questions of law are in the last instance solved by vote in the adjudication, and I don't think that the formation of majority opinions in a legal-scientific community would radically differ from "voting" in this respect. Nevertheless, minority or dissenting opinions in a supreme court are seldom regarded as *unjustified*, even less dissent in legal science. The actual acceptance or potential acceptability of a certain *NS* in a certain audience is a contingent social fact which is conceptually independent of its justifiability. Courts and scientific communities can and do accept unjustified opinions and reject justified opinions.

The version of negative coherence theory advanced here does not make every *NS* automatically justified. For a *NS* to be justified the condition (3c) must also be fulfilled. Hence the *NS* may not be objectively defeated either. This connects the theory of legal justification to the theory of legal argumentation. A lawyer may feel to be subjectively justified in his believing in a certain *NS* because he has not taken into consideration possible defeaters. Aulis Aarnio, Robert Alexy and Thomas Perry, for example, have emphasized that rationality in legal argumentation or in legal reasoning is above all *procedural.*[21] In order to be rational, legal argumentation has to follow certain rules about communicative and intellectual honesty, formal consistency, material adequacy, and so on. This procedural conception of legal argumentation can easily be explained by the negative coherence theory of legal justification. The subject is justified in keeping his *NS* only if he has according to the rules of rational legal discourse checked the existence of possible defeaters; if he has found some, he has to find positive reasons for rejecting them.

There are no absolutely objective defeaters in the legal community. Every legal source can e.g. be overruled by another even though normally the more binding "must" sources of law overrule less binding "should" or "may" sources of law.[22] In other words, there are no in-advance given objectively valid defeaters for a certain *NS*, but no *NS* is subjectively justified if its advocate has not followed the procedural rules of legal argumentation and checked whether his position is warranted, that is, not objectively defeated. What counts as an objective defeater for the subject depends at the last instance on his own beliefs. Even in legal science, the contention remains valid that nobody can break out from the circle of his own beliefs.[23] The search for objective defeaters is, anyhow, dictated for every member of the legal-scientific community as the most elementary principle of the scientific method. Dissent as such is never unjustified.

University of Helsinki

NOTES

[1] Swain, p. 45.
[2] Cf. Quinton, 112–3.
[3] On the concept "transformation inside the law", see Aarnio, Alexy and Peczenik, 136–41 and 150–8.
[4] This proposition is often taken as a piece of common sense; see e.g. MacCormick, 48.
[5] The most illuminating instance of this phenomenon is perhaps the reception of foreign law and legal science as justification for norm statements about domestic law.
[6] Cf. Aarnio, Alexy and Peczenik, 429.
[7] Cf. e.g. Alexy's "second basic rule of general practical discourse", in Alexy (1978), 234: "Jeder Sprecher darf nur das behaupten, was er selbst glaubt."
[8] Hamlyn, 86.
[9] See e.g. Aarnio, Alexy and Peczenik, 275–8, with further references, and Aarnio (1982), 121.
[10] Cf. Pollock, p. 93, and Quinton, 119.
[11] Cf. Pollock, p. 101.

[12] Cf. Pollock, pp. 109–11.
[13] By "classical" I understand the period in the history of epistemology before the so-called Gettier problem was formulated; see Hamlyn, 81.
[14] See e.g. Aarnio (1982), 166, and (1981), p. 34.
[15] Cf. Pollock, p. 101.
[16] Aarnio (1981), p. 45.
[17] Cf. Pollock, p. 101, 103.
[18] Pollock, p. 110.
[19] Cf. Pollock, p. 96.
[20] Cf. Perry, 213: "To be sure, when he (the judge – NJ) remains in doubt about how a case should be decided after using the criteria first mentioned above, and after considering the legal rules they yield, a judge must normally ask *himself* what rule for the case would be most desirable or practicable. This is because there is no official record or canon of the moral consensus for him to consult. Indeed, on a good many issues there would be no consensus in our society. And even in more homogeneous societies, we would hardly expect to find a consensus on many moral questions arising in technical legal contexts."
[21] See Aarnio (1982), 169–178, Alexy (1981) *in passim*, and Perry, 85–92, especially what he writes on page 88: "It will not make sense to speak of the legally right decision as far as the context of the courts reasoning and judgement is concerned, although there are always definitely *wrong* ways to decide such a case. But we can still demand that the judge decides such a case only after as thorough a study and as disinterested an analysis as his abilities and the time available permit. If he does so, and does not fall into legal or logical or factual error, then he will have decided the case rightly, in the only sense 'rightly' can have here."
[22] See Aarnio, Alexy and Peczenik, 151.
[23] Cf. Pollock, p. 106.

BIBLIOGRAPHY

Aarnio, A.: 1981, 'On Truth and Acceptability of Interpretative Propositions in Legal Dogmatics', in *Rechtstheorie*, Beiheft 2, Berlin (W), pp. 33–52.

Aarnio, A.: 1982, *Oikeussäännösten tulkinnasta*, Helsinki 1982 (forthcoming in English: *Rational as Reasonable*, Reidel, Dordrecht-Boston-N.Y.).

Aarnio, A., Alexy, R. and Peczenik, A.: 1981, 'The Foundation of Legal Reasoning', *Rechtstheorie* **12**.

Alexy, R.: 1978, *Theorie der juristischen Argumentation*, Frankfurt am Main.

Alexy, R.: 1981, 'Die Idee einer prozeduralen Theorie der juristischen Argumentation', in *Rechtstheorie*, Beiheft 2, Berlin (W), pp. 177–88.

Hamlyn, D. W.: 1980, *The Theory of Knowledge*, Hong Kong.

Pappas, G. S. (ed.): 1979, *Knowledge and Justification*, Dordrecht.

MacCormick, N.: 1978, *Legal Reasoning and Legal Theory*, Bungay.

Perry, T. D.: 1976, *Moral Reasoning and Truth. An Essay in Philosophy and Jurisprudence*, Bungay.

Pollock, J. L.: 1979, 'A Plethora of Epistemological Theories', in Pappas (ed.), pp. 93–114.

Quinton, A.: 1973, *The Nature of Things*, Boston & Henley, London.
Swain, M.: 1979, 'Justification and the Basis of Belief', in Pappas (ed.), pp. 25–40.

GERT-FREDRIK MALT

DEONTIC PROBABILITY

1. INTRODUCTION

In this paper I shall discuss a concept of what I call "deontic" – or "normative" – probability and the corresponding kind of norms to be called "probabilistic norms". Deontic probability is thought of as a deontic/normative counterpart to what has traditionally been regarded as probability – but which I will rather choose to call declarative probability. Both declarative probability (in German called "Wahrscheinlichkeit") and normative probability should be regarded as instances of a more general concept of probability (which we in German could rather call "Gültigscheinlichkeit").

By a probabilistic norm, I will understand a norm that has a logical structure – to be explained below – similar to statements of declarative probability, the only difference being that the declarative probability statement is determined (marked) by a declarative operator or illocutionary force, while the norm is determined by a normative operator/illocutionary force.

I regard probabilistic norms as one kind of what we might call "weak norms". Some of these kinds would fall under a wide notion of probabilistic qualification, others would not. I will of course not be treating all such kinds of weakness. I will not deal with the kind of weakness and types of probability which we might call syntactical or pragmatical, e.g. having to do with the utterer's commitment, with the validity, with reasons for its assertion, or its effectiveness and application. The concept of probability should rather be regarded as a kind of *semantic* notion of (objective) probability.

I assume that the logical form of the material content of the norm can be represented as having the form of a conditional: if q, then r. Probability is then a way of qualifying the conditional – or more specifically: the quantitative relation between the antecedent and the consequent in the conditional, e.g. in the following way:

Given such and such facts q, (determined in the antecedent to the norm) then – with such and such deontic probability, i.e. such and such a relative frequency of cases – *shall* also r (determined in the consequent) be the case.

General probability propositions can be regarded as "less stringent counterparts of laws that have the universal conditional form."[1]

E. Bulygin et al. (eds.), Man, Law and Modern Forms of Life, 233–240.

I will assume that to every probability proposition there can be associated a qualitative and/or quantitative probability "measure" or "indicator", *p*, to be interpreted as indicating the degree of probability.

I shall in general limit the discussion to the treatment of probabilistic norms of what Hempel calls "basic statistical form".

2. SOME EXAMPLES – AND ON HOW TO IDENTIFY PROBABILISTIC NORMS

I will now indicate some *examples* of norms that at least under one interpretation can be represented as having a probabilistic logical form. Of course, probabilistic norms are like other norms in that they can only be established as such after a process and decision of interpretation, based on existing syntactic, pragmatic and semantic evidence.

I assume that one single norm-formulation or norm-sentence can be interpreted as having one, two or more semantic contents – through what is called the phenomenon of "meaning accumulation".

First: *Explicit occurrences* of probabilistic norms are rare. This is no surprising fact, of course, if what we mean by explicit occurrences is occurrences of words like "probable" or "wahrscheinlich".

Some expressions, however, that I feel will often have this meaning, are expressions like the following:

– if *q*, then *as a rule r*;
– if *q*, then *generally r*;
– if *q*, then *in most cases r*;
– if *q*, then *preferably r*.

Expressions like these occur rather often in legal literature, but are, as said, rather rare in positive law. In Norwegian law there are some few examples; one of them being

Constitution, Section 109: "As a *general rule* every citizen of the State is equally bound to serve in the defence of the Country for a specific period, irrespective of birth or fortune."

Another one is this: The Act on Guardianship, Section 71: "The funds administered by the board of guardianship should *preferably* ("helst") be lent out only against mortage."

Second: A seemingly universal norm can have such exceptions that the norm can only be recognized as being implicitly of a probabilistic kind. Such a probabilistic interpretation is rather frequent. This is especially the case in relation to the broad and vague norms which we call principles or "prima facie norms". However, also inside the legal system do we find such norms – first of all as unwritten metanorms (of argumentation and of competence), but also as positive law.

Third: The occurrence of certain "*weak*" deontic and other specific *expressions* inside a norm may often give rise to an interpretation of the norm as being a probabilistic one.

Fourth: A particular interesting class of occurrences of probabilistic norms is established through interpretation of certain norms, often called "*discretionary norms*", in cases where these norms, at the same time as conferring discretionary powers on some authority with regard to some result (decision) also contain, embedded, norms indicating some of the arguments to be taken into account in the decision. Such discretionary norms can generally be interpreted as containing two norms:

(a) The whole norm, or metanorm, with the general function of a norm conferring powers and else regulating the application of the underlying norm.

(b) The embedded norm, to be called a subnorm, which regulates *in a probabilistic manner* the relation between the indicated fact or arguments on the one side and the possible result on the other.

I will mention just one example:

Section 32, second paragraph of *the Children Act*, starts by stating that "When the child has reached the age of 12, he shall have the right to express his opinion before decisions regarding the child's personal matters are taken, also including law suits concerning with whom of the parents the child shall live". And then there is a norm saying, "*Considerable weight* is to be attached to the opinion of the child."

In this case the norm sentence should as said be regarded as expressing a double norm:

(a) (The metanorm): "The norm applying authority (the Court) shall take account of the child's opinion in the decision."

(b) (The probabilistic subnorm): "If the child has opined F, then, with some normative probability p the result r is to follow."

Fifth: There is a difference of degree between the cases mentioned above, where we are able to read a probabilistic norm into another norm as contained in it, and cases where the use and existence of probabilistic norms are tacitly presupposed by another norm, or cases where we establish such dependent probabilistic norms through interpretation by other means. The clearest examples of the need and utility of establishing secondary probabilistic norms can perhaps be seen in the case of the so-called "*rationalization*", i.e. the development of arguments and their relative importance, in relation to so-called "*legal standards*" or "*Generalklauseln*". In such cases, the existence of the legal standard is readily seen at the same time as a norm conferring discretionary powers on some authority, and as a reference to some explicit or implicit underlying probabilistic norms related to each of the arguments.

3. THE MATERIAL CONTENT OF PROBABILISTIC NORMS

There are no limits in principle as to the possible material content probabilistic norms may have, compared to other norms.

Even if the most typical probabilistic norms may be what has been called "norms of qualification", the probabilistic norms can also be norms of competence, of duty/action, of location, of existence etc.

4. THE GENERAL MEANING OF PROBABILISTIC QUALIFICATION AND THE DETERMINATION OF PROBABILITY MEASURES

As said I will distinguish between two types of probability measures – or coefficients – to be called qualitative and quantitative measures. By a *qualitative* measure I mean the kind of measures that Carnap calls "classificatory" and "comparative", including in these concepts also measures that are undetermined and measures indicating that there is a "high", "low", "strong" or other non-quantitatively qualified degree of probability. A *quantitative* measure is a measure consisting of a determined probability coefficient p, where $0 \leqslant p \leqslant 1$.

Both qualitative and quantitative probability measures can be determined *arbitrarily* – e.g. as part of the enactment of a norm.

A probability measure can also be determined *logically*, e.g. through the development of methods analogue to Carnap's inductive logic.[2] Of course, theorems and rules of deduction and induction that have been used within theories of declarative probability cannot automatically be applied to normative probability.

Thus, in some cases an analogue to the so-called laws of multiplication and of conditional probability will be applicable, in others not. Inverse probabilities will be even more problematic in normative contexts than they are in declarative contexts. Also if a given norm is interpreted as a biconditional probabilistic norm, then the probability measure has to be established independently for the two conditionals that are parts of the biconditional.

Is it also possible to determine qualitative and quantitative probability measures *statistically* – in a way similar to to the analytical and statistical methods used in determining empirically declarative measures of relative frequency? It is not at all evident what such an analogous procedure in the case of norms should look like. It will, of course, in such cases be possible to establish – through known methods of statistical analysis, description, estimation, tests etc. – all the same *declarative* hypotheses concerning the material, as will be the case in pure declarative contexts. There is, however, one important difference between declarative and normative probabilistic qualification. To establish a general norm concerning the future is to *evaluate* the possible characteristics (relative frequencies of the antecedent conditions or "situations" and the consequent conditions) of the world, and then *decide* on how we want them to be or how they rationally "ought" to be.

A pure descriptive-statistical treatment of the future as an extension of the past will not be appropriate. Even if it is possible to use the descriptive analysis of past cases as a point of departure, one is neither obliged nor does one have the right to accept without further ado that the future will be like the past, or even necessarily to accept that the past decisions are valid. Of course, if the past cases have the authority of High Court decisions or the like, you may be (or feel) obliged to take them for granted and as expressing valid *instances* of the probabilistic norm, but the decision as to which definite probability measure to choose is still in the last resort a matter of *responsibility* towards the future and the past taken as an evaluated whole. If we think of a probabilistic measure, indicating the (limit of) relative frequency as valid for a potentially infinite class of instances (this corresponds to the traditional understanding of general norms), the determination procedure will then – ideally – have to consist in first figuring out all possible cases where the antecedent condition is fulfilled and then *deciding* whether the consequent is to follow or not.

A difficult question is the question of the relation and possible *translation* of a qualitative measure into a quantitative and vice versa. This question has implications for the possible mechanical application of probabilistic norms. If we assume the possibility of applying at all probabilistic norms with quantitative probability coefficients, then I think we should also accept the possibility of functional equivalence between the two kinds of measure, and even a principle of *correspondence* between qualitative and quantitative probability measures.

In practice, of course, such correspondence can be difficult to establish.

5. THE APPLICATION OF PROBABILISTIC NORMS IN INDIVIDUAL CASES

Probability propositions and measures are established through the inductive analysis of the relation between classes of events, and have immediate application only to events as members of such classes.

The most a probabilistic statement can say about a particular case, is then that given an event of a particular type or class that corresponds to the antecedent of the norm, then a particular result will (have to) happen in a certain frequency of *such* cases. This applies also to explicit individual probabilistic norms or individual instances of general probabilistic norms. As long as such norms are properly understood there is no problem in accepting them as probabilistic norms along with the general ones. In any case, it is not possible, out of a probabilistic norm as such, to state either that the type of result will/shall in fact take place or not. The reason for this is of course that the norm does not say exactly in which of the cases classified as falling under the antecedent the particular result will in fact happen – whether it be this particular case that we are regarding or not. If the probability measure established has a strong value, then we can perhaps reckon that there will or shall be *more* cases with the given result than not. Perhaps we can even say that among all the cases that we as a competent authority have to decide, there will at most be a few out of a thousand that should have a negative result (or a positive one, depending on the values that are correlated), but still *we do not know which*. This is obviously also the case where the norm indicates that a given argument shall be taken into account or given especial "weight" in each case of a particular type. The norm makes the norm-applying authority responsible for the taking into account of the argument in each case, but it still does not say – as such – anything of whether the argument is *decisive* in a particular case or not. The responsibility is so to say only a responsibility in the long run – or in considering this case as a typical member of a class. Accordingly, we are in the first place in a situation of indecision. Now, assuming that there is a normative problem to be solved, there is *a need for a decision* on the application or instantiation of the norm. But *who* shall make the decision, and *how*?

Let us for the moment only assume that the decision is to be taken by a court or a civil servant, after a decision process called "legal argumentation". How can a probabilistic norm be used in such a process?

A first way of applying a probabilistic norm in a particular situation could be to interpret every such norm also as qualifying directly or analogously each of the possible instances that could be subsumed under the antecedent. That is, if the norm contains a probability measure corresponding to a probability higher than .5, then the result is to be determined according to the result qualified in the consequent. However, it is evident that this method is not viable. First of all for the reasons, touched upon above, that in the long run such an "immediate" application would really amount to *breaking* the norm – because it would not cause *any* of the antecedent-determined cases to have the other result not-*r*.

But such an application would also lead to *inconsistencies* of the same type as those which have been described in the theory of explanation of phenomena through use of declarative probability propositions. The reason for this is that a given event (situation) has various characteristics that may function as the argument (antecedent) of different probabilistic propositions with quite opposite content. I will refer to this problem as the problem of probabilistic ambiguity.

A second way of application and a way of solving the problem of probabilistic ambiguity may now be to identify *other* arguments – i.e. other probabilistic norms – that can be applied in the given case, according to a principle called the "principle of total evidence".

In order to decide on a given case, the norm-applier will thus first have to identify the complete body of arguments and norms, or "evidence", associated with the case. The next step will then be to establish more *complex probabilistic norms* containing arguments of the form: if *q and r, and s* ... then with probability *p, t*. The process of harmonization (combination) of the different norms cannot stop before we have reached a norm which is such that no further arguments, restricting the antecedent class, will change the probability measure. In this case the resultant, combined norm will comply with a condition to be called the *requirement of maximal specificity*.

Only after having complied with the requirement of maximal specificity can a probabilistic norm be applied "directly" in a given case.

In this paper I have explained norms containing indications of the weight of arguments generally as complex norms containing both a (meta-)norm to the effect that an argument of the kind is to be taken account of in the indicated manner, and a probabilistic (sub-)norm relating the given argument to a certain result. I have further understood the probabilistic norm as primary, in the sense that the decision process mentioned in the metanorm is regarded as a process of correct application of the sub-norm. And, in the end, I have explained that the correct application of such a probabilistic norm is only possible through a process of harmonizing the given probabilistic norm with the whole set of other norms (the "evidence"), in such a way that the norm is expanded or transformed into a complex norm complying with the requirement of maximal specificity. This may, however, be a rather disappointing conclusion as it really amounts to saying that what is needed in order to make a decision in a particular case, is the development of one "complete" probabilistic norm containing all the particular (i.e. the "relevant") arguments of the case. Only if there are no more relevant arguments and thus competing probabilistic norms to take account of, are we able to conclude from the established norm to a determinate result. And here a further problem arises:

Even after having found no further arguments – if the norm we have established is of a probabilistic form, *we still do not know*, i.e. we have to decide, whether *the given case* shall have the result or not. The only way of being *sure* of how to treat this particular case, is to have a norm established that not only is probabilistic but really is universal. In the declarative case – if we have established a statement complying with the requirement of maximal specificity – we have done all we can do. We can perhaps further bet on the given result, but we must then let nature or some God decide for the rest. In the normative case, on the other hand, the one who decides is ourselves, so we cannot stop the argumentation but must continue – or stop arbitrarily. The indication of a probability measure is in itself an indication that the argumentation is not complete!

University of Oslo

NOTES

[1] Cf. Hempel (1965).
[2] Carnap (1962).

BIBLIOGRAPHY

Carnap, R.: 1962, *Logical Foundations of Probability*, Chicago.
Eckhoff, T.: 1976, 'Guiding Standards in Legal Reasoning', *Current Legal Problems*, 205–19.
Hempel, C. G.: 1965, *Aspects of Scientific Explanation*, New York.
Sundby, N. K.: 1974, *Om normer*, Oslo.

ANDERS STENING

EVIDENCE AND STATISTICS IN LEGAL REASONING

I would like to start by giving an example which I hope will show the problem that I want to discuss.

Let us assume that the police carry out a speed check on a well-defined part of a road. According to the records, 10 cars were registered and 9 of these drove too fast. Unfortunately the policeman on duty dropped some of his papers, with the result that it was no longer possible to individualize the speed of every single car. If we pick out any driver among those 10, it is perfectly correct to say that the probability that he was speeding is 90%.

Nevertheless I believe – and I hope – that no court would sentence any of these drivers for speeding. This is very obvious at least in the case where the court has to try all ten drivers, one after the other.

One question is then: what role does this kind of information – that is very useful in everyday life – play in the court procedure?

Another question is how this kind of information should be combined with ordinary kinds of evidence, e.g. that of a witness.

Before I am able to deal with this problem, I have to go a step backwards and present my theoretical and terminological starting points.

Discussion in Sweden of the theory of evidence after the procedural reform of 1948 – when the principle of free evaluation of evidence was codified – has started from the question as to what rules or principles there might exist for the estimation of evidence and proofs of different kinds, rules not legal but still confining the judge, rules given by science rather than by the law.

Per Olof Ekelöf was the one to start this development towards a new theory of evidence. Later these ideas have been further developed by philosophers, statisticians and lawyers. I should now like to use my own presentation from my book *Bevisvärde* (Evidentiary Value) from 1976.

The basic evidentiary relation is that between two states of affairs or circumstances, from the existence of one of which we can infer the existence of the other. This inference is inductive and based on our knowledge of the state of affairs in general. The fact from which the inference is drawn is called the evidentiary fact, *A*, and the fact inferred is called the evidentiary theme, *B*. The proposition 'if *A*, then *B*' is suggested by a law of general experience.

E. Bulygin et al. (eds.), Man, Law and Modern Forms of Life, 241–249.

The extent to which an evidentiary fact entitles us to infer an evidentiary theme depends on the existence of certain other facts that are relevant without being directly connected with the theme. These facts (called auxiliary facts) only affect the evidentiary value of the evidentiary fact. Thus two kinds of knowledge are necessary: factual knowledge of the concrete situation and abstract knowledge of relations and events in general.

The relationship between these concepts can be exemplified by a case where skidmarks are the evidentiary fact and the speed of the car the evidentiary theme. The skidmarks have no evidentiary value unless our experience tells us that skidmarks of a certain length appear at a certain speed. This experience may be our knowledge of a found frequency based on statistical investigations but it can also be simply a vague notion of a correspondence based on unsystematized observations. It is obvious that skidmarks at a certain speed vary according to the situation in which they occur. On a dry surface the skidmarks found indicate one speed while the identical skidmarks on a wet surface would indicate a lower speed. The fact that the road was wet is no evidentiary fact in relation to a certain speed but it affects the evidentiary value of the skidmarks by pointing to a special experience.

In probabilistic terms this means that we are looking for the probability of the hypothesis that "the evidentiary theme is proved by the evidentiary fact", instead of the probability of the evidentiary theme given the evidentiary fact.

This way of emphasizing the evidentiary relation I have called "the evidentiary value model" and the other "the theme probability model". There is an important difference between these models:

– one can always assess an individual value for each single piece of evidence, usually using a scale from 0 to 1, where 0 means that the evidentiary fact has no implicative force related to the evidentiary theme, and 1 means that the evidentiary fact proves the existence of the theme. The value 0.5 means that the evidentiary fact in five cases out of 10 proves the existence of the theme, while in the rest of the cases it gives no implicative information about the existence of the theme.

– the value 0 means according to the theme probability model that we know that the theme does not exist, while according to the evidentiary value model it means that there is no empirical relation between the evidentiary fact and the theme. The difference lies in the way of formulating the knowledge.

The most problematic part of this general evidentiary relation is the proposition linking the two main facts together, which is based on experience.

The inference in question is inductive or constitutes an extension of limited observations and is consequently only probable. The problem of induction has been subject to much discussion; I here only want to point out that any attempt to prove the inductive inference in a more or less deductive manner will be futile because of the conjectural quality inherent in the inductive process. What we can do is to find criteria of what can be considered a reasonable conjecture.

This part of the evaluation of evidence is an empirical question and open to 'subjective' influence. The only way to achieve some degree of objectivity is by insisting on an open account of all arguments relevant to the decision. Ekelöf and Halldén suggest that causality is the criterion.[1] If one fact is caused by another, then the latter is proved by the former. I here disagree with them. Causality is a convenient means of expressing a relationship constituting evidentiary value but it is in no way a method of making the evaluation 'objective'; the criteria of causality are the same or at least as difficult to define as are those of evidentiary value. The only means of controlling the evaluation and of preventing it from being purely 'subjective' in a negative way, is by expressing the different propositions suggested by experience as clearly as possible.

Even if we have to accept this uncertainty in the result of the evaluation of a single piece of evidence, it does not necessarily mean that all evidentiary problems are to be treated as intuitive processes. In looking for evidentiary value rather than the probability of the evidentiary theme it is possible to combine all relevant evidence in a case analytically – that is, to calculate the joint effect without any further empirical knowledge than the evidentiary values of the evidentiary facts involved in the combination. The idea is that instead of having one event – the theme – with a changing probability (Bayes) we have several "events" consisting of the relation between the evidentiary fact and the theme. We are then able to apply the usual axioms of probability. There are three evidential combinations: chain, concurrence and contradiction.

When the evidentiary fact itself is not certain it has to be proved by introducing a new piece of evidence. We then have a chain from the new piece of evidence, *C*, via the original evidentiary fact, *A*, to the evidentiary theme, *B*. Of course the chain can be much longer than this.

A chain means a multiplied uncertainty. The optimal situation – where no uncertainty exists – is when every evidentiary fact has full evidentiary value, in other words when it proves its evidentiary theme. Consequently we look for the probability of *C* proving *A* ($bv1$)[2] and *A* proving *B* ($bv2$). This could be said to be a joint event, and applying the usual axioms of probability we get

$$P(bv1 \text{ and } bv2) = P(bv1) \times P(bv2/bv1).$$

If $P(bv2/bv1)$ equals $P(bv2)$ the events are independent and the formula for the total evidentiary value of a chain is

$$P(bv1 \text{ and } bv2) = P(bv1) \times P(bv2).$$

There is often more than one piece of evidence in favour of an evidentiary theme. These different pieces of evidence interact and must somehow be added together. In such a case we look for the probability of either *A* proving *C* ($bv1$) or *B* proving *C* ($bv2$).

$$P(bv1 \text{ or } bv2) = P(bv1) + P(bv2) - P(bv1 \text{ and } bv2).$$

Using the chain formula we then get

$$P(bv1) + P(bv2) - P(bv1) \times P(bv2).$$

The independence required in this case can be written $P(bv2) = P(bv2/{\sim}bv1)$.

Edman has shown that the presented formula for adding pieces of evidence together only provides a lower limit for the factual total evidentiary value.[3] This is due to the fact that the evidentiary value of a piece of evidence depends on the prior probability of the theme in question, even though the dependence is very small as long as this probability is neither very high nor very low. The idea is that the added evidence increases the prior probability which affects the evidentiary value. It can be shown, however, that the result of the presented formula is practically correct in all cases where the evidentiary values are high enough to make a trial possible.

There are also cases where there is evidence in favour of a theme contradictory to the main evidentiary theme. This will of course affect the total evidentiary value. If *A* proves *B* ($bv1$) and *C* proves $\sim B$ ($bv2$), $bv1$ and $bv2$ are contradictory. In order to be able to decide whether *B* or not, we must know that *C* does not prove $\sim B$ and that *A* proves *B*, which means $P({\sim}bv2 \text{ and } bv1)$.

Again the usual axioms of probability can be used and we get $P(bv1) - P(bv1) \times P(bv2)$.

The required independence can here be written $P(bv1) = P(bv1/{\sim}bv2)$, which means that the evidentiary value of the first piece of evidence must not be affected by the fact that the other has no evidentiary value at all. In the case of contradictory evidence the effect of the prior probability is more disastrous to the presented formula. As a matter of fact this formula is correct only in cases where either one or both evidentiary values are very low. Fortunately the effect of contradictory evidence can be formulated in a manner not based on prior probabilities:

$$\frac{P(bv1) - P(bv1) \times P(bv2)}{1 - P(bv1) \times P(bv2)}$$

This short presentation of the evidentiary value model shows that:

1. We are looking for the probability of an evidentiary relation = the evidentiary value instead of the probability of the evidentiary theme. The theory gives no real answer to what the criterion is of evidentiary value, although the terminology makes it easier to analyze the information given.
2. The model gives us the possibility of calculating the combined effect of independent singular pieces of information.

However, sometimes we have information of a kind that it is possible to express in terms of theme probability. This was the case in my example in the beginning, and is often the case when forensic scientists are involved in the trial.

The question is then how this information should be used as a whole, and especially how it should be combined with other information with evidentiary value (e.g. testimony). Different answers have been given to the latter question. Ian Hacking and Ekelöf have both – obviously independently of each other but with reference to Bernoulli – tried to solve the problem by using a system of squares.[4]

Ekelöf explains it by means of Figure 1. There are 100 small squares in the big one. The knowledge we have through the evidentiary fact (let us say 0.9) can be expressed by saying that the theme is proved by the evidentiary fact in the 90 squares marked with lines, while the remaining 10 dotted squares represent cases where we do not know whether the theme exists or not. If we then in one way or another know that the probability of the theme is 0.8, Ekelöf says that we can say about those remaining 10 cases that 8 out of them – those dotted as well as marked with lines – represent cases where the theme exists, and the remaining 2 cases where the theme does not exist. The result is then that the theme exists in 98 cases out of 100 = 0.98 or 98%.

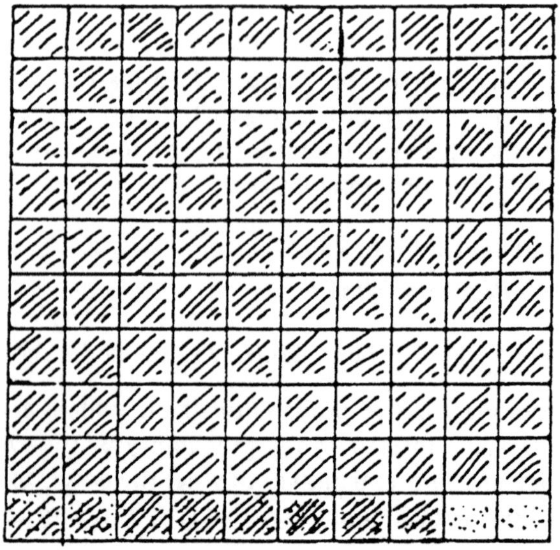

Fig. 1.

Let us then see what the formula of concurring evidence leads to: $0.8 + 0.9 - 0.8 \times 0.9 = 0.98$, or the same as the square model.

Is this possible? It seems surprising considering what I have said about the difference between knowledge of evidentiary value and knowledge of the theme probability.

Let us make a test by using an example.

I know that a friend of mine usually lives in the United States at this time of the year. I am not quite certain, but I estimate the probability as 80% or 0.8. This means, according to what I have said earlier, that – if we make the unrealistic assumption that my friend can only be at home or in the States – the probability that he will be at home is 20% or 0.2. One day I catch a glimpse of him in the crowd. I take a closer look, but because of the crowd I cannot reach him to make sure that it really is him. I estimate the evidentiary value of my observation as 0.9.

Following Ekelöf and Hacking, the fact that it is very improbable that my friend is at home today, should in one way or another be *added* to the knowledge that lies in my observation, and hereby the total probability of the theme – that he is at home – should increase instead of decrease.

This seems absurd and indicates that the use of the concurrence formula must be a mistake.

Intuitively this mistake has to do with the information involved in the example. As a starting point I have a very general knowledge about where my friend usually stays at this time of the year. When I think I see him in the crowd the former information is replaced by the information given by my observation, which is much more specific. It seems natural to consider these two situations as representing different *stages of knowledge*: the general probability is consumed by the specific probability that involves much more knowledge about the particular case that we are interested in.

Can this problem be explained in a more formal manner?

The basic idea is that the pieces of information or knowledge involved are not entirely independent of each other. Using the concurrence formula, we have to test whether the requirement of independence is fulfilled! The two "events" involved are

(1) the theme exists;

(2) the evidentiary fact proves (is caused by) the evidentiary theme.

In the concurrence case we are looking for the probability that either (1) or (2) is at hand = P (1 or 2). If the requirement of independence is fulfilled, $P(2) = P(2/{\sim}1)$. This means that the probability that my observation proves that my friend is at home must not be affected by the knowledge that he is not in the United States. This is not the case: with my unrealistic assumption we then know that he is at home. (Even without this assumption it is obvious that the first probability is affected.) Especially if we talk in terms of causality, it is obvious that if we know that a certain fact does not exist, then we also know that this fact cannot be the cause of the evidentiary fact we know.

This shows that we cannot use the concurrence formula.

If we cannot combine information that can be expressed as an evidentiary value with information that can be expressed in terms of theme probability, it has a great practical impact upon the use of forensic information in court. As far as I can see, there are two ways out of this dilemma:

(1) we have to choose one or the other, or

(2) we have to transform the theme probability into a shape that fulfils the requirement of independence.

1. The choice must be made taking into consideration partly what kind of knowledge we prefer from a legal point of view, partly in what piece of information we can find the most accurate knowledge.

If we have an evidentiary fact with an evidentiary value that is higher than the statistical probability attached to the theme, it is natural to use the evidentiary value, which obviously contains the best knowledge in the particular case.

If, instead, we know that the statistical distribution gives a higher probability than is implied by the evidentiary value, it is from a purely theoretical standpoint natural to use the former.

However, there are legal reasons to be careful with this kind of knowledge, since it does not in the same way as the evidentiary value attach to the particular case.

Let me turn back to the initial example. There is no doubt that the probability of speeding is 90% for any single car. Still it seems quite unrealistic to sentence any of these ten drivers for speeding. The reason is that the driver has no chance to show that he was the one that did not speed. Even if he could find proof, this means that the burden of proof has been placed on the accused, which is not acceptable.

This solution is of course very radical, and means e.g. that a handwriting analysis with a probability of 0.8 should be ignored if the case includes an "ordinary" evidentiary fact with an evidentiary value of 0.85, or even that all statistical knowledge should be ignored. Intuitively this seems to be a bad and somewhat arbitrary solution.

2. Is it then possible to transform statistical probability into evidentiary value?

The statistical evidence is sometimes (esp. when forensic science is involved) based on such low frequencies that experience and common sense tell us e.g. that the peculiarity in question is unique, and then we obviously talk about the particular case. However, we have to remember that the evidentiary value of such evidence is dependent upon how certain you are that the low frequency implies uniqueness, not upon how low the frequency is. If a fingerprint expert has found that a combination has occurred only once in 10 million prints, it can be natural to believe not that we will find another if we investigate 10 more million prints, but rather that this is a unique combination. The evidentiary value is 0.9 if the expert estimates that his conclusion about uniqueness is correct in 9 cases out of 10.

This means that when a statistical probability is extreme enough it turns out to be comparable to evidentiary value.

If it has been established in this way that some peculiarity is unique, it is possible e.g. to deduce that the accused is the one who wrote the text. In this way we are able to replace the theme with the state of affairs that the peculiarity is unique, and then this piece of evidence can be made independent of other pieces of evidence. It is then possible to use the concurrence formula.

As an example we can look at the case where we have a testimony proving that the text is written by the accused, and the material of an expert showing that a certain peculiarity in the text is unique and that the accused writes in the same way. Note that this material is not supposed to prove that the text is written by the accused, although this is the case if the material shows that the peculiarity is unique. However, the case where the peculiarity is *not* unique does *not* imply that the accused did not write the text. The requirement of independence is then that the probability that the testimony proves that the accused wrote the text must not be affected by the fact that we know that the material of the expert does not prove that the peculiarity is unique. Of course it does not! It is very possible that the accused wrote the text although the peculiarity turned out to be a mistake.

This means that the statistical information can be combined with ordinary evidentiary facts, but the figures given to the courts must not be the statistical probability. However, this is not the place to investigate when the statistical information can be transformed in this way.

I do not have courage enough to say that this is the way all forensic information of this kind should be treated. However it is interesting to see that what I have said is already applied by fingerprint experts. They have often been criticized for not giving statements before they are absolutely certain that there cannot be another person with the same combination.

What can be said is that forensic scientists must be very careful when they are using figures in their statements, since lawyers might use these as comparable to ordinary evidence, which is obviously wrong.

University of Örebro

NOTES

[1] P. O. Ekelöf, 'Topik und Jura', in *Akten des Weltkongresses für Rechts- und Sozialphilosophie*, Brussels 1971, p. 52; S. Halldén, 'Indiciemekanismer', *Tidsskrift for Rettsvitenskap* 86 (1973), 55.

[2] The notation '*bv*' stems from the term in Swedish, 'bevisvärde'.

[3] M. Edman, 'Adding Independent Pieces of Evidence', in *Modality, Morality and Other Problems of Sense and Nonsense. Essays Dedicated to Sören Halldén*, Lund 1973.

[4] I. Hacking, 'Combined Evidence', in S. Stenlund (ed.), *Logical Theory and Semantic Analysis*, Dordrecht 1974, p. 113; P. O. Ekelöf, *Rättegång* vol. 4, 4th edition, Stockholm 1977, 37.

LUCINDA VANDERVORT

EMPIRICAL UNCERTAINTY AND LEGAL DECISION MAKING

The rationality of law and legal decision making would be enhanced by a systematic attempt to recognize and respond to the implications of empirical uncertainty for policy making and decision making. Recognition of the existence of uncertainty with regard to the accuracy of facts and the validity of assumptions relied on to make inferences of fact is commonly avoided in law, because it raises the spectre of paralysis of the capacity to decide issues authoritatively. The view is widespread that the illusion of general certainty is more conducive to social order than the recognition and acceptance of limited certainty would be. This is a short-sighted view whose roots are found in primitive mechanical models of relationships in the empirical and social world – those of objective causality and determinism.

Within those limited frameworks it is assumed that if we had sufficient data a clear and unequivocal answer would be available to each question. Admission of uncertainty is thus seen as a sign of insufficiency, incompetence, impotence, and is avoided whenever a decision that must be seen to be rational, taken on the basis of valid reasons, cannot be avoided. The result is avoidance of some decisions (which is itself a decision with consequences) and duplicity in others.

Law making and decision making in law therefore must be restructured in a manner that permits the legal process first to take cognizance of the tentative, provisional, and context-bound validity and relevance of the models we use to conceptualize and order our understanding of phenomena, and then to utilize this awareness as an instrument in the production of legal policies and decisions that will be authoritative precisely because they are honestly accurate and socially responsible. "Honestly accurate" is here taken to mean validly grounded on what is recognized to be limited knowledge. Responsibility in policy and decision making is possible only when the implications of relative ignorance are taken fully into account, and thus is possible only in a legal process which admits that "honest accuracy" with regard to empirical and social relationships and facts, not "absolute truth", is the most its fact-finding processes can purport to achieve.

And it is only with such a transformation, whereby serious effort is made to evaluate the quality of the information and the validity of the assumptions

E. Bulygin et al. (eds.), Man, Law and Modern Forms of Life, 251–261.

used in legal reasoning, that law can purport to be "just". For law can be just only insofar as statutes enacting policy in legal form, and the policy making required by statutory interpretation in individual decisions, apply legal and societal norms to information that is honestly accurate. Policy development undertaken on the basis of misleading information or utilizing invalid or inapplicable reasoning processes cannot, except through accident, result in a plan, design or set of criteria that constitutes an effective and appropriate (or rational and reasonable) instrument for achieving stated social goals. Such misuse of legal authority, created as a means and granted only for the purpose of generating policy for the implementation of legitimate social goals, cannot be "just" in the fundamental sense, even if the misuse occurs through ignorance or inadvertance.

Likewise, decision making in individual cases, requiring an application of law and policy to the "facts", cannot be "just" if it is based on erroneous assumptions and errors of fact and inference. On occasion individual cases must be decided that require the application of a law embodying an irrational policy. Here the hands of the decision maker are all but tied. It is difficult to "justly" apply an inherently unjust law in an individual case. Individual decision makers can, of course, fictionalize the facts, read them up or down, or use any other discretion they have, to achieve a more appropriate result, but this will occur only insofar as a law is regarded as ill-advised or unreasonable by a particular decision maker.[1] Equal relief thus will not necessarily be made available in all cases.

The observation, that to be "just" law requires: (1) that legal policy be based on accurate information and rationally related to social goals; and (2) that decisions applying policy to individual fact situations be based on assumptions that are both relevant and accurate, in itself sounds very familiar. And indeed it is. For it reiterates some of the most fundamental concepts of the prerequisites of just decision making. The significance of its implications for legal systems only becomes apparent when the legal process is re-examined in some detail with an active awareness of the limits of the validity and relevance of the diverse conceptual frameworks that may be presupposed by the law in the 20th century in its attempt to regulate the broad range of human activities and interactions. The remainder of this discussion will do precisely that in a preliminary and provisional manner with reference to selected aspects of the legal process.

1. REASONS FOR DETERMINATIONS OF FACT

At present, at least in the common law jurisdictions, reasons are not given for determinations of fact or conclusions based on mixed fact and law. Appeals are based on errors of law, including procedural errors, and misdirection of the trier of fact as to the law, but not on errors of fact. There must be sufficient evidence (itself an issue of law) to enable the trier of fact to arrive at the conclusion of fact, or fact and law, in issue. The reasoning processes used to determine sufficiency of the evidence, and to arrive at the conclusion of fact, or fact and law, are not scrutinized. Insufficiency of the evidence may be made the basis of an appeal. But when this occurs, the appeal court makes its decision on the basis of a review of the reported evidence, not by an examination of the reasoning *process* used by the trier of fact in the lower court.

At the trial level the validity and relevance of assumptions, on which inferences about facts in issue could be based, are not themselves at issue unless specifically raised. When the knowledge and expertise of a specialist is seen to be required, and an expert is called as a witness to give opinion evidence, the validity of the propositions and assumptions relied on by the expert may itself become an issue. This leads, typically, to a "battle of experts", presentation of yet further experts to confirm or rebut the "truth" of previous expert opinion evidence.

Where the validity and relevance of assumptions are not actively placed in issue, it is assumed that the trier of fact will draw from his experience of the world to supply the assumptions required to determine the facts. Yet time, place, and life experience do augment and vary the pool of experience which the average trier of fact will have available. A judge or jury from the 15th century, hearing a 20th-century case, could be expected to require considerable assistance from specialists in 20th century life were they to arrive at a valid determination of liability or guilt, presupposing complex inferences about states of mind, intention, recklessness or negligence. A vast amount of knowledge about the empirical and social world is commonly assumed for the purposes of making the conclusions of fact required for judicial decisions, and this undeniably makes the accuracy of the conclusion dependent on the relevance and validity of the assumptions on which it is based. Yet, once a fact is determined from evidence that is regarded in law as sufficient, the fact is not subject to further scrutiny and is relied on absolutely for the purpose of determining the legal result.

Why are findings of fact once determined so sacrosanct in law? Why is more attention not given to errors of fact and invalid inferences from facts? A wrong decision is no less so merely because it results from a mistake in inference of fact rather than a mistake of law. Mistakes of law are seen to be matters of public concern because they may constitute precedent for other similar cases. Is the same not true of decisions made in reliance on inferences based on invalid or irrelevant assumptions about the empirical or social world? Habitual reliance on established modes of conceptualizing certain questions of fact may surely have as pervasive an effect in introducing error into whole classes of legal decisions as unchallenged mistakes of law do. And, if so, surely at minimum a legal decision should be challengeable on the grounds, not that the decision was made on the basis of a particular factual error – for this might be said of each and every case, but on the grounds that the reasoning process used to arrive at the inference of fact is itself invalid, either because the process used or assumptions relied on are invalid or not applicable to the phenomenon in question. Only if reasons for determinations of fact were given, as they are for determinations of law, could legal decisions be challenged on this expanded ground. Without reasons for determinations of fact, as long as there is sufficient evidence in law to enable a properly instructed trier of fact to arrive at the determinations in question, the reasoning process used remains undisclosed and hence its validity and applicability to make a particular determination of fact cannot be examined.[2] What cannot be examined cannot be challenged.

Assume then that we have before us once more our 15th-century jury charged by a judge in a 20th-century case. It is alleged that the defendent was negligent in that he did *X* although he knew or ought to have known that a particular result was a probable consequence of that act. The judge has determined that there is sufficient evidence to ground a finding of liability. No matter what the result at which the jury arrives, is it not the case that one can't help but wonder whether the assumptions relied on by the jury to arrive at the decision were valid or relevant? And if one would agree in this case that the assumptions used in drawing inferences from the facts should be available for scrutiny and subject to challenge, ought that ground not be as appropriate a basis for challenging the findings of a 20th-century jury charged in the same case? Mere contemporaniety, especially in a heterogeneous society, surely does not confer on the trier of fact a flawless grasp of that which it is reasonable, or reasonable beyond a reasonable doubt to assume, depending on the standard of proof, when one must make determinations of fact and conclusions of fact and law from available evidence.

The rationale for reliance on juries for fact finding is based on the notion that community beliefs, as embodied or represented by the jury, do represent that which can be reasonably assumed. While the present proposal does not require rejection of that general view, it does imply at minimum that reliance on assumptions properly the subject of expert evidence without the benefit of such evidence, illogical reasoning, or reliance on irrelevant assumptions should all be grounds for appeal. Thus the key consequence of this proposal is that the presumption that the trier of fact is reasonable will cease to confer on the trier of fact an unconditional license to apply private modes of logic and theories of social and natural science. Only with disclosure are challenges possible.

2. "REASONABLE" AND "NECESSARY" AS SOCIAL CONSTRUCTS

If triers of fact were required to provide reasons for their determinations of fact, thus establishing a record for the purposes of an appeal on expanded grounds as proposed, the next problem would be to establish an appropriate measure of the validity of the assumptions relied on by the trier of fact. In borderline cases there would be a strong temptation for the appellate court to substitute a test of "objective validity" for the reasonable man tests it is now assumed the trier of fact, whether judge or jury, will apply. Tempting though this might be, it is ultimately not a solution for it will only serve to beg all important questions. "Objective" criteria are of limited utility in legal decision-making because their social meaning is derivative. Objective tests also obscure the influence of normative considerations on assessment of what constitutes a valid and relevant consideration. Their use presupposes that normative conflict has been resolved. Moreover, even from an "anormative" perspective, insofar as there is such a thing, many of the issues with which contemporary legal decisions must deal cannot be conceived of within the conceptual framework with which the term "objective" has been strongly associated – a simple deterministic model of causality and a correspondence model of truth. Thus, quite independent of dispute arising from normative conflicts, there will be many issues that cannot be discussed, possible outcomes that cannot be described, other than in terms of probabilities valid only for the class as a whole, not each member. With regard to other issues even the probabilities associated with the class as a *whole* are the subject of mere speculation, not experience.

It is essential that means be devised within the legal process to recognize that "reasonableness" is a social construct. Failure to do so is an invitation to duplicity in policy and decision making. Our use of the phrases "undue risk", "public interest", "reasonable", and "necessary" reflects only the weight we choose to give conflicting social values and goals when we must make decisions in relative ignorance of all the consequences.

It is futile, for example, to suggest that "objectivity", in a primitive sense referred to above, be the test of the validity of empirical assumptions relied on in arriving at the determination that an industrial by-product poses an "undue risk to the public", that the "public interest" will be harmed by the program policies of a publicly licensed broadcaster, or that a prisoner should continue to be detained "to protect the public". In each of these examples the risk, harm, or hazard to be avoided is vaguely defined and itself must be specified, given concrete content, before the question (whether the particular activity in question will contribute to the prohibited outcome) can be addressed. Even if this has been done it is often impossible to say unequivocably that "but for *X, Y* will occur". In such cases there may *be* no unequivocable answer because particular outcomes can only be predicted in terms of probabilities, not certainties, and the model, though accurate on the average over all cases, is subject to a high error rate when applied to individual cases. The first problem frequently arises when statutory powers are created to deal with broadly defined problems before detailed policy questions have been resolved. In the absence of secondary legislation, judges and other decision makers exercising statutory powers find it necessary to expand the legal definition of key terms before attempting to apply the law to the facts. This can lead to disparate treatment of similar cases and a branding of judges as unduly activist. The only solution is actual legislation of detailed policy or some other device, such as policy hearings leading to policy determinations that are then applied to all individual cases.

The second problem – that of justifying a decision about an individual case on the basis of probabilities accurate only for the class of cases as a whole – also invites disparity in disposing of similar cases. Where decisions must be made (cannot be avoided) on a case-by-case basis, and no criteria exist that can be used to predict accurately the relevant future behaviour or outcome, the decision maker is in a no-win situation. Flipping a coin doesn't fit within his job description, but would demonstrate as much integrity as purporting to apply the law to facts indistinguishable in their relevance to the legal issue. Requiring individual decisions to be made on the basis of probabilities descriptive of a class only as a whole thus not merely invites, but demands, an arbitrary, capricious, intuitive, subjective (and thus private) use of decision-making power in the guise of a determination of objective fact. Here the terms "arbitrary and capricious" reflect the conclusion that a decision cannot be "judicial" if it *can only be made* in response to *non-legal* factors. Legal factors are those facts whose significance for the issue to be decided is sufficiently unequivocal to permit them to be used as criteria for the purposes of legal decision making. These observations imply that with no loss of "justice" we could opt to determine individual outcomes in cases involving insufficient criteria for non-arbitrary decision making by flipping coins, reading chicken entrails, or observing sunsets. The problem with these alternatives is that though they would be as "just" as the other approach they would not be apprehended to be so. The illusion of state power being used in a measured, deliberate and responsible manner would be lost.

Other alternatives exist. The preferred alternative is: (1) to invoke the evidentiary principles of natural justice to invalidate all laws that authorize *individual* decisions to be made on the basis of probabilities descriptive only of outcomes across a whole *class* of cases, and (2) to enact only those laws that both articulate a clear policy and establish clear criteria for its application. The consequence of the latter approach to law-making will be development of explicit social policy in areas characterized by empirical uncertainty to replace the general and vague standards now commonly used in law when legislators see themselves as obliged to "do something", but find it convenient to avoid political responsibility for the consequences by delegating both the authority to develop policy and criteria for implementation and the power to decide individual cases.

In areas where rational decisions about individual cases cannot be made on the basis of the merits of the particular case, other decision making mechanisms will be required if cases within a class are to be subjected to differential legal treatment. In each instance, however, the preliminary question will be whether there are social policy reasons for dealing with the whole class of cases by either refusing to permit the activity or, at the other extreme, imposing no restrictions on the activity and thus refusing to attempt to regulate it, the reason in each case being the absence of any rational means to distinguish one case from another within the class. The significance of conflicting collective societal values and norms in situations marked by uncertainty becomes apparent when a choice of this sort must be made. Assume the question is whether an industrial process, whose by-products are known to be hazardous to human health, is to be: (1) permitted, and (2) regulated. Assume further that considerable uncertainty surrounds the efficacy of waste storage and disposal techniques as well as determination of "safe" exposure levels. Depending on the relative importance attached to the industrial activity and its products as opposed to human life and health, uncertainty will be seen either as an indication that the activity should be permitted without legal controls or that it should be prohibited outright.

Where the activity is seen to be of sufficient present benefit to override most but not all concern about future consequences, and where the value attached to human health and life is not strong enough or is not perceived to be sufficiently at risk to outweigh that attached to present pursuit of the activity, the resultant political tension creates a climate in which there may be a strong temptation to attempt to find a compromise between competing values. It is precisely this type of tension that tends to spawn vague policy and irrational decision making mechanisms like those criticized above. In this example, if it were permitted to evolve in a typical manner, legislators would enact a law providing for regulation of the activity in the "public interest". The statute itself would receive broad support because it would be couched in terms general enough to alienate none even if it pleased none. All would see it as providing an opportunity to enlist the power of the state on behalf of their own notion of the public interest. Powers to inspect and make licensing or other regulatory decisions would be created, to be exercised with reference to criteria to be established through subordinate legislation and individual case decisions. The question of whether a rational basis existed for either the subordinate legislation or differential treatment of individual applicants under the legislation would not be squarely raised.

Preventive detention of purportedly dangerous persons presents a similar temptation to duplicity. The values balanced against one another are individual liberty and protection of society from undue risk of harm from acts of violence. Widespread public clamour for enhanced protection places political pressure on persons with statutory authority and encourages decision makers to view the powers they have as expansive. The attempt to achieve a compromise and protect both values, rather than only one or the other (life sentences for all those persons seen as posing a risk *versus* abolition of detention used solely for the purpose of incapacitation), is often seen to require the creation of mechanisms to dispose of individual cases. This is invariably the case when the alternative, creation of mandatory dispositions in accordance with set criteria established by statute, is perceived as "unjust" because it necessarily ignores the "special features" presented by a few cases. The illusion that individualized justice is the only "real" justice dies hard. Hence we have the creation of decision-making power with discretion to evaluate each case on its merits. Because this is seen as a responsible exercise of benevolence, the provision of a mechanism whereby a few appropriate candidates will be released rather than none, few people stop to consider whether the information used to justify differential dispositions of individual cases has any relevance to the individual case and, if relevant, whether it is sufficiently complete to be useful. The illusion that a rational decision making process is involved is protected by the significant symbolic value of the process itself. Effort expended by all participants, allocation of public resources to collect information and evaluate it, even the hope invested by the subject of the inquiry in its outcome, all serve to bolster the credibility of the process and discourage examination of the actual rationality of the purported decision making process.

Are there alternatives to such a charade? Yes, but implementation requires that the evidentiary issues be openly examined in the political arena and explicit policy choices be made by statute or some other similar legal instrument for which there is public accountability. Assume, for example, that the "public interest" is seen to require that all industries producing *X* tons of sulphur per *Y* % of GNP per year cease operation or that all persons who have caused personal harm of *X* severity to *Y* persons through acts of violence in the last *Z* years be detained. Assume further that in each case the legal provision adopted was designed to be a responsible collective response in the face of limited knowledge to a problem seen to be one of general societal significance. Rights and freedoms are thereby constrained on the ground that this is deemed "necessary" in the face of relative ignorance to prevent the creation of unknown future negative consequences or to achieve certain social goals.

If such provisions are alleged to violate constitutional or human rights protections how can the claim of "necessity" be defended? Can desire to prevent feared but unknown future possibilities justify interference with specific present rights? The "necessity" claimed here is not the necessity of the simple deterministic model; there is no proof beyond reasonable doubt that "but for" infringement of the right or freedom in question a specific, or even any, harm to society will occur. (The lack of evidence of precisely this sort was seen above to make the attempt to engage in individualized decision making "unjust".) Rather the "necessity" in this case is that of moral and political reasoning. To assert that an infringement on particular rights and freedoms is "necessary" is to claim that the preference structure of a society attaches sufficient weight to certain values and goals to unilaterally override the claims of competing values and goals whenever a choice must be made. If the priorities among preferred values are clearly and strongly held, this obviously may occur even where there is only suspicion, not actual knowledge, of a grave threat to preferred values. Thus the perceived "necessity" that a law be enacted and enforced is as much a social construct as are the "reasonableness" tests used to assess beliefs and choices. Development of collective social consciousness, which of course includes knowledge about the empirical world, over time alters the consensus about what is "necessary". The label can be successfully attached even to strongly repressive measures where there is a collective apprehension that preferred values otherwise may be placed at unacceptable risk. By the same reasoning repressive measures may be rejected even in the face of grave risk where those measures are themselves seen as posing a greater risk to a preferred value.

Thus although, as argued above, it often may be unjust to purport to use goal related criteria to differentiate between members of a single group precisely because the differentiation cannot be "rational", that same group, as long as it is dealt with as a whole, in some cases may justifiably be given more preferential or disfavorable treatment than other groups, as long as no other choice would be "responsible" in view of the values believed to be potentially affected. In each case explicit recognition, not avoidance and denial, of empirical uncertainty, is a crucial factor in the determination of "reasonable" and "responsible" social policy.

It is therefore to be concluded that law must alter its aspirations and recognize that rational decision-making is a process that can occur only within the parameters set by present knowledge and societal preference structures. Only by recognizing and consciously working within the constraints imposed by these parameters is it possible to achieve "just" decisions. Where no rational basis for differentiating cases exists, "individualized justice" must be avoided and public policy articulated in law applied uniformly to all cases in a class. The terms "reasonable" and "necessary", used to describe policy and its consequences for specific cases, must be understood to represent provisional societal assessments, attempts to implement societal preference structures in the face of limited knowledge. Heightened awareness of the limited nature of our knowledge can only result in legal policies that have a more explicit normative basis and are more readily seen as merely provisional.

University of Saskatchewan

NOTES

[1] Cf. Ch. Perelman, *Justice, Law, and Argument: Essays on Moral and Legal Reasoning*, Dordrecht, 1980, 141–143.

[2] Legal decisions are subject to challenge, of course, on the ground of abuse of discretion,

consideration of matters irrelevant in law to exercise of the decision making power. A decision maker who does this is acting in excess of jurisdiction. Where this ground is used to challenge a decision it is often alleged that had only relevant and proper factual considerations been relied on there would have been insufficient evidence to arrive at a conclusion. Hence this ground often collapses, in effect, into that of insufficient evidence.

GEORG HENRIK VON WRIGHT

IS AND OUGHT

1. The two figures of this century who have most deeply influenced its social science are – there can be little doubt – Hans Kelsen and Max Weber. (A comparable influence has only been exerted by Karl Marx but he died long before the century was born.) Both represent a spirit which can, with due caution, be labelled "positivist" although the philosophic tradition in which they were reared was neo-kantianism rather than 19th-century positivism. Common to both was a passionate urge to "purify" science from ingredients which they thought extraneous to an uncompromising pursuit of truth. Weber saw the threat to scientific purity in valuations and professed the ideal of a value-free science (*eine wertfreie Wissenschaft*). Kelsen's vision was of a *reine Rechtslehre*, a legal science uninfected by teleological and moralistic argumentation.

The climate of opinion which these two giants represented has changed and is much less characteristic of recent decades than it was of the mid-century years when "logical positivism" was dominant in philosophy and exerted a strong influence on scientific methodology. Criticism of positivism was for some time a fashion, and if the *Positivismusstreit* no longer appears exciting this is because it has effected a change from which no return seems possible to the positions which were then attacked. But there is also a danger that some important clarity attained by the genius of men like Kelsen and Weber got obscured in the debate and will have to be regained through a new process of "purification". My paper is intended as a modest effort in this direction.

2. In a paper from the early 1950's called "Was ist die Reine Rechtslehre?" Kelsen emphasizes two features of his "pure theory".[1] One is the sharp distinction between fact and norm, the other is the logico-analytical character of a "scientific" jurisprudence.

"Die logische Unterscheidung zwischen Sein und Sollen", he says, "und die Unmöglichkeit im Wege einer logischen Schlussfolgerung aus dem Bereich des einen in den des anderen zu gelangen, ist eine der wesentlichen Positionen der Reinen Rechtslehre." And, he adds, "Die Logik, die die Reine Rechtslehre sozusagen erst entdeckt hat, ist die *allgemeine Norm-Logik*, das heisst: eine

E. Bulygin et al. (eds.), Man, Law and Modern Forms of Life, 263–281.

Logik des Sollens oder der Soll-Sätze, die Logik einer auf Normen, und nicht auf die natürliche Realität gerichteten Erkenntnis." This logic of norms he also calls "die Voraussetzung für eine korrekte Rechtslehre".

There is something problematic, not to say ironic, about Kelsen's juxtaposition of the two features. Because the sharp distinction between Is and Ought is the very thing which makes it doubtful whether there *can be* a "logic of norms" at all – particularly if, as is the case with Kelsen, the separation of fact and norm goes together with a so-called non-cognitivist conception of norms as directives or prescriptions which cannot be true or false. For a reason which I shall mention presently Kelsen seems to have been unaware then of the difficulties of reconciling with one another the sharp Is-Ought distinction, a non-cognitivist position, and the idea of a logic of the normative.[2] But I shall also argue that a reconciliation is, in fact, possible.

3. The history of the Is-Ought debate is often traced back to a well-known passage in Hume's *Treatise*[3] – and the idea that there is "an unbridgeable gap" separating fact from value and norm is sometimes also referred to as "Hume's *Guillotine*".[4] The attribution of the separation thesis to Hume may not be historically entirely fair.[5] But it was certainly forcefully defended by the neo-Humeans of the logical positivist movement who shared with Hume a phenomenalistic epistemology, the denial of natural necessity, and an emotive theory of morality.

In this context, a saying by the French mathematician and philosopher of science Henri Poincaré, is also often quoted to the effect that from premisses in the indicative one cannot draw conclusions in the imperative mood.[6] Ought-sentences and value-judgements are then regarded as imperatives and exclamations in linguistic disguise, so to speak.[7] A more refined version of this view – associated above all with the name of the English philosopher Richard Hare[8] – says that from (purely) descriptive premisses one cannot draw prescriptive conclusions.

But if norms are imperatives or otherwise "prescriptive", how can they enter into logical discourse at all? Relations of contradiction and of logical consequence (entailment) seem to presuppose that the related entities have truth-value. But imperatives certainly are neither true nor false, and the same presumably holds good of prescriptions of all kinds, too. Can even a simple subsumptive inference which a judge draws when he applies a general law to an individual case claim to be logically valid?

Axel Hägerström and some of his followers in Scandinavian jurisprudence had the courage to give a frank 'No' in reply to the question.[9] The logical positivists found this separation of norms from logic difficult to stomach, although they appreciated the problematic nature of any attempt to create a logic of norms. The difficulty is still sometimes referred to as Jørgensen's Dilemma after the Dane Jørgen Jørgensen who gave a particularly clear expression to the difficulty of reconciling the sharp Is-Ought dichotomy with the aspirations of logicians to penetrate with their instruments also the realm of the normative.[10]

4. After the heyday of positivism in the mid-century years the climate of opinion in philosophy gradually changed.

The success of some logicians in the 1950's in creating a "deontic logic" which, at least from a purely formal point of view, was easy to integrate into the mainstream of modern logical research, made it doubtful whether Hume's Guillotine really constituted an obstacle to "logicizing" the Ought-side, too, of the Is-Ought dichotomy. It was partly under the impression of these developments that Kelsen in his 1953-paper expressed his confidence in a *Normenlogik* – although he was a bit too egocentric, I think, in attributing its discovery to the Pure Theory of Law.

However, with further changes in the philosophic climate some began to doubt even the *existence* of the infamous "guillotine". Perhaps the Is-Ought gap was just an illusion.

A forceful attack on the received doctrine was made by John Searle first in a paper "How to Derive 'Ought' from 'Is'" and subsequently with some modifications in his very influential work *Speech Acts.*[11] I shall here present Searle's argument in a somewhat "compressed" form which, nevertheless, should do justice to his main point:

First premiss:	*A* promises to do *p*.
Second premiss:	By promising to do *p, A* has placed himself under an obligation to do *p*.
Conclusion:	*A* ought to do *p*.

The performance of actions and existence of obligations are facts. Searle does not explicitly deny that it also is a fact that *A*, who gave a promise, ought to act accordingly. His point is rather that an Ought-statement has been derived from obviously factual statements. So there *is* a "bridge" from Is to Ought.

Shortly after Searle's first paper, Max Black presented an even simpler argument against the Is-Ought separation.[12] His reasoning runs as follows:

A and *B* are playing chess. *A* wants to checkmate *B*. The situation is such that unless he makes a certain move he cannot mate his opponent. Therefore he should now make this very move.

Since Searle and Black wrote their papers the Is-Ought debate has been in full swing again – and there is no sign in recent years that it has abated.[13] Opinions are sharply divided. Also, the nature of the issue has become vastly more complicated. That Ought-sentences may be derived from Is-sentences does not necessarily show that normative conclusions are derivable from factual premisses. There is also the possibility to be considered that Ought-sentences, or *some* such sentences, actually state facts – and the possibility that Is-sentences sometimes express norms. We have to consider here, not only the syntactical form of some sentences, but also the semantics of their interpretation.

5. As already hinted at (p. 264), the question whether the alleged gap between Is and Ought can be bridged or not is crucially related to the question whether norms can be true or false. One may distinguish two positions on this last question:

The first position I shall call cognitivist (or descriptivist). According to it, some norms are true, *i.e.* such that one can in their case truthfully say that something or other ought to or may be. One can, moreover, distinguish two forms of this position according to whether the truths are held to be contingent empirical facts to be ascertained through observation of the social reality or whether they are thought of as a kind of necessity to be grasped through reflexion on the nature of law and morality. I shall call the two positions naturalist and non-naturalist cognitivism (descriptivism), respectively.

Various systems of normative ethics and ideas about so-called "natural law" exemplify non-naturalist cognitivism. The norms of natural law may then be regarded as a measure whereby positive law, the law of the state, is judged adequate or inadequate in relation to a universally valid standard of justice. Thus Cicero in a well-known passage in his *Republic* (Bk. III, Ch. 32) wrote:

> There is a true law (. . .) that conforms to nature; this law directs men to the good by its commands, and detours them from evil by its prohibitions, (. . .) It is impermissible to oppose it by other laws, nor to derogate its precepts (. . .). It cannot be different in Rome or in Athens, and it will not be in the future different from what it is today; but one and the same law, eternal and immutable, will impose itself upon all peoples for ever.

One may smile at the lack of a sense of "cultural relativity" revealed in Cicero's words. The philosophic difficulties encountered by a natural law theory with such universalistic claims as Cicero's are all too obvious. But it would be quite wrong to think of the idea itself as obsolete, belonging only to the past. Thus an influential work on political theory from recent years, Robert Nozick's *Anarchy, State and Utopia* opens with the statement: "Individuals have rights, and there are things no person or group of persons may do to them (without violating their rights)".[14] The author does not mean rights actually conferred on people by (positive) legislation, but rights, presumably, "eternal and immutable", which men have by virtue of being individuals and which set a standard for what the state and its officials may "legitimately" do.

I think myself the tendency pernicious to try to remove the "ought" and "may" of norms from the realm of contingent facts of the world to a "non-natural" realm of timeless truths. A removal of the norms from the world of facts is also a removal of them from the realm of truth.

The second position on our question I shall call non-cognitivism or prescriptivism. According to it, norms do not describe or state anything which is true or false, but prescribe what ought to or may be (or be done). This is a position usually taken by philosophers who would label themselves "positivists". But it is certainly not confined to philosophers of that particular denomination.

The term "prescriptivism" suggests that norms are issued by some norm-*authority* as I shall call it and directed to some agents or groups of people, the norm-*subjects*. The basic pattern is that of a master imposing duties and giving permissions to his servants. But the master can also be a legislature, composed of members selected according to some rules (norms) and enacting laws (norms) in accordance with regulations (norms) for its procedures. Or the authority can be the group itself which, in the course of generations, has evolved customs and other precepts for the conduct of its members. He can also be a fictitious figure of a remote past, like Lycurgus, or a fictitious supernatural authority, like the Jahve who handed to Moses the tablets on Mount Sinai.

6. It is an essential feature of norms that they should be expressible in language, in what I propose to call norm-formulations. Some norms may never be expressed and yet "exist", for example in the form of "instinctively" observed customs or taboos. And when formulated they need not be written.

There are standard forms of norm-formulations using deontic words such as "ought", "should", "must(-not)", "may". But also forms of sentence, the primary use of which is for describing, and not for prescribing, are quite frequently used as norm-formulations. I have seen it stated that some legal codes have been deliberately written in the indicative mood. For example, using sentences of the type: "Whoever does so and so will be sentenced to such and such". This may be a pretty accurate description of what actually happens in a society and a basis for reliable predictions. But as a fragment of a legal text, *i.e.*, as a norm-formulation, the form of words is neither descriptive nor predictive, but prescriptive. It says what ought to happen consequent upon such and such facts.

If norms, by definition, are to the effect that certain things ought to or may be, then all norms are also expressible in deontic language. And I think one may say that, from the point of view of understanding their logic, it is preferable that norms be thus expressed.

It is a great merit of the Swedish philosopher Ingemar Hedenius to have clearly noted and exploited an ambiguity which is characteristic of deontic sentences.[15] I shall refer to it as their descriptive and prescriptive interpretation; Hedenius himself called legal sentences in the descriptive interpretation "spurious", and in the prescriptive interpretation "genuine". A legal sentence "it ought to be the case that so and so" can be read either as a norm or prescription, *e.g.* for the reader's own conduct: he is urged to behave in a certain way. But the same sentence can also be read as a statement that there is (exists) a norm to this effect. That a certain norm exists or does not exist is a fact. It may therefore be uncontroversially true that, according to, say, Finnish law such and such ought to be the case or be done.

To notice the ambiguity inherent in deontic sentences is, of course, not to "bridge the gap" between Is and Ought. But it can be said to throw light on the distinction. In a certain sense the Is-Ought distinction *is* the difference between description and prescription, the difference which comes to light in the descriptive and the prescriptive use of a peculiar type of linguistic discourse, *viz*. deontic sentences.

7. We can now give to the traditional Is-Ought problem a slightly new formulation: Can prescriptions follow logically from descriptions? We can supplement this with the converse question: Can descriptions follow logically from prescriptions? And we can add a third question: Can prescriptions follow from other prescriptions?

I think that the answer to all three questions is a firm No. The reason is simple: Logical consequence is a truth-preserving relationship. If from A follows logically B then either A is false or A and B are both true. Since prescriptions are neither true nor false they can figure neither as premisses nor as conclusions in logically valid inferences. It is a consequence of this that no combination (conjunction) of descriptions and prescriptions can perform in these rôles either.

These statements may sound dogmatic. They are certainly much more radical than the views usually held by authors on legal theory or argumentation – even by writers who take an otherwise guarded attitude to the problem of bridging the gap between Is and Ought. I must therefore try to argue in defense of my position.

Before considering the Is-Ought case I shall say something about what may be termed the Ought-Is and the Ought-Ought cases.

The former is the question, already raised, whether a description can follow logically from a prescription. Some writers think this possible. They often use as a supporting example a famous principle associated with the name of Kant, *viz*. the principle that Ought entails or implies Can. That something or other can be the case or can be done may be regarded as a factual statement. It could rightly be said that a law-giver who enjoined the impossible would behave irrationally, since his will could not be fulfilled. We may therefore make it a maxim of rational or reasonable law-giving that only possible things (actions) be subject to norm. But this maxim is itself a norm, or something norm-like, and the "inference" "you ought so therefore you can" is not a logical entailment but an affirmation of the reasonableness of the command.

Of greater importance to our theme is the question whether there can exist logical relations such as consequence and contradiction between prescriptions, *i.e.* prescriptively interpreted norm-formulations. This question takes us to the topic of deontic logic or the logic of norms.

Deontic logic as a systematic study came into existence some thirty years ago. It can be said without exaggeration, not only that it has acquired an established status as a branch of (modern) logic, but also that it has aroused unusual interest outside the circle of logicians, among social scientists and legal and moral philosophers.

It is, I hope, not too self-centered to tell here the following story. When Kelsen in 1952 made his first and only visit to Finland he was very excited about the prospects which deontic logic seemed to open for vindicating some basic tenets in his own "pure" theory of law. In particular, he looked for support in logic for his idea that a legal order is of necessity closed, *i.e.* that there are no "gaps" in the law, and for the idea that a legal order must be free from "contradictions".

I do not remember exactly how I answered him, but presumably my reply was encouraging. I certainly believed myself then that, for example, "it ought to be the case that *p* and it ought to be the case that not *p*" was a *logical* contradiction. And this in spite of the fact that I – and Kelsen too – held norms to be neither true nor false. It seemed to me then that, with the invention of deontic logic, logic had somehow transcended the borders of truth and falsehood and subjected a wider realm of conceptual entities to its laws.

But this opinion was premature – and, I now think, false.

We already noted that deontic sentences are characteristically ambiguous. They can be used for expressing norms, *i.e.* prescribing modes of conduct. Or they can be used for describing or stating what norms, prescriptions, there are. Under the second use deontic sentences are said to express norm-propositions.

The formulas of deontic logic are schematic representations of deontic sentences. Noting the ambiguity one can ask: Is deontic logic a logic of (genuine) norms, or of norm-propositions? If the second, there is no question of truth-values being transcended. Because norm-propositions are true or false as the case may be.

I find it surprising that this problem has been but little discussed among logicians. (An exception are the writings of Alchourrón and Bulygin.[16]) Authors generally regard it as clear what deontic logic is about and assume that standard logical techniques can be used for handling its formulas. My own view was for a long time that deontic logic is concerned with norm-propositions, although it also embodied some conceptual elements relating to norms proper.

If this opinion were correct it would indeed be the case, for example, that two norms could not co-exist if the one enjoined something which the other norm prohibited. By suitably moulding the notion of existence when applied to norms this could be made true by definition. But it would be in flagrant conflict with the fact that contradictory norms actually appear in legal orders[17] – not only in the sense that they are duly enacted by the same legislature but also in the sense that they are both applied – sometimes the one, sometimes the other – by the judiciary when deciding legal cases. Do they not then co-exist? I think it would be absurd to deny that they do. But then the contradiction is not between norm-propositions. And if norms have no truth-value then contradiction, it seems, cannot be between the norms either. So where *is* the contradiction? Is there a *logical* contradiction at all?

The last two questions are in fact quite easy to answer. There is a straightforward logical contradiction between the *contents* of the two norms. This is so because it is logically impossible for one and the same agent both to do and refrain from doing the same thing on the same occasion. And this contradiction betwen the norm-contents is obviously the reason why we call the norms themselves (and the correlated norm-propositions) contradictory, although this is really a misnomer.

Calling norms contradictory is a signal that something is "unsatisfactory" about them. In order to see what it is we must, I think, reflect on the purpose of norms and of norm-giving activity such as legislation.

The one who issues an order or prohibition – be it an individual commander or a legislative assembly – can normally be said to *want* or to "*will*" that things be as prescribed. And the one who gives permission is prepared, if not to encourage, so at least to *tolerate* that the permission-holders avail themselves of the permission. I think this is true and important – notwithstanding difficulties which in other respects may be encountered by a so-called "will theory" of norms.

In order to enforce his will, the law-giver normally also prescribes various measures, such as punishment and fines, to be taken against those who do not comply with his (primary) prescriptions. As has often been said, a legal order is a coercive order. Use of coercion and force are of its essence – even if some valid norms may be (legally) broken with impunity.

If a law-giver issued norms with mutually contradictory contents he would be acting *irrationally* in the sense that he wanted something to be the case which is logically impossible. *Ordering* something and its contradictory is possible, but having both orders *satisfied* is impossible. Similarly, if a law-giver permitted something of which – for reasons of logic – nobody could ever avail himself, the "permission" could rightly be labelled irrational, silly, no permission at all.

Generally speaking: a legal order and, similarly, any coherent code or system of norms may be said to envisage what I propose to call an *ideal* state of things when no obligation is ever neglected and everything permitted is sometimes the case. If this ideal state is not logically possible, *i.e. could not* be factual, the totality of norms and the legislating activity which has generated it do not conform to the standards of rational willing. Deviations from these standards sometimes occur – and when they are discovered steps are usually taken to eliminate them by "improved" legislation.

I think this characterization is substantially correct – ignoring here some complications connected with the *unity* and possible *hierarchical* structure of normative codes. Any such code may be said to contain an implicit description of a state of affairs, *viz.* the ideal state envisaged by the law-giver. This description is almost certainly *false* in the sense that it does not agree completely with reality, the factual state of things. But unless it *could be true* it cannot be *rationally willed* by the law-giver either. In order to be rational to entertain, the ideal must be a picture of a *possible world* which is, to use a happy phrase coined by Jaakko Hintikka, *deontically perfect.*[18]

Anything which is possible at all is logically possible, but not anything which is logically possible is also physically possible, *i.e.* possible according to the laws of nature. And not anything physically possible is also humanly possible, *i.e.* possible to achieve through human action. In view of the fact that (most) norms are rules of action it seems reasonable to demand that the ideal world envisaged by a system of norms should be not only logically but also humanly possible to realize, but such stronger demands we need not consider here.

Deontic logic, to put it in a nutshell, is the study of logical relations in deontically perfect worlds. The fact that norms are neither true nor false constitutes no obstacle to this study. Deontic logic is not concerned with logical relations between prescriptions (norms) but with logical relations between the ideal states the descriptions of which are implicit in norms.

I think it is a good characterization of the activity of the discipline called *legal dogmatics* to say that its task is to expound and make clear the exact nature of the ideal state of affairs which the law envisages. It clarifies the content of the law. Sometimes it is clear from the norm-formulations which this content is. But sometimes it is not clear and the activity of the legal dogmatist has to assume a hermeneutic or interpretative character. He makes a proposal or recommendation about how the law should be understood. The proposed content is stated in true or false propositions – but the proposal itself cannot be assessed as true or false. It can, however, be justified by various means of legal argumentation, and it may be assessed as reasonable or not according to a variety of standards which need not, incidentally, mutually agree.

8. From the platform which we have now reached new vistas open on the Is-Ought question.

First, I think we can demolish the myth of a separate Realm of the Normative – ein *Reich des Sollens* in which Oughts and Mays exist in isolation from the actual world. The myth demolished, what remains of the "realm" is a description of an alternative, "ideal" world constituted by the norm contents of a given normative code or order. This description can, point by point, be compared with reality and will then normally be found to be partly true, partly false of our real world. Calling the description false does not mean that it describes what is sometimes called a "false ideal". It means that the actual world is not perfect, the ideal not realized.

The function of norms, one could say, is to urge people to realize the ideal, to make them act in such a way that the description of the real approximates to the description of the ideal. In an important sense we could say that the purpose of norms is to "bridge the gap" between Is and Ought, although *not* in the sense of establishing a deductive bond of entailment between the two. Such a bond is out of question, cannot possibly exist – for the simple reason that norms are prescriptions and relations of entailment can exist only between descriptions or, if you wish, between propositions expressed by descriptive sentences.

I am presumptuous enough to think that what has been said contains, *in nuce*, a solution to the much debated Is-Ought problem. It is a solution which both preserves the underivability of the ideal from the real *and* accords to the existence of norms the same robust reality as other (social) facts.

This said, there still remains a formidable task before us. It is to examine those arguments which have recently been brought forward to show that it *is* sometimes possible to derive an Ought from premisses which look undoubtedly factual .

9. Let us first consider Searle's argument. A man by performing a certain action which constitutes a promise, commits himself to a further action, *viz.* to fulfilling his promise. The statement that he gave the promise is a statement of fact. From it follows logically, it seems, that now he ought to do a certain thing. Is this not deducing a norm from a fact?

It certainly is not – but to see this clearly is not quite easy.

There is a norm of promise-keeping. It goes as follows: It ought to be the case that, if someone promises to do something he also does this thing. Or, which says the same: It must not be the case (*i.e.* is forbidden) that someone gives a promise without fulfilling it. Now *A* promises to do *p*. It follows that he then ought to do *p*.

Since the conclusion was drawn from the factual statement that *A* gave a promise in conjunction with the norm of promise-keeping, one may feel inclined to say as follows: Searle has not shown that an Ought may be inferred from (just) an Is, but that it can be inferred from an Is in combination with an(other) Ought. So Searle is not entirely right, only half-right.

But this is to concede too much. First, one may doubt whether one premiss was normative. Was it not rather the norm-proposition to the effect that *there is* a norm of promise-keeping? If so, both premisses were factual. Secondly, it is not clear either whether the conclusion is normative. If it too were factual, Searle's argument would have no bearing at all on the Is-Ought issue, *i.e.* on the question whether *normative* conclusions can follow from (purely) *factual* premisses. It would only show that sometimes a factual statement to the effect that something ought to be (done) follows logically from some other factual statements one or several of which are to the effect that certain obligations under norm exist.[19] And that such entailments are possible nobody could ever seriously have doubted.

However, Searle's argument *is* much more interesting than this. We can leave unanswered the question whether one of its premisses is a norm or a norm-proposition. We focus attention on the conclusion that *A* ought to do *p*. Of it I shall say that it is neither a norm – in the sense in which the rule of promising is a norm or the laws of the state are norms – nor a norm-proposition. So what is it then?

We are here confronted, I maintain, with another "ought" – equally common as the deontic or normative ought of moral or legal norms. I shall call it a *technical* Ought. When in this "technical" sense it is said of something that it ought to be or to be done, this is an elliptic statement the full meaning of which is that *unless* this thing is (done), something else will (also) fail to be the case. For example: If I have given a promise, I ought to (must, have to) fulfil it *in order to* satisfy the obligation constituted by the norm which prohibits breach of given promise.

The technical Ought expresses a requirement, a practical necessity, and it is also often – and perhaps better – rendered by the word *must*. The thing, for which something is required can be called, quite generally, an *end* and the thing required a *means*. The formulation in language of the means-end relationship can also be called a *technical norm*; it is closely related to that which Kant called "hypothetical imperatives".

The technical Ought must not be confused with the Ought of genuine norms. There is a strong tendency to do so. It is nourished by the use of the same word "ought" (or "must") in both cases. It would be pedantic and contrary to sound linguistic practice to try to reserve the word "ought" for the obligation imposed by norms and "must" for the practical necessities stated in hypothetical imperatives. The fact is that both "oughts" are intimately connected. The "ought" of norms engenders "oughts" of practical necessity – as witness Searle's example. And the "ought" of a hypothetical imperative very often engenders "oughts" of a normative character: when we want to make true that for which certain actions are practical requirements we urge people to perform those actions by telling them that they ought to be done. This last is norm-giving activity giving rise to genuine norms (commands, orders).

We can now see what is wrong with Searle's purported argument to show that one can deduce an Ought from Is. From the fact that there exists an institution of promising, *i.e.* a norm to the effect that given promises ought to be kept, and the fact that a person has given a promise it follows logically that he ought to do a certain thing. That he ought to do this is then an elliptic formulation and short for the statement that unless he does it he will not satisfy his obligation. His obligation, however, is not to do the thing in question *simpliciter* but his obligation, that which he, in the normative sense, ought to do, is either not to promise or, once he has promised, to keep his word. By having promised he has created for himself a practical necessity of doing the promised in order to fulfil his obligation. This is true, a fact, not a norm. But *ought* he not then to keep his promise – in the normative sense of "ought"? If he hesitates to do the thing he promised someone else may urge him on, saying "promises ought to be kept". This is prescriptive use of language. Or the promisee, who is interested in getting for himself the promised thing but perhaps does not care much about moral duties, may say "you ought to do what you promised me". This too is prescriptive activity. Such activity may occur after a promise has been given. But whether it does or not is contingent. At no stage is there anything which could rightly be called the deduction or derivation of an Ought from an Is, *i.e.*, of a norm from some facts.

10. We can now also deal with Black's example of the chess-player who is anxious to mate his opponent and will not (cannot) do this unless he makes a certain move. Does it "follow logically" that he ought to make this move then? Black prefers to say "should" rather than "ought to" but admits that the difference between the two deontic verbs is immaterial here.[20] He, furthermore, does not say that the should-sentence which is the conclusion of the argument is prescriptive (nor that it is normative). But he says that it has a "distinctively performative aspect"[21] and that it has the practical function of *advising* ("prodding") the player.[22] One can grant the correctness of these observations about the rôle of the should-sentence. They do not substantially affect the issue. But we must disagree with Black on the question whether some non-factual conclusion here follows from factual premisses. An advice does not "automatically" follow from the facts of the case – as a propositional conclusion would do, even if there were nobody to "draw" it. An advice requires an advisor and an advisee, and whether any

advice is forthcoming or not in this case depends upon a number of factors other than those mentioned in the premisses of Black's inference schema. What follows logically, however, is that unless player *A* makes a certain move he will forfeit his objective (in the game against *B*). This is a technical norm which can be expressed elliptically in the sentence "*A* should make move *M* now". Also other things follow logically in the sense that they are true if the premisses are true – for example that if *C* is to give honest (correct) advice to *A* on how *A* shall mate *B* he must advice *A* to make move *M* now. And this he can do by saying to *A* "you should now make move *M*". But whether *C* actually gives this advice or not depends on circumstances other than the facts that *A* wants to checkmate *B* and that the one and only way in which *A* can achieve this is by making move *M*.

Also in the context of chess-playing genuine *norm*-giving may occur. The captain of the chess team may tell one of the members never to make a certain move in such and such a situation. This is an order (norm) – and there may even be some sanction attached to it. But the reason for giving the order may be the captain's firm conviction that if the member in question does not observe this norm the team is in for defeat. Here a technical Ought can be said to "back" or to justify a deontic Ought. This is a common type of situation. It is also prominent in legislation. Laws are usually enacted with a view to some end or purpose which the legislator considers important. The purpose may be outlined in a preamble stating the motivation for the law. The purpose is often debated publicly. Do, for example, very strict regulations about speed-limits for vehicles promote safety on the roads? If not, why issue them? Drivers tend not to observe them very strictly and this again may encourage disregard for regulations generally, including those which obviously serve important purposes. These are familiar arguments.

The question might be raised: Is it theoretically conceivable that all laws of the state could be given a backing in technical norms? So that every Ought of a legal norm could be, as it were, translated into the Ought of a technical norm which says that *unless* certain things are the case (citizens and officials observe a certain conduct) the lawgivers' aims will be forfeited?

To the best of my knowledge no law-code is written in the form of technical norms. Maybe a code could, "in principle", be thus written. This would not show, however, that the normative "Ought" is reducible to the "Is" of technical "Oughts". Because the law-code would not be "meant" to be read as a description of what is required if certain aims are to be attained – but it would be "meant" as an urge to "all those concerned" to live up to the ideal. Its "meaning" *qua law* would be prescriptive, not descriptive.

11. I shall try to summarize my position on the Is-Ought issue.

Norms pronounce certain things (actions or states) obligatory, permitted or forbidden. Such pronouncements are neither true nor false. Neither between norms mutually nor between norms and facts can there exist logical relations, for example, relations of contradiction or entailment. In this sense Is and Ought are separated by an "unbridgeable gap".

Norms prescribe something and do not describe anything. But the contents of norms, *i.e. that which* norms pronounce obligatory, permitted or forbidden, may be said to describe an ideal world. Between the constituent parts of it logical relations can obtain. The formal study of such relations is the subject matter of deontic logic, also called, somewhat misleadingly, the "logic of norms".

Given a norm, one may consider what has to or may be done in order to satisfy it. And the result of such considerations will be that unless such and such is done the norm is not satisfied. So therefore, if the norm is to be satisfied such and such ought to be done. This is a different kind of Ought from the one enunciated in the norm. It is what I have called a "technical" Ought stating a fact which is *internal* to the assumed existence of a "normative" Ought. The technical Ought, one could say, is an Is – and nothing normative "follows" from it, although something normative may be presupposed in it.

12. The term "legal positivism" embraces a variety of positions between which there is a family resemblance.[23]

A common feature of many members of the family is the idea of a sharp separation of Is and Ought. Another is the non-cognitivist view that norms are prescriptions and therefore neither true nor false. As a third we may count the view that norms are "posited", *i.e.* have come to exist and often also passed out of existence in the course of the history of societies – sometimes as a consequence of acts of legislation, sometimes as commandments of a trusted authority or leader, sometimes as a result of gradually formed societal habits, customs, and traditions, to mention only a few of the sources of origin of norms.

At least in the above three respects I should myself wish to defend a "positivist" position in the philosophy of norms, legal or moral. Some main arguments for this position I hope I have succeeded in presenting in this paper.

The impossibility of deriving an Ought from an Is is a *consequence* of the non-cognitivist view of norms. There is also another view which I mentioned and called non-naturalist cognitivism (above p. 266). On it, too, there is no derivation of norms from facts. But norms may be, in their own right so to say, true or false. We must still say something about this.

The law of the state says that we ought this and that. But ought we, without exception, to obey the law? The same question can be raised about morals: Ought we to be moral? And if so, why?

Such questions must be taken seriously. They concern the topic called civil disobedience and also, though less directly, human rights.

The person who says he ought not to do what the law commands usually claims to have a *right* to dissent. He would perhaps call it a moral right which overrides his legal duty. Or he may appeal to a principle of so-called natural law which the law of the state is thought to violate.

What is the logical nature of such a claim? Is it a truth-claim? So that the claimant could say that *it is true that* he ought not to obey the law, *i.e.* true that he is free, permitted, has a right to disobey.

To construe the claim as a truth-claim would, in my opinion, be a serious mistake. The foundation of the claim is not truth but something which I propose to call *assent*.

A person who obeys the law may do so unreflectingly, just "because it is the law". Most conduct in conformity with law is, I presume, of this kind. Sometimes one obeys for reasons of expediency, thinking perhaps that being caught and punished for disobedience is a risk one better not take. Sometimes, finally, one obeys thinking it *right* to do so – either because one considers the thing decreed right as such, or because one considers it right to obey the law of the state as such. Then one assents to the legal Ought.

One can refuse assent and still obey – for example for reasons of expediency. Or one can refuse assent and disobey. In both cases one would say that one *ought* not to obey.

To assent to a norm is not to affirm a truth – and to dissent is not a denial (of truth). To assent (dissent) is more like an act of legislation or norm-giving itself. By assenting to the norm given him by some external norm-authority, the agent gives the same law unto himself so to speak – transforms it from heteronomous to autonomous. In this same sense of "assent" a subject may also create norms for his own conduct. Assenting, one could also say, is prescriptive and not descriptive (mental) activity.

In assenting or dissenting a subject evidences his moral attitude to a norm, his conception of what is right and what is not. When legal matters are concerned what is right is said to conform to an ideal of *justice*.

Attitudes of assent to norms are also reflected in legislation and in the interpretation of law by jurists and lawyers. From the legislator's point of view it is *expedient* that the citizens should assent to the laws. The less assent, the more civil disobedience and the more complaints about injustice. This may even become a threat to the stability of the legal order. Therefore legislation usually tries to adjust to prevailing conceptions of what are the "demands" of justice.

Such demands express the moral consciousness of a society. This consciousness is not uniform. It varies from one individual to another and it changes in the course of history. The prime movers of change are usually some outstanding individuals: such as the founders and reformers of a religion, moral philosophers, or experienced and prestigious judges. These individuals may be said to "mould" the notions of justice and morality which come to prevail in a society. Their rôle as "moulders" places them "ahead of developments" – and sometimes in tragic conflict with the moral consciousness of the majority of their contemporaries.

Morality can be said to "transcend" legality in the sense that it censures laws and the decisions of courts. For this reason morality can never be fully embodied in the kind of coercive order which the laws of the state constitute. In order to function as a standard whereby the rightness of law is judged, moral principles cannot be turned into positive law. If they were, this would be the end of morality.

Legal positivism is right when it maintains that law and morals are essentially different things and when it combats doctrines of "natural law" which blur this distinction. But legal positivism is wrong if, in the name of the "purity" of law, it insists on excluding considerations of a moral nature from legislation, legal decision making, and the hermeneutic aspects of legal dogmatics.

Academy of Finland

NOTES

1 H. Kelsen, 'Was ist die Reine Rechstlehre?', in *Demokratie und Rechtsstaat*, Festschrift für Zaccaria Giacometti, 1953. Quoted after O. Weinberger, 'Kelsens These von der Unanwendbarkeit logischer Regeln auf Normen' in *Die Reine Rechtslehre in wissenschaftlicher Diskussion*, Manzsche Verlags- und Universitätsbuchhandlung, Wien 1982.

2 Towards the end of his life, however, Kelsen changed his views towards a "nihilistic" position, reminiscent of that of Hägerström, with regard to the possibility of a "logic of norms" or "deontic logic". See the paper by Weinberger referred to in note 1 and, for

further details, Weinberger's book *Normentheorie als Grundlage der Jurisprudenz und Ethik, eine Auseinandersetzung mit Hans Kelsens Theorie der Normen*, Duncker & Humblot, Berlin 1981.

[3] *A Treatise on Human Nature*, Bk. III, Pt. I, Sect. 1 (the end).

[4] The title is an invention of Professor Max Black's in his well-known essay 'The Gap between "Is" and "Should"', first published in *The Philosophical Review* **73** (1964); reprinted in Max Black, *Margins of Precision*, Cornell University Press, Ithaca 1970.

[5] See the paper by A. MacIntyre, 'Hume on "Is" and "Ought"', *The Philosophical Review* **68** (1959).

[6] Henri Poincaré, *Dernières Pensées*, Flammarion, Paris 1913, 225.

[7] See R. Carnap, *Philosophy and Logical Syntax*, Psyche Miniatures, Kegan Paul, London 1935, 23: "It is easy to see that it is merely a difference of formulation, whether we state a norm or a value-judgment. A norm or rule has an imperative form. (. . .) actually a value statement is nothing else than a command in a misleading grammatical form."

[8] R. Hare, *The Language of Morals*, The Clarendon Press, Oxford 1952.

[9] A. Hägerström, *Till frågan om den objektiva rättens begrepp*, I, 1917. Included in Axel Hägerström, *Inquiries into the Nature of Law and Morals*, ed. by Karl Olivecrona, transl. by C. D. Broad, Almqvist & Wicksells, Uppsala 1953.

[10] J. Jørgensen, 'Imperatives and Logic', *Erkenntnis* **7** (1937–1938).

[11] J. Searle, 'How to Derive "Ought" from "Is"', *The Philosophical Review* **73** (1964) and J. Searle, *Speech Acts, An Essay in the Philosophy of Language*, Cambridge University Press, Cambridge 1969. Searle calls the Is-Ought dichotomy a distinction between Fact and Value. (*Speech Acts*, 175.) He does not explicitly contrast facts with norms, nor descriptions with prescriptions in the context of his discussion. This, however, does not change the issue. It is true that "ought" sometimes is used as an evaluative term, but to call it evaluative in the example which Searle discusses and which is concerned with obligations arising from promises seems to me not very natural.

[12] In the paper referred to in note 4 above.

[13] As witnessed, for example, by the collections *The Is-Ought Question, A Collection of Papers on the Central Problem in Moral Philosophy*, ed. by W. D. Hudson, Basingstoke, London 1979, and *Ethics: Foundations, Problems, and Applications*. Proceedings of the 5th International Wittgenstein Symposium, ed. by E. Morscher and R. Stranzinger, Vienna 1981.

[14] R. Nozick, *Anarchy, State and Utopia*, Basic Books, New York 1974.

[15] I. Hedenius, *Om rätt och moral*, Tidens förlag, Stockholm 1941. See especially 65 ff.

[16] C. E. Alchourrón, 'Logic of Norms and Logic of Normative Propositions', *Logique et Analyse* **12** (1969) and C. E. Alchourrón and E. Bulygin, *Normative Systems*, Springer Verlag, New York-Wien 1971.

[17] Alchourrón and Bulygin, *Op. cit.*, 63 ff.

[18] J. Hintikka, 'Deontic Logic and its Philosophical Morals', *Models for Modalities*, D. Reidel, Dordrecht, Holland 1969, and J. Hintikka, 'Some Main Problems in Deontic Logic' in *Deontic Logic: Introductory and Systematic Readings*, ed. by R. Hilpinen, D. Reidel, Dordrecht, Holland 1971.

[19] It is perhaps revealing that Searle in one place (*Speech Acts*, 182) should say that the Ought in the conclusion of his argument "is relative to the *existence* of the obligation". (My italics.)

[20] Black, *Margins of Precision*, 27.

[21] *Ibid.*, 29.
[22] *Ibid.*, 31.
[23] See A. Aarnio, 'The Form and Content of Law. Aspects of Legal Positivism'. *Archivum Iuridicum Cracoviense*, Vol. XIII, 1980. Reprinted as Ch. 3 in Aarnio, *Philosophical Perspectives in Jurisprudence*, Acta Philosophica Fennica vol. 36, Helsinki 1983.

JERZY WRÓBLEWSKI

PRESUPPOSITIONS OF LEGAL REASONING

INTRODUCTION

1. 'Presupposition' is a term referring to one of the instruments used in logical analysis. It seems, however, that it can be convenient also for analytical purposes not to presuppose this kind of philosophical approach. Legal reasoning covers a great variety of various processes of discovering and/or justifying statements in legal discourse.

In this situation one has to determine the key concepts in question, by way of choosing or reconstructing some of them from the current language or even constructing new ones. The last-mentioned approach seems neither necessary nor convenient. I will therefore determine the concepts in question basing my study as much as possible upon the current linguistic use.

2. The line of my argument starts from the determination of presupposition as a technical term of my essay (Section I) and the choice of a particular field of legal resoning as the scope of a detailed analysis (Section II). This field is the judicial interpretative reasoning and I will single out its presuppositions (Section III). In conclusion, I will comment the problem of presuppositions of legal reasoning in general (Section IV).

I. A CONCEPT OF PRESUPPOSITION

3. The concept of presupposition elaborated within the framework of the analytical philosophy of natural language serves the purposes of an analysis of assertive statements: X is a presupposition if and only if the truth of X is the condition of either Y being true or the negation of Y being true.[1] This concept is not adequate for an analysis of legal discourse. The latter deals with norms and evaluations which cannot be given truth claims without controversial and very complicated operations. In legal discourse we are interested in the sort of justification and justifiability of various statements which cannot be reduced to verification in terms of truth.[2]

4. In the present essay 'presupposition' is treated as a technical term used

E. Bulygin et al. (eds.), Man, Law and Modern Forms of Life, 283–298.

for an analysis of a legal discourse in a language used in this analysis or in the discourse itself. The distinction between a language and its meta-language is not relevant for our present purposes, and we use the term 'legal discourse' as a corollary of legal reasoning in a rather ample and not strictly defined way.

By *X* and *Y* we symbolize any meaningful complex statements in the language of legal discourse, i.e. propositions, evaluative statements, norms, as well as expressions of a mixed sort. We assume that in this language one can link them with the functors used in a natural language.

According to the proposed definition *X* is a *presupposition* of *Y* if and only if the acceptance of *X* is the necessary and sufficient condition of a pragmatic sense of *Y* and *Y*'s negation in a given discourse.

The "acceptance" is determined by the concrete features of *X* and *Y*, that is, acceptance is understood differently depending on whether the values of these variables are propositions, evaluative statements, or rules. The term 'condition' is used in its standard meaning, i.e. *A* is a necessary and sufficient condition of *B* given that (i) if *A* exists, then *B* exists and (ii) if *A* does not exist, then *B* does not exist.

The meaning of the new term 'pragmatic sense' is more complicated. This sense is contrasted with a semantic sense. A linguistic expression *EL* has a *semantic* sense in a language *L* if it has a meaning according to the meaning rules of a given language *L*.[3] Pragmatic sense deals with a concrete discourse: a linguistic expression *EL* has a *pragmatic sense* in a given discourse if *EL* has a semantic sense in *L* and *EL* or its negation can be justified in this discourse or is accepted as its axiomatic assumption.

5. The definition of presupposition can be used for all statements meaningfully formulated in legal language and used in legal discourse. It can be also applied in the study of any natural language and any practical discourse. Our definition takes into account the whole complexity of legal language and of legal discourse, and does not exclude by convention any of its elements.

II. LEGAL DISCOURSE AND LEGAL REASONING

6. Legal discourse, roughly speaking, means any sort of discourse about law. Law, on the other hand, can be defined in many ways.

Legal discourse involves rather differentiated types of audiences and varied sorts of activities.[4] It deals with the practice of law-making and decisions of the application of law. Both of the latter involve large audiences of professionals and laymen. Legal discourse covers also the theoretical examination of law as a set of rules (norms), social facts or complex phenomena, and is restricted to professional audiences.

It is an interesting question whether these types of legal discourse are linked with legal reasonings whose aim is to discover some truth or value or to justify some statements before the said audiences. I assume here that one can analyze legal reasoning and its various types without taking into account the features of the corresponding audiences, although their expectations are relevant for explaining characteristics of legal reasoning.

7. There are many typologies of legal reasoning which take into account who reasons and in what situations, and what are the purposes and/or functions of the reasoning in question.

One of the typologies is based on the traditional distinction between theoretical and practical reasoning which, in spite of controversies concerning its applicability, still remains classic and can be used for modelling purposes.

We may single out as ideal cases the purely *theoretical* legal reasoning, the purely *practical* legal reasoning, and a case of *mixed* reasoning which seems to be a compromise between both these extremes.

As a case of purely theoretical legal reasoning one can take a "pure" description of some data, either consisting of rules of law (e.g., "Reine Rechtslehre" according to its own methodological postulates) or of some facts (e.g., of "law-as-fact" in a consequently behavioral description).

As a case of purely practical legal reasoning one can take the decision-making of a judge deciding a concrete case, e.g. making an operative interpretation, accepting some proof, or determing the legal consequences of a fact in a case at issue.

Legal dogmatic reasoning has a mixed character. The fact that there is some intertwining of theory and practice in the reasoning of legal dogmatics makes it methodologically complex and interesting: it is neither pure research nor pure decision-making.[5]

These three types of legal reasoning are presented here as directions of reasoning only. They do not suggest the actual existence of any "pure" theoretical legal reasoning (in the sense of axiological indifference) or a "pure" practical reasoning (in a sense of epistemic indifference). The former idea is problematic, and the latter would be absurd.

8. There is, however, the question if there exists a form of legal reasoning which covers all the three types mentioned above. It seems to me that it is

possible to speak about such a sort of reasoning if one uses a sufficiently high level of abstraction.[6] The same holds for the sort of legal reasoning which is common to various types of law singled out in macro-comparativist research, e.g. to statutory law and common law systems.[7]

While I accept this possibility, I would, however, like to discuss the presuppositions of legal reasoning by way of taking up a particular kind of legal reasoning included in one of the types singled out above. This sort of reasoning should, as far as possible, meet the following conditions; (a) not overlook the complexity of legal reasoning; (b) not depend too much on controversial assumptions of some particular legal theory; (c) not depend on the specific features of particular types of legal system or branches of law.

Condition (a) excludes the sorts of reasoning linked e.g. with decisions concerning systemic validity.[8] Condition (b) excludes the sorts of reasoning which depend on the notion of law as a specific cultural entity, such as e.g. in the regional ontology of the egological theory of law.[9] Condition (c) rules out the reasonings that seek to establish a *ratio decidendi*[10] as well as reasonings in criminal law excluding *ex lege* some types of analogy.[11]

A form of legal reasoning that seems to meet criteria (a)–(c) is the interpretative reasoning justifying a judicial interpretative decision.

Legal interpretation is highly relevant in legal practice and in legal doctrine, and it is also one of the crucial issues of legal theory. Legal interpretation is specifically linked with legal discourse and the theoretical background of legal language, legal system and practical legal decision-making.

Judicial interpretative reasoning indeed seems to meet well the above-mentioned conditions for a representative sort of legal reasoning. It is sufficiently complex and does not simplify the issues. It does not depend too much on general assumptions controversial in legal doctrine, because it is based mostly on some commonly acknowledged facts of operative interpretations. It is not too heavily related with some particular types and branches of law: there are several common features of judicial interpretative reasoning and common problems of the ideologies (or normative theories) of interpretation which are equally problematic in different types of legal systems.[12]

III. PRESUPPOSITIONS OF JUDICIAL INTERPRETATIVE REASONING

9. Presuppositions of legal reasoning as a whole can be typologized in many ways.[13] Philosophically one can discern presuppositions e.g. in ontology, epistemology, axiology, or in logic *sensu largo*. This typology is relevant especially when one seeks to ascribe the foundations of legal reasoning a

particular philosophical standpoint or philosophical theses.[14] It seems to me that this sort of approach opens up interesting perspectives, but only after one has elaborated the comprehensive theory of legal reasoning itself.

I shall not, therefore, make use of this extensive typology in my essay which deals primarily with one kind of practical legal reasoning only. It will be sufficient for my purpose to single out three groups of presuppositions in judicial interpretative reasoning: (a) rule-presuppositions concerning legal language, legal reasoning and legal system; (b) fact-presuppositions; (c) value-presuppositions.

10. An examination of the presuppositions of judicial interpretative reasoning must be based at least on a necessary "minimum" of theory of legal interpretation. In the present essay I can neither elaborate nor justify this theory. Therefore I shall only single out the theoretical theses assumed in the present essay.[15] I think, however, that these theses are acceptable within the framework of most present-day legal theories which see law as a system of rules (rules conceived as meaningful linguistic statements interpreted in operative interpretation).[16] I shall examine only the justification of interpretative decision based on the texts of judicial decisions.[17] I shall leave aside the process of making the decision which can be described either as a kind of psychological process[18] or as a transformation of informations used by the decision-maker.[19]

11. Legal rules are expressed in a fuzzy language. We assume that in a language there are names (descriptions) and each of them singles out a linguistic class A referring to some part of reality, x. In a fuzzy language there are three situations concerning the relation of an x and A. According to the characteristics of this language, there are some x for which the statement "$x \in A$" is true (i.e., A has a positive core of meaning), some x for which the negation of "$x \in A$" is true (A has a negative core of meaning), and some x for which the semantic rules of this language are not strong enough to tell us whether the former or the latter is the case.[20]

In operative interpretation made during an act of law-application, one typically has to remove a doubt (i.e., an uncertainty) concerning the meaning of a rule which could be applied to the case. The doubt arises in the concrete use of a norm on pragmatical level. The decision-maker is supposed to remove the uncertainty by finding out whether a part of reality x belongs or does not belong to the linguistic class A. In a fuzzy language this decision cannot be made without using some instruments which, however, are *not* semantic rules. The interpretative decision should be justified in legal discourse. Therefore we would expect that these instruments are rules of *some* sort, i.e. directives of legal interpretation and evaluations, which do justify the decision in question.

12. Interpretative directives are rules which connect the meaning of a legal rule with the elements of the context in which it is used and which is relevant for its meaning.[21]

In my opinion the relevant context has three parts: the *legal language* in which the rule is formulated; the *legal system* to which the rule belongs; and the *sociofunctional context* of the creation or application of the rule.[22] Let us call the directives of interpretation indicating the use of these three contexts the first-level directives (DI^1). There are also *second-level* directives (DI^2) which indicate how to use DI^1 (DI^2 of procedure) and what to do in case that the results of an application of DI^1 are in conflict with each other (DI^2 of preference).[23]

Directives of legal interpretation often refer to evaluations determining interpretative behaviour. There are conflicts between these directives and so one has to choose between them, taking some evaluative criteria as given.

One can group the basic values determining the choice in *static* values (certainty, security, predictability, stability) and *dynamic* values (adequacy of law and life, effectiveness, equity, just decision, and so on).

13. On the basis of these general theoretical features of operative interpretation I shall now single out the elements of a justified judicial interpretative decision.

A decision is *internally justified* (rational) if is inferred from the premisses accepted by the decision-maker. These premisses are the legal language (*LL*) in which the rule is formulated, the system to which the rule belongs (*LS*), the situational context of the operative interpretation (*SC*), two levels of directives of legal interpretation (DI^1, DI^2) which are being applied, and the evaluations which are used for the choice and application of the directives in question (V^1, V^2).

The standard formula of the interpretative decision is: "The rule *N* formulated in legal language *LL* in the legal system *LS* has the meaning *M* applied in the situational context *SC* according to $DI^1_1, DI^1_2, \ldots, DI^1_n$ and evaluations $V^1_1, V^1_2, \ldots, V^1_n$ and $DI^2_1, DI^2_2, \ldots, DI^2_n$ and evaluations $V^2_1, V^2_2, \ldots, V^2_n$."

The particular point of the operative interpretation in comparison with a doctrinal one is the reference to the situational context of decision (*SC*) and the obligation to determine the meaning in a manner enabling the formulation of a decision. The decision of interpretation, as a rule, concerns a valid legal rule or at least an applicable legal rule. The problems of validity, although practically linked with interpretation, can be theoretically separated and are left outside the discussion in this essay.[24]

14. The presuppositions of judicial interpretative reasoning can be now presented in their relation with the formula of interpretative decision. We may ask whether there are presuppositions concerned with: legal language (*PLL*), legal reasoning expressed in directives of interpretation (*PLR*), legal system (*PLS*), facts relevant for interpretation (*PFI*), and axiology of interpretation expressed in evaluations (*PAI*).

If such presuppositions are necessary for the justification of interpretative decisions (cf. point 4), then they can be arranged in three groups: rule-presuppositions (*PLL, PLR, PLS*), fact-presuppositions (*PFI*) and value-presuppositions (*PAI*) (cf. point 9).

15. Presuppositions concerning legal language (*PLL*) are linked with the theoretical background of legal interpretation based on the semiotic features of legal language (cf. point 11). The following *PLL* seem to be necessary for interpretative reasoning.

(*PLL*1) Some features of legal language are relevant for the meaning of the legal rules expressed in it.

This is a necessary condition of justifying any interpretative decision which takes into account the formulation of an interpreted rule. Without this there would be no interpretation of the rule, and this is analytically true. The degree of the relevance in question is not, however, presupposed, and is stated differently in various theories of interpretation and/or, in particular, normative theories (or ideologies) of legal interpretation.

(*PLL*2) There are cases of application of a legal rule in which it is impossible to determine the meaning of the rule solely by virtue of the strength of the semantic rules of the legal language in which the rule is formulated.

This presupposition should be understood as a concise qualification of the legal language as a fuzzy language (cf. point 11). The rejection of this presupposition would reduce interpretative reasoning either to a purely analytical (i.e., logical) task or to an act of empirical verification. Both of these possibilities are unacceptable from the point of view of our theoretical assumptions (points 11–13). The corollary of this presupposition is the emphasis on the role of the decision-maker in interpretative activity.

16. Presuppositions concerning legal reasoning (*PLR*) do not concern the general basis of legal reasoning as a whole,[25] but only the operative interpretation.

(*PLR*1) Application of rules of legal reasoning is necessary for the justification of interpretative decision.

This is an analytical truth in so far as it is implied by our definition of presupposition and the meaning of the term 'justification' accepted here (point 4). Without a reasoning one cannot give reasons for an interpretative decision. These reasons were singled out in the formula of the decision in question (point 13). The presupposition does not, however, assume any particular form of justification, but only its "ruleness". That is, it can be stated in a formula (point 4) and be treated as a "transformation",[26] as a "game",[27] or the like.

The problem of the content of the rules of legal reasoning will not be discussed here. It seems that these rules include several postulates singled out in the theory of legal reasoning. The peculiarity of the rules of legal interpretative reasoning is that they are mainly formulated as the directives of interpretation (point 12). These directives, in spite of their fuzziness, are the necessary condition of justifying interpretative decision, but they are not the sufficient condition because of the role of evaluations.

(*PLR*2) The premisses of legal interpretative reasoning are at least in part independent of the decision-maker.

This presupposition is necessary for any operative interpretation. First, operative interpretation is thought of as an interpretation of a legal rule formulated in legal language and belonging to a legal system; the elimination of this presupposition in an extreme case would mean that the decision-maker freely creates the rule, the language and the legal system. Secondly, the decision-maker cannot freely invent all the directives he uses, although he has a possibility of choosing them and creating some of them. The negation of this presupposition would mean that there are no rules of legal interpretative reasoning or that there are only *ad hoc* rules. The former is not an acceptable proposition, and the latter would mean treating legal language not as a genuinely fuzzy language but as a "soft" language, which is evidently counter-intuitive.

(*PLR*3) The premisses of interpretative decision are "internally consistent", i.e., their knowledge-content does not involve contradictions and the evaluations contained in them are not contradictory.

This presupposition is an application of a general postulate of consistency.[28] It must be mentioned here because it implies, *inter alia*, the consistency of the legal system to which the interpreted rule belongs as well as the consistency of the evaluations used (at least) in a given operative interpretation. (We assume here that the meaning of the terms 'consistency' and 'contradiction' is well enough defined for the area of legal reasoning and thus in legal discourse.)

17. Presuppositions concerning the legal system (*PLS*) are not controversial:

(*PLS*1) An interpreted rule is a part of a legal system.

This presupposition corresponds to the basic feature of law as a system of rules and "systemic interpretation".[29] It should be noticed, however, that there are various notions of legal system[30] and especially of its features (e.g., consistency, completeness, hierarchy, openness)[31] and its structure (static, dynamic, mixed).[32]

(*PLS*2) Some features of the legal system are relevant for determining the meaning of interpreted rules.

This presupposition is closely linked with the preceding one. Were this not so, then the belonging of the interpreted rule to a legal system would not be relevant for interpretation, which is an untenable idea.

18. Presuppositions concerning facts relevant for legal interpretation (*PFI*) need a preliminary general comment.

Any decision-making activity, including interpretation, presupposes some ontology, i.e., the existence of several types of facts. Roughly speaking, one must assume that the world, a society and its members exist. This basic ontology will not be dealt with here. I will limit my remarks to the presuppositions necessary for interpretative reasoning, which only in part cover those mentioned above. I shall, however, take up the basic presuppositions when dealing with hypotheses concerning presuppositions of legal reasoning (point 22 below).

(*PFI*1) There exist the following realities: rules formulated in legal language, situations which make the use of this language pragmatically meaningful, legal system, and directives of legal interpretation which are in part independent of the interpreter.

This presupposition is linked with those formulated above (points 15–17) and can be treated as their ontological corollary.[33] The elimination of any part of this presupposition is impossible, because it would result in the negation of a justified decision of operative interpretation.[34]

(*PFI*2) A legal rule is interpreted in a situational context existing independently of the interpretator.

This is *ex definitione* a necessary condition of an existence of any operative interpretation. For other types of interpretation the situational context can be imagined or can be outside the discourse, as in some kinds of legal dogmatic interpretation dealing with a systematization of rules. An open question is whether this situational context or some part of it is relevant for interpretative decision. This is the problem for a descriptive theory of legal interpretation and for postulates of a normative theory (or ideology) too.[35]

19. Value-presuppositions of the axiology of interpretation (*PAI*) deal with some features of evaluative elements in the justification of interpretative decision (cf. point 12).

(*PAI*1) Evaluation is relevant in operative interpretation at least for the choice and use of some directives of interpretation.

This role of evaluations is determined by the properties of fuzzy legal language when used in situations undecidable by its semantic rules only (point 11), and by the features of the directives of legal interpretation and of their use (point 12). This presupposition is highly relevant for differentiating pure theoretical discourse from the practical one (point 7).

(*PAI2*) Evaluations are part of the reasons justifying interpretative decision.

This is a necessary presupposition of interpretative reasoning as a type of general practical reasoning. One can treat this presupposition as the corollary of the preceding one, and it is expressed in the formula of interpretative decision (point 13).

20. Our examination of presuppositions of judicial interpretative reasoning leaves open several problems for particular descriptive and normative theories (or ideologies) of legal interpretation. For instance, one can ask whether there is any possibility of making the theory of presuppositions stronger by singling out some elements of the justification of interpretative decisions as generally valid.

There are indeed two such elements: common directives of legal interpretation and common evaluations.

There are directives of legal interpretation which are commonly accepted by contemporary normative theories (ideologies) of interpretation, i.e. they are neutral as to the choice between static and dynamic values (point 12).[36] These directives are connected with some salient features of legal language or legal system. One can argue, however, (a) that these features of a language or a legal system are postulates or working practical hypotheses rather than statements of facts, and (b) that if they are postulates, then they are necessary only within some legal culture having certain shared common values.

This remark leads us to the problems of common evaluations. It seems that one should take into account two things. First, evaluations referred to in directives of interpretation or functioning in the justification of interpretative decision are terms covering different contents (e.g., justice, equity, good reasons, and so on). Secondly, the unity of evaluations can be explained by some common cultural background of the decision-makers who share the same evaluative beliefs. This can be treated as a definitory feature of a common legal culture, or more amply as signifying participation in a common "form of life".[37] In any case this evaluative element in justification should have some sort of a relativizing clause and thus does not have the sort of necessity which the presuppositions dealt with in this essay do have.

IV. PRESUPPOSITIONS OF LEGAL REASONING

21. The presuppositions analyzed above (Section III) do not cover all types of judicial reasoning. We have not examined the sorts of reasoning used in

justifying judicial decisions on validity, evidence, or the choice of consequences. *A fortiori*, the set of presuppositions discussed here does not cover the presuppositions operative in other types of legal reasoning, i.e. in theoretical reasoning and in a mixed reasoning in legal dogmatics (point 7). Moreover, each type appears as a complex of several kinds of reasonings.

It seems, however, that taking the analysis of interpretative reasoning as a starting point, one can formulate some general hypotheses concerning the presuppositions of all sorts of legal reasoning.

22. There are three very general groups of presuppositions of legal reasoning: rule-presuppositions, fact-presuppositions, and value-presuppositions. The features of presuppositions in each group vary depending on the type of reasoning referred to. I will now give a rough outline of each group.

Rule-presuppositions were already discussed, and we saw that they are relevant in judicial interpretative reasoning. They concern the particular features of legal language, legal reasoning and legal system. It seems that in legal reasoning common presuppositions are that legal rules are formulated in a fuzzy language, that they function as a part of a legal system, that legal statements are either justified by rules of legal reasoning or are accepted as axioms of a given discourse, and that legal reasoning is based on the principle of non-contradiction.

Fact-presuppositions deal with an ontology. Legal reasoning presupposes some world *sensu largo* including, in particular, nature, society and human beings. It presupposes their existence and some key characteristics of each of them. It would be interesting to discuss in more detail the characteristics of these three domains of reality and their possible differences from the entities presupposed in an extra-legal discourse. There is also the question whether and how an epistemic attitude proper to legal reasoning is linked with general cultural notions and orientations and with sets of beliefs characterizing particular forms of life. The fact-presuppositions of interpretative reasoning are rather limited (point 18). They cover, however, issues relevant for all legal reasoning, such as the existence of legal language, legal system and some directives of legal reasoning. It is clear that also the existence of several other domains of reality is presupposed in each reasoning in the area of any practical discourse.

Value-presuppositions deal with legal axiology. It seems that at least when one formally describes values in terms of their content, procedures of justification and systemic relations, any legal reasoning presupposes some set of values necessary for the justification of statements in legal discourse.

It is an open question whether and how these presuppositions are interrelated, and whether some ordered sets of beliefs implied by particular "forms of life" can be ascribed to them. Extrapolating the result of our analysis, we seem to be right in saying that there is a possibility of such an ascription.

23. By way of a conclusion, one is well warranted in maintaining that legal reasoning does imply several sorts of presuppositions. The study of them, starting with an analysis of a particular type of legal reasoning, supports the hypothesis that these presuppositions deal with rules, facts and evaluations. Their analysis obviously can be a step towards a theory of legal reasoning as a part of a comprehensive legal theory.[38]

University of Łódź

NOTES

[1] Cf. P. Strawson, *Introduction to Logical Theory*, London-New York 1952, 175–9; J. Woleński, *Z zagadnień analitycznej filozofii prawa* (The Problems of Analytical Legal Philosophy), Warszawa-Kraków 1980, 51ff.

[2] See J. Wróblewski, 'Verification and Justification in the Legal Sciences', in *Rechtstheorie*, Beiheft 1, Berlin (W) 1979, pp. 195–213 (1979a); id., 'Justification of Legal Decisions', *Revue internationale de philosophie* **33** (1979), 127–8, 277–93 (1979b); A. Aarnio, *Philosophical Perspectives in Jurisprudence*, Helsinki 1983, chapter 8; A. Aarnio, R. Alexy and A. Peczenik, 'The Foundation of Legal Reasoning', *Rechtstheorie* **12** (1981), 133–158, 423–448. The justifiability of legal decisions is connected with the conception of their rationality; see the texts referred to above. I share the standpoint that "Reason alone cannot wholly determine what we ought to do" (N. MacCormick, *Legal Reasoning and Legal Theory*, Oxford 1978, 265). An analysis of justification is also presented in the form of various arguments used, e.g. by rules, consequences, analogy, principles, authority, and so on. I should mention that there are also ideas about using a special conception of truth as "legal truth"; cf. L. Ferrajoli, 'La semantica della teoria del diritto', in U. Scarpelli (ed.), *La teoria generale del diritto. Problemi e tendenze attuali*, Milano 1983, pp. 86–97.

[3] Cf. K. Ajdukiewicz, 'Sprache und Sinn', *Erkenntnis* **4** (1934), 100–138; J. Wróblewski, 'The Problem of the Meaning of the Legal Norm', *Österreichische Zeitschrift für öffentliches Recht* **14** (1964), 3/4, 253–66, reprinted in J. Wróblewski, *Meaning and Truth in Judicial Decision*, Helsinki [2]1983, 1–21 (1983a).

[4] About the notion of audience, see Ch. Perelman, *The New Rhetoric and the Humanities*, Dordrecht-Boston-London 1979, chs. 1, 2 and 5; id., *Justice, Law and Argument*, Dordrecht-Boston-London 1980, ch. 6; id., *L'empire rhétorique*, Paris 1977, ch. 2; Aarnio (1983), ch. 9.

[5] E.g. A. Aarnio, *Denkweisen der Rechtswissenschaft*, Wien-New York 1979, chs. 2, 3 and 4; id., *On Legal Reasoning*, Turku 1977, Pt. III ch. 4; id., 'Truth and Acceptability

of Interpretative Propositions in Legal Dogmatics', in *Rechtstheorie*, Beiheft 2 (1981), pp. 33–51; id. (1983), 215–20; W. Krawietz, *Juristische Entscheidung und wissenschaftliche Erkenntnis*, Wien-New York 1978, pars. 1, 2, 19–24; J. Wróblewski, 'Wybrane zagadnienia metodologiczne dogmatyki prawa' (Selected Methodological Problems of Legal Dogmatics), in J. Wróblewski (ed.), *Zagadnienia metodologiczne prawoznawstwa* (Methodological Problems of the Legal Sciences), Wrocław-Warszawa-Kraków-Gdańsk-Łódź 1982, pp. 120–42 (1982a); Z. Ziembiński, *Szkice z metodologii szczegółowych nauk prawnych* (Essays on the Methodology of the Particular Legal Sciences), Warszawa-Poznań 1983, chs. 1 and 2; E. Zuleta Puceiro, *Paradigma dogmatico y ciencia del derecho*, Madrid 1981, ch. 4. The practical character is also ascribed to legal theory; cf. e.g. M. Jori, *Il metodo giuridico tra scienza e politica*, Milano 1976, ch. 6; E. Pattaro, 'Per una mappa del sapere giuridico', in U. Scarpelli (ed.), *op. cit.*, pp. 276–9; U. Scarpelli, 'La teoria generale del diritto: prospettive per un trattato', in U. Scarpelli (ed.), *op. cit.*, pp. 287–91.

[6] E.g. Aarnio, Alexy and Peczenik, *op. cit.*, 134–5.

[7] E.g. J. C. Cueto-Rua, *Judicial Methods of Interpretation of Law*, Louisiana State University 1981, 4 and *passim.*

[8] Cf. J. Wróblewski, 'Tre concetti di validità', *Rivista trimestrale di diritto e procedura civile* **36** (1982), 586–91 (1982b); id., 'Three Concepts of Validity', *Tidskrift utgiven av Juridiska Föreningen i Finland* (1982), 5/6, 408–414 (1982c); A. G. Conte, 'Validità', in *Nuovo Digesto Italiano*, Torino 1975, pp. 418–25.

[9] J. Wróblewski, 'Law and Liberty in the Egological Theory of Law', *Österreichische Zeitschrift für öffentliches Recht* **16** (1966), 1/2, 1–26 and lit. cit.

[10] E.g. Cueto-Rua, *op. cit.*, ch. 3 (8, B).

[11] E.g. E. Betti, *Interpretazione della legge e degli atti giuridici*, Milano ²1971, ch. 6.

[12] See Wróblewski, *Sadowe stosowanie prawa* (Judicial Application of Law), Warszawa (1972a), ch. 7.4; id., 'L'interprétation en droit: théorie et idéologie', *Archives de philosophie du droit* **XVII** (1972), 51–69 (1972b). There are, however, particular features of justification of judicial decisions, and especially of interpretative decisions, in statutory law systems: see J. Wróblewski, 'La règle de la décision dans l'application judiciaire du droit', in Ch. Perelman, P. Foriers (eds.), *La règle de droit*, Bruxelles 1971, pp. 68–93; id., 'Motivation de la décision judiciaire', in Ch. Perelman, P. Foriers (eds.), *La motivation des décisions de justice*, Bruxelles 1978, pp. 111–35.

[13] Presuppositions are not thought of in the present essay as a kind of *Vorverständnis*. See e.g. Cueto-Rua, *op. cit.*, ch. 5.1; Ch. Weinberger and O. Weinberger, *Logik, Semantik, Hermeneutik*, München 1979, 191; J. Esser, *Vorverständnis und Methodenwahl in der Rechtsfindung*, Frankfurt a.M. 1972, 11ff., 43ff., 53ff., 134ff. On the hermeneutical background of this concept see Aarnio (1983), 133, 199–200; S. Jørgensen, 'Hermeneutik und Auslegung', *Rechtstheorie* **9** (1978), 67. Neither are presuppositions in the present essay thought of as legal assumptions concerning the "historical law-maker", "rational law-maker", "perfect law-maker", "proper legal system", "perfect legal system" and so on. Some of these notions are accepted in traditions of positivistic thought (e.g. R. J. Vernengo, *La interpretación juridica*, Mexico 1977, chs. 6, 7), some are reconstructed in present-day legal reasoning or are postulated (e.g. G. Tarello, *L'interpretazione della legge*, Milano 1980, pars. 62–66, 69; L. Nowak, *Interpretacja prawnicza* (Legal Interpretation), Warszawa 1973, chs. 3–8; Wróblewski (1982a), pp. 133–42 and lit. cit.)

[14] J. Wróblewski, 'Law and Philosophy', *Öst. Z. f. öff. Recht* (1977), 214–5.

[15] Cf. J. Wróblewski, 'Semantic Basis of Legal Interpretation', *Logique et analyse* **6** (1963), 21–24, 397–415; id., 'Legal Reasonings in Legal Interpretation', *Logique et analyse* **12** (1969), 45, 3–31, reprinted in Wróblewski (1983a), 22–48, 71–103; id. (1972a), chs. 7, 10.3.; id., *Zagadnienia teorii wykladni prawa ludowego* (Problems of Interpreting Socialist Law), Warszawa 1959, chs. 2, 3.

[16] L. Ferrajoli, 'Interpretazione dottrinale e interpretazione operativa', *Rivista internazionale di filosofia del diritto* **43** (1966), 1, 290–304; K. Makkonen, *Zur Theorie der juridischen Entscheidung*, Turku 1965, par. 5; E. Betti, *Teoria generale dell'interpretazione*, Milano 1955, ch. 8; Wróblewski (1959), ch. 3, pars. 1–2: id. (1972a), ch. 7.

[17] Wróblewski (1972a), ch. 2.1., 3.2.; id. (1983a), 59–62.

[18] E.g. Cuato-Rua, *op. cit.*, ch. 3.

[19] Cf. Wróblewski (1972a), ch. 3.3.; id., 'Computers as an Aid to the Judicial Process', *Systema* (1972), 1, 57–9; Vernengo, *op. cit.*, chs. 1, 8.

[20] Cf. J. Wróblewski, 'Fuzziness of Legal System', in *Essays in Legal Theory in Honour of Kaarle Makkonen, Oikeustiede-Jurisprudentia* **XVI** (1983), pp. 315–9 (1983b). The concept of fuzziness implies several logical problems; cf. C. E. Alchourrón, 'Negación y tercero excluido', *Rivista latinoamericana de filosofia* **7** (1981), 1, 75–77.

[21] This position does not assume any standpoint between the "hyletic" conception of norms and the "expressive" conception of norms; cf. C. E. Alchourrón and E. Bulygin, 'The Expressive Conception of Norms', in R. Hilpinen (ed.), *New Studies in Deontic Logic*, Dordrecht-Boston-London 1981, pp. 95–121.

[22] Wróblewski (1959), chs. 5–7; id. (1972a), 123ff.; R. Zippelius, *Einführung in die juristische Methodenlehre*, München [3] 1980, 64–68.

[23] For the enumeration of these directives, cf. Wróblewski (1972a), 126–39; Tarello, *op. cit.*, ch. 8 and cf. chs. 3 and 9–13. These directives are treated as "individual norm-transformation" rules in A. Peczenik, *The Basis of Legal Justification*, Lund 1983, chs. 2.3.2.–2.3.6., and as traditional arguments of legal reasoning in G. Kalinovski, *Introduction à la logique juridique*, Paris 1965, ch. 4 par. 3b.

[24] Cf. Wróblewski (1983b), pp. 319–322, 326–329; Aarnio (1977), 20ff.; id. (1981), pp. 44, 49ff.; MacCormick, *op. cit.*, 63, 65, 244; E. Bulygin, 'Time and Validity', in A. A. Martino (ed.), *Deontic Logic, Computational Linguistics and Legal Information Systems*, Amsterdam-New York-Oxford 1982, pp. 65–82; cf. also note 8 above.

[25] About this basis, cf. R. Alexy, *Theorie der juristischen Argumentation*, Frankfurt a.M. 1978, Part C; Aarnio, Alexy and Peczenik, *op. cit., passim*; J. Wróblewski, 'Towards Foundations of Judicial Reasoning', in W. Krawietz and R. Alexy (eds.), *Metatheorie juristischer Argumentation*, Berlin (W) 1983, pp. 233–252 (1983c).

[26] Cf. Aarnio, Alexy and Peczenik, *op. cit.*, part I; Peczenik (1983), chs. 1.1., 1.2., 2.3.1., 2.3.2., 3.1., 3.2.

[27] Aarnio (1977), part II, chs. 1, 2; id. (1983), 193–5; J. Wróblewski, 'Games of Explanation and Justification and Their Theoretical and Ideological Background', in A. Peczenik and J. Uusitalo (eds.), *Reasoning on Legal Reasoning*, Vammala 1979, pp. 107–114.

[28] R. Alexy, *op. cit.*, 234ff. Postulates of normative and narrative coherence are singled out in MacCormick, *op. cit.*, 89–92.

[29] This appears as the common feature in operative and doctrinal interpretation: Aarnio (1977), part III, ch. 4; id. (1979), ch. 4.1.3.; Tarello, *op. cit.*, pars. 20–23,

53–55, 68; Vernengo, *op. cit.*, ch. 4; Wróblewski (1959), ch. 6; id. (1972a), ch. 8.3.2. – There is also the question what types of rules belong to a legal system (e.g. Wróblewski (1983b), pp. 319–22), and especially whether "principles" (and in which sense of this term) belong to it (cf. R. Dworkin, 'The Model of Rules', in J. Feinberg and H. Gross (eds.), *Philosophy of Law*, Encino-Belmont 1975, pp. 81–92; R. Benditt, *Law as Rule and Principle*, Stanford 1978, ch. 4; R. Alexy, 'Zum Begriff des Rechtsprinzips', in *Rechtstheorie*, Beiheft 1, Berlin (W) 1979, pp. 59–88; MacCormick, *op. cit.*, 231ff., 245). The principles thus in some conceptions of a legal system are also rules which are interpreted.

[30] E.g. C. E. Alchourrón and E. Bulygin, *Normative Systems*, Wien-New York 1971; L. M. Friedman, *The Legal System*, New York 1975; J. Raz, *The Concept of a Legal System*, Oxford 1970; H. L. A. Hart, *The Concept of Law*, Oxford 1961, chs. 5–6; G. di Bernardo, *L'indagine del mondo sociale*, Milano 1979, part I, ch. 2; id., *Le regole dell'azione sociale*, Milano 1983, 184–209.

[31] E.g. E. Bulygin and C. E. Alchourrón, 'Incompletezza, contradittorietá e indeterminatezza degli ordinamenti giuridici', in G. di Bernardo (ed.), *Logica deontica e semantica*, Bologna 1977, pp. 291–306; A. G. Conte, *Saggio sulla completezza degli ordinamenti giuridici*, Torino 1962; id., 'Completezza e chiusura', in *Scritti in memoriam di W. Cesarini Sforza*, Milano 1968, pp. 159–179; H. Kelsen, *Allgemeine Theorie der Normen*, Wien 1979 (posth.) chs. 57–59; O. Weinberger, 'Über die Offenheit des rechtlichen Normensystems', in *Festschrift für Walter Wilburg*, Graz 1975, pp. 439–451. Cf. also 29 above.

[32] Cf. H. Kelsen, *Reine Rechtslehre*, Wien ^{2}1960, pars. 34–5; O. Weinberger, 'Die normenlogische Basis der Rechtsdynamik', in U. Klug, Th. Ramm, F. Ritter and B. Schmeidel (eds.), *Gesetzgebungstheorie, Juristische Logik, Zivil- und Prozessrecht*, Heidelberg 1978, pp. 173–190; id., 'Die Struktur der rechtlichen Normenordnung', in *Rechtstheorie und Rechtsinformatik*, Wien-New York 1975, pp. 110–132; J. Wróblewski, 'Systems of Norms and Legal System', *Rivista internazionale di teoria del diritto* **49** (1972), 2, 224–5 (1972c); id., 'Modelli di sistemi giuridici e potenzialità dell'informatica giuridica', *Logica, informatica diritto* **4** (1978), 1, 55–76.

[33] Cf. e.g. about "*logische Ontologie*": O. Weinberger, 'Normenlogik und logische Bereiche', in A. G. Conte, R. Hilpinen and G. H. von Wright (eds.), *Deontische Logik und Semantik*, Wiesbaden 1977, pp. 177–180.

[34] A presupposition of facts is necessary for the justification of the validity of decisions using a factual concept of validity; see Wróblewski (1982b), 591–593; id. (1982c), 414–417; M. D. Farrell, *Hacia un criterio empirico di validez*, Buenos Aires 1972, ch. 3. Facts are used for an objective justification of the validity of norms; see S. Cotta, *Giustificazione e obbligatorietà delle norme*, Milano 1981, ch. 5. Also the existence of norms has been treated as equivalent to their validity; e.g. Kelsen (1979), ch. 44. II; C. E. Alchourrón and E. Bulygin, *Sobre existencia de las normas*, Valencia 1979.

[35] Wróblewski (1959), chs. 5–7; id. (1972a), ch. 7.3.; Cueto-Rua, *op. cit.*, chs. 2.2., 3.

[36] Wróblewski (1959), ch. 8, par. 2; id. (1972a), ch. 7.3.4.

[37] Aarnio (1977), 102; id. (1981), p. 48ff.; id. (1983), 181–3, 185–208; cf. also di Bernardo (1983), ch. 5.

[38] Aarnio, Alexy and Peczenik, *op. cit.*, 136; MacCormick, *op. cit.*, 259: "A satisfactory theory of legal reasoning requires and is required by a satisfactory theory of law."

ALEJO DE CERVERA

PROBLEMS WITH PRESUPPOSITIONS

Comments on Wróblewski

As Professor Wróblewski himself says (9, 23),* legal reasoning – as any reasoning, we may add – has presuppositions the use of which cannot be avoided, that necessarily are implied or involved in legal reasoning. An important task for analysis is to make a typology of them. But another, very demanding thing is to establish clearly which those presuppositions are, what they are, and to see them clearly in their organization. Wróblewski sets out to do just this: To elaborate a theoretical conception of the presuppositions in legal reasoning.

Such a task is a very large one, and Wróblewski proceeds to establish some limits. Legal reasoning includes various processes of discovery and justification (6), but he takes up only the presuppositions of judicial interpretative reasoning. He observes that it is necessary "to determine the key concepts" involved (1). But, although his discourse shows that he has in mind three types of presuppositions (cf. 9, 22), it turns out very soon that he is only interested in those presuppositions that are *propositions*. This is a very legitimate attitude since facts and values must be integrated in propositions to play any role in legal reasoning. His "definition of presupposition can be used for all statements meaningfully formulated in legal language and used in legal discourse" (5). Both enunciative (descriptive) and normative propositions can play the role of presuppositions (3, 4), in a sequence which goes from the enunciative ones to the correlative normative ones immediately postulated by them. As a matter of fact, Wróblewski expressly establishes the role of enunciative propositions only, but it is evident that all of these imply other, normative ones.

His examination of presuppositions proceeds through an analysis of the analysis that legal reasoning, legal discourse in particular, implies; that is, of the propositions used in the latter analysis. His approach is a very analytical one, and most of his conclusions are analytical. On several occasions his analytical effort is quite explicit. For instance, it is an analytical way of proceeding to tell us that there is a use of the word 'presupposition' which only involves truth, and then to conclude that the concept involved is not adequate in normative thinking (3, 12). Besides, he observes several times

* The numbers refer to corresponding points in Wróblewski's essay.

E. Bulygin et al. (eds.), Man, Law and Modern Forms of Life, 299–309.

that the proceedings are analytic (16), or that the conclusion is *ex definitione* (16, 18), or frequently also that the presuppositions are "corollaries". Several of these analytical points give important information on the inferential and conceptual furniture of legal reasoning and may be thus considered achievements. They do not always contain "new" insights as such, but help us to see many controversial points in a proper context.

I. ACHIEVEMENTS OF THE STUDY

In what follows, Wróblewski's points have undergone some – perhaps a bit audacious – sharpening, including sometimes a somewhat different use of words. One aim of this is to further emphasize such points, another aim is to shed some more light on the "presuppositions" of Wróblewski's own way of thinking.

1. It is an achievement to promote the idea and the feeling that an analysis of the analysis implied in both legal reasoning and legal thinking is necessary. As was to be expected, the presuppositions found out by Wróblewski are propositions, and enunciative propositions at that. As was also to be expected, all of these presuppositions follow from definitions of some key concepts such as the first one, the concept "operative interpretation". Consequently, the presuppositions are all analytically true, "in the manner of axioms", as Wróblewski says on more than one occasion.

2. Taking into account the care with which Wróblewski proceeds in his analysis, there are no objections against the way he reaches his results and corollaries. However, he seems to somewhat belittle one significant analytical point by talking about facts and values as presuppositions regarding which the analytical effort would be senseless. This point naturally is regained if facts and values are couched in terms of propositions; then the propositions of course are the subject matter, not the facts or the values themselves.

3. It is also an achievement to make clear that all presuppositions are not immediately derived from the key concepts or found in direct connection with them. The point is that there is a hierarchy organizing such presuppositions; this is pointed out by calling most of the latter "corollaries", although at times several corollaries are put at the same level. This all implies that there is what we can call a "master presupposition", which is at the highest level in the hierarchy of presuppositions.

4. Wróblewski recognizes very correctly that the "presented conception of presuppositions" of judicial reasoning does not say much about the way how the norms of legal interpretation function as more or less generally valid directives (20). Given the analytical approach, interwined as it is with a mainly descriptive effort, it hardly could have been otherwise. In view of this shortcoming, Wróblewski belittles the analytical approach by conceding its weakness and by wondering "whether there is any possibility of making the theory of presuppositions stronger by singling out some elements of the justification (. . .) as generally valid" (20). Such elements are in fact found, and it is probably here that Wróblewski is at his most inspirational moment.

5. Wróblewski takes a very measured standpoint on the problem of the relationship between enunciative and normative propositions. He observes that their relationship is controversial and complicated (3). It is, naturally, very prudent to affirm that the question is not fully settled. However, Wróblewski also lets us know his own standpoint. He points out a difference of quality between these two types of propositions. He says that normative propositions "cannot be reduced to verification in terms of truth" (3). Of course, he cannot be expected to be more precise without a very extensive and intensive investigation, taking into account the most recent contributions.[1]

6. Wróblewski tells us that one of the typologies of legal reasoning is based on the dichotomy "theoretical-practical", a controversial but still classic dichotomy which often is used for modelling purposes (7). As this dichotomy and the preceding one (cf. preceding par. here) cross each other, the relationship between both must be still more controversial. In a way geared towards further insights, Wróblewski points out that if it is question of a descriptive-enunciative mode of thinking the reasoning is theoretical; if not, practical; if both descriptive and evaluative, the reasoning has a mixed character (7).

7. Wróblewski also emphasizes something which is many times neglected or unrecognized especially among analytical thinkers, namely, that "there are conflicts between (the different) directives (of interpretation)", "making some evaluative criteria" necessary (12).

8. Following current use, Wróblewski includes the concept "legal reasoning" in the concept "legal discourse". He points out that there are different types of legal discourse, and discusses the criteria needed to establish the types. Sure enough, he accepts the main types of legal discourse that are currently

distinguished, that is, enunciative and normative ones. He does not, however, go further, because legal discourse as a whole is beyond the scope of his study (6).

9. Although he does not say it explicitly, Wróblewski sees interactions between enunciative and normative thinking, possibly even necessary influences. This is one step towards the clarification of the relationship involved. At the very least, it seems to exclude the idea that these realms had nothing to do with each other. But he also lets us understand that the distinction between enunciation and normativeness seems to be impossible to obliterate.

10. Subsumption – classification, characterization or qualification, as the legal thinking in the English language prefers to say – is recognized as being a key legal operation, probably the most important step in the application of law.[2] In subsumption, three situations are possible between some event or fact relevant to the operation of the law and a linguistic formulation of the legal rule (11). To be true, Wróblewski on this point speaks as though only concerned with enunciative thinking ("a linguistic class *A* referring to some part *x* of reality"; see 11).[3] Of course, in both cases, subsumption is a limit act.

II. SOME PURELY INFORMATIVE QUESTIONS

In relation to Wróblewski's basic viewpoints, some questions of substance may be raised. However, they do not necessarily involve or claim any grave discrepancies between his viewpoints and mine.

1. One wonders about the hesitation with which Wróblewski, by "presupposition", is ready to understand both enunciative and normative propositions. At first sight, one would be tempted to say that he is only concerned with enunciative thinking and propositions. One is inclined to conclude so in view of (a) what he says about "presuppositions" being circumscribed to the enunciative realm only since an analysis of an analysis must be enunciative (4), (b) what he says about the inadequacy of the presuppositions-framework as regards normative thinking, and (c) his conditions for the selection of the type of legal reasoning to be examined (8). But such a conclusion would be unwarranted, since Wróblewski, by the term 'presupposition', also understands "evaluative statements or rules" (see also the last part of his par. 5). He explicitly mentions that there is a "concept of presupposition" that is

of no help to us because it involves verificationist truth claims and we are dealing with norms and evaluations (3). Wróblewski himself is clearly inclined to think that there do seem to be evaluative statements that also can be considered enunciative. It definitely seems to me that Wróblewski seeks to find out this sort of solution to the problem of the relationship between enunciative and normative propositions. This is shown for instance when he says, with respect to a presupposition, that "the premises of interpretative decisions" should be internally consistent *both* concerning knowledge *and* concerning evaluations and commands (16).

2. I find it somewhat difficult to pin down the meaning of the term 'operative interpretation', despite its definition (16). It is made apparently equal with "interpretative decision" (11). Would we thus be licensed to simply say "interpretation", "operative" being only an epithet? In the language of semantics, following Carnap,[4] "operative" would then be an adjective which adds quality without modifying the extension and the intension of the substantive. However, "operative interpretation" is later opposed (13) to the "doctrinal interpretation", using the reference to the situational context (or the lack of it) as a criterion. There is also the claim that there are "other types of interpretation" (18) as well.

III. OBSCURITIES RAISING DISCREPANCIES

I shall now proceed to discuss some questions that do allow for discrepancies, in view of the way Wróblewski grapples with problems.

1. It seems to me that Wróblewski indulges in an unwarranted putting together of the civil law and the common law (8). Of course, and despite his assertion that there are "common features" and "common problems", he acknowledges that there are differences between the two. But the differences are greater than he probably thinks. It is no coincidence that legal analytical considerations, as the ones made by Wróblewski, on the basis of the civil law, do not raise any deep concern as soon as we enter the field of the common law, nor are consequential in view of the way the common law proceeds. This is an experience repeated over and over again, on several occasions. It is apparent that Wróblewski only has in mind the concept "*norm*" when he is dealing with the problems of application and interpretation, thus neglecting the problems attendant to the use of *precedents*. However, the situation is quite another when we deal with the concept

"precedent", which, to be sure, does not coincide with the concept "norm". Common law jurists are bound to have and do have the impression that a heavily norm-oriented analytical jurisprudence is alien to them. And the adherents of the civil-law way of thinking just cannot smugly retort here that this is a shortcoming of the common law. Using Wróblewski's terminology, it is fair to say that, although there is in effect less interest for legal reasoning in the common law than in the civil law, legal discourse is analysed in the former as much as in the latter.

2. Next, I shall take up a point which I find very important. Many readers are likely to wonder about the fact that Wróblewski does not list any *concept* – the word "concept" appearing only a few times (1, 2, and 3) – among his presuppositions, a fact which, apart from being at odds with a very respectable tradition, involves a rather debatable attitude. The subsequent perplexity is compounded by the additional fact that his efforts stop at the level of propositions, thus neglecting the analysis of the concepts involved in those propositions. Of course he is fully entitled to do so. But is this approach to be thought to have a deliberate significance? We do know that any proposition in fact involves at least one concept.

It so happens that such an analysis of concepts, in turn demanding an analysis of the context in which they are used, perhaps would improve Wróblewski's own approach. For instance, there is all reason to emphasize (which Wróblewski does not do) that there is the *word* 'presupposition' on the one side, and the *concept* "presupposition" on the other. Neither does he sufficiently emphasize the difference between words and concepts as entities; concepts are one thing, and words a very different one. Nor does the relationship between words and concepts seem to come up with adequate sharpness. The view that I myself advocate is that words stand for meanings and/or referents; that some referents are concepts, so that concepts are meant and referred to by words; and that in contrast – as against a rather commonly held opinion – concepts do not stand for anything, that a concept is not a sign, that a concept has nothing to be referred to. Recall that at times concepts are called "*termini*"; [5] concepts imply the end of the line.

As this paper is about to make some rather unexpected suggestions, it is pertinent to go on and say that concepts come first. Beyond a certain degree of elaboration, all concepts claim for a denomination until, if the process of elaboration continues, a name is given. Hence, linguistic analysis boils down to the analysis of the meanings and/or referents of words, i.e. *inter alia* to the analysis of concepts: What they are, and how they are. All of this implies the examination of their characteristic features.

Concepts are put in connection with life through the process of subsumption. Concepts are used for the classification of the events and facts pertinent to the law, through this process. I want to emphasize the role of this process because it is apt to give us the clue with regard to the notion that concepts stand for other things. As the one who makes the subsumption is deciding that the event or fact in question has such a texture that coincides with the concept sanctioned by the legal order, it does appear that concepts have referents. But, of course, subsumption does imply a decision in each case, and not simply reference. Strictly speaking, that concepts are to be used for subsumption excludes any question concerning what they stand for.

Duly aware of the significance of subsumption, we may consider now the use of the verb "to be" in those cases which only involve the relationship between something and a concept, that is, at the level of words, between two words, one of them meaning and/or referring to a concept. The conclusion would seem to be that such a use should be avoided because it is apt to give the impression that by saying the word meaning and/or referring to the concept we are giving an explanation or a detail of the thing of which we so say. Of course, we *are* doing something to that effect, but only indirectly, by way of a subsumption in the concept, so that it all depends on the way the invoked concept is understood. If our interlocutor or audience is not familiar with the invoked concept, then the use of the verb is fruitless. An exactly similar thing happens when we just put a name to mean something largely unknown. To this very extent, we are saying nothing. For instance, we say that a certain phenomenon *is* inertia as though we were giving an explanation, while in reality we are doing nothing of the kind. Consequently, when we say that a transaction between two parties *is* a deposit, the use of the verb "to be" only means the postulated appropriateness of the subsumption, and only reveals that we have made an operation of subsumption.

If this is so, although we must go on using concepts, at least we should always keep in mind what the operation with concepts implies. Otherwise we shall remain, more or less, prisoners of the very thing we have elaborated, without being aware of our predicament. There is, then, a key *word* ('presupposition'), and a key *concept* ("presupposition"), the former standing for the latter. The proper thing would be to say that 'presupposition' is a technical word referring to a concept used in the analysis of the legal discourse (1, 4).

For the same reasons, although against a usage in which most legal writers coincide, it would be perhaps better to say, by way of a rectification already suggested in this paper, "the concept 'presupposition'", instead of "the concept *of* presupposition". It is perhaps best to generally use the formulation "the concept '*X*'", without the preposition.[6]

It so happens that the usage criticized here may easily invoke confusions. For instance, to say "the concept *of* State" is to presuppose that on one hand there is a concept, a State which cannot be identified with the French State, the Spanish State and so on, and on the other hand there are the French State, the Spanish State, and so on, as individual realities. As the concept must be named, also another thing is involved: the name given to the concept.

In these circumstances, a confusion is bound to appear because, to name the concept, we make use of the same name as the one designating those individual realities. As the expression itself is meant to refer only to one thing, it is difficult to avoid a confusion of the concept and its name or a confusion of the concept with the other realities. In both cases, the consequences will be dire. To avoid the first confusion we may be driven to overlook any distinction between the concept and the French State, the Spanish State etc. We may be even tempted to think that everything resolves into concepts, which only would be admissible against the backdrop of very idealistic positions. To avoid the second confusion we may be driven to overlook the distinction between the concept and its name.

It would seem possible to forestall all of this if we always keep in mind that concepts have a name, or are to be named, and if we understand that there is a concept and a name given to the concept, by speaking for instance of the "concept 'presupposition' " (and likewise when dealing with deposits, servitudes, testaments, and so on). The reason why I have elaborated this point at such a length is that the sort of terminological policy I am advocating seems to best correspond with Wróblewski's own approach. After all, he uses 'presupposition' as a technical term referring to a concept in legal discourse, but also emphasizes that such a general analytical concept is not to be confused with various sorts of actual presuppositions which are being examined in terms of the framework provided by this concept (cf. e.g. 5).

3. Wróblewski ventures the opinion that there is a type of legal reasoning which covers "the purely theoretical legal reasoning, the purely practical legal reasoning, and a case of mixed reasoning" (7, 8). But it would seem to be more accurate to say that (a) if we reach an enunciative proposition which would cover everything enunciative, still everything normative would remain out, and (b) we may likewise reach a normative proposition which would cover everything normative, and still everything enunciative would remain out. It appears legitimate to say in this context that Wróblewski still struggles here with the relationship between enunciative and normative thinking.

This very struggle and attendant uncertainties seem to put Wróblewski's standpoint on the verge of contradiction. This conclusion seems to be warranted by the fact that by "presupposition" he understands primarily an enunciative effort, while in effect he uses the word to refer to both enunciative and normative reasoning.

4. Concerning the very analysis employed by Wróblewski, the problem does not always lie in the correct selection of words, but in the power – to a great extent discretionary – to select the conceptual determinations so that the *continua* involved were handled in the most efficacious manner. Using such a discretionary power, and disregarding some more traditional classifications, Wróblewski belabors for instance at two or more types of "interpretations". It is always a difficult thing to succeed in doing something better or more on target. At times, Wróblewski's approach reminds us of those specialists who, in a quite discretionary way, proceed to the elaboration of various concepts (and to the organization of whatever results) by starting from the meanings and/or referents of well-known words, in which they make differentiations, and carefully try afterwards to make explicit the organization of the newly elaborated concepts. The result sometimes is a complex of concepts and their interrelations requiring much retentive to avoid getting lost, despite (or because of!) the familiarity of names suggesting a familiar meaning and the acronyms used on occasions. Afterwards, of course, the consequences are determined by the way the concepts have been elaborated (13, 14).

5. At those points where Wróblewski is at his most interesting, he exhibits a somewhat hesitating but clearly relativistic attitude (e.g. 16) which is difficult to make compatible with his idea of propositions-as-presuppositions, apart from raising the age-long debate of whether there are absolutes in law. But I will not go into this here. There is no reason to enter now the overpowering debate between relativists and absolutists and to start enlisting the quasi-infinite varieties of both.

IV. CONCERNING THE ANALYTICAL APPROACH

Wróblewski's contribution is apt to renew the polemics concerning the relative merits of the analytical approach to legal problems. There are no difficulties in pointing out these problems: To attain a better understanding of legal phenomena, especially of the ways followed and the finalities pursued by legal doctrine, by those who apply the law, and by those who contribute to the system and to the systematization of legal provisions.

Although an analytical approach does not presuppose the so-called analytical philosophy,[7] and although Wróblewski points out that he understands analytical philosophy in a broad sense (1), the intimate association of this particular approach and this particular philosophy is not easy to overcome. This renders the "analysis of the analysis" to which Wróblewski has recourse vulnerable to the same objections usually made with regard to analytical philosophy: It is necessary, but probably not the most fruitful endeavor concerning the legal problems.

There is no doubt that it is necessary. There seems to be no philosophy which denies the necessity of logical or linguistic analysis; a philosophy denying it would be incomprehensible. And it must also be admitted that an "analysis of an analysis" is bound to have a clarifying impact on the basic philosophical outlook itself, so that our insights will be improved and more and more intricacies apt to be extricated. The point for Wróblewski and those who are in the same spirit is to establish in both normative and descriptive theories (11, 15, 16) – some would say, in a "formal" way – a listing of propositions coherent with one another, the elements of which then could be filled up with data given by legal life, wherefrom we could reach conclusions which we can claim to be correct. The complementary – some would say "material", or "contentual" – job is the incumbency of another discipline. Wróblewski says, of several of his propositions-presuppositions, that they have "analytical truth" (e.g. 16). But this is not yet to gain much. Notice that he also says that the "problem of the content of (. . .) legal reasoning will not be discussed here" (16). The formula of interpretative reasoning given by Wróblewski (13) is an attractive one. But it is difficult to see in which way it may help a court to make a decision. Only the so-called "analytical philosophy" – in some of its versions – would think that such an analysis is the most important endeavor, or even the endeavor by *antonomasia*, of legal theory.

Wróblewski is fully aware of the above. Only, he has decided to remain in the analytic field. On several occasions he takes us to the borders of what is not analytic, in a change of quality, only to end up by saying us that a given problem "is an open question" (22), precisely when we feel that what is most interesting lies beyond. Again, there is also a theory of legal reasoning to be elaborated or re-elaborated; even, as he says, a "comprehensive legal theory" (23). One cannot help but missing something here, while feeling that the analytical examination is only preparation (23). It remains as a fact that such an analysis is necessary. Only after it is established how we are to use the words, how they are to be or happen to be related – by virtue of the concepts they refer to – in legal reasoning, and which are the presuppositions of the latter, the ground is prepared for the analysis proper, that is, the analysis of the law.

This is why we must be thankful to Professor Wróblewski. He has made the analytical instruments more incisive. But it would seem that impatience takes over when there is a promise to begin the analysis proper. It would seem also that such an impatience accompanies any investigation which remains purely analytical.

University of Puerto Rico

NOTES

1 See J.-L. Gardies, 'Le problème logique et le problème philosophique du passage de l'être au devoir être', *ARSP* **68** (1982), 281–298.
2 See for instance A. Aarnio, *On Legal Reasoning*, Turku 1977, 64.
3 Concerning the enunciative thinking, "the application has indisputably even the form of subsumption, whether or not this is conscious" (N. Hartmann, *Zur Grundlegung der Ontologie*, Meisenheim am Glan 1948, 302). In the same vein: "even though the blueprint of the syllogism is one merely of subsumption, this most simple function of subsumption is central to conceiving, where it is not consciously performed as well" (N. Hartmann, *Möglichkeit und Wirklichkeit*, Meisenheim am Glan 1949, 474). (My translations.)
4 R. Carnap, *Meaning and Necessity*, The University of Chicago Press 1958, 2.
5 "Traditional logic uses this word in a completely vague way, without any attempt to determine it further, and in a narrowly limited sphere". (E. Husserl, *Formale und Transzendentale Logik*, Den Haag 1974, 312, appendix I, § 15.) Husserl adds that it is very usual to say "concept" instead of "terminus", even though the word "concept" has also many significations. (My translation.)
6 See N. Hartmann, *Der Aufbau der Realen Welt*, Meisenheim am Glan 1949, 108–109.
7 We may say concerning this analytical philosophy as applied to law that it hopes to find a better understanding of the legal phenomena through the empirical investigation of the historically given natural languages used in the different positive laws; such an investigation can also be called "legal pragmatics", "a kind of analysis that has long been carried out by linguists and philosophers, especially analytic philosophers" (Carnap, *op. cit.*, 233, Suppl. D).

LIST OF EDITORS AND CONTRIBUTORS

Eugenio Bulygin, Professor, Faculty of Law, University of Buenos Aires. Arroyo 963, 1007 Buenos Aires, Argentina.

Jean-Louis Gardies, Professor, Dept. of Philosophy, University of Nantes. 2 rue Tournefort, F-44000 Nantes, France.

Ilkka Niiniluoto, Professor, Dept. of Philosophy, University of Helsinki, Unioninkatu 40 B, SF-00170 Helsinki, Finland.

Timo Airaksinen, Professor, Dept. of Philosophy, University of Helsinki, Unioninkatu 40 B, SF-00170 Helsinki, Finland.

Junichi Aomi, Professor, Faculty of Law, University of Tokyo, 3–1 Hongo 7-chome, Bunkyo-ku, Tokyo, Japan.

Michael D. Bayles, Professor of Philosophy, University of Florida, Gainesville, FL 32611, U.S.A.

Edgar Bodenheimer, Professor of Law Emeritus, University of California at Davis, CA 95616, U.S.A.

Jan M. Broekman, Professor, Instituut voor Grondslagenonderzoek van het Recht, Katholieke Universiteit Leuven, Tiensestraat 41, B-3000 Leuven, Belgium.

Alejo de Cervera, J. S. D. (University of Columbia, N.Y.), Professor of Law, University of Puerto Rico, Rio Piedras, PR 00931, U.S.A.

John H. Crabb, J. D. (Harvard Univ.) and LL.M. (New York Univ.), 38 chemin de la Planche Brûlée, F-01210 Ferney-Voltaire, France.

Risto Hilpinen, Professor, Dept. of Philosophy, Florida State University, Tallahassee, FL 32306, U.S.A.

Jaakko Hintikka, Professor of Philosophy, Florida State University, Tallahassee, FL 32306, U.S.A.

Niilo Jääskinen, LL.Lic., Assistant, Institute of Jurisprudence, University of Helsinki, Hallituskatu 11–13, SF-00100 Helsinki, Finland.

Mikael M. Karlsson, Dr., Docent in Philosophy, University of Iceland, IS-101 Reykjavik, Iceland.

Roberta Kevelson, Director, Program in Semiotic Research in Law, Government and Economics, Dept. of Philosophy, Pennsylvania State University, Berks, Reading, PA 19608, U.S.A.

Hannu Tapani Klami, LL.D., B.A., Professor, Faculty of Law, University of Turku. Ratsukonkatu 1 as. 23, SF-20880 Turku, Finland.

Gert-Fredrik Malt, Dr., Research Fellow, Institute of Private Law, University of Oslo, Karl Johansgate 47, Oslo 1, Norway.

John B. Oakley, Professor of Law, University of California at Davis, CA 95616, U.S.A.

Andrew Oldenquist, Professor of Philosophy, The Mershon Center and Dept. of Philosophy, Ohio State University, 350 University Hall, Columbus, OH 43210, U.S.A.

Kazimierz Opałek, Professor, Faculty of Law, Jagellonian University of Kraków. Ul. Mazowiecka 2/3, 30–036 Kraków, Poland.

Peter G. Sack, Dr., The Research School of Social Sciences, The Australian National University, GPO Box 4, Canberra, ACT 2601, Australia.

Michael Saltman, Dr., Senior Lecturer, Dept. of Sociology and Anthropology, University of Haifa, Mount Carmel, 31999 Haifa, Israel.

Mihály Samu, Professor, Eötvös Lorand University, Egyetem tér 1–3, Budapest V, Hungary.

Anders Stening, Dr., Rector of Örebro University, Box 923, S-701 30 Örebro, Sweden.

Timothy Stroup, Associate Professor of Philosophy, John Jay College of Criminal Justice, City University of New York, 444 West 56 Street, NY 10019, U.S.A.

Lucinda Vandervort, Assistant Professor, College of Law, University of Saskatchewan, S7N OWO Saskatoon, Canada.

Georg Henrik von Wright, Member of the Academy of Finland, Professor, Dept. of Philosophy, University of Helsinki, Unioninkatu 40 B, SF-00170 Helsinki, Finland.

Jerzy Wróblewski, Professor Dr., Dept. of the Theory of State and Law, University of Łódź. Al. Kosciuszki 46 m 9, 90 427 Łódź, Poland.

INDEX OF NAMES

Proceedings of the 11th World Congress on Philosophy of Law and Social Philosophy, held in Helsinki, August 14–20, 1983. General theme of the Congress:

PHILOSOPHICAL FOUNDATIONS OF THE
LEGAL AND SOCIAL SCIENCES

1. D. Reidel Publishing Company: In the *Law and Philosophy Library*

   MAN, LAW AND MODERN FORMS OF LIFE. Edited by E. Bulygin, J.-L. Gardies and I. Niiniluoto, with an introduction by M. D. Bayles.

2. Verlag Franz Steiner Wiesbaden GmbH: 'Beihefte' of the *Archives for Philosophy of Law and Social Philosophy* (*ARSP*), containing contributions in English, German and French

   TRADITION UND FORTSCHRITT IN DEN MODERNEN RECHTSKULTUREN. Edited by S. Jørgensen, J. Pöyhönen and C. Varga, with an introduction by J. Llompart.
   I. *Genese und Geltungsgrundlagen des zeitgenössischen Naturrechtsdenkens*: C. D. Johnson, A. Kaufmann, G. Lanata, J. López Medel, G. Lübbe-Wolff, R. Lukic, G. Soaje Ramos, R. Tokarczyk, F. Viola, S. O. Welding; II. *Strukturen moderner Rechts- und Staatstheorien*: G. Antalffy, C. Despotopoulos, A. Levine, W. Maihofer, N. Nenovski, W. Weichelt; III. *Begriff, Grundlagen und Entwicklung der Rechtskulturen in vergleichender Perspektive*: G. Haney, J. Ojwang, B. Ranchod, N. Sanajaoba, A. Tay, V. Tumanov, F. Wieacker, M. Yasaki; IV. *Menschen- und Bürgerrechte als Erfindung gegen den Machtmissbrauch*: P. Bénéton, J. Blahož, J. Feinberg, S. Cotta, M. Villey, N. Kobayashi, S. Leader, E. Moutsopoulos.

   SOZIALE GERECHTIGKEIT UND INDIVIDUELLE VERANTWORTLICHKEIT IM WOHLFAHRTSSTAAT. Edited by J. M. Broekman, K. Opałek and D. Kerimov, with an introduction by C. Wellman.
   I. *Moralische und rechtliche Prämissen materialer Gerechtigkeit*: L. Garcia Alonso, J. R. Lucas, A. Macleod, S. Panou, J. Parain-Vial, V. Peschka, V. Petev, T. Sampaio Ferraz Jr., D. Scheltens, O. Weinberger; II. *Mensch und Menschenbild im Recht*: M. Alliot, A.-J. Arnaud, P.

Braun, B. Edelman, F. Lachmayer, E.-J. Lampe, S. Latouche, E. Mock, A. Oldenquist and M. Lynn, J. Van Peteghem, H. Rodingen, K. S. Tollett, W. Zitscher; III. *Recht und Rechtsstaat in wohlfahrtsstaatlicher Perspektive*: J. Bell, E. Kamenka, L. Lombardi Vallauri, N. B. Reynolds, L. Tower Sargent, M. Urso, R. Voigt; IV. *Soziale Verantwortung und strafrechtliche Zurechnung*: R. W. Burgh, S. Gbadegesin, N. Jareborg, N. Lacey, R. Lahti, W. Lang, A. Mabe, R. Martin, A. Papsthart, Ch. Sharma.

GELTUNGS- UND ERKENNTNISBEDINGUNGEN IM MODERNEN RECHTSDENKEN. Edited by N. MacCormick, S. Panou and L. Lombardi Vallauri, with an introduction by R. Dreier.

I. *Prinzipien und Regeln im Recht*: R. Alexy, S. Axinn, M. Henket, J. Llompart, J. W. Murphy, Th. Schramm, R. A. Shiner, C. Wellman; II. *Wachstumsbedingungen des Erkenntnisfortschritts im Recht*: J. Dalberg-Larsen, E. V. Heyen, T. Sampaio Ferraz Jr., D. Töllborg, V. Villa, A. H. de Wild, E. Zuleta Puceiro; III. *Modernes Recht und Wahrheitstheorien*: H. Aoi, O. A. Ghirardi, T. Gizbert-Studnicki, D. Lyons, I. Niiniluoto, F. Ost, J. Woleński.

3. Verlag Duncker & Humblot, Berlin: 'Beihefte' of *RECHTSTHEORIE, Zeitschrit für Logik, Methodenlehre, Kybernetik und Soziologie des Rechts*, containing contributions in English, German and French

JURISTISCHE LOGIK, RATIONALITÄT UND IRRATIONALITÄT IM RECHT. Edited by A.-J. Arnaud, R. Hilpinen and J. Wróblewski, with an introduction by R. J. Vernengo.

I. *Logik im Dienste des Rechts*: J.-L. Gardies, M. P. Golding, S. Gram Jensen, V. Knapp, A. A. Martino, A. Menne, H. Schreiner, R. Sève, L. Åqvist; II. *Grundlagen und Grenzen der Rationalität im Rechtsdenken*: V. Arévalo, R. Dreier, A. Edel, M. D. Farrell, Å. Frändberg, U. Lohmann, N. MacCormick, E. Pattaro, D. A. J. Richards, N. Roos, A. Sajó, L. Sheleff, F. Terré, H. Ph. Visser't Hooft, R. Weimar, E. Zalten, Z. Ziembiński, M. Zirk-Sadowski; III. *Bürgerrechte und ziviler Ungehorsam*: M. D. Bayles, J. Ellin, L. D. Eriksson, V. Gulyev, J. Kleinig, T. Laker, A. Łopatka, B. J. Narain, B. Nazarov, J. Paust, R. Tamayo, K. E. Tranøy.

SOZIOLOGISCHE JURISPRUDENZ UND REALISTISCHE RECHTSTHEORIE. Edited by E. Kamenka, R. S. Summers and W. Twining, with an introduction by A. Peczenik.

I. *Recht und Gesellschaft in rechtsphilosophischer Perspektive*: A. J. Aristegui, E. Backman, W. Eichhorn, K. Fabian, Ph. Gérard, H. Klenner, V. Luizzi, V. Nersesiants, K. Penegar, P. Popoff, A. Visegrady, T. Wilhelmsson; II. *Theorien des Rechts und Rechtssoziologie*: M. Borucka-Arctowa, K. Liebl, L. Mazor, K. Mollnau, M. Mikkola, D. Nelken, H. Rottleuthner, S. Sariola, C. Varga, E. Zalten; III. *Voraussetzungen und Folgen des Rechtsrealismus*: J. Bjarup, S. Castignone, C. Faralli, S. Jørgensen, A. Lagerqvist-Almé, F. Michaut, E. Pattaro, J. W. F. Sundberg.

VERNUNFT UND ERFAHRUNG IM RECHTSDENKEN DER GEGENWART. Edited by T. Eckhoff, L. M. Friedman and J. Uusitalo, with an introduction by O. Weinberger.

I. *Systemische Grundlagen der Rechtsvernunft*: C. J. Bax, H. J. M. Boukema, E. Flower, D. J. Galligan, L. Gianformaggio, H. P. Graver, M. Laclau, A. Peczenik, A. Sajó, M. Sintonen, J. Strangas, J. Uusitalo, J. M. Van Dunné, J. Vanderlinden; II. *Systematisierung in Rechtsdogmatik*: A. Aarnio, C. Alchourrón, J. Boguszak, E. Bulygin, P. Dauchy, M. Van Hoecke, R. J. Vernengo; III. *Das Rechtssystem und seine gesellschaftliche Basis*: A. G. Conte, H. Fenge, L. M. Friedman, R. Guastini, N. Intzessiloglou, W. Krawietz, J. B. Oakley, M. Pavčnik, J. Raz, G. Robles, M. Rodriguez Molinero, J. de Sousa e Brito, R. Tamayo, J.-L. Vullierme: IV. *Ökonomische Analyse des Rechts*: J. Axinn, W. Balekjian, E. E. Dais, V. Laptev, R. S. Summers, J. Tolonen, R. Weimar.

GPSR Compliance

The European Union's (EU) General Product Safety Regulation (GPSR) is a set of rules that requires consumer products to be safe and our obligations to ensure this.

If you have any concerns about our products, you can contact us on ProductSafety@springernature.com

In case Publisher is established outside the EU, the EU authorized representative is:

Springer Nature Customer Service Center GmbH
Europaplatz 3
69115 Heidelberg, Germany

Batch number: 10815964

Printed by Printforce, the Netherlands